T0389046

African Political Activism in Postcolonial France

African Political Activism investigates the relationship between African immigrant political activism, government surveillance, and the social welfare state in postcolonial France. This book weaves together three interrelated areas of historical scholarship—the history of immigration to France, the political lives of immigrant communities, and policy making—to offer a new appraisal of postcolonialism and neocolonialism in the 1960s and 1970s.

Gillian Glaes is a Visiting Professor at the University of Montana-Missoula.

The Routledge Global 1960s and 1970s series

As the decades that defined the Cold War, the 1960s and 1970s helped shape the world we live in to a remarkable degree. Political phenomena including the almighty tussle between capitalism and communism, the Arab-Israeli conflict, apartheid in South Africa, uprisings against authoritarianism and independence from colonial rule for a large swathe of the nations of the Global South helped define the period, but the sixties and seventies were as much about cultural and social change, with lives the world over altered irretrievably by new standpoints and attitudes. Traditionally, analysis of the era has largely been concerned with superpower posturings and life in Europe and America, but this series, while providing full coverage of such impulses, takes a properly global view of the era.

Titles in the series include:

Postcolonial Conflict and the Question of Genocide
The Nigeria–Biafra War, 1967–1970
Edited by A. Dirk Moses and Lasse Heerten

African Political Activism in Postcolonial France
State Surveillance and Social Welfare
Gillian Glaes

African Political Activism in Postcolonial France

State Surveillance and Social Welfare

Gillian Glaes

LONDON AND NEW YORK

First published 2019
by Routledge
2 Park Square, Milton Park, Abingdon, Oxon OX14 4RN

and by Routledge
711 Third Avenue, New York, NY 10017

Routledge is an imprint of the Taylor & Francis Group, an informa business

British Library Cataloguing-in-Publication Data
A catalogue record for this book is available from the British Library

Library of Congress Cataloging-in-Publication Data
A catalog record has been requested for this book

ISBN: 978-1-138-04400-5 (hbk)
ISBN: 978-1-315-17269-9 (ebk)

Typeset in Times New Roman
by codeMantra

To Sean, who was there from the very beginning
And to Chloe, who came at the very end

Contents

List of figures

List of abbreviations

AEE	Association Evangile et Enfance
AAE	Amicale des Algériens en Europe
ACAFOM	Association culturelle et amicale des familles d'outre-mer et migrants
ACMSB	Association de centre médico-social Bossuet
ACTAF	Association culturelle des travailleurs africains en France
ADSSD	Archives départementales de la Seine-Saint-Denis
ADVDM	Archives départementales du Val-de-Marne
AEF	Afrique équatoriale française
AFTAM	Association française des travailleurs africains et malgaches résidant en France
AMM	Archives municipales de Montreuil
AMSD	Archives municipales de Saint-Denis
ANOM	Archives nationales d'Outre Mer
AOF	Afrique-Occidentale française
APP	Archives de la préfecture de police
APS	Association pour la promotion de la culture et de la langue soninké
ASSOTRAF	Association pour l'aide sociale aux travailleurs africains
ASTI	Association de solidarité avec les travailleurs immigrés
ATA	Association des travailleurs africains
ATANRP	Association des travailleurs de l'Afrique noire de la région parisienne
ATM	Association des travailleurs maliens
ATMF	Association des travailleurs maliens en France
ATM-SSD	Association des travailleurs maliens, section Saint-Denis
ATSRP	Amicale des travailleurs sénégalais de la région parisienne

BDIC	Bibliothèque de documentation internationale contemporaine
BDS	Bloc démocratique sénégalais
BN	Bibliothèque nationale François Mitterrand
CAN	Centre des archives nationales
CANC	Centre des archives nationales contemporaines
CFDT	Confédération française démocratique du travail
CFTC	Confédération française des travailleurs chrétiens
CGT	Confédération générale du travail
CGTA	Confédération générale du travail-autonome
CIEMI	Centre d'information et d'études sur les migrations internationales
CIMADE	Comité inter-mouvements auprès des évacués
CMSB	Centre médico-social Bossuet
CNDCT	Comité national de défense contre la tuberculose
CNPF	Centre national du patronat français
DSSAOF	Direction des services de sécurité de l'AOF
ESNA	Études sociales nord-africains
FAS	Fonds d'action sociale pour les travailleurs étrangers
FASTI	Fédération des associations de solidarité avec les travailleurs immigrés
FEANF	Fédération des étudiants d'Afrique noire en France
FETAF	Fédération des travailleurs africains en France
FETRANI	Fédération des travailleurs d'Afrique noire en France
FLN	Front de libération nationale
FO	Force ouvrière
FRAMOM	Fédération régionale afro-malgache et d'Outre Mer
GIP	Groupe interministériel permanent
GP	Gauche prolétarienne
HLM	Habitation à loyer modéré
INSEE	Institut national de la statistique et des études économiques
MRAP	Mouvement contre le racisme, l'anti-semitisme et pour la paix (to 1977); Mouvement contre le racisme et pour l'amitié entre les peoples (since 1977)
ONI	Office national de l'immigration
PCF	Parti communiste français
PS	Parti socialiste
PSU	Parti socialiste unifié
SAT	Service d'assistance technique de la préfecture de police
SLCTKM	Service de lutte contre la tuberculose de Kayes au Mali
SLPM	Service de liaison et de promotion des migrants

SONACOTRA(L)	Société nationale de construction de logements pour les travailleurs (algériens)
SOUNDIATA	Association pour le soutien, l'union et la dignité de l'accueil aux travailleurs africaines
UCJG	Union chrétienne de jeunes gens
UGEESS	Union générale des étudiants, élèves et stagiaires sénégalais
UGTAN	Union générale des travailleurs d'Afrique noire
UGTMF	Union générale des travailleurs maliens en France
UGTSF	Union générale des travailleurs sénégalais en France
UGTSRP	Union générale des travailleurs sénégalais de la région parisienne
UNTM	Union nationale des travailleurs maliens
UTN	Union des travailleurs nègres

Acknowledgements

I wrote a book about migration and movement during a period in my life when I could not quite stay in the same place. The project as it stands now started off with an interest in immigration developed at the University of Oregon as a Master's student and shifted direction when I became a PhD student at the University of Wisconsin-Madison. Over the course of writing it, I lived in four states and three different countries. It grew and developed over employment at two different institutions: Carroll College and the University of Montana-Missoula. In reflecting on this journey, I see that that my interest in immigration emerged from my own inability to set down roots as I moved about to different cities, states, countries, and institutions.

Rudy Koshar once said during a graduate seminar that interesting adventures awaited us during our fieldwork. He was right. At one point, I ended up reviewing inventories in a closet at the Paris Archives. One day, the roof at the temporary location for the French National Archives leaked and rain cascaded down on my computer. Luckily, the documents remained unharmed. Most harrowing of all, though, was the *dérogation* process, or the process of securing the right and privilege to use classified documents in France. Thank you to all who guided me through this, including Monsieur Arnaud de Castelbajac. This book would not have been possible without his advocacy, support, and guidance.

As I unearthed more information than I knew what to do with at archives, libraries, and research centers, many others contributed as well. Thanks to all of the archivists and librarians who assisted with the research process, including those at the AN, CAN, BDIC, CIEMI, BN, the Paris Archives, the Paris Police Archives, the Overseas Archives, the Saint-Denis Municipal Archives, the Ivry Municipal Archives, the Montreuil Municipal Archives, the Departmental Archives of the Seine-Saint-Denis and the Val-du-Marne Departments, and many others. I would like to especially thank the staff at the University of Montana-Missoula's Mansfield Library and the Corette Library at Carroll College, respectively, for finding books and articles for me in English and in French from far-flung places.

This project benefitted financially from several funding sources. The *Institut d'études politiques* (Paris) Exchange Fellowship and the Dorothy Leet

Grant supported initial fieldwork. Thanks, too, to the University of Wisconsin-Madison Graduate School for its generous financial support through the Vilas Fellowship and various Vilas Travel Grants. I would like to thank the Carroll College Faculty Development Committee for awarding the travel grants that made return trips to France possible, while also supporting conference travel, which provided the opportunity to present various portions of this book. The Jerry Berberet Summer Research and Writing Grant proved critical in providing funding for additional research. A semester-long sabbatical from Carroll College created the time and space necessary to make significant progress on the project overall.

Several people and personalities shaped this project. The friendships that I developed over the years as a graduate student and a faculty member have proven invaluable and there are many people whom I want to thank for their unwavering support and constant encouragement. Doug Palmer was my first friend in graduate school. I met Derek Hoff on a Friday afternoon at a tiny Greek restaurant in Eugene, Oregon. He read the book proposal and various chapters and his insight and feedback made me think harder and more deeply about key issues than I perhaps wanted to at times. Our parallel career tracks have given us much to discuss on ski slopes and hiking trails. Ian and Candy Rush were part of an incredible group of friends in Oregon who welcomed me in. George Sheridan, Jr. and Ulf Hedatoft introduced me to the history of immigration. At the University of Wisconsin-Madison, Karen Spierling was my oracle, giving sound advice and perspective at every turn. Kristin Walton was one of the first people I met in the department. Rob Lewis and Holly Grout adopted me into their cohort. Molly Todd and Meredith Terretta introduced me to Latin American and African history, respectively. Lisa Cline showed me the ropes in Paris, helping me to find housing and the archives all at the same time. David Ciarlo reminds me of what it means to be a good historian. I was grateful for the friendship of Mariah Devereaux Herbeck and Jason Herbeck. My advisor, Laird Boswell, supported me at every turn, even as my tendency to wander took me far away from Madison. He was the first to suggest that I shift my focus to the West African community in France. Rudy Koshar, Suzanne, Desan, Florence Bernault, Mary Louise Roberts and the late Patrick Harries lent their insight and their tremendous talents as scholars.

At Carroll College, I found an unwavering champion in my chair, Robert Swartout, Jr. Jerry Berberet became a mentor and a friend. Elvira Roncalli, Debra Bernardi, and Kay Satre commented on an early version of chapter 4 through our faculty writing group. Through the Annette Moran Faculty Colloquium, co-chaired by Charlotte Jones, I had the opportunity to present the project to my colleagues. Their feedback was invaluable. Jenn Glowienka, Jamie Dolan, Nisan Burbridge, Dawn Gallinger, Doreen Kutufam, Bill Parsons, Heather Barnes, Chris Fuller, Martha Gonzalez, Kyle Strode, John Ries, Jeremy Johnson, Leslie Angel, Candie Cain, and Colin Thomas provided friendship, laughter, and support. Stephanie Lammers reiterated time and again how important it is to love what you do.

Sometimes life takes unexpected twists and turns. When I decided to step away from my position at Carroll, I was fortunate to find myself at the University of Montana-Missoula, where I met a whole new set of incredibly talented and accomplished colleagues and friends. Kyle Volk has championed this project from the time that I met him, reading everything from the book proposal to the introduction and various chapters along the way. The Lockridge Colloquium shaped this book in numerous ways, from providing the opportunity to present two chapters to creating a space for ongoing historical discourse and dialogue. Robert Greene has extended numerous teaching opportunities and encouragement. Daisy Rooks and Erin Saldin have provided friendship, support, and perspective to me as colleagues and friends. Anya Jabour has been a mentor, pointing me to new opportunities while providing sage advice. Tobin Miller Shearer provided my first opportunity to teach at UM and has been a tremendous colleague and friend. He also took time out of his schedule to read the introduction. Jody Pavilack lent me books that proved critical for chapter 3 and provided several key philosophical suggestions. Patrick O'Connor consistently provided terrific feedback. Dan Spencer was a joy to teach with in the Davidson Honors College. Amy Kinch extended numerous opportunities to me as a faculty member. Nancy Clouse kept my teaching universe organized and on track. My job would not have been as enjoyable over the past few years without the invaluable support of Diane Rapp. Students at Carroll College and at the University of Montana-Missoula pushed me to think about history in new and innovative ways.

Making the transition to the University of Montana-Missoula also afforded me the privilege and the honor of teaching at my alma mater. As an undergraduate, Paul Lauren, Richard Drake, Harry Fritz, Fred Skinner, Dave Emmons, Ron Perrin, and Bill Farr all served as role models and mentors. The late Robert Lindsay was my first formal advisor. The late Michael Laslovich made me work harder as a student and scholar while reminding me of the importance of my roots.

Several friendships beyond academia have nurtured me through the process of bringing this book to life. Kari Swartz Dilloo provided unwavering support, humor, and encouragement. Michelle Huie always made time to talk, even as she started a new company. Melissa Wilson brought a smile to my face with her boundless energy and enthusiasm. The Hanson family—Brenda, Eric, Emily, and Brynn—reminded me to hit the ski slopes and take time for Saturday football games. Alison Lambert has kept me laughing for over twenty years. Candi Jones always encouraged my interest in history. The Shull family—Jason, Andrea, Max, and Mara—have been great friends and travel companions. In Missoula, I was able to reconnect with old friends, including Rebecca and Luke Jackson, Ted and Carrie Schuster, Jennie and Graham Roy, Torrey and Diana Holmquist, Kendra Lee, Erica Woodahl, Anne Labbe, Tao Rohitsathian, Crystal Sampson, Maria Nicholl Hawk, and Elise Guest. I am in awe of Sean, Jennifer, and Emma Swartz's strength and courage. We all miss Kole.

When it comes to writing, I have learned that accountability and support are key. I want to thank Melissa Hibbard for keeping me on track over the years and showing me all sorts of technological innovations that could help me do so. This manuscript became a book because of her optimism, resourcefulness, and friendship. I had the pleasure of working with Laura Brade at the very end of this project and I appreciated her suggestions and support. Michelle Boyd helped me understand the importance of planning, accountability, time off, and task lists. My faculty writing group at UM—Theresa Floyd and Libby Metcalf—assisted me with goal setting. Erica Zins, Rebecca Wood, Daisy Rooks and I met twice a week for over three years while we all worked on various projects. I could not have completed this book without their support, encouragement, and presence. My thanks also to my neighbor Claudine Tobalske for help with the French translations.

The opportunity to publish with Routledge came about at a delightfully unexpected time. I want to thank my editor, Robert Langham at Routledge, for his support for and advocacy for this book and the series in which it appears. Thank you to Michael Bourne and Julie Fitzsimmons for answering my seemingly endless questions about the publication process. I would also like to thank the anonymous reviewers and the editing team at Routledge, whose suggestions and feedback made this book better. Any mistakes, though, are my own.

Over the course of developing this project, I met numerous colleagues and friends in and beyond the field of history whose talent, dedication, and focus inspire me to be a better scholar and teacher. Thank you to Kathleen Keller, Rebecca Scales, George Trumbull IV, Rebecca Puljus, Louisa Rice, Jennifer Sessions, Elizabeth Foster, Jennifer Miller, Dominic Thomas, Sung Choi, Jennifer Boittin, Mary Dewhurst Lewis, Clifford Rosenberg, Eric Reed, Jennifer Sweatman, Gregory Mann, David Messenger, Jonathyne Briggs, Paula Lee, Louisa Rice, Nicole Richardt, Rachel Chrastil, Rachel Nunez, Melissa Byrnes, Félix Germain, Burleigh Hendrickson, Samuel Kalman, Ethan Katz, Pape Drame, Raissa Binga, Jeanine Stefanucci, Katherine Curtis, Brian Baucom, Katie Williams Baucom, Jeff Wiltse, Jennifer Brothers, Ken Lockridge, Catherine Wihtol de Wenden, Philippe de Witte, Riva Kastoryano, Patrick Weil, and Jacques Barou. Thank you to my colleagues at the Gilder Lehrman Institute of American History's Slave Narratives Seminar, the Fulbright German Studies Seminar, and the United States Holocaust Memorial Museum Silberman Seminar for making me think more carefully and critically about issues ranging from slavery to immigration to genocide. Special thanks to Kathleen Keller for reading the manuscript in its entirety and providing incredibly helpful feedback. Thanks, too, to the numerous co-panelists, chairs, commentators, and audience members who made my work better over the years at academic conferences throughout the U.S. and internationally.

In my hometown of Missoula, Montana I was fortunate to grow up in a community thriving with artists, writers, and intellectuals. The late Jim Welch graciously agreed to an oral interview—my first—when I was 13 years old.

David Quammen continues to provide writing advice, support, and encouragement and has been like a family member. Bill Bevis still has time for a chat when I see him around town. The late Jim Kriley and the late Dave Alt inspired me to pursue an academic career. I hope that Missoula's history of welcoming immigrants and refugees will continue.

I owe a debt of gratitude beyond words to my family, whose faith, support, and encouragement made it possible to finish this book. My mom and dad, Keith and Carol Glaes, are two of the strongest people I have ever known. My mom's unflagging belief in me and in this project helped in more ways than I can articulate here. She has gently pushed me my entire life to achieve what she always thought I was capable of and for that I am grateful. My dad first introduced me to history over dinner table conversations and during outdoor adventures. My parents' lifelong love of learning and reading inspires me every day. Together, they showed me how to think and dream bigger than I ever thought that I could. My sister, Samantha Glaes keeps me laughing and grounded. She also helps me to remember what is important in life. My grandparents on both sides made my education possible and I will always be appreciative of their thoughtfulness and care. My in-laws—Al, Sharlane, Gretchen, and Jeff—welcomed me into their family. I want to thank them for their hospitality and generosity. My nieces Abigael and Cynthia invite me see the world through their eyes.

Finally, my husband Sean Kissane was with me every step of the way with this project. He gracefully encouraged me to pursue my career, even as we found ourselves living apart for almost a decade. His belief in me when I decided to step away from a tenured position and change course made it possible to do so. This book is a testament to his capacity for love, patience, and understanding. Sean, I owe you more than a few hikes, ski trips, and backpacking adventures. Finally, our daughter Chloe arrived two weeks after I finished this manuscript. Every day with her has been a true joy. Chloe, you have helped me to understand love in a whole new way. It is to Sean and Chloe that I dedicate this book.

Preface

The Saint-Denis Riot

In his 2006 article, Didier Fassin argued that in response to the 2005 riots in France, "[s]uddenly a previously unacknowledged colour bar was discovered."[1] Long before these riots, though, the colour bar that Fassin refers to was acknowledged in the aftermath of a riot in Saint-Denis outside of Paris.[2] The 1960s and 1970s were two tumultuous decades internationally, with uprisings occurring in Europe, the United States, and around the world. France was no exception as riots and racial violence occurred throughout this era. While moments such as the upheaval of May of 1968 left a lasting impact, clashes involving immigrant communities proved more fleeting, spurring the popular media to debate and discuss them, after which they receded to the back of public consciousness.[3] As Fassin argues, "[n]ewspaper articles and television reports revealed how difficult it was for Arabs or Black people to get a job or a flat, how they were stigmatized at school and humiliated by the police."[4] That same cycle had played out in response to the 1963 Saint-Denis riot and other similar events. The reactions to the 2005 riots were another manifestation of this cycle, which began decades before.

So how can we recover the memory and meaning of the Saint-Denis riot in the early 1960s, which is now all but forgotten, and how does this event play into the larger trajectory of African immigrant political activism in France after decolonization? The story begins in a *banlieue* outside of Paris. About a month before the Reverend Dr. Martin Luther King, Jr. delivered his "I Have a Dream" speech as the culmination of the "March on Washington" in the United States and three years after France's former colonies in Sub-Saharan Africa gained independence, a clash occurred outside of Paris. On July 22, 1963, Algerian and Mauritanian immigrants fought in Saint-Denis in a bloody conflict that pitted against one another two seemingly disenfranchised and dislocated groups struggling in a host country that was also a former colonizer. The brawl on a hot July evening received news coverage around the world, from West Germany to the United States and throughout France. Over one hundred men took to the streets in what one witness describes as a "riot like you'd see in the movies."[5] Observers locally, nationally, and internationally took note. The riot in Saint-Denis marked one of the first moments in the early postcolonial era when protests undertaken by African immigrants were visible to the rest of French society, making it an early turning point for postcolonial African political activism.[6] Amidst worldwide debate over human rights and civil liberties, African workers and other immigrants confronted racism and discrimination throughout metropolitan France, a place that was theoretically "color blind" according to the tenets of French republicanism and citizenship and their emphasis on integration.[7]

Although its pattern echoed other instances of collective violence, the riot differed from other similar incidents in the postwar era. Unlike similar events occurring in the U.S. in the 1960s, in Britain in the 1970s, 1980s, and 1990s, and in France in 2005—which all stemmed in part from conflicts between local residents and police—this one originated from a landlord–tenant dispute. On July 21, Mauritanian immigrant Gata Sirakhata was accused of stealing a pair of shoes belonging to Algerian Ali Ouahab. As a result, Algerian hotel owner Habil Saïd decided to evict the group of Mauritanians living in his hotel at 14 rue du Landy in Saint-Denis. The Mauritanians denied any wrongdoing and demanded that Saïd return part of the rent, a request that he immediately refused. The initial allegation led to a shoving match between the two sides, with some participants sustaining minor injuries.[8] Accusations of theft were not uncommon against immigrant groups such as the Mauritanians living at 14 rue de Landy, which points to a broader societal tendency to link immigration and "blackness" with criminality, and which, in this case, triggered a much larger conflict.[9] Dating back to at least the 1920s, fears of immigrant criminality helped shape the modern immigration controls enacted in the interwar period, which persisted into the postwar and postcolonial eras as well.[10]

The Saint-Denis riot was not the first incidence of conflict between these two immigrant groups. Authorities detailed other violent incidents in France in the late 1950s, just before decolonization in *Afrique-Occidentale française* (AOF or French West Africa) and especially as the struggle for independence from the French in Algeria grew increasingly brutal. One such incident occurred on March 6, 1956 at the Bar Coloniale in Marseille, an establishment frequented by Senegalese civilians and soldiers. That night, employees asked an inebriated Algerian patron to leave because of public drunkenness. The situation escalated when the patron returned with dozens of friends, who, following a heated discussion, clashed with Senegalese customers. Media reports placed the number wounded at between 10 and 12 people. This incident came on the heels of a few others in the same neighborhood in Marseille. During the next evening, another brawl occurred on the rue des Dominicaines involving at least 60 people.[11]

Just over a year later, two more conflicts erupted in southern France, home to immigrant communities from North and Sub-Saharan Africa. In March 1957, a confrontation occurred in the Bar Lenscale in Frejus between Senegalese soldiers and Algerian civilians. When the Senegalese soldiers entered the bar, the Algerians began to disparage France, the French, and

Senegalese military personnel, taking issue with the role of Senegalese colonial forces in Algeria.[12] These remarks revealed the ways in which events on the African continent shaped the dynamic between these two communities in France. The Senegalese Chief Warrant Officer, who spoke Arabic, attempted to defuse the situation, but a fight broke out. It took a Senegalese taxi driver living in Frejus to intervene and break up the conflict.[13] Another confrontation occurred a few months later in St. Raphaël, located on the southern coast of France. On the night of October 20, following a soccer match between the Frejus team and a team from St. Raphaël, an African player by the name of Pape Ba became embroiled in a confrontation with Ali Hamidou, an Algerian member of the St. Raphaël club, at the Templiers bar. A fight ensued, with Hamidou losing several teeth. The police report noted that, while the African player instigated the confrontation, the Algerian, who was "usually very calm and well regarded in Frejus" was drinking that night.[14] News of the incident quickly spread through both communities. At least 30 of Hamidou's friends organized a retaliation, which resulted in a second confrontation.[15]

By 1963, then, there were precedents for conflict between these two groups. Media coverage highlighted the idea of an interracial rivalry between them as a contributing factor. Referencing the conflicts in March, 1956, one report from the *Renseignements généraux*, the French police's intelligence service, of Marseille explained, "Between Arabs and the Senegalese there is a racial rivalry that has been reflected repeatedly in past brawls, which were even more violent than those that have occurred in recent days."[16] Newspaper reports further attributed the conflicts to the close proximity of these two groups, each of which lived near the Saint Charles train station.[17] Police had invoked the same explanation, explaining that, "About 600 Senegalese live in this [Arab] quarter … In principle, North Africans and blacks do not frequent the same establishments and contact between the two is limited but sometimes it takes very little for an incident to flare up."[18]

In the case of the conflict in Saint-Denis, what started out as a small, localized disagreement over a pair of shoes grew quickly into a full-blown riot. On July 22, 1963, Saïd started the eviction process against his Mauritanian tenants. The two sides confronted one another again and a brawl ensued.[19] Several groups of Algerian, Senegalese, Mauritanian, and Malian immigrants lived along the street. Word of the altercation spread, attracting more and more participants who had little or nothing to do with the initial confrontation. Neighbors and passers-by joined in, the riot grew in scope, and several blocks of the neighborhood became engulfed in the melee. At its height, at least 30 Mauritanians and upwards of 100 Algerians fought each other on the streets of Saint-Denis. As more and more people joined in, witnesses barricaded themselves into their homes in an effort to escape the mayhem.[20] The *Préfecture de police* (Police Headquarters) later referred to the altercation as a "battle."[21] For almost an hour, chaos dominated the rue du Landy.

This was not a spontaneous riot, but one that grew out of long-simmering tensions between two immigrant communities, as revealed by previous incidents. Housing was frequently a source of disputes as hundreds of immigrants from North Africa and Sub-Saharan Africa lived side by side on the rue du Landy and other streets around Saint-Denis and throughout the Paris region.[22] In this case, the mounting friction exploded into conflict. Because participants arrived armed with a variety of weapons, the Saint-Denis riot, like those before it, resulted in casualties.[23] Newspapers estimated that between 15 and 28 participants were injured. A police report indicated that over 20 participants were transported to the Saint-Denis and Beaujon hospitals. Several were hospitalized. Three remained in critical condition, with injuries ranging from a skull fracture to a laceration to the chest and a collapsed lung. Neither the media nor the *Préfecture de police*, however, reported any deaths.[24]

This riot marked an important moment in the history of immigrants from Sub-Saharan Africa in France because it underscored the challenges that African immigrants faced in terms of housing and tensions with other immigrant groups after decolonization. A crisis was mounting in the outer neighborhoods of Paris and the *banlieues*, one that would attract attention from officials across a range of French governmental organizations as well as from media outlets and advocacy organizations. The African immigrant community and the struggles its members encountered across the 1960s and into the 1970s would come to shape social welfare policies and surveillance tactics for generations while also continuing an important tradition of immigrant political activism that dated back to the interwar period. While confronting a rapidly expanding surveillance state, African immigrants procured housing and health care benefits from the French government that resulted directly from policies seeking to control them. In doing so, they challenged conceptualizations and stereotypes shaped by colonialism and colonial racism that persisted into the postcolonial era. This riot also reflected myriad forms of political protest undertaken by the African immigrant community in response to their plight, underscoring their active participation in the political sphere throughout the 1960s and 1970s. Various forms of political protest—including rioting—underscored the challenges that African immigrants faced, including in the area of housing, and attracted the state's attention as authorities feared that mounting political activism by non-western immigrants could destabilize an already fragile republic.

The many ways that African immigrants expressed themselves politically, including through riots such as that in Saint-Denis, the conditions that shaped this activism, and the ways in which the French state responded represents the critical issues evaluated in this book. The Saint-Denis riot represents a central idea discussed throughout these pages: that immigrants, including African workers, were political actors who shaped the policies of the Fifth Republic following decolonization. The riot was a critical moment in the early history of postcolonial African migration to France. As such, the riot provides insight into interethnic violence in postcolonial France. This riot elucidates an important moment of conflict between the two immigrant groups, which reflects the uneasy relationship and ongoing tensions that spanned the colonial and postcolonial eras while also highlighting the power dynamics at play.[25]

The riot also revealed the ways in which African immigrants could use collective violence to protest their situation.[26] This incident represented an attempt by those involved to assert their position within an urban area and vocalize their frustrations at the limited opportunities available to them.[27] Just three years into postcolonial immigration, African workers grew increasingly troubled that their experiences in France fell far short of their expectations. In this instance, they resorted to rioting.[28] Looking at the history of immigrant communities in France reveals that conflict between the host population and immigrant communities or between different ethnic groups within a host society was not uncommon. The Saint-Denis riot represented a continuation of this historic trend.[29] This event and the place in which it occurred reflected several key facets of economic migration, including the sometimes contentious relationship between immigrant groups as well as the municipal response to the growing presence of immigrant workers. A variety of factors contributed to the riot's outbreak, from the heightened tensions between immigrants from North Africa and Sub-Saharan Africa exacerbated by competition for jobs to the challenges around housing, where Algerian landlords frequently rented to African tenants. The Saint-Denis riot further reinforced the identities of these two immigrant communities in opposition to one another. This increasingly adversarial relationship was not only a cause of the riot, but also a consequence. The factors that contributed to the riot reflected the challenges that immigrants from Sub-Saharan Africa and elsewhere faced, from deprivation and dislocation to geographical proximity and the inability of political structures to adequately respond to important postwar and postcolonial shifts in the French labor market and changes in immigration patterns to France.[30] Thus the color bar that Fassin discussed shaped policies, conditions, and immigrant responses for generations before the 2005 riot.

A few final notes. Throughout this book, I use the French term *banlieue*, which has no direct translation to English. From a linguistic perspective, this term most accurately represents the areas outside of urban areas and referred to in English as "suburbs." For consistency and clarity, I refer to French-controlled West Africa during the colonial era, including after World War Two, as Afrique-Occidentale française (AOF) or French West Africa, despite the changes in status that it underwent after World War Two, prior to decolonization. Finally, many of the names of immigrants in this book have been changed to protect the identities of those whose records were kept by organizations such as the Ministry of the Interior and in accordance with policies related to the use of classified documents. I have, however, kept the names of well-known figures intact, including that of Sally N'Dongo.

Notes

1 Dider Fassin, "Riots in France and Silent Anthropologists," *Anthropology Today* 22, no. 1 (February 2006): 2.

2 An earlier version of this preface appeared as the article "Africans against Algerians, the exploited against the exploited': Media Representations of the 1963 Saint-Denis Riot" in *The Proceedings of the Western Society for French History*, 36 (2008): 309–321.

3 Peter Kivisto, *Multiculturalism in a Global Society* (Oxford: Blackwell, 2002), 142; Carole Fink, Philipp Gassert, and Detlef Junker, eds., *1968: The World Transformed* (Cambridge: Cambridge University Press, 1998); Kristin Ross, *May '68 and Its Afterlives* (Chicago: University of Chicago Press, 2002).

4 Fassin, "Riots in France and Silent Anthropologists," 2.

5 AMSD 18 ACW 22/23 "Les habitants de tout un quartier de Saint-Denis ont vécu une soirée de panique: la bataille de la rue du Landy," *Paris presse intransigeant*, 24 July 1963. Jean Dannemuller, "1.000 Algériens par jour 1.000 Sénégalais par mois ... A l'ère de la décolonisation, la France réduite à l'hexagone est envahie par les ressortissants de son ancien empire," *Carrefour*, 31 July 1963. "A Saint-Denis, une bataille rangée a mis aux prises Mauritaniens et Algériens 24 blessés," *Union républicaine de la Marne*, 25 July 1963. "L'exploitation de la misère des noirs à déclenché la révolte," *Croix du Nord*, 25 July 1963. "La misère (exploité) à l'origine de la bagarre qui opposa Mauritaniens et Nord-Africains, l'autre nuit à St.-Denis," *L'Echo (La Liberté)*, 24 July 1963.

6 Daniel A. Gordon, *Immigrants and Intellectuals: May '68 and the Rise of Anti-Racism in France* (Pontypool: Merlin Press, 2012), 53.

7 Rogers Brubaker, *Citizenship and Nationhood in France and Germany* (Cambridge: Harvard University Press, 1992), 1–17; Patrick Weil, *Qu'est-ce qu'un français? Histoire de la nationalité française depuis la révolution*, Édition revue et augmentée (Mesnil-sur-l'Estrée: Folio, 2005), 11–20; Dominique Schnapper, *Qu'est-ce que l'intégration?* (Paris: Éditions Gallimard, 2007), 11–25. Tariq Modood, "The Politics of Multiculturalism in the New Europe" in Tariq Modood and P. Werbner. *The Politics of Multiculturalism in the New Europe: Racism, Identity, and Community* (Palgrave Macmillan, 1997), 5.

8 Didier Lapeyronnie, "Primitive Rebellion in the French *Banlieues*: On the Fall 2005 Riots," trans. Jane Marie Todd in Charles Tshimanga, Didier Gondola, Peter J. Bloom, eds., *Frenchness and the African Diaspora: Identity and Uprising in Contemporary France* (Bloomington: Indiana University Press, 2009), 24, 27; CANC 19940023 art. 20 Préfecture de police, "A. S. des incidents de Saint-Denis entre Algériens et originaires d'Afrique Noire" Paris, 24 July 1963; 18 ACW 22/23. "Bataille rangée à Saint-Denis entre Noirs et Nord-Africains," *Le Monde*, 24 July 1963. "Moslem Clash with Negroes in Paris; 15 Injured," *New York Herald Tribune*, 24 July 1963. "Saint-Denis: L'Exploitation de la misère des noirs à déclenché la révolte," *La Croix*, 25 July 1963. "La bagarre de la nuit dernière à Saint-Denis: drame de la misère des déracinés," *Nord littoral Calais*, July 1963.

9 Dana S. Hale, *Races on Display: French Representations of Colonized Peoples, 1886–1940* (Bloomington: Indiana University Press, 2008), 23–45

10 Clifford Rosenberg, *Policing Paris: The Origins of Modern Immigration Control Between the Wars* (Ithaca; London: Cornell University Press, 2006), 6–7.

11 CANC 19850087 art. 9 "Bagarre à Marseille entre une cinquantaine de Sénégalais et de Nord-Africains: Cinq grands blessés," *Franc-Tireur* 8 March 1956; "Grave bagarre á Marseille ou des Nord-Africains attaquent par principe les gens de race noire: 10 blessés" *L'Aurore* 9 March 1956; Renseignements généraux Marseille 807/4e Section to M le Préfet Directeur des R. G. (Renseignements

généraux) Paris, M le Préfet des B. D. R., M le Directeur Départemental et M le Commissaire Central, Marseille, 9 March 1956.

12 For an exploration of the role of African soldiers in the French army during the era of decolonization and specifically on their role in the Algerian war, see Ruth Ginio, *The French Army and Its African Soldiers: The Era of Decolonization* (Lincoln; London: The University of Nebraska Press, 2017), 105–140.

13 CANC 19850087 art. 9 Direction des renseignements généraux et Direction générale de la sureté nationale "Objet: légers incidents entre Nord Africains et militaires sénégalais du GITCM à Fréjus" 20 March 1957.

14 CANC 19850087 art. 9 Direction des renseignements généraux et Direction générale de la sûreté nationale, "Objet: Léger incident entre Nord Africains et Sénégalais à la suite du match de football" 22 October 1957. Original French: "habituellement très calme et bien considéré à Fréjus."

15 Ibid.

16 CANC 19850087 art. 9 Renseignements généraux Marseille 807/4e Section to M le Préfet Directeur des R.G. (Renseignements généraux) Paris, M le Préfet des B.D.R., M le Directeur Départemental et M le Commissaire Central, Marseille, 9 March 1956. Original French: "Il existe entre arabes et sénégalais une rivalité raciale qui s'est traduite á plusieurs reprises dans le passé par des rixes qui furent encore plus violentes que celles qui se sont produites ces derniers jours."

17 CANC 19850087 art. 9 "Bagarre à Marseille entre une cinquantaine de Sénégalais et de Nord-Africains: Cinq grands blessés," *Franc-Tireur* 8 March 1956.

18 CANC 19850087 Renseignements généraux Marseille 807/4e Section to M le Préfet Directeur des R.G. (Renseignements Généraux) Paris, M le Préfet des B.D.R., M le Directeur Départemental et M le Commissaire Central, Marseille, 9 March 1956. Original French: "Environ 600 Sénégalais vivent dans ce quartier … En principe, Nord-Africains et noirs ne fréquentent pas les mêmes établissements et les contacts sont limités. Mais il suffit parfois de peu de chose pour que l'incident éclate."

19 CANC 19940023 art. 20 Préfecture de police, "A.S. des incidents de Saint-Denis entre Algeriens et originaires d'Afrique Noire" Paris, 23 July 1963.

20 AMSD 18ACW 22/23 "Saint-Denis: L'Exploitation de la misère des noirs à déclenché la révolte," *La Croix*, 25 July 1963. "Après la bagarre de Saint-Denis: Cinq Mauritaniens et quatre Algériens restent à la disposition de la justice," *Le Parisien libéré*, 25 July 1963. Bordeaux, "'Nos gris-gris protègent des balles,'" *France-Soir*, 24 July 1963. Robert Buchard, "'Les Algériens nous exploitent' m'a dit le 'chef' des noirs de la rue du Landy," *Paris presse l'intransigeant*, 25 July 1963.

21 CANC 19940023 art. 20 Préfecture de police, "A.S. des incidents de Saint-Denis entre Algeriens et originaires d'Afrique Noire" Paris, 23 July 1963.

22 Ibid.

23 Ibid.

24 AMSD 18 ACW 22/23 Roger Maria, "Après les incidents des Saint-Denis: propos déformants," *Droit et liberté*, 15 October 1963. "L'exploitation de la misère des noirs a déclenché la révolte," *Croix du Nord*, 25 July 1963. "La bagarre de la nuit dernière à Saint-Denis: drame de la misère des déracinés," *Nord Littoral Calais*, 23 July 1963. "Bataille rangée à Saint-Denis: 100 Algériens et 30 Africains s'affrontent sauvagement pendant trois quarts d'heure 24 blessés 78 arrestations," *Le Populaire du Centre*, 24 July 1963. "La Bagarre nord-africains et africains dans les rues de la banlieue parisienne a fait 24 blessés," *L'Agence ivoirienne de presse*, 25 July 1963. "Cette nuit folle de Saint-Denis est un drame de la misère," *Paris jour*, 24 July 1963. "Les habitants de tout un quartier de Saint-Denis ont vécu une soirée de panique: la bataille de la rue du Landy," *Paris presse intransigeant*, 24 July 1963. "La misère (exploite) à l'origine de la bagarre qui opposa Mauritaniens et Nord-Africains, l'autre nuit à Saint-Denis," *L'Ècho*, 24 July 1963. "Rixe monstre

à Saint-Denis: Entre Noirs et Algériens 15 blessés ... arrestations," *L'Oise matin*, 24 July 1963. "Saint-Denis: L'Exploitation de la misère des noirs a déclenché la révolte," *La Croix*, 25 July 1963. Gérard Bordeaux, "'Nos gris-gris protégent des balles,' hurlaient les noirs en attaquent l'hôtel des Nord-Africains," *France-Soir*, 24 July 1963. Guy Teisseire, "C'est un ancien tirailleur qui a commandé la bataille de Saint-Denis entre noirs et nord-africains: 28 blessés, 80 arrestations," *L'Aurore*, 24 July 1963; CANC 19940023 art. 20 Préfecture de police, "A.S. des incidents de Saint-Denis entre Algériens et originaires d'Afrique Noire" Paris, 24 July 1963.

25 Charles Tilly, Louise Tilly, and Richard Tilly, *The Rebellious Century* (Cambridge: Harvard University Press, 1975), 24. Edward Shorter and Charles Tilly, *Strikes in France, 1930–1848* (Cambridge: Cambridge University Press, 1974).

26 Charles Tilly outlines various forms of collective violence, which directly informed this analysis of an immigrant-led riot. See Tilly, *The Politics of Collective Violence* (Cambridge, U.K.; New York: Cambridge University Press, 2003).

27 See Stephen Castles and Mark J. Miller, *The Age of Migration: International Population Movements in the Modern World* Second Edition (London: Macmillan Press, 1998).

28 Cornelia Beyer, *Violent Globalisms: Conflict in Response to Empire* (Abingdon: Ashgate, 2008), 10.

29 Manchuelle, "Background to Black African Emigration to France: The Labor Migrations of the Soninké, 1848–1987," (Phd diss., University of California-Santa Barbara, 1987), 544.

30 Daniel J. Myers, "Racial Rioting in the 1960s: An Event History of Local Conditions," *American Sociological Review* 62, no. 1 (February 1997): 94.

Introduction

The Saint-Denis riot was not the first instance when the dangerous conditions endured by African immigrants and other immigrant groups made their way into newspaper headlines and broader public discourse. Still, this riot in a Parisian *banlieue* with a growing African population marked an important early moment in the postcolonial era when immigrant political protest in the form of rioting became unambiguously visible to the rest of France. It was also a turning point for postcolonial African political activism, as the riot's African participants challenged long-held ideas about the apolitical African immigrant, which ignored an important tradition of political activism going back to the interwar era.[1]

While rioting served as one means of protest, it was not the only approach available in France, a country with a rich history of political engagement, including among immigrants. In his 1975 autobiography, *Voyage forcé: Itinéraire d'un militant*, Senegalese immigrant and labor activist Sally N'Dongo detailed the challenges facing his fellow workers. He explained:

> I cannot not speak about the conditions of reception and lodging for African workers in France or for immigrants in general, because for me this is the key problem. The slum-ghettos, where our countrymen are stuck, serve as a propaganda instrument for fascist groups with which to provoke racism against immigrants.[2]

N'Dongo argued that colonial-era exploitation continued after independence through immigration to France, the former colonizer, a point that scholars in a variety of disciplines highlight.[3] Regional migration patterns within French West Africa, N'Dongo explained, had become global, taking African workers to France and major cities such as Paris and Marseille.[4] The reality that they confronted, though, was much different than they envisioned. Life in metropolitan France proved taxing, with exploitive working conditions, dilapidated housing, unemployment, racism, and loneliness.

Sally N'Dongo's advocacy on behalf of the African immigrant community in France and the state's response to his efforts and those of his contemporaries reflect the three key issues upon which this book focuses:

the multiple forms of immigrant political activism undertaken by African workers, the state's ever-growing surveillance of this community, and the social welfare programs that emerged as a result. *African Political Activism in Postcolonial France* positions political activism not as the anti-colonialism of previous generations but in terms of anti-racism in mainland France and other diasporic contexts. I emphasize the transcolonial and transnational aspects of immigrant advocacy from an historical perspective, bringing them together with other types of political activism that reflected different yet related forms of representation. The African immigrants discussed here endured racism and discrimination within French society and responded to it in complex and multifaceted ways. In the early decades after decolonization, they were engaged politically in much more complicated ways than acknowledged in studies focused on the contemporary era. Through visible political activism, African immigrants shaped state policies toward immigration, just as they had influenced colonial governance in *Afrique-Occidentale française* (AOF or French-controlled West Africa).[5] Together with other immigrant communities, African political activists such as N'Dongo and their organizations helped to transform Paris into a postcolonial city, even as they confronted a neocolonial society.[6] Through the political sphere, African immigrants and other groups influenced the development of several state initiatives, from surveillance to social welfare programs. State efforts on behalf of African immigrants proved more substantial and enduring than acknowledged in previous accounts. While the state intended to use these kinds of initiatives to control the African community, African workers at times procured benefits from the very social welfare policies meant to restrict and survey them.

African Political Activism in Postcolonial France offers new ways of thinking about the lives of African immigrants in France after decolonization. This analysis contributes to the growing discourse on mobility throughout the world. These pages explore the plight of African workers in France between 1960, the year of independence for France's West African colonies, and 1981, when the law of associations was liberalized and immigrants could found them. Although the focus here is on one immigrant group in the Paris region, it reflects the importance of movement between countries, between France and Sub-Saharan Africa, between Paris and the *banlieues*, between northern France and southern France, and between rural and urban regions. This is also the first analysis of postcolonial African immigrants to assess the relationship between political activism and the state's response. At the core of African immigrants' participation in the political sphere was a response to the challenging conditions they faced on multiple fronts, from housing to health and employment. Initiatives such as the opening of the *Centre Bossuet* and the initiation of the relocation program addressed issues underlying the political responses of many African immigrants, including struggles with disease and housing, respectively. African political activism shaped the state's response to this population by drawing its attention to key issues and the state in turn dictated the contours of that activism.

In investigating how African political activism shaped state policies, *African Political Activism in Postcolonial France* seeks to better understand how immigrants fought against a system that not only dissuaded them from staying, but that was also, at least on some levels, influenced by colonial notions of race and ethnicity, despite the French state's premise of equality dating back to the the French Revolution. A range of organizations and individuals, including N'Dongo, provided racial advocacy when French society and the state struggled to do so for African immigrants and other groups. Their efforts contributed to the global black radical tradition dating back to the Saint-Domingue revolution of the late eighteenth century and continuing with the abolitionism of the nineteenth century and the struggle for civil rights and against colonialism and apartheid in the twentieth century.

African Political Activism in Postcolonial France engages with several areas of scholarly inquiry, ranging from the study of immigrants to the investigation of surveillance and the legacy of colonialism. Within migration studies, many important analyses have focused on integration, yielding critical contributions to our understanding of immigration and identity.[7] My work moves in a different direction. Factoring in the dynamics of colonialism, decolonization, and their effect on immigrant political activism and state policy in the postcolonial, Cold War era reveals that immigrants from francophone Sub-Saharan Africa were key players who shaped the development of public policy toward immigrants. Through this approach, we can understand how republicanism, colonial ideology, immigration policy, and immigrant political activism intersected in the postcolonial era, shaping the reception of African workers and affecting their lives and experiences in France.[8] State organizations such as the Centre Bossuet, for example, were modeled on colonial-era institutions in France and French West Africa. Rather than emphasizing citizenship and integration for non-western immigrant groups, including African workers, French officials in the postcolonial era sought to contain them in order to preserve the social and political order in France, which they perceived as being threatened by immigrant political activism, especially as it seemed increasingly allied with the *Parti communiste français* (French Communist Party or PCF) and other leftist organizations. This reflected not only the paranoia on the Left and the Right embedded in the Cold War, but also the state's lingering suspicion of African organizations in light of the success of anti-colonial movements in fighting for the independence of France's African colonies. Various facets of African immigration highlighted the emergence of a neocolonial society in France after decolonization.[9] Postcolonial African immigration to France, then, reflects the legacy of colonialism and its impact on the trajectory of French society and politics long after the end of France's empire.

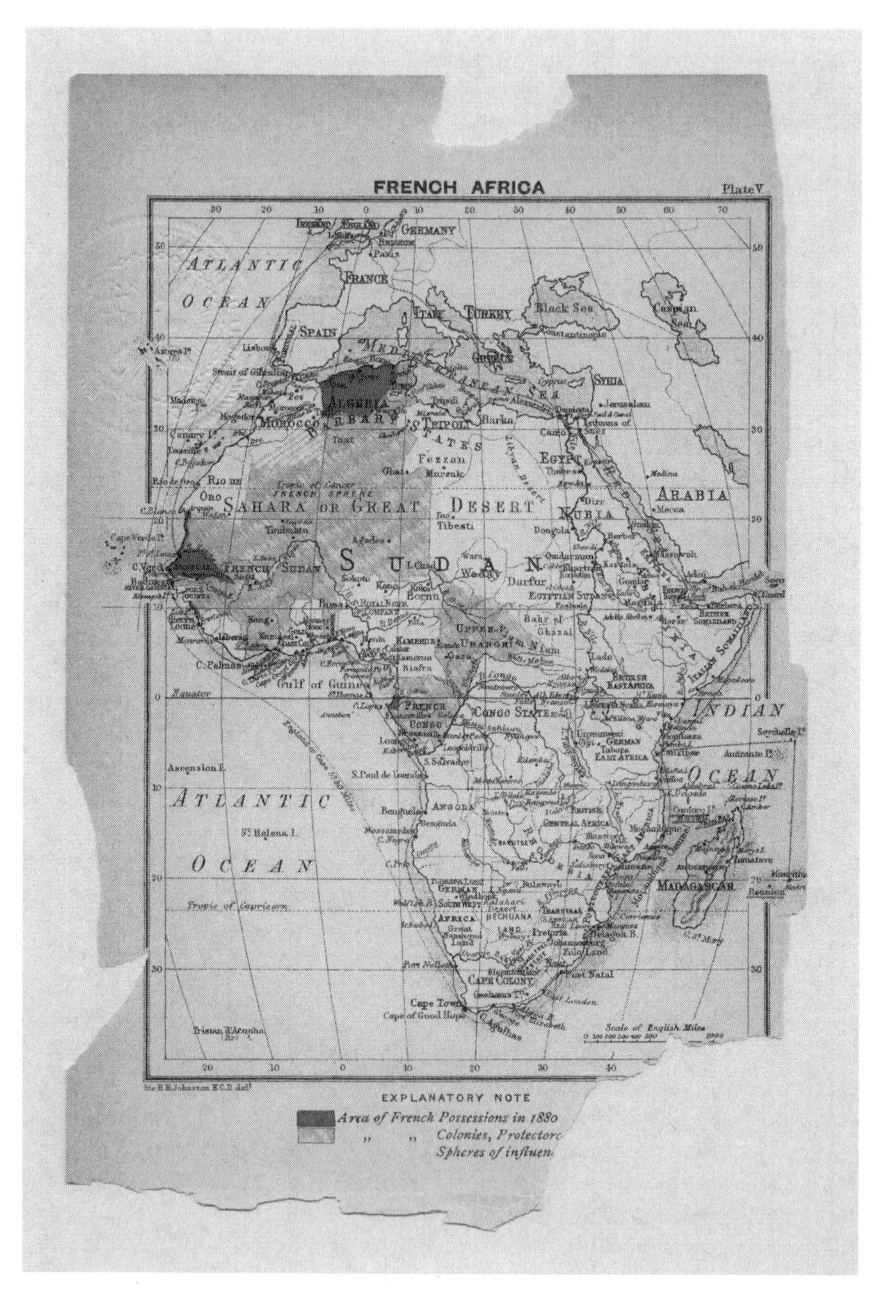

Figure I.1 French Africa. Image courtesy of Schomburg Center for Research in Black Culture, Jean Blackwell Hutson Research and Reference Division, New York Public Library Digital Collections.

There is ample room historiographically for a study that takes into consideration the political lives, experiences, and activism of African immigrants after decolonization. Earlier scholars of immigration to France focused primarily on migration from other European countries, including Italy and Poland and, later, Spain and Portugal, emphasizing integration as a key theme.[10] More recent contributions point to the importance of immigration from French colonies in North Africa, Sub-Saharan Africa, and Southeast Asia throughout the nineteenth and twentieth centuries, adding considerably to our understanding of the history of global migration to France and how it is that colonialism itself shaped those immigration patterns.[11] This new direction in migration studies was prompted, in part, by the growing body of scholarship on French colonialism in those regions.[12] Additionally, the emphasis on postwar, Cold War history has helped scholars to historicize post-colonial migration from various colonies, indicating the ways in which the colonial empire influenced the French economy, politics, and society long after its collapse. Much of the newer scholarship in this area, however, focuses on the Algerian and, more broadly, North African communities. Obviously, this is an important area of scholarly inquiry, but incorporating immigrants from Sub-Saharan Africa and their political activities into the story of postwar, postcolonial French history is critical to a more complete understanding of twentieth-century immigrant political activism. Workers from Sub-Saharan Africa who were recruited to work in France throughout the 1960s and into the 1970s shaped the direction of French immigration and social welfare policies through political activism for the better part of two decades. The politicization of African immigrants raised their profile in terms of public visibility, placing them at the center of important broader debates regarding identity and community within French society in the postwar, postcolonial, Cold War era.

This study also joins other recent contributions that challenge the colonial–metropolitan divide, bridging it through an assessment of an immigrant community from former colonies in French West Africa.[13] Several histories of the black community in France consider the colonial empire and its effects on metropolitan France during the interwar period.[14] The same must be done for the postwar era and African immigrants who arrived during and after decolonization. Decolonization was not a rupture in terms of immigration policy. Important continuities between the colonial and postcolonial eras need to be taken into account to truly understand the experiences of postcolonial African immigrants in France as well as those of other immigrant groups. The state's interpretation of immigrant political activism, for example, was shaped by colonial understandings of race and ethnicity, which in turn influenced some of the policies developed in response to the African community's growing presence. Questions arose over who could be integrated based on colonial notions of race and ethnicity, while important patterns of politicization undertaken by African workers in

Sub-Saharan Africa and France during the interwar period continued after World War Two and decolonization.

African Political Activism in Postcolonial France contributes to literature focusing on what Dominic Thomas and other scholars refer to as "black France." Recent scholarship assesses the lives and contributions of black workers and black activists from multiple perspectives over the course of the twentieth century, reflecting the diversity of emphases and types of analysis undertaken by scholars working in a variety of disciplines. In *Des Africains noirs en France*, for example, Mall Far argues that throughout the twentieth century, Africans were powerful social and political actors, albeit often overlooked as such.[15] Brent Hayes Edward's *The Practice of Diaspora* traces the contours of black internationalism during the interwar years, looking at the complex and diverse places where members of the international black community connected with one another and the subsequent results in what he terms "the discourses of black internationalism."[16] Through his focus on the poets turned politicians Aimé Césaire and Léopold Senghor of Martinique and Senegal, respectively, historian Gary Wilder's *Freedom Time* explains that both figures represent efforts to secure decolonization through self-determination rather than state sovereignty.[17] Senghor and Césaire envisioned "colonial emancipation and (an) alternative global order that would promote civilizational reconciliation and human self-realization."[18] These two key figures also believed in the centrality of Africans and Antilleans to, as Wilder phrased it in his first book, the French imperial nation-state.[19] Shifting to the postcolonial period, in *Decolonizing the Republic*, Félix F. Germain explains that the colonial relations established during the interwar period and chronicled by scholars such as Hayes Edwards persisted after decolonization. Black workers from Sub-Saharan Africa and the Caribbean became what he terms "agents of decolonization" in France from the 1950s to the contemporary period.[20] Germain's work also factors in gender and provides insight into the lives of African and Antillean women living in France after decolonization. In *La parole immigrée*, Jean-Philippe Dedieu argues that in understanding how it is that immigrants from Sub-Saharan Africa participated in the public sphere through associations and other types of organizations, we can more easily discern the influence of African states on the former colonizer. Doing so also allows for a greater understanding of how democracies resist or accept the contributions of immigrants within public discourse.[21] Pap N'Diaye, in *La condition noire*, explores the multiple factors that contribute to the complex identity that has emerged for black residents of France.[22] Thomas argues in *Black France* that a symbiotic relationship exists between France and Africa as relayed through the cultural contributions of writers from several African nation-states, including Senegal, Cameroon, the Congo, Ivory Coast, and beyond. Placing them within a comparative framework, Thomas explains, provides "new ways of thinking about the symbiotic dimension of relations and population flows between France and the Francophone world."[23]

These studies have enriched our understanding of the worldwide African diaspora and its contributions to, for example, the black radical tradition and developments such as decolonization, civil rights, and human rights. Through these and other important works, we have come to understand the rich political lives of the African diaspora in France during the interwar period with workers' movements, the early postwar era with the student activism in the 1950s, and the *sans-papiers* of the late 1990s.[24] *African Political Activism in Postcolonial France* argues that the political activism undertaken by the African immigrant community in France during the era of decolonization contributes to this important global tradition of black radical politics.

Until recently, though, few works accounted for the vibrant political lives of African workers across the 1960s and into the 1970s. Those that have looked at African political activism after World War Two usually do so from the students' perspective, as we see with Fabienne Guimont's *Les étudiants africains en France*.[25] Thus, the state's responses to African political activism after 1960—and how this activism influenced the Fifth Republic's policies toward immigrant communities—are not well understood. Little of the existing scholarship engages with archival records from the police or, more broadly, the Ministry of the Interior. There is ample evidence, however, to suggest a robust reaction from the state to an increasingly politicized African immigrant community. Appalled and concerned by this activism, the French state dealt with what it saw as threatening political behavior, revealing how it was that immigration itself shaped state policy after decolonization.

To spotlight the activism of the African community itself, *African Political Activism in Postcolonial France* examines a full range of political activities of African immigrants, from rent strikes to political protests and the creation of formal organizations such as the *Union générale des travailleurs sénégalais en France* (General Union of Senegalese Workers or the UGTSF). In fact, political activism undertaken by African immigrants influenced state policy to a much greater extent than previously acknowledged, revealing the "give and take" relationship that developed between the Fifth Republic and the African immigrant community. Although the state undertook extensive monitoring and surveillance of this community, some of the social welfare programs that it developed benefitted Africans, including those in the area of health and medicine. Others, however, proved disruptive and dislocating, including the relocations undertaken in what was known as the anti-slum campaign. All the while, long-standing colonial conceptualizations of this community shaped state initiatives while the African community itself carried on an important tradition of political activism in France that dated back to the interwar period.

Sally N'Dongo ties together all of these stories. He arrived in France in the late 1950s as an unknown immigrant in search of work, reflecting one of the main reasons for which African immigrants came to France. N'Dongo not only witnessed the deplorable living and working conditions that his fellow African immigrants endured, but he also experienced them first-hand

and became politically active in response, as did many of his fellow workers. In the early 1960s, N'Dongo founded what would become one of the most powerful African immigrant organizations in France, the *Union générale des travailleurs sénégalais en France* (UGTSF). By the early 1970s, members of the African immigrant community had created a vibrant political sphere for themselves, built in part on the model of trade unions found in France and AOF. N'Dongo and other immigrants, subject to French law regarding the founding of organizations, transformed these unions into powerful advocacy organizations while also providing private social welfare services, including housing, to fellow immigrants. N'Dongo became a prominent spokesperson for the African immigrant community, growing more critical of the French state as conditions for African workers worsened. Like his politically active predecessors of the interwar period, N'Dongo's police file grew thicker as authorities became alarmed over his sharp rhetoric aimed at the French state and what he deemed its exploitive immgration policy. From the perspective of policy makers, though, N'Dongo should never have existed because they interpreted African workers as apathetic towards the political sphere. Yet there he was, at the center of postcolonial grassroots African political activism.

N'Dongo's story is unique in that few African immigrants achieved his level of prominence in France after decolonization. Yet his increasingly powerful position reflected that of his predecessors in the *Négritude* and Pan-African nationalist movements of the interwar period, including Lamine Sénghor, a former Senegalese soldier turned revolutionary political activist in France by the 1920s.[26] N'Dongo used the framework of colonial exploitation that Pan-African nationalists such as Sénghor shaped to explain what was happening to African immigrants in France after decolonization. From N'Dongo's perspective, it was the legacy of colonialism itself that explained the racism and discrimination that African workers experienced in France. Workers from former French colonies such as Senegal, Mali, and Mauritania, who expected to find financial enrichment, instead confronted poverty, destitution, and discrimination in the very country that promoted itself as purveyor of the "civilizing mission" embedded within French colonialism. From N'Dongo's perspective, the exploitation undertaken in the colonies continued in France. One African worker called this the "mirage of fortune," reflecting the stark reality that life in France did not live up to the idea of fortune and opportunity that drew many immigrants in the first place. They responded with a wide range of political activities unexpected by the French officials observing them.

N'Dongo's growing reputation as an immigrant activist, then, reflected the overall politicization of France's African immigrant community. The tradition of activism established during the interwar period and carried forward by African students into the early postwar era continued after independence in Sub-Saharan Africa. This continuance occurred much to the surprise and alarm of French state officials, who watched as the African immigrant community grew in size and in visibility. N'Dongo was but one of thousands of African immigrants who created and joined organizations and protested through rent strikes and other demonstrations. These activists were willing to risk deportation in order to make the point that France was failing the very immigrants it had recruited as a labor source during the dramatic economic expansion after World War Two.

How did this political awakening happen? How is it that thousands of African immigrants established and joined trade unions and openly protested throughout the late 1960s and early 1970s, risking deportation as authorities increasingly viewed them as dangerous and a threat to the French political and social order after the end of empire? How did a group of immigrants perceived to be politically neutral in the early 1960s become the target of aggressive Fifth Republic surveillance and social welfare programs amidst the expansion of the welfare state across postwar Europe?

The answer begins with a look at the history of immigration to France. The arrival of African workers after 1960 was part of the large-scale labor migration to France that occurred after World War Two. Despite hesitations over the use of workers from the colonies and former colonies, various French governments emphasized immigration from Europe and beyond as a solution to France's ongoing demographic challenges, dating back to the nineteenth century and, in the twentieth century, exacerbated by the devastation

Figure I.2 French colonies in Africa circa 1920. Image courtesy of Wikimedia.

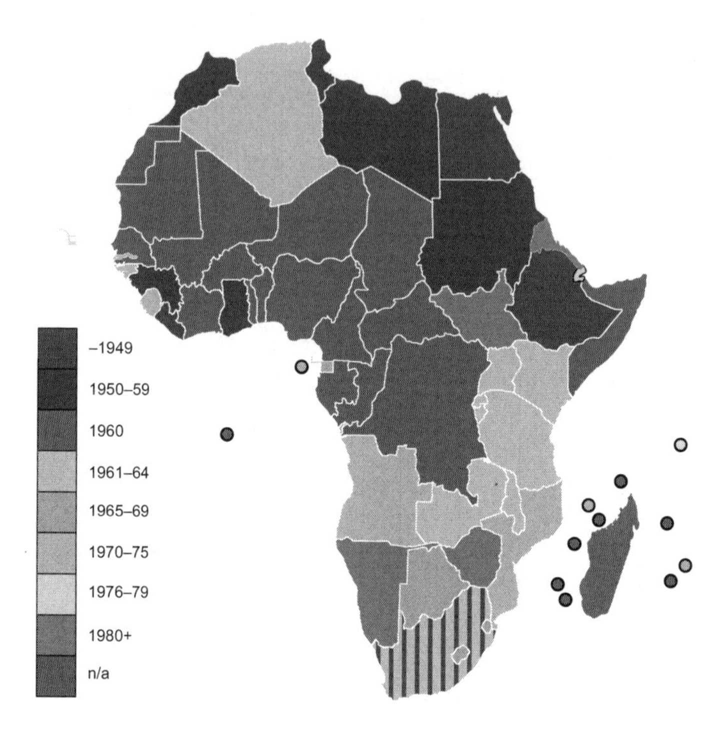

Figure I.3 Map of decolonization in Africa. Image courtesy of Wikimedia.

of two world wars.[27] Concerns about plummeting birth rates and the need for white regeneration dated back to the Third Republic and increased with the demographic decimation of World War One. By the late 1940s, the Fourth Republic had created an immigration policy that prioritized the recruitment of European workers while attempting to reduce migration from the Mediterranean region, the Middle East, and Africa.[28] As Patrick Weil argues, officials ranked immigrants of European origin much higher than those from the colonies and former colonies.[29] Workers from French-controlled North Africa and West Africa were considered racially inferior and problematic. In addition, some of their social, cultural, and religious norms, from the practice of polygamy to the practice of Islam, were seen as incompatible with the values of French society.[30] Despite lingering racism and these negative connotations, though, workers from Sub-Saharan Africa and North Africa continued to arrive and find employment in a variety of French industries, including manufacturing and construction.

Decolonization and its impact also factor into this story. As restrictions on Algerians entering France increased amidst the intensifying war in Algeria and despite skepticism over their ability to adapt to urban life in Paris, African workers became more attractive to employers by the late 1950s and early 1960s.[31] Entrenched in a brutal conflict in Algeria after losing its former colony in Indochina, the French government sought to avoid another protracted military conflict in Sub-Saharan Africa. Former colonies such as Senegal, Mali, and Mauritania became sovereign nation states in 1960 as France relinquished its colonial empire in AOF amidst the "Thirty Glorious Years" of postwar economic growth.

As the empire collapsed, the French government and private companies struggled to find enough workers to fill the labor needs of the postwar economy. Labor migration from European countries continued, but French industries from construction to car manufacturing competed against booming nations such as West Germany and Italy for these European workers.[32] Demand for workers outpaced supply in economies throughout Western Europe. Whereas West Germany recruited Turkish guest workers to shore up its labor pool, the French economy looked within and beyond Europe, turning to its colonies and former colonies.[33]

More specifically, as the Algerian war grew increasingly violent by the early 1960s and immigration from Algeria became more difficult, industries and the French government looked to its former colonies in Sub-Saharan Africa for workers as independence came to these regions.[34] What they encountered were already-established labor migration patterns between Sub-Saharan Africa and cities such as Paris and Marseille dating back to the interwar period.[35] Both the *Office national de l'immigration* (National Immigration Office or ONI), established in 1945, and private companies tapped into this migration network.[36] By 1956, Algerians were required to have official visas to enter France, thereby making labor migration that much harder to facilitate for private companies looking for supplemental labor sources. The number of Algerian immigrants entering France dropped precipitously in the late 1950s, with more Algerians leaving than entering the country. In 1955, 194,000 Algerians came to France. One year later, the number fell to 79,000.[37] With continued economic growth, French industries recognized the labor shortage that they faced on all fronts: too few European immigrants, too many restrictions on Algerian workers until after 1962, and too few French citizens willing to work in low-level and low-paying jobs. These developments opened the way for African immigrants to enter France and its labor market at higher numbers than previously seen.[38]

Workers from Sub-Saharan Africa, like their Algerian counterparts until 1956, when they faced new visa restrictions in the midst of the Algerian War, could come to France with few impediments to immigration. Companies began sending representatives to French cities such as Marseille and Le Havre to recruit African workers already living there, many of whom had already begun to take up employment in small factories. Automobile industry executives seized an opportunity to bring these immigrants to Paris. Renault, for example, tried to convince African workers in Marseille to relocate to the Paris basin and work at the factory in Billancourt.[39] Even the Paris city government participated, recruiting Soninké workers as street sweepers.[40] These recruiters utilized the networks established by African workers, including those from the Soninké ethnicity, over the first half of the twentieth century.[41] For the most part, African immigrants were clustered in a small number of industries, and especially in automobile manufacturing. Many African immigrants worked for two of the major French automobile manufacturers: Renault and Citroën. Workers from Sub-Saharan Africa also found employment as metalworkers and in the construction and textile industries.[42]

Because of this emphasis on labor recruitment in and beyond the colonies and former colonies, postwar and postcolonial immigration and the French Fifth Republic developed together. Despite shifting citizenship status with independence, African immigrants retained many of the same rights in the early postcolonial era, including free circulation between France and their new African nation states.[43] As the Fifth Republic emerged in 1958 from the ashes of its predecessor the Fourth Republic, an uptick occurred in the number of immigrant workers arriving from the colonies of Senegal, Mali, and Mauritania. Authorities in the Ministry of the Interior and elsewhere in the French government took notice.[44] By the 1960s, as thousands of African immigrants arrived in the Paris region, officials grew increasingly alarmed about how their presence would affect French society. The very language that they used to describe this immigrant group was borrowed directly from the colonial realm as officials appropriated French colonial terms for a variety of African ethnic groups, including the Soninké.[45]

The reality of African immigration and official perceptions of it were often in conflict with one another. Accounts of this community in the 1960s labeled it "numerically very weak."[46] By the late 1950s, a few hundred African workers arrived per year.[47] That number grew to several thousand per year by the mid-1960s after independence in Sub-Saharan Africa. The African immigrant community's size increased to between 28,000 and 70,000 by the mid-1960s.[48] Government officials ranked Africans last in terms of suitability for industrial work and yet private-sector recruitment efforts were well under way. Between 1960 and 1974, which brought the suspension of labor migration to France, African immigration was dominated by Senegalese, Malian, and Mauritanian immigrants. One 1969 study estimated that 40 percent of Africans in France originated from Mali, while 25 percent came from Senegal and 25 percent hailed from Mauritania.[49] Official estimates varied of course, but one placed 2,000 African workers in France in 1953 and 15,000 by 1956.[50] By 1963, that figure had grown to between 22,000 and 30,000.[51] The *Préfecture de police* estimated the African population in France at 22,000 in 1969.[52] Other sources cited figures as high as 50,000.[53] The difficulty in identifying the precise African population stemmed from the growth of undocumented immigration after 1963. African workers sometimes arrived without work contracts, medical documentation, or guaranteed housing. As early as 1964, several government agencies began investigating the number of undocumented African workers, ushering in an era of increased scrutiny and surveillance across the 1960s and into the 1970s.[54]

Several factors continued to shape African immigration to France, from citizenship status to changing international borders. Because of decolonization, the early 1960s brought important changes in nationality for African workers. Immigrants from France's former colonies in Sub-Saharan Africa were now "Senegalese," "Malian," or "Mauritanian" nationals rather than French citizens, a status they held during the late colonial period, which meant that they assumed a new national identity. The closing of national borders during independence also shaped immigration from Sub-Saharan Africa. Those border closings disrupted long-standing Soninké migration patterns, which amplified immigration to France because migration to Europe served as a viable alternative to movement between African nation states. A priest working in Mali argued at the time that, "traditional migration became difficult because of the closure of neighboring countries."[55] Even if they could not move as easily between the new African nation-states created out of former colonies, between 1960 and 1963, African workers could still freely circulate between their nation-states and France. While gaining the citizenship of their new nation-states, they could also obtain French citizenship through a declaration guided by the law of July 28, 1960, which recognized French citizenship of those born in former AOF colonies by judicial declaration.[56]

Between 1963 and 1964, the situation changed again, as France signed bilateral migration treaties with Mali, Mauritania, and Senegal. Agreements between France and its former colonies based legal entry into France on the stipulation that immigrants would arrive in possession of a labor contract and a medical certificate guaranteeing their health.[57] Because of the long-standing tradition of migration between Sub-Saharan Africa and France, many African workers continued to arrive without the labor contracts or medical examinations mandated by the agreements. Without the proper papers, though, they were technically categorized as undocumented immigrants and could be subject to deportation, which added a layer of uncertainty to what quickly became an already tenuous existence in France.[58] The status of African workers who came to reside in France, then, was often transformed through independence from that of colonial subjects or citizens to that of foreign nationals.[59]

With that transition, the state viewed African immigrants as more dangerous than previously perceived, even as they provided a source of labor. This change in status followed broader shifts from a regime of immigration in the nineteenth century to one of migration marked by increased restrictions in the twentieth century.[60] For the first time since the establishment of France's colonies in Sub-Saharan Africa, immigrants from that region were neither colonial subjects nor colonial citizens—they were, in many cases, categorized as foreigners. Through a process of negotiation, French officials had to adjust how they addressed what they perceived as a new category of immigrants and they did so by relying on previous colonial policies and earlier approaches to immigration, many of which were developed during the interwar period.[61]

Authorities' use of the term "*problème noir*" or "black problem" signified the state's struggle in addressing this supposedly new population of immigrants even though France was home to a long-standing African immigrant community. Although concerns over politicization and leftist influence among African immigrants preoccupied authorities monitoring their presence, the "black problem" also came to signify in the official imagination what, exactly, they were dealing with: a "problem" of sorts as contextualized in the era of decolonization and the collapse of the French empire. That officials used the term "problem" in referring to African immigration reinforced racial subjugation and racism in the postcolonial era. The idea of the African presence in France as a problem to be solved wove its way into the official imagination in regard to workers from Sub-Saharan Africa. This in turn influenced the state's outlook on this immigrant community as it enacted increasingly restrictive policies toward immigrants over the course of the twentieth century. As Carole Reynaud-Paligot argues, a "veritable culture of race was thus a staple in Western society from the 1850s to the Second World War."[62] Following World War II, as Reynaud-Paligot explains, prevailing understandings of race were discredited, but as revealed here, they did not disappear.[63]

Because of these concerns, the state, which had monitored African workers since the interwar period in France, continued to do so in the postwar and postcolonial eras, even as it understood African workers initially as apolitical, especially in comparison to their Algerian counterparts.[64] As African immigrant politicization became more visible over the course of the 1960s, administrators began to acknowledge the political tendencies of African workers to a much greater extent, while also panicking about the possibility of leftist influence within this immigrant community. State surveillance and social welfare became intimately connected.[65] As Ann Laura Stoler argues, "the personal was highly political" and, conversely, one can argue that the political was highly personal in the surveillance of immigrant communities.[66]

After 1960, what Gary Wilder labels the imperial nation-state was transformed into a post-imperial country with significant colonial influences, retaining policies and attitudes developed in its colonial regimes throughout the world.[67] This occurred largely because of the influence of French colonialism in post-colonial immigration policy and the ways in which it shaped officials' perceptions of African immigrants and, in turn, policies such as social welfare initiatives. Administrators who had once worked in the colonies looked back to them for inspiration while continuing the trajectory of migratory controls, tracking, monitoring, and social welfare programs established in the interwar period, continued into the Vichy years, and carried over into the postwar era.[68] Emphasizing how daily life shaped the political realm, for example, historian Shannon Fogg argues that during World War Two, foreigners and anyone seen as an outsider experienced challenges in accessing basic goods despite the rationing system.[69] After decolonization, outsiders, including Sub-Saharan Africans, were still under suspicion, as they were before and during World War Two in AOF and France. Authorities refined the system of surveillance honed in the colonies and in the metropolitan context.[70] Spanning three important eras in twentieth-century French history—the interwar period, the Vichy years of World War Two, and the postwar era—authorities developed and sometimes withheld resources using the information that they gleaned through surveillance, which included, for example, the infiltration of meetings and the tracking of prominent figures, including N'Dongo. Thus this was the context in which African workers found themselves living as they arrived in France.

As they navigated the intricacies of citizenship status, immigration regulations, and ideas of race, African Workers who arrived after 1960 settled in the Paris region, France's industrial center at that time and the focus of this book.[71] These immigrants reconvened in specific neighborhoods in Paris and the *banlieues*, such as Saint-Denis, which had rich political histories and traditions of their own. For most of the twentieth century, for example, the French Communist Party found substantial support in *banlieues* such as Bobigny, creating what historian Tyler Stovall labeled a political "red belt" surrounding Paris.[72] He and other scholars point to the long-standing tension between Paris and its periphery as workers were pushed to the city's outer edges, beginning with the nineteenth century's urban renewal projects and continuing into the twentieth century.[73]

As part of a generation born colonial subjects in AOF during the 1920s and 1930s, these immigrants responded to the precarious living and working conditions that they encountered in those neighborhoods and *banlieues* by building on a tradition of political activity and trade unionism in Sub-Saharan Africa and France. They created labor unions, held demonstrations, staged strikes, and, at times, rioted, all the while raising their profile and creating awareness about their plight. Politicized by the appalling living and working conditions that they confronted, African immigrants extended and transformed the vibrant political culture created by their predecessors during the interwar period into the postwar and post-colonial eras. The political activities undertaken by African immigrants challenged the neocolonial society that emerged after decolonization, while also surprising the officials who initially perceived them as apolitical, despite the strong affinity for political activism displayed by previous generations of African workers.[74] By participating in riots and demonstrations, mounting rent strikes, and formally organizing through associations such as the UGTSF, the postcolonial African immigrant community forced the French government to acknowledge its shortcomings in improving the immigrant experience.

The transition from the colonial to the postcolonial era provided a foundation for this politicization. Weil argues that from 1968 on, immigration became a central aspect of public and political debate and policy.[75] Even earlier than Weil acknowledges, immigrant political activism and specifically that of African workers played a prominent role in making immigration both a public and a political issue. The "immigration question" emerged within public discourse due to the activism undertaken by African workers and other immigrant groups and the legacy of this activism as immigrants themselves shaped public discourse and the state's response to their presence. Through their advocacy, leaders such as Sally N'Dongo and organizations such as the UGTSF forced the plight of African workers in France into the public sphere. This story is important to postwar and post-colonial French, African, and global history because it has much to tell us about how immigrant communities used political tactics in response to their plight and how the state reacted through social welfare policy initiatives often designed for other immigrant groups with different demographic profiles, including Algerians.

An international dialogue about human rights also shaped these political tactics. Although France was never home to a U.S.-style postwar Civil Rights Movement, immigrants from around the world who resided in France utilized the language of human rights, civil rights, independence, and autonomy. The social and political activism undertaken by African immigrants emerged within the context of an international movement focused on human rights, one that eschewed racism, discrimination, and segregation.[76] From the perspective of African immigrants, one of the most accessible templates upon which to base their approach to political activism was that of the anti-colonial movements in Sub-Saharan Africa. Yet the quest for civil rights in the U.S. and beyond, which in turn was heavily influenced by the postwar emphasis on human rights, shaped the discourse of African immigrants in the public sphere throughout the post-colonial period.[77] French radicals and trade unionists also contributed to this movement and many of the organizations founded by African immigrants represented a blend of these various political styles, approaches, and tactics.

To discuss these important and interconnected issues, *African Political Activism in Postcolonial France* uses a range of sources from various archives throughout France. Much of the documentation supporting this book is drawn from police surveillance and government reports generated by several ministries over many decades of the twentieth century. The *Archives nationales d'Outre Mer* provided documentation through the SLOTFOM files regarding the surveillance of African immigrants in France during the interwar period. Both the *Centre des Archives Nationales* and the *Centre des archives nationales contemporaines* house important documents regarding African immigrants on issues ranging from health to housing to various organizations. Regional archives such as those of the Val-de-Marne and Seine-Saint-Denis departments provided important materials on African organizations, political activity, housing, health, and education. Municipal archives, such as those in Saint-Denis and Ivry, offered critical documentation on specific events, including the Saint-Denis riot and the Ivry rent strike, respectively. Each of these archives also included interviews and personal correspondence between African immigrants and their friends and family as well as political tracts circulated by both African organizations and French groups supporting their cause. Published reports and books at the *Bibliothèque nationale François Mitterand* (Francois Mitterand National Library or BN), the *Centre d'information et d'études sur les migrations internationales*, and the *Bibliothèque de documentation internationale contemporaine* contributed several different types of sources, incuding published volumes, to this book as well. The BN's newspaper holdings proved invaluable and the *Institut national de l'audiovisuel* provided unique and important radio and television reports and interviews.

In drawing on these sources, *African Political Activism in Postcolonial France* is divided into two sections. The first section examines various forms of African immigrant political activism, from the creation and trajectory of the UGTSF to a rent strike in Ivry outside of Paris to the protests that followed the deaths of five immigrants in Aubervilliers outside of the capital. Chapter 1 investigates the UGTSF's founding in response to the challenges African immigrants faced in France, initial activities in housing and education, and its later politicization in order to understand the early postcolonial political trajectory taken by African immigrant groups. The group evolved from socially focused to politically oriented over a 20-year span. Chapter 2 explores a large-scale immigrant-led rent strike in Ivry within the context of the growing, diverse, and sometimes unexpected forms of African political activism across the 1960s and 1970s. Chapter 3 considers the deaths of five African immigrants at Aubervilliers in January of 1970 from several perspectives, looking at the bereavement experienced by the African immigrant community as well as the responses of advocacy groups, leftist political organizations who advocated for immigrants, public intellectuals, and the media.

The second section examines the state's response through social welfare initiatives, including the establishment of a medical clinic in Paris and the anti-slum campaign, which undertook the physical relocation of African immigrants and other immigrant groups throughout the capital city and its *banlieues*. Bridging the two is a chapter focused on surveillance and the ways in which the Fifth Republic monitored the African immigrant community. Chapter 4 explores how the French state watched African immigrants and the ways in which this monitoring was influenced by factors such as immigrant political activism, the Cold War, discourse on international human rights, and decolonization and independence. Chapter 5 argues that, through the Centre Bossuet, medicine and medical care became a space for surveillance and what Neil MacMaster and Jim House describe as the penetration of an immigrant community. Yet the Centre Bossuet also provided critical medical and social welfare services.[78] African immigrants benefitted from the clinic's services and made it their own, demonstrating the reciprocity that developed between state authorities and African workers. Chapter 6 uses the relocation of African immigrants across the Paris region to understand the impact of political protest, state surveillance, and social welfare initiatives on the African immigrant community.[79]

This story, then, shows the dynamic between state officials and African immigrants in a new way. On the one hand, they clashed with one another. But on the other hand, they worked together through unexpected channels. The state not only attempted to enact political repression but also extended programs that benefitted the African immigrant community, including assistance with housing, medical care, and educational opportunities, including job training. Although the French government constructed itself as in control of this community, it was not always the powerful entity that it portrayed itself to be. African immigrants carved out an important niche within the social and political spaces of French society, in large part because of their dealings with the state.

Notes

1 Daniel A. Gordon, *Immigrants and Intellectuals: May '68 and the Rise of Anti-Racism in France* (Pontypool: Merlin Press, 2012), 15.
2 Sally N'Dongo, *Voyage forcé: Itinéraire d'un militant* (Paris: François Maspero, 1975), 12. Original French: "Je ne peux pas ne pas parler des conditions d'accueil et de logement des travailleurs africains en France ou des immigrés en général, car pour moi c'est un problème clé. Ces taudis-ghettos où sont parqués nos compatriotes servent d'instrument de propagande aux groupes fascistes pour provoquer le racisme contre les immigrés."
3 For discussions of the colonial legacy in France from a variety of perspectives, see Nicholas Bancel, Pascal Blanchard, and Dominic Thomas, eds., *The Colonial Legacy in France: Fracture, Rupture, and Apartheid* (Bloomington: Indiana University Press, 2017).
4 N'Dongo, *Voyage forcé*, 12.
5 Elizabeth Foster, *Faith in Empire: Religion, Politics, and Colonial Rule in French Senegal, 1880–1940* (Stanford: Stanford University Press, 2013), 4–5.
6 Jennifer A. Boittin, *Colonial Metropolis: The Urban Grounds of Anti-Imperialism and Feminism in Interwar Paris* (Lincoln: The University of Nebraska-Lincoln, 2010), xv.
7 For example, sociologist Riva Kastoryano has written on the question of integration. See Kastoryano, *Negotiating Identities: States and Immigrants in France and Germany* trans. Barbara Harshav (Princeton: Princeton University Press, 2002); Kastoryano, *Être Turc En France: réflexions sur les familles et communautés* (Paris: Éditions l'Harmattan, 2004). Patrick Weil writes on this issue as well: see Patrick Weil, *La France et ses étrangers: L'aventure d'une politique de l'immigration 1938–1991* (Paris: Calmann-Levy, 1991). See also Dominique Schnapper, *Qu'est-ce que l'intégration?* (Paris: Éditions Gallimard, 2007). Gérard Noiriel's seminal work on immigration to France largely introduced the topic to scholarly and historiographical discussion: see Gérard Noiriel. *Le creuset français: Histoire de l'immigration XIXe–XXe siècle* (Paris: Éditions du Seuil, 1988).
8 Alice Conklin, *A Mission to Civilize: The Republican Idea of Empire in France and West Africa, 1895–1930* (Stanford: Stanford University Press, 1997), 2.
9 Ibid., 8.
10 For example, see Marie-Claude Blanc-Chaléard, *Les Italiens dans l'est parisien: une histoire d'intégration (1880–1960)* (Rome: École française de Rome, 2000); Pierre Milza, ed., *Les Italiens en France de 1914 à 1940* (Rome: École française de Rome, 1986); Marie-Christine Volovitch-Tavares, *Portugais à Champigny, le*

temps des baraques (Paris: Autrement, 1995); Maria do Céu Cunha, *Portugais de France: essai sur une dynamique de double appartenance* (Paris: L'Harmattan, 1988).

11 See for example Clifford Rosenberg, *Policing Paris: The Origins of Modern Immigration Control between the Wars* (Ithaca; London: Cornell University Press, 2006); Neil MacMaster, *Colonial Migrants and Racism: Algerians in France, 1900–62* (Houndmills; Basingstoke; Hampshire; New York: Palgrave Macmillan, 1997); Amelia Lyons, *The Civilizing Mission in the Metropole: Algerian Families and the French Welfare State during Decolonization* (Stanford: Stanford University Press, 2013); Philippe Dewitte, *Les mouvements nègres en France, 1919–1939* (Paris: Éditions L'Harmattan, 1985).

12 Tony Chafer, *The End of Empire in French West Africa: France's Successful Decolonization?* (Oxford and New York: Berg, 2002); Conklin, *A Mission to Civilize*; Gary Wilder, *The French Imperial Nation-State: Négritude and Colonial Humanism between the Two World Wars* (Chicago; London: The University of Chicago Press, 2005); George R. Trumbull IV, *An Empire of Facts: Colonial Power, Cultural Knowledge, and Islam in Algeria, 1870–1914* (Cambridge: Cambridge University Press, 2009); Martin Thomas, *Empires of Intelligence: Security Services and Colonial Disorder After 1914* (Berkeley; Los Angeles: University of California Press, 2008).

13 Foster, *Faith in Empire*, 8.

14 Boittin, *Colonial Metropolis*, xxii–xxviii.

15 Mar Fall, *Des Africains noirs en France: Des tirailleurs sénégalais aux . . . Blacks* (Paris: Broche, 2000), 9–11.

16 Brent Hayes Edwards, *The Practice of Diaspora: Literature, Translation, and the Rise of Black Internationalism* (Cambridge; London: Harvard University Press, 2003), 9.

17 Gary Wilder, *Freedom Time: Négritude, Decolonization, and the Future of the World* (Durham: Duke University Press, 2015), 1–3.

18 Wilder, *Freedom Time*, 2.

19 Ibid., 6–7; Wilder, *The French Imperial Nation-State*, 3–23.

20 Félix F. Germain, *Decolonizing the Republic: African and Caribbean Migrants in Postwar Paris (1946–1974)* (East Lansing: Michigan State University Press, 2016), xii.

21 Jean-Philippe Dedieu, *La parole immigrée: Les migrants africains dans l'espace public en France (1960–1995)* (Paris: Klincksieck, 2012), 18.

22 Pap Ndiaye, *La condition noire: Essai sur une minorité française* (Paris: Éditions Calmann-Levy, 2008), 45–55.

23 Dominic Thomas, *Black France: Colonialism, Immigration, and Transnationalism* (Bloomington; Indianapolis: Indiana University Press, 2007), 3.

24 Fabienne Guimont, *Les étudiants africains en France (1950–1965)* (Paris: L'Harmattan, 1997); Thierry Blin, *Les sans-papiers de Saint-Bernard: mouvement social et action organisée* (Paris: L'Harmattan, 2005); Catherine Raissiguier, *Reinventing the Republic: Gender, Migration, and Citizenship in France* (Stanford: Stanford University Press, 2010).

25 Guimont, *Les étudiants africains en France*, 11–17.

26 Dewitte, *Les mouvements nègres en France, 1919–1939* (Paris: L'Harmattan, 1985), 51–52.

27 Joshua Cole, *The Power of Large Numbers: Population, Politics, and Gender in Nineteenth-Century France* (Ithaca: Cornell University Press, 2000), 2; Patrick Weil, *La France et ses étrangers*, 54.

28 Weil, *La France et ses étrangers*, 56.

29 Patrick Weil, "L'ordonnance de 1945: l'aboutissement l'un long processus," *Plein droit* 22–23 (1993) http://www.gisti.org/spip.php?article3899.

30 Weil, *La France et ses étrangers*, 48–75.
31 François Manchuelle, *Willing Migrants: Soninké Labor Diasporas, 1848–1960* (Athens: Ohio University Press, 1997), 213–214. François Manchuelle, "Background to Black African Emigration to France: the Labor Migrations of the Soninké, 1848–1987" (PhD diss., University of California-Santa Barbara, 1987), 490. See also Martin S. Alexander, J. F. V. Keiger, eds., *France and the Algerian War, 1954–62: Strategy, Operations and Diplomacy* (London; Portland, OR: Frank Cass, 2002).
32 For more on postwar European economic growth see Barry J. Eichengreen, *The European Economy since 1945: Coordinated Capitalism and Beyond* (Princeton: Princeton University Press, 2007); T. Iván Berend, *An Economic History of Twentieth-Century Europe: Economic Regimes from Laissez-Faire to Globalization* (Cambridge, UK; New York: Cambridge University Press, 2006).
33 For more on Turkish guest workers in Germany, see Jennifer A. Miller, "Postwar Negotiations: The First Generation of Turkish 'Guest Workers' in West Germany, 1961–1973" (PhD diss., Rutgers University, 2008); Miller, "Her Fight Is Your Fight: 'Guest Worker' Labor Activism in the Early 1970s West Germany," *International Labor and Working Class History* 84 (Fall 2013): 226–247; Miller, "On Track for West Germany: Turkish 'Guest-Worker' Rail Transportation to West Germany in the Postwar Period," *German History* 30, no. 4 (1 December 2012): 550–573.
34 Manchuelle, *Willing Migrants*, 213.
35 Ibid., 197–203.
36 Catherine Wihtol de Wenden, *Les immigrés et la politique: Cent cinquante ans d'évolution* (Paris: Presses de la Fondation Nationale des Sciences Politiques, 1988), 85.
37 Manchuelle, *Willing Migrants*, 213.
38 Ibid., 214; Manchuelle, "Background to Black African Emigration to France," 490.
39 Manchuelle, *Willing Migrants*, 213–214.
40 Ibid., 214; Manchuelle, "The 'Patriarchal Ideal' of Soninké Labor Migrants: From Slave Owners to Employers of Free Labor," *Canadian Journal of African Studies/ Revue canadienne des études africaines* 23, no. 1 (1989): 108.
41 Manchuelle, *Willing Migrants*, 215–219.
42 CANC 19960311 art. 6 "L'étude sur l'immigration des travailleurs africains." 1969.
43 AN Fla 5136 Préfecture de la Seine, "Étude problème noir région parisienne." Paris.
44 AN FIa 5136 Gérard Esperét, Conseil économique et social, *Journal officiel de la république française: Avis et rapports du conseil économique et social*, session de 1964, "Problèmes posés par l'immigration des travailleurs africains en France." séance du 23 juin 1964.
45 AN Fla 5136 Préfecture de la Seine, "Étude problème noir région parisienne." Paris.
46 AN Fla 5135 "Chapitre 1: Les Africains noirs en France avant l'indépendance" in "Immigration et conditions des travailleurs africains noirs en France." Paris, 1964.
47 AN FIa 5136 Gérard Esperét, Conseil économique et social, *Journal officiel de la république française: Avis et rapports du conseil économique et social*," session de 1964, "Problèmes posés par l'immigration des travailleurs africains en France," séance du 23 juin 1964.
48 Ibid.
49 CANC 19960311 art. 6 "L'étude sur l'immigration des travailleurs africains." 1969.

50 Manchuelle, "Background to Black African Emigration to France," 498. One official from the *Préfecture de police* estimated the population of Malians, Senegalese, and Mauritanian immigrants in 1960 at 1,000, considerably lower than Manchuelle's figure. ADVM 2018 W. art. 20 Maurice Grimaud to M le Ministre de l'Intérieur, 1969.
51 Manchuelle, "Background to Black African Emigration to France," 498.
52 ADVM 2018 W. art. 20 Maurice Grimaud to M le Ministre de l'Intérieur, 1969.
53 CANC 19960311 art. 6 "L'étude sur l'immigration des travailleurs africains." 1969. AMSD 18 ACW 22/23 "40,000 noirs vivent en France, la plupart dans des conditions épouvantables." *Les Échos*, Paris, 1963.
54 CAN F1a 5136 "Les travailleurs originaires d'Afrique noire." Paris, 10 November 1964.
55 AMSD 18 ACW 22/23 "40,000 noirs vivent en France." *Les Échos*, Paris 24 July 1963. Original French: "les migrations traditionnelles sont devenues difficiles par suite de la fermeture des États voisins."
56 CANC 19960311 art. 6 "Programme du gouvernement du résorption." 2 November 1970.
57 Manchuelle, "Background to Black African Emigration to France," 533–534. ANC 19960134 art. 15 Jacques Aubert to M le Premier Ministre, 1963. Sous-direction des étrangers et de la circulation trans-frontière to M le Premier Ministre, December 1970.
58 Manchuelle, "Background to Black African Emigration to France," 533–536.
59 For more on changes in colonial status, including citizenship, see Frederick Cooper, *Citizenship between Empire and Nation: Remaking France and French Africa, 1945–1960* (Princeton: Princeton University Press, 2014). Although Cooper does not discuss changes in citizenship status for Sub-Saharan Africans after decolonization, he details them throughout the early postwar era to 1960 and the "year of independence" for Africa.
60 Mary Dewhurst Lewis, *The Boundaries of the Republic: Migrant Rights and the Limits of Universalism in France, 1918–1940* (Stanford: Stanford University Press, 2007), 3; Rosenberg, *Policing Paris*, 6–7.
61 See, for example, Rosenberg's discussion of the creation of modern immigration controls during the interwar period. Rosenberg, *Policing Paris*, 6–12. Lewis also discusses the shift to an immigration regime during the interwar period. See Lewis, *The Boundaries of the Republic*, 3.
62 Carole Reynaud-Paligot, "Construction and Circulation of the Notion of Race in the Nineteenth Century," in Nicholas Bancel, Thomas David, and Dominic Thomas, eds., *The Invention of Race: Scientific and Popular Representations* (New York: Routledge, 2014), 97.
63 Ibid., 97.
64 Dewitte, *Les mouvements nègres en France*; Manchuelle, *Willing Migrants.*
65 Ann Laura Stoler discusses the intimacy within colonial rule, which can also be uncovered in the post-colonial surveillance of immigrant communities. See Stoler, *Carnal Knowledge and Imperial Power: Race and the Intimate in Colonial Rule* (Berkeley; Los Angeles; London: University of California Press, 2002),
66 Ibid., 6.
67 Wilder, *The French Imperial Nation-State*, 1–23.
68 Rosenberg, *Policing Paris*; Lewis, *Boundaries of the Republic*; Lyons, *The Civilizing Mission in the Metropole.*
69 Shannon L. Fogg, *The Politics of Everyday Life in Vichy France: Foreigners, Undesirables, and Strangers* (Cambridge: Cambridge University Press, 2009), 3.
70 For a discussion of the tracking of migrants in France during World War Two, see Fogg, *The Politics of Everyday Life in Vichy France*, 3.

71 Manchuelle, "Background to Black African Emigration to France," 522–523; CANC 19960311 art. 6 "L'étude sur l'immigration des travailleurs africains." 1969.
72 Tyler Stovall, *The Rise of the Paris Red Belt* (Berkeley: University of California Press, 1990).
73 On nineteenth-century urban reconfiguration in Paris, see Michel Carmona, *Haussmann: His Life and Times, and the Making of Modern Paris.* trans. Patrick Camiller (Chicago: I. R. Dee, 2002); David Van Zanten, *Building Paris: Architectural Institutions and the Transformation of the French Capital, 1830–1870* (Cambridge; New York: Cambridge University Press, 1994); David H. Pinkney, *Napoleon III and the Rebuilding of Paris* (Princeton, NJ: Princeton University Press, 1958).
74 For more on African political activism throughout the twentieth century, see for example: Dewitte, *Les mouvements nègres en France*; Frederick Cooper, *Decolonization and African Society: The Labor Question in French and British Africa* (Cambridge: Cambridge University Press, 1996); Jean-Philippe Dedieu, *La parole immigrée*; Fabienne Guimont, *Les étudiants africains en France.*
75 Patrick Weil, *La France et ses étrangers*, 74. Original French: "la question immigrée est donc devenue une question publique et politique."
76 Mary L. Dudziak, *Cold War Civil Rights: Race and the Image of American Democracy* (Princeton: Princeton University Press, 2000); Paul Gordon Lauren. *The Evolution of International Human Rights: Visions Seen.* 2nd ed. (Philadelphia: University of Pennsylvania Press, 2003).
77 Jean-Philippe Dedieu, *La parole immigrée*, 18, 20.
78 Jim House and Neil MacMaster, *Paris 1961: Algerians, State Terror, and Memory* (Oxford; New York: Oxford University Press, 2006), 66.
79 Georges Mauco, *Les étrangers en France et le problème du racisme* (Paris: LaPénsée universelle, 1984), 87.

1 Immigrant politics and the *Union générale des travailleurs sénégalais en France* (UGTSF)

In 1967, the *Union générale des travailleurs sénégalais en France* (UGTSF) hosted a gathering in the Parisian *banlieues*, which also served as a fund-raiser. Afterward, the *Chef du bureau d'action sociale d'ambassade du Sénégal à Paris*, M. Aumardier, gave an interview to Radio France. He explained that the event was intended to highlight African folklore while also further acquainting those who attended with African culture and the continent of Africa overall. Aumardier argued that Africa was disassociated from the rest of the world and events such as this could raise awareness regarding African cultural contributions. That same radio broadcast included an interview with Lamine Guéye, who highlighted the agricultural internships developed by the UGSTF. He emphasized that the organization worked year-round—including during summers—to ensure these kinds of opportunities for African workers. In particular, Guéye drew attention to internships provided in the Tarn-et-Garonne, where young workers learned the benefits of cooperative agriculture. By the late 1960s, the UGSTF not only provided social, cultural, and material support for members of the African immigrant community but also developed economic opportunities that could benefit both African workers in terms of skills and their countries of origin in terms of agricultural production.[1] The diverse and multifaceted nature of the UGTSF reflected its position within the African immigrant community and the key role that it had come to occupy.

The UGTSF became one of the most important immigrant groups of the postcolonial period and reflected the influence and legacy of Pan-African nationalism after decolonization. Advocating for various African nationalities residing in France, it provided multifaceted support to African workers. Even as it became more politicized by the 1970s, at its core it remained an advocacy organization. Kwame Nantambu argues that there are four periods of Pan-African nationalism, the last of which occurred in the twentieth century and included the works of activists and writers such as W. E. B. DuBois and Kwame Nkrumah. The UGTSF and similar types of organizations in France suggest that we could add a fifth category to that list: postcolonial Pan-African nationalist movements such as those created by immigrant communities in France and other countries with a growing

African immigrant population.[2] Yet there was also an emphasis placed on development in Senegal, reflecting the nationalist objectives of members of the African diaspora, a tension that had existed within diasporic communities dating back to the colonial period.[3]

At its peak, the UGTSF contradicted many of the assumptions often made about immigrant organizations. Scholars led by Stephen Castles and Mark J. Miller have argued that, at least initially, most immigrant organizations focus on developments in the country of origin rather on the migrant community in the host country.[4] Yet in its first decade of existence, the UGTSF concentrated on the basic, local needs of African immigrants, such as housing and health care, rather than on political and social issues in Senegal or other Sub-Saharan African countries. The former were among the most pressing problems that African immigrants faced. In doing so, the group solidified the social networks that attracted Africans to Paris in the first place. This association and others like it served as a nexus for political activism while creating a system of social welfare for African immigrants as the French state increasingly struggled to do so. Through its various programs, the UGTSF challenged French perceptions of African immigrants as rural, apolitical, and incapable of surviving in an urban setting. For instance, in a 1965 article published by *Cahiers north african/ESNA (North African Notebooks, later referred to as ESNA)*, Michel Massenet, director of the *Fonds d'action sociale pour les travailleurs étrangers* (Social Action Fund for Immigrant Workers or FAS, a government organization), argued:

> Now, these are people who have not had contact with urban life and are even less familiar with industrial life; their adaptability to work is therefore an area of concern and in all cases necessitates an effort for adaptation before they can perform at a satisfactory level.[5]

While officials grappled with how to address this immigrant group, the UGTSF harnessed its political power and facilitated social services and educational opportunities, demonstrating the importance of immigrant-driven social welfare programs to everyday survival. The organization and its endeavors provide an important perspective on the circumstances of postcolonial African immigration and the conditions in which immigrants found themselves living. This group and others like it served as precursors to contemporary racial advocacy and debates about equal opportunity policies in contemporary France.

By the 1970s, founder Sally N'Dongo and his organization had become more overtly politicized, critiquing Senegal's first president, Léopold Senghor, and dissecting French neocolonialism. As authorities became increasingly suspicious of the group's activities, it struggled to maintain its position. In the 1980s, amidst multiple shifts within the African immigrant community and increased official scrutiny, the organization collapsed, losing its state authorization. It was overtaken by ethnicity-based organizations, cultural associations, and gender-oriented groups. This reflected the pattern of "organization, mobilization, and collapse" identified by Gary Wilder in his discussion of postcolonial Panafricanism, connecting the UGTSF to broader developments within the history of black radical politics in France.[6]

Sally N'Dongo, immigrant activist

The story of the UGTSF's emergence begins with that of one of its founders, Sally N'Dongo, who was born in 1926 in Sinthiou-Garba, Senegal. After working as a merchant in Dakar, N'Dongo migrated to Nice, France, in 1956 to seek employment as a domestic servant.[7] He spoke almost no French and felt isolated in what he referred to as his "village prison," receiving little news of his family or friends back home in Senegal.[8] N'Dongo's experiences as an African immigrant residing in France in the late 1950s, 1960s, and 1970s resembled those of thousands of other workers from Sub-Saharan Africa, North Africa, and Europe.

In 1960, the year of Senegal's independence, N'Dongo moved north to the capital city after enduring four years of low pay, no vacation, no social security, and no health benefits. He characterized his departure as an escape from an exploitive situation—one that African immigrants endured, from his perspective, all too often in France. A much different life awaited him. In his first job in Paris, he worked as a chauffeur for the Senegalese consulate and observed the challenges confronting other African immigrants.[9] One year after arriving in the capital city, he was in the midst of creating an influential immigrant association, the UGTSF. A police report referred to him as "the spokesman of Senegalese workers in the Paris region."[10] N'Dongo's rise to political and social prominence from anonymity was swift, and, for more than two decades, he remained one of the foremost leaders of the African immigrant community.

Under N'Dongo's guidance, the UGTSF became one of the most active immigrant groups of any nationality in France during the postcolonial era. In contrast to the riot in Saint-Denis, it became a sustainable way for immigrants to voice their political and social concerns. Thus, the UGTSF provides an important means through which to understand African immigrant political activism in the postcolonial era. The group's aggressive approach to social welfare and political activism also make it a compelling case for understanding the challenges faced by African immigrants after decolonization, especially poor living and working conditions, and their responses through political activism.[11]

African trade unions: historical context

In order to contextualize the UGTSF's political evolution, it is helpful to briefly examine the twentieth-century history of immigrant politicization in France. Political activism among immigrant groups dates back to the late nineteenth century and the emergence of Polish and Italian associations.[12]

When workers from Europe and refugees entered France in the 1920s and 1930s, associations created by immigrants played an important role in creating and sustaining their social and political world.[13] The post–World War Two era witnessed the expansion of the Algerian independence movement, and some Algerian immigrant organizations, including the *Fédération de France du front de libération nationale* (French Federation of the National Liberation Front), actively demanded the end of colonialism.[14] Portuguese immigrants in France created one of the most organized associational networks of any twentieth-century immigrant group.[15]

The UGTSF's approach to associational activism not only had historical precedent in French-controlled West Africa during the colonial era but also in France during the interwar and early postwar period. African workers residing in France during the 1920s and 1930s created a vibrant network of trade unions in cities including Paris and Marseille.[16] During the 1920s and 1930s, the *Union des travailleurs nègres* (Union of Black Workers or UTN) established a template on which postcolonial African labor organizations patterned themselves.[17] The UTN created an important link between AOF and France and influenced the historical trajectory of African workers' groups. Through organizations such as the *Union inter-colonial* (Inter-Colonial Union or UIC), African workers mingled with Antillean migrants from Guadeloupe, Martinique, and other areas of the Caribbean while also interacting with the *Parti communiste français* (French Communist Party or PCF).[18] Several prominent political activists, including Lamine Senghor, became involved in the PCF-led anti-colonial movement.[19] As historian Philippe Dewitte argues, organizations such as the UIC created a culture of political militancy for Antilleans and Africans living in France during the interwar period.[20] The UGTSF was only the most recent incarnation of African political organizations dating back to the interwar period, and its methods and ideology borrowed heavily from its predecessors.

In AOF after World War Two and before decolonization, the *Union générale des travailleurs d'Afrique noire* (General Union of Black African Workers or UGTAN) became one of the most powerful colonial trade unions, reflecting the growing role of these organizations in the struggle for independence.[21] According to one historian, the UGTAN advocated for "the end of the colonial regime, the emancipation of workers and the protection of public and individual liberties."[22] Of the 500,000 workers in French West Africa by 1956, 35 percent participated in trade unions.[23] Labor activist, *Confédération générale du travail* (General Labor Committee or CGT) leader, and future Guinean president Sékou Touré and his associates struggled with how to proceed with the African labor movement throughout the 1950s. New unions independent of those in France emerged, including the *Confédération générale du travail-autonome* (Independent General Workers' Union or CGTA) and the *Confédération africaine des travailleurs croyants* (African Confederation of Christian Workers or CATC).[24] By 1957, the *Union générale des travailleurs d'Afrique noire* had emerged, the organization that Sally N'Dongo used as a template in forming the UGTSF in Paris after decolonization.[25] In Senegal, the *Bloc démocratique sénégalais* (Senegalese Democratic Bloc or BDS), led by future Senegalese president Léopold Senghor, attempted to incorporate organized labor into its coalition while working to appeal to a broader constituency.[26] The AOF's burgeoning labor movement became an integral part of the independence struggle there, which in turn inspired the postcolonial African immigrant community in Paris as it mobilized politically.

After decolonization, immigrant organizations modeled on African and French trade unions continued to dominate the political and social landscapes of the African community in France. By emulating the union model of organization, African immigrants extended to postcolonial French society the political culture created in AOF and metropolitan France during the interwar and early postwar eras. Unions provided social and economic support while drawing attention to the community's plight. Although the UGTAN and other organizations contributed to the independence movement in Sub-Saharan Africa, African associations such as the *Association des travailleurs de l'Afrique noire de la région parisienne* (Association of Black African Workers of the Paris Region or ATANRP) emerged in the last few years of the 1950s, before independence. Led predominantly by white-collar professionals, this group nonetheless foreshadowed the social and political activism undertaken by African workers after decolonization.[27]

The UGTSF, identity, and the African diaspora

By emulating the union model of organization, African immigrants after 1960 blended the political culture created in the colonies with a long-standing tradition of immigrant activism. The UGTSF's centrality to the African immigrant trade union movement reflected important shifts within the African diaspora itself in the wake of decolonization. This organization and its name pointed to the labor-oriented nature of African immigration between 1960—the collapse of France's empire in AOF—and 1974, the end of labor migration to France. African associations founded during the 1950s, for example, reflected the importance of educationally driven migration at that time. As labor immigration from Sub-Saharan Africa picked up in the late 1950s and early 1960s, the UGTSF's self-identification as a group of "Senegalese workers" signaled the scope of postcolonial migration and the partition of the African community into various social and political categories.[28] Its association with Senegal reflected the rise of nationality-based organizations that echoed Pan-African movements in French West Africa, which developed under French colonial regimes and continued after decolonization. The UGTSF and other organizations, such as the *Union générale des travailleurs maliens en France* (General Union of Malian Workers in France or UGTMF) and the *Association des travailleurs maliens* (Association of Malian Workers or ATM), pointed to the national identities of nascent Sub-Saharan African countries emerging from colonialism in the late

1950s and early 1960s.[29] Such names also foreshadowed the development of ethnically based political mobilization, which would come to the forefront of immigrant activism by the 1970s and 1980s.[30]

The UGTSF and other similar organizations incorporated grassroots nationalism into their agendas, which emphasized national identities over ethnic, local, or regional approaches. N'Dongo and other activists shifted the organizational terminology away from advocacy for "Africans" or "blacks" to that for "Senegalese," "Mauritanian, and Malian" immigrants. This rhetorical metamorphosis occurred within the context of continued discussions of human rights in the postwar era, an ongoing battle against the overt racism associated with colonialism and World War Two, and the struggle over civil rights in the U.S. The new linguistic approach was, as historian Todd Shepard argues, a consequence of decolonization itself.[31] Whereas interwar and postwar African organizations utilized the more general terminology of the colonial era, early postcolonial organizations adopted a more specific means of communicating their identities. The French state reclassified them as well in an effort to erase the colonial past.[32]

The UGTSF: establishment and expansion

Because of the UGTSF's nature as a familiar, stable, and officially recognized organization, membership and participation were important means of political activism and reflected the approaches taken by immigrant communities residing throughout France and Europe. N'Dongo shaped and directed the organization's agenda over its two-decade existence. The UGTSF's sustained visibility in French society from the early 1960s through the late 1970s was a consequence of N'Dongo's media-savvy approach. The group drew attention to the plight of African immigrants through newspaper articles, public support of political activities such as rent strikes and other protests, radio and television appearances, and the publication of several books in conjunction with François Maspero, a major French publisher.[33]

The group's genesis coincided with N'Dongo's arrival in Paris. By 1961, N'Dongo was involved with the African immigrant trade union movement. After observing other migrants' living conditions and enduring his own exploitive situation, N'Dongo concluded that an African-based organization could best address housing problems and other challenges.[34] His work at the consulate put him in a unique position to form an organization for Senegalese workers in Paris and the surrounding communities using consular resources. Immigrants from Sub-Saharan Africa after 1960 did not possess the right to create associations under French law because they either lacked full-fledged French citizenship or arrived in France as undocumented workers.[35] N'Dongo, however, faced no such legal impediment. He maintained French citizenship as a former resident of the French Union who arrived in France before decolonization and retained his ability to live and work in France after the collapse of the French empire in Sub-Saharan Africa.[36]

N'Dongo's first organization, the *Amicale des travailleurs sénégalais de la région parisienne* (Alliance of Senegalese Workers in the Paris Region or ATSRP), collided with political tensions after decolonization. An attempted overthrow of President Léopold Senghor in Senegal by Prime Minister Mamadou Dia placed N'Dongo in an awkward position with the Senegalese consulate in Paris. Like N'Dongo, Dia was ethnically Toucouleur, and the Prime Minister drew political support from this and other ethnic groups who inhabited the Soninké River valley. Consular authorities interpreted the ATSRP as a potential source of support in France for Dia.[37] The situation convinced N'Dongo of the danger of ethnic factions, a position that would influence the early course of the UGTSF after its founding. Pan-African nationalists such as Senghor and others warned of the specter of factions dating back to the interwar period. Although N'Dongo shared this concern after 1960, authorities worried about his personal loyalties and his relationship to the political situation in Senegal.

As tensions increased between N'Dongo and the consulate over the attempted coup, a schism emerged between N'Dongo and the president of the ATSRP, Abdoulaye N'Dao. N'Dongo and N'Dao accused each other of fostering divisions among Senegalese workers for their own personal gain.[38] N'Dao produced a tract entitled "*Mise au point*," charging N'Dongo with swindling African workers out of their hard-earned money, and, as president and unofficial treasurer, of "never having presented the association's budget or accounting practices" to the group's members.[39] N'Dao and N'Dongo remained adversaries throughout the 1960s. In 1969, N'Dao accused N'Dongo of utilizing the UGTSF's resources for his own personal gain.[40] This schism served as a reminder that relations were not necessarily cordial between various African associations and their members, even when they shared the same nationality and pursued similar goals.[41]

As the fallout deepened, N'Dongo left the ATSRP, and in October of 1962 he formed the *Union générale des travailleurs sénégalais de la région parisienne* (General Union of Senegalese Workers of the Paris Region or UGTSRP).[42] At an assembly in Paris in March 1964, N'Dongo's organization changed its name to reflect its broader aims, calling itself the *Union générale des travailleurs sénégalais en France* (UGTSF). Soon affiliate organizations formed in cities, such as Rouen, Marseilles, and Le Havre. Those cities were home to large populations of African workers because of the migration of Senegalese sailors and dockworkers to French port towns dating back to the early twentieth century.[43] Under N'Dongo's guidance, the UGTSF became one of the most visible immigrant organizations in France throughout the 1960s and 1970s. The second article of its organizational charter established that, "This association aims to strengthen the connections between Senegalese workers in France and to improve their living conditions through social and professional assistance."[44] N'Dongo maintained this official focus into the 1970s and 1980s, even as the group became critical of Senegalese politics and politically active in France.

Figure 1.1 Flier of an event hosted by the UGTSF. Image courtesy of the Bibliothèque de Documentation Internationale Contemporaine.

The organization recruited members directly from African *foyers* (dormitories) throughout the Paris region. After its founding, the UGTSF maintained a close relationship with dormitory residents, supporting several rent strikes—including one in the Paris *banlieue* of Ivry in 1969—while working to improve housing conditions for African immigrants throughout the Paris region.[45] The group created social and political space for African immigrants outside of the *foyers* while drawing on them for membership and support. Observers such as Madeleine Trébous, writing for the magazine *Esprit* in 1966, argued, "The small solidarity funds were created over many years in the dormitories, cellars, or attics, which are the basis for the creation of the *Union générale des travailleurs sénégalais en France*."[46] Leaders of the African community succeeded in creating and expanding organizations such as the UGTSF because of their political and social connections in AOF and in France. Before arriving in Paris, N'Dongo and others resided in urban areas such as Dakar, where French colonial authorities replicated France's bureaucratic structure.[47] As colonial residents, they became familiar with the French language and bureaucracy while observing the growth of the African trade union movement.

Once in France, this generation of immigrant workers was well suited to guide the transition from colonial to national citizenship within the metropolitan context.[48] For example, N'Dongo's work for the Senegalese consulate enhanced his political and social connections. The UGTSF drew its leadership from the same socio-economic class as its members, primarily workers recruited by the French government through the *Office national de l'immigration* (National Immigration Office or ONI) and through business enterprises such as the car manufacturer Renault, which employed approximately 1,000 African workers at its Billancourt plant by 1964.[49] The trade union format was an ideal one for African immigrant political activism after 1960: useful, relevant, and conducive to support from African governments and their consulates in Paris.[50]

By creating a more formal, permanent, and in some ways individualized form of immigrant activism, the UGTSF influenced the African immigrant community in numerous ways. The organization achieved its concrete goals of opening an all-African dormitory while providing educational opportunities through agricultural internships and literacy courses. In large measure, the UGTSF proved more effective than French bureaucrats and private organizations in providing housing and education for African immigrants living in squalor. The group not only assisted fellow African workers, but its success also drew attention to the plight of immigrants and revealed the tiered system of integration that existed within French political culture. The UGTSF recognized these challenges early on, worked to rectify them, and in doing so revealed the shortcomings of French immigration policy and its ability to address the needs of migrants amidst decolonization.

Beyond providing social welfare assistance, the UGTSF's structure and focus fostered a sense of social interaction, created important networks of sociability, and increased the amount of social capital available to African participants. Because N'Dongo and the group's leadership understood that the social networks that encouraged African immigration to France in the first place also extended support to migrants once they lived in France, the UGTSF worked to foster connections among various ethnic and national groups. In addition to ordinary organizational meetings, the group organized lunches and evening soirees, including a 1973 gala that served as a fundraiser for victims of drought in Sub-Saharan Africa.[51]

By facilitating social connections between immigrants throughout France, N'Dongo and the UGTSF worked to reduce the exclusion and marginalization that many individual migrants experienced.[52] Writing in October of 1964, Massenet described the role of immigrant organizations in assisting African workers this way:

> But given the urgency that certain problems pose, such as housing or the improvement of health, each association has taken initiatives to address the misery of African groups to whom they are particularly close. A word should be said about African associations in France. They certainly have a role to play amongst their compatriots, a role of the

> moral kind; in particular it's incumbent on them to maintain a connection between the migrants and their country of origin. I do not believe, however, that they can intervene without danger in a domain that is the responsibilities of the French state, that of lodging nationals from African countries.[53]

Groups like the UGTSF could help immigrant workers overcome the geographical distance within the urban realm, which could prove challenging to the creation of close-knit groups. N'Dongo intended to combine the kinship networks that facilitated African immigration with the social connections facilitated by immigrant organizations.[54] In one report, N'Dongo described the typical immigrant experience, noting, "at his arrival in France he is welcomed and taken in by the African community. [The community] takes responsibility for finding him a job. It tends to him, feeds him and lodges him, gives him a bit of money in his pocket."[55]

This social-welfare approach worked, contributing to the organization's large membership base. At its founding, the organization claimed 800 members.[56] The Ministry of the Interior reported that in March 1963, 1,400 members belonged to the organization.[57] *Journal Officiel*, a French governmental publication, cited a membership of 5,000 by 1964.[58] By 1965, the group claimed 6,800 members.[59] Historian François Manchuelle lauds but qualifies this number, arguing that even if it were in actuality much smaller, it was still an important indication of the group's early success, given the small size of the African community overall.[60]

N'Dongo's vision for an inclusive approach to community organization and politicization influenced his group's organizational structure, which, although focused on one nationality, attempted to represent the diversity within the African population in France and indeed in Senegal. Reflecting its Senegalese origins—a Muslim country with a Catholic minority population—the group allowed Christians and Muslims alike as members.[61] The organization's statutes prohibited political and religious affiliations and discussions.[62] Delegates elected by migrants from departments throughout France comprised the UGTSF's national board. Its bylaws mandated representation for each African ethnic group in France. No single ethnicity could dominate leadership positions. The trade union approach adopted by the UGTSF also appropriated the message of pan-African nationalism and *Négritude* dating back to the interwar period. Senghor and others feared the "balkanization" of Sub-Saharan Africa and promoted the idea of a federation to unify rather than divide newly independent nation-states.[63] This message of unity within Pan-African nationalism influenced not only the postwar independence movement but also the type of social and political activism undertaken by African immigrants through organizations such as the UGTSF as well as the organization's structure.[64] Members of African ethnic groups, including the Soninké, Toucouleur, and Mandigue, could hold the group's offices of president, secretary general, and deputy secretary general.[65] The UGTSF worked to create an identity within the African community that transcended national, ethnic, and religious identity, emphasizing unity rather than division within the African diaspora while also utilizing a grassroots approach to social and political organization.[66]

Despite its official recognition by French authorities, the UGTSF maintained a close relationship with the newly independent state of Senegal and its government.[67] Although an outsider from the French perspective, N'Dongo was an insider within Senegalese political circles. He developed close ties to the Senegalese embassy, first as an employee and then as a community leader. These affiliations helped him in gaining official backing for the UGTSF in its efforts to support the development of the African community as it grew after 1960.[68] One of the organization's most important programs aimed to assist with development in Sub-Saharan Africa by placing young African men in agricultural internships in rural France so that they could contribute to Senegal's agricultural sector after returning home. Because of its emphasis on economic development and social welfare, the Senegalese government and its diplomatic representatives in Paris during the 1960s provided support. N'Dongo explained the group's early objectives in the following manner: "The only goal of our Union—which is an association and not a syndicate—is to bring to our workers social and technical assistance while aiding them in their advancement."[69]

Although he patterned the UGTSF directly on earlier trade unions in French-controlled West Africa and France, in stressing the social nature of the UGTSF, N'Dongo made an important distinction between an association and a union. French authorities indeed interpreted immigrant associations as less threatening than trade unions, so N'Dongo deflected officials' suspicion of the group as inherently politicized and therefore dangerous. As the UGTSF emerged in the early 1960s, French authorities perceived African immigrants as incapable of politicization. A Ministry of the Interior report from 1964 characterized African workers in the following manner: "Workers from black Africa in France remain attached to their African traditions and clothing. They are for the moment rarely susceptible to political or other propaganda and they generally seem unenthusiastic about attempts made to penetrate their circles."[70] Yet N'Dongo's connections to Senegal and the Senegalese embassy and the organization's emphasis on social welfare and development pointed to its complex and multifaceted nature and its propensity for political engagement early on in its history.

The organization's desire to contribute to the growth of the Senegalese economy through training and education also garnered early support from officials in the Senegalese embassy.[71] From the Senegalese government's standpoint, the creation of an organization allied with its own policies and objectives was a means of securing the loyalty of Senegalese immigrants.[72] Although the group also relied on membership dues, contributions, and private donations, the Senegalese government's assistance proved critical. Senegalese President Senghor, a former resident of France during the colonial era and an important figure in the pan-African nationalist movement and African intellectual diaspora, supported the UGTSF's development.[73] Senghor kept in close contact with N'Dongo for the better part of the 1960s, despite the ethnic affiliation and perceived alliance with Dia during the coup attempt.[74] Because of French authorities' concerns over connections between immigrant groups and foreign governments, the UGTSF publicly kept financial distance from the Senegalese and French governments. Yet it appealed to both for support to accomplish various goals, most importantly the construction of dormitories for African immigrants.[75]

Social welfare: housing

As the UGTSF fostered social networks and navigated its relationship with the Senegalese government, it also achieved several objectives related to the challenges faced by African immigrants. A primary goal was to create better housing. In the organization's own words, "The problem of finding suitable lodging … constitutes the first challenge for everyone upon arrival in France."[76] In an open letter, N'Dongo wrote, "Lodging conditions have been and continue to be terrible. Also, workers live … in cellars, attics, hangars, old hotels … run, in general by North Africans."[77] Indeed, N'Dongo and Africans living throughout the Paris region too often resided in slums, basements, and attics marred by dim lighting, poor air circulation, humidity and dampness, little to no viable source of heat, and more often than not no suitable bathroom or shower facilities. According to authorities and eyewitness reports, slums lacked any semblance of hygiene. Overcrowding contributed significantly to these already grave problems. One report claimed that it was not rare to see 40 Africans squeezed into one 30 by 40-meter room where all the inhabitants slept, cooked, ate, and used the bathroom facilities. This makeshift housing was beyond the control of state regulation. Many residents utilized dangerous butane burners to reheat food and provide warmth on cold, damp evenings. Multiple residents throughout the day and night slept in beds placed end to end. Suitcases lay on the floor, suggesting the precarious nature of their living conditions as well as their hopes of returning home. But residents continued to occupy problematic dwellings simply because they saw few alternatives, short of homelessness.[78] These slums—as undesirable as they were— also came at a price. Despite their rundown condition, landlords who rented them often charged at least 30–60 francs per month to each inhabitant. Workers in textile manufacturing made 70–90 francs per week or 280–360 francs per month.[79]

Hotels offered an alternative. Most often, they constituted an inexpensive yet unstable and decrepit housing option. Life in such squalid hotel settings closely resembled that of other rundown housing options, with residents living in rooms that lacked running water and proper bathroom facilities. Unscrupulous "landlords" or hotel owners charged high rates ranging from 12 Francs per day to 200 Francs per month. These hotels became makeshift studio apartments for their residents, who chose hotels when possible over slums but lived with the specter of expulsion and displacement.[80] These types of living conditions proved devastating for immigrants who sought a better life and found themselves living in squalor.[81]

In an attempt to alleviate these housing problems, the UGTSF opened and operated its own *foyers*. As early as 1963, N'Dongo sought funds from the Senegalese consulate to open a dormitory on the rue de Charenton in the 12th *arrondissement* of Paris, where, along with the 11th, 18th, 19th, and 20th *arrondissements*, a substantial population of African immigrants already lived.[82] French authorities became alarmed over what they saw as ethnic enclaves of African immigrants and other groups who, they perceived, challenged the republican idea of integration.[83] A May 1963 report by the Ministry of the Interior described the situation in the following manner:

> The black African colony quickly dispersed into the neighborhoods of Paris and the surrounding communities where Muslims from North African were ahead of them, namely the 19th, 20th, 18th, 11th, and 13th *arrondissements*, and St. Denis, Clichy, and Aubervilliers. At the moment, rare are the Africans who are lodged in individual locations. In the most favorable cases, they live eight or ten in hotel rooms that formerly housed half as many Algerians.[84]

A sociological report produced by the Prefecture of the Seine in 1965 argued that, "Africans regroup themselves in Paris by village community."[85] This assessment reflected authorities' concern that African workers tended to seek out what they characterized as the "communitarian life," preferring to live with other African immigrants rather than on their own.[86] A July 1964 article in *Journal Officiel* placed the total number of African immigrants in France at 27,674, with 15,000 of those residing in the Seine department, which included Paris.[87] That meant that thousands of African workers maintained a lifestyle perceived as problematic by authorities, who became increasingly alarmed at these kinds of settlement patterns.

While officials struggled to provide decent housing for a growing population of African immigrants, the UGTSF hoped to bolster the strength of the African community throughout Paris by establishing African-run dormitories. The UGTSF feared that *foyers* under government or third-party control, such as that of the *Association pour le soutien, l'union et la dignité de l'accueil aux travailleurs africaines* (Association for the Support, Union, and Dignity in the Reception of African Workers or SOUNDIATA)[88] would break up social, cultural, and political networks through relocation and dispersal.[89] SOUNDIATA's first president, Robert Buron, served in several key governmental positions, including within the ministries of economic affairs, overseas territories, and finances from 1949 to 1955, and knew France's former colonies in West and Central Africa quite well.[90] Buron constituted the very type of former colonial administrators whom the UGSTF feared.[91] African residents who lived in *foyers* managed by the state and private organizations such as SOUNDIATA and the *Association pour la formation technique de base des africains et malgaches résidant en France* (Association for the Basic Technical Training of Africans and Malagasy Living in France or AFTAM) could encounter racism and discrimination resembling what they endured in the colonies.[92]

N'Dongo sought to break this cycle. By running its own dormitories, the UGTSF and its leaders could improve housing conditions on their own terms. Through these accommodations, the group was able to address specific African expectations, including the desire for common cooking and eating areas. The UGTSF also viewed the amelioration of housing conditions by Africans themselves as a means to improve community development.[93] In December 1965, the group opened a foyer for 150 African residents in Roubaix, which became a cornerstone of the UGTSF's social welfare program, revealing how an immigrant organization could beat the French at their own game when it came to creating social welfare programs for immigrants.[94] In addition to creating and overseeing *foyers*, the UGTSF became involved in political struggles related to immigrant housing. By 1969, for example, it supported a rent strike at the foyer run by the *Association pour l'aide sociale aux travailleurs africains* (Association for Assistance to African Workers or ASSOTRAF) on the rue Pinel in Saint-Denis, publishing the tenants' demands in its 1970 book, *Le livre des travailleurs africains en France* (*The Book of African Workers in France*).[95] This publication also contained letters from one of the leaders of the Ivry rent strike addressing the struggles between the foyer's residents and its landlords.[96]

N'Dongo and the UGTSF took public positions on many of the housing problems that garnered media attention in the late 1960s and early 1970s. In response to the deaths of five Malian workers of asphyxiation in a foyer on the rue des Postes in Aubervilliers in January 1970, for example, N'Dongo stated in an article in *Le Monde*, "I have to have you make a visit to the dozens of places like that on the rue des Postes, where my compatriots are exploited in scandalous conditions."[97] Such political activities and statements aroused the interest of authorities, who thought leftist organizations controlled the UGTSF, just as they believed Maoists and other extremist groups directed various rent strikes staged by immigrants throughout the Paris region.[98]

Social welfare and development: agricultural internships

While focusing on housing, the UGTSF also promoted development in Senegal and Sub-Saharan Africa through educational programs in France. According to the group, farms served as "classrooms" and farm work constituted the "assignments." Beyond providing instruction in basic French literacy for African workers, the UGTSF sought opportunities for its members to acquire agricultural skills, despite the fact that many UGTSF members worked in the industrial sector, especially automobile manufacturing, construction, and metallurgy.[99] Still, the push for agricultural education makes sense when one considers that many of the organization's members originally emigrated from rural areas throughout the Soninké river valley in Mali, Mauritania, and Senegal. In other words, agricultural skills would be the most readily applicable when students returned to their countries of origin.

N'Dongo and the UGTSF's leadership spent considerable time seeking out opportunities for agricultural training for immigrants largely employed in the industrial sector. The organization focused on communal agriculture in rural areas throughout France, investigating how farmers organized themselves into agricultural syndicates and what types of benefits they gained from doing so. While visiting farmers such as Gérard Bignon and Emmanuel Grandemange, who ran a small dairy commune, the UGTSF observed not only a jump in productivity and the sense of "family" created among commune members but also a resulting increase in leisure time. Bignon found more time to administer the *Centre national des jeunes agriculteurs* (National Center for Young Agriculturalists), while Grandemange participated more actively in the *stages d'information agricole* (agricultural internships). The UGTSF's delegation noticed that women also benefitted from cooperative agriculture because farmers' wives got two out of three Sundays off from their work, with extra time to attend the cinema, play with their children, and visit with friends.[100] Eventually, the UGTSF's leadership hoped to apply the ideas garnered from participation in cooperative agriculture in France to farming in Senegal.[101]

To facilitate this knowledge transfer, the UGTSF established internship programs throughout France to train young Senegalese migrants in the technical aspects of farming. In its other programs, in line with its founding principles, the organization rarely made distinctions concerning the nationality or ethnicity of its members. But here, it did. Through these internships, though, N'Dongo and the UGTSF hoped to improve Senegal's agricultural output by training Senegalese migrants. The internship programs were largely run in the Tarn-et-Garonne through a partnership between the UGTSF and the *Fédération Léo Lagrange*, an organization with socialist roots intended to provide educational opportunities. N'Dongo conducted several interviews with young participants, their parents, and directors of farming co-ops, trying to glean how they organized their own internship and training programs, how they viewed and organized agricultural cooperatives, and what types of benefits they derived from them.[102] While the UGTSF viewed its affiliation with the *Fédération Léo Lagrange* as a means of facilitating agricultural development in Senegal, authorities in France interpreted it as another sign of increasing politicization and contact with left-leaning organizations.

The UGTSF and the *Fédération Léo Lagrange* used this opportunity to familiarize young workers with the technological aspects of cooperative farm work with an eye toward development in Sub-Saharan Africa. In interviews, N'Dongo discussed how the mechanization of various tasks—such as the milking of cows—lessened the workload of rural farmers and simplified their lives. One technological development that especially captured his imagination was the tractor. Through internships and excursions to farms, young Senegalese immigrants could learn to drive tractors, earn their driver's licenses, and gain an understanding of how tractors could improve agricultural production in Senegal.

These educational opportunities also created a point of contact between French farmers and their families and young Senegalese immigrants. Often the farmers themselves instructed their young charges in the operation of various types of machinery. For example, Ba Demba, a Senegalese internship participant, learned to drive a tractor over the span of eight days with the assistance of Monsieur Luans, the director of the *Syndicat des jeunes agriculteurs de Nègrepelisse* (Union of Young Agriculturalists of Nègrepelisse).[103] In a 1994 article, N'Dongo noted the important rapport that developed between the interns and the French farmers overseeing their work:

> We were pleasantly surprised at the very beginning by the warmth of these families for we were prepared for some hostility, as this population has less contact with the black population than urban dwellers. The opposite happened, though, and many have sympathized immediately and cooperation has been fruitful.[104]

Despite what N'Dongo characterized as a surprisingly hospitable reception, he noted that Senegalese farmers struggled to acquire technical skills, and hoped that their French counterparts could serve as an inspiration for acquiring them. For example, Diambele Diao, encouraged by N'Dongo to take advantage of the opportunity to leave Paris for a while, participated in an internship program in Aignan (Gare) during July 1965. In his final report, Diao observed that French peasants' collective outlook was different that the individualist attitude he perceived as pervasive in Paris. The experience benefitted him in large part because he discovered so much in common with the peasants he encountered and the experience of life in rural areas. N'Dongo perceived the French peasantry as more "communitarian," resembling that of his home village in Senegal. The familiarity suggested that rural internships might assist African workers not only in acquiring technical skills but also in transferring skills applicable in the agricultural realm back to Senegal and other Sub-Saharan African countries. N'Dongo believed that such programs would contribute to the important project of postcolonial economic development through African immigrant-directed initiatives rather than outside organizations and former colonial powers such as France.[105]

More broadly, N'Dongo's commitment to transferring agricultural skills to rural Senegal illustrated his vision for Sub-Saharan African immigration and his critique of neocolonialism. From his vantage point, migration from Senegal and other African countries to France was not permanent. African emigration was supposed to be economically productive, with the migrants learning valuable skills before returning home. If young Senegalese workers such as Diao did not return home to assist in developing Senegal, then, the large-scale migration was a missed opportunity. The goal of returning skilled workers to Sub-Saharan Africa was one of the reasons that the UGTSF worked to improve the social conditions of workers throughout the 1960s. Migrants could not acquire critical skills, such as cooperative agriculture production, to take back to their home countries if they languished in *bidonvilles* or shantytowns, isolated, malnourished, sickly, and unable to communicate.[106]

The UGTSF's focus on development reflected its belief that the immigrant experience should afford the opportunity to acquire new skills applicable in the Senegalese and African economies. The time spent in cities such as Paris as temporary labor migrants aiming to return home provided a critical opportunity to expand knowledge in the agricultural and industrial realms. To miss that opportunity was, from the UGTSF's perspective, unacceptable. While working to improve conditions for African immigrants in France, N'Dongo and the UGTSF also examined the factors that facilitated immigration from Sub-Saharan Africa. One of the key mechanisms that contributed to this migratory pattern was agreements signed between France and its former colonies in Sub-Saharan Africa. N'Dongo labeled these agreements "neocolonial." In *"Coopération" et néo-colonialisme* (*Cooperation and Neocolonialism*), he argued, "Far from streamlining emigration, the current system permits a whole crowd of traffickers without scruples."[107] He further explained:

> It is well known that African workers do not come to France with the intention of settling there permanently. They stay two to three years maximum, enough time to save the money that allows them to take on a small business when they return home and to bring to France another member of their family as well as a dowry for their wedding. The implementation of a free circulation of peoples would certainly require a reduction of the time spent in France to one year.[108]

Not only did emigration from Sub-Saharan Africa pull workers away from emerging economies, but it also perpetuated the dependence fostered by the colonial regime into the postcolonial era and stymied economic growth in the sending region. The social welfare programs and the neocolonial critique of immigration policy hinted at the emphasis that N'Dongo and the UGTSF would place on Senegal and other African countries by the early 1970s. The UGTSF's concern over migration to France pointed to another important priority: economic development in Senegal and Sub-Saharan

Africa, a priority that was part of the broader international push to transform developing countries in the wake of decolonization.

From the social to the political

While the U.S. established the Peace Corps and the French government created what critics such as N'Dongo referred to as neocolonial policies in former colonies, immigrant-based organizations such as the UGTSF contributed to a global discussion about how best to transform countries emerging from colonial control.[109] Although the UGTSF's emphasis on social welfare remained, by the early 1970s the organization's discourse focused on the political, social, and economic challenges faced by Senegal and other former French colonies. This emphasis on development not only shaped the UGTSF's agenda but also placed it under greater scrutiny by French officials, who perceived this focus as overtly political and therefore threatening. The politicization of which French officials initially believed African immigrants to be incapable in the early 1960s manifested itself in a critique of neocolonialism in Sub-Saharan Africa and a more overt political tone overall for organizations such as the UGTSF. As he emphasized development, N'Dongo became increasingly critical of the relationship that emerged after decolonization between France and Senegal, characterizing it as "neocolonial." In numerous publications—including two books—and in radio and television appearances, N'Dongo adamantly opposed continuing French influence in the region, arguing that it inhibited the growth of the Senegalese economy and nation-state, both of which became dependent on foreign and particularly French capital, investment, and trade.[110] N'Dongo argued: "'Independent' Senegal only has value as defined by foreign capital. Senegal's wealth, including its most important resource, its labor force, is sold off to benefit foreign capital."[111] The French government exerted its influence through migration policies favorable towards its economy, importation of goods such as peanuts that perpetuated the reliance on cash crops into the postcolonial era, and investment in industries that benefitted the international markets rather than the Senegalese economy as a whole.[112] For their part, French officials did not try to hide their desire to maintain a presence in Senegal and other former colonies. Speaking in 1964 to the French National Assembly, Prime Minister Georges Pompidou explained: "There are also economic and political reasons for cooperation … France has no reason to hide that it wishes to maintain a certain influence and a certain political, moral, and cultural presence."[113] Economic influence was but one of the ways in which France sought to maintain its presence in Sub-Saharan Africa after decolonization.

From N'Dongo's perspective, the connection between pre-colonial, colonial, and postcolonial dominance was obvious. In *"Coopération" et néocolonialisme*, N'Dongo traced the origins of this relationship to the nearly four-centuries long trans-Atlantic slave trade. Slavery and the slave trade, he argued, made Africa vulnerable to outside influence in numerous ways. He explained:

> But the consequences of this pillage cannot be considered solely from the standpoint of demography. In effect the destruction, the permanent insecurity resulting from this exploitation completely disrupted the societies that were victims ... Colonial penetration was largely facilitated by the blood spilled through this exploitation of blacks.[114]

The long history of exploitation through the slave trade weakened the region, leaving it vulnerable to formal colonization. From N'Dongo's perspective, the colonial emphasis on agricultural production favoring one crop—peanuts in Senegal and cocoa in Ghana and Cameroon—left the region without much industrial infrastructure and little in the way of economic diversity or stability.[115] "Curious independence that 'allows' Africans to become more and more exploited, whether in Africa or in France," he explained.[116] For example, Senegal's peanut farmers relied on international demand for their crop after decolonization. Buyers, however, shifted their interest away from peanut oil to olive oil. The price of peanut oil fell over the course of the 1960s from 22 francs per kilogram in 1960 to 17 francs in 1969. While the Senegalese economy became increasingly dependent on French foreign aid, the Côte d'Ivoire's agricultural sector—also a legacy of colonial policies—produced coffee and cacao, two valuable commodities on the international market.[117]

Taking this development-oriented focus further, in the 1970s the UGTSF also began focusing on "country of origin" politics and set out overtly political objectives. With the publication of works such as *La coopération franco-africaine* (*Franco-African Cooperation*), the UGTSF and N'Dongo expanded the organization's concern for development in Sub-Saharan and the relationships between former colonies and their one-time colonizers. Above all, N'Dongo criticized the French government for maintaining neocolonial domination over the Senegalese economy into the postcolonial era. This critique marked an important shift from the organization's earlier emphasis on social welfare for the African community in France. A seemingly newfound emphasis on overt political critiques attracted the attention of French authorities, who realized that they had misread the possibility for politicization among African immigrants.

Official suspicion, competition, and collapse

As they became more overtly political, the UGTSF and similar organizations attracted considerable attention from French authorities because of the long-standing history of trade union political activism in both Sub-Saharan Africa and France. During the late 1960s and 1970s, officials monitoring African immigrants in France grew increasingly paranoid that political critiques regarding neocolonialism issued by the UGTSF and N'Dongo might morph into a more radical and dangerous movement, which could destabilize the social and political order in France.[118] The tensions and anxieties surrounding decolonization in the Francophone context intersected with increased African immigration. While authorities worried about increasingly vocal political activism among a growing population of African immigrants in the Paris region, the French state expanded its monitoring of organizations such as the UGTSF, including of its founder and leader, Sally N'Dongo, and of other key members.

By 1973, authorities were describing the UGTSF as openly hostile to President Senghor's regime in Senegal. In a report dated April 5 of that year, one official from the *Direction de la réglementation* (the Regulatory Directorate) within the *Préfecture de police* discussed one of the organization's meetings slated for the next day with an anticipated turnout of between 100 and 150. Scheduled as a means of protesting the Senegalese government's crackdown on political protest, the group labeled Senghor a "criminal."[119] Together with the *Union générale des étudiants, élèves et stagiaires sénégalais* (General Union of Senegalese Students and Interns or UGEESS), the report explained:

> Both organizations invite 'all democrats, men who support peace, justice, and liberty to show their solidarity with the struggle of Senegalese teachers who are in danger, to push for their immediate liberation and to denounce the suppression of political and organizational liberties in Senegal.'[120]

The UGTSF's public stances on political developments and its cooperation with other organizations, such as the UGEESS, troubled French authorities.

This increasingly overt politicization also caused trouble, in turn, for the UGTSF. A 1977 report by the Ministry of the Interior identified an alliance between the UGTSF and unnamed organizations on the extreme political Left. This same report recommended that the state refuse to renew the group's authorization as a legally sanctioned organization.[121] Indeed, in August 1978, the Ministry of the Interior, in consultation with the Ministry of Foreign Affairs, denied the UGTSF's standard application for authorization to the *Préfecture de police* in accordance with the 1901 law governing immigrant associations in France.[122] The organization's growing reputation for radical political positions drove this decision. As a whole, the African community, which, in the early 1960s, authorities perceived as apolitical and docile, now appeared more politically motivated, connected, and threatening to French society. Ultimately, shutting down African organizations like the UGTSF was one of several actions the French state took in response to perceived radicalization in the aftermath of 1968 and the political upheaval that gripped France, Czechoslovakia, the U.S., and other countries that year.[123]

In the wake of this upheaval, officials expanded their efforts to detect individuals and groups within the African immigrant community whom they believed to be radical and dangerous. From a broader perspective, the

UGTSF was but one such organization that authorities monitored throughout the 1970s. By 1977, for example, authorities were linking several members of the *Regroupement des Sénégalais de l'Oise* (Coalition of Senegalese in the Oise Region) to the CGT, labor unions, and Marxists in Africa.[124] The long-standing surveillance of organizations such as the UGTSF and individuals such as N'Dongo eventually led to a decision by the *Préfecture de police* to deny authorization for the group's continuance in France.

As the UGTSF contended with anxious government officials, the nature of immigration itself had changed by the 1970s, in turn weakening the UGTSF. Competing associations such as the ATMF (*Association des travailleurs maliens en France* or Association of Malian Workers in France) and less formal routes of political activism, such as rent strikes, were drawing members away from the UGTSF.[125] Active engagement required time away from work, which few immigrants could spare, given the industrial and often tenuous nature of their employment and a weakening economy.

Meanwhile, the grassroots nationalism of the UGTSF and other labor organizations was shifting to an emphasis on ethnicity and the recovery of pre-colonial identities and cultures.[126] By the 1970s, the UGTSF also experienced increasing competition for members from organizations such as the *Association pour la promotion de la culture et de la langue soninké* (Association for the Promotion of Soninké Culture and Language or APS), an ethnicity-based group that emerged in the Paris *banlieue* of Saint-Denis. The growth of the APS reflected the shift in the trajectory of African immigrant politicization and grassroots organization. As Pan-African nationalism faded in the decades following decolonization and French authorities cracked down on overtly political immigrant organizations, groups such as the APS grew in popularity, while those modeled on trade unions, such as the UGTSF, declined. Beyond ethnically focused groups, those promoting African culture also emerged, including the *Association culturelle des travailleurs africains en France* (Cultural Association of African Workers in France or ACTAF).

By the mid- to late-1970s, women and children came to dominate African immigration to France, contributing to a sea-change in the composition and mission of African immigrant associations. In 1974, a year after the global economy confronted the oil shock, the French government ended labor migration—the postwar policy that had sustained recovery and growth for almost three decades.[127] However, an allowance for family reunification was maintained, which led to more women and children arriving in France to join their husbands and fathers and hence a more permanent African community in France. Whereas the UGTSF was a male-dominated organization, women's organizations became a dominant feature of African associational life. As authorities cracked down on overtly political groups such as the UGTSF, associations that organized themselves along gender and ethnic lines proved more appealing. The union-based model gave way to the more ethnicity- and immigration status–oriented organizations of the 1980s and 1990s, including the APS and the *sans-papiers*, or undocumented worker movement. The UGTSF privileged social welfare during the 1960s, but later groups focused on the promotion of ethnic groups such as the Soninké over Senegalese and other national identities within the African community in France.

Rather than appealing to a collective "African" identity or a national identity such as that of the Senegalese, the APS and other similar groups attracted members of particular ethnicities. This represented the ethnic splintering that early Pan-Africanists and members of the *Négritude* movement feared—that the ethnic identity would overwhelm other broader identities. In some ways, African immigrant organizations in France "balkanized," representing more specialized interests than their earlier counterparts, such as the UGTSF, had.[128] In other ways, however, the APS and other such organizations demonstrated that the associational realm could adapt to the changing nature of African immigration itself. The UGTSF and other union-based organizations became outdated, no longer appealing to an immigrant group that was quickly diversifying and growing.

The UGTSF and its leader, Sally N'Dongo, came to represent the broader plight of the African immigrant community in Paris and the *banlieues* throughout the 1960s and 1970s. This organization grew from one that provided social welfare services to its members to one that became increasingly politicized and visibly critical, not only of French policy in Sub-Saharan Africa but also of the Senegalese political scene and Senegal's first president, Léopold Senghor. Along the way, authorities became increasingly suspicious of the organization, which was seemingly innocuous at first. As the group became more vocal, authorities became more interested and the group entered into important debates about integration, belonging, and identity in postcolonial France. In fact, authorities became so concerned about its political affiliations with leftist organizations that eventually, it was denied official recognition. By then, however, its relevance was being called into question, as the second generation of African immigrants together with their parents sought new and different ways to express themselves socially, culturally, and politically. Despite its collapse, the contributions of the UGTSF to the development of the postcolonial African immigrant community in Paris and throughout France cannot be overlooked. Nor can its focus on development in Senegal and other Sub-Saharan African nations, an issue that the organization championed throughout its existence.

Notes

1 Institut national de l'audiovisuel "*L'Union générale de travailleurs sénégalais en France*" radio broadcast 1 June 1967.
2 Kwame Nantambu, "Pan-Africanism versus Pan-African Nationalism: An Afro-Centric Analysis," *Journal of Black Studies* 28, no. 5 (May 1998): 570.
3 Hakim Adi, "Pan-Africanism and West African Nationalism in Britain," *African Studies Review* 43, no. 1 (April 2000): 69–82.
4 For an analysis of why immigrant organizations typically focus first on the situation in the country of origin and then shift their focus to the immigrant

community in the host country, see Stephen Castles and Mark J. Miller, *The Age of Migration: International Population Movements in the Modern World* Revised Second Edition (London: Macmillan Press, 1998); Stephen Castles and Alastair Davidson, *Citizenship and Migration: Globalization and the Politics of Belonging* (New York: Routledge, 2000); Robin Cohen and Zig Layton-Henry, eds., *The Politics of Migration* (Cheltenham, UK; Northampton, MA: E. Elgar, 1997).

5 CIEMI Michel Massenet, "Le fonds d'action sociale et les travailleurs d'Afrique noire en France" in ESNA/Cahiers Nord-Africains, *Approche des problèmes de la migration noire en France* (Paris: ESNA, 1965), 60. Original French: "Or, il s'agit de gens qui n'ont pas eu de contacts avec la vie urbaine et encore moins avec la vie industrielle; leur adaptabilité au travail est donc sujette à caution et en tout cas nécessite un effort d'adaptation avant que leur rendement soit satisfaisant."

6 Gary Wilder, "Panafricanism and the Republic Political Sphere," in Sue Peabody and Tyler Stovall, eds., *The Color of Liberty: Histories of Race in France* (Durham: Duke University Press, 2003), 239.

7 Fla 5136 Police report on Sally N'Dongo, December 1965.

8 Sally N'Dongo, *Voyage forcé: Itinéraire d'un militant* (Paris: François Maspero, 1975), 9–11; Sally N'Dongo, *Exil, connais pas …* (Paris: François Maspero, 1976), 7, 19.

9 François Manchuelle, "Background to Black African Emigration to France: the Labor Migrations of the Soninké, 1848–1987" (PhD diss., University of California-Santa Barbara, 1987)," 528.

10 Fla 5136 Police report on Sally N'Dongo, December 1965. Original French: "le porte-parole des travailleurs sénégalais de la région parisienne."

11 For sociological and anthropological perspectives, see Jacques Barou, *Travailleurs Africains en France* (Grenoble: Presses Universitaires de Grenoble, 1978) and Catherine Quiminal, *Gens d'ici, gens d'ailleurs: Migrations soninké et transformations villageoises* (Paris: Christian Bourgeois Éditeur, 1991).

12 For a discussion of the Italian immigrant community in France, see Pierre Milza, et al, eds., *L'intégration italienne en France: Un siècle de présence italienne dans trois régions françaises: 1880–1980* (Bruxelles: Éditions Complexe, 1995); Pierre Milza, ed., *Les Italiens en France de 1914 à 1940* (Rome: École française de Rome, 1986); Marie-Claude Blanc-Chaléard, *Les italiens dans l'est parisien: une historie d'intégration: 1880–1960* (Rome: École française de Rome, 2000). For the Polish immigrant community and the Polish-Jewish immigrant community, see Yves Frey, *Polonais d'Alsace: pratiques patronales et mineurs polonais dans le bassin potassique de Haute-Alsace, 1918–1948* (Besançon: Presses universitaires franc-comtoises, 2003); Didier Epelbaum, *Les enfants de papier: Les juifs de Pologne immigrés en France jusqu'en 1940: l'accueil, l'intégration, les combats* (Paris: B. Grasset, 2002).

13 For a discussion of asylum in interwar France, see Vicki Caron, *Uneasy Asylum: France and the Jewish Refugee Crisis, 1933–1942* (Stanford: Stanford University Press, 1999).

14 Neil MacMaster and Jim House, "*La fédération de France du FLN et l'organisation du 17 octobre 1961*" *Vingtième siècle. Revue d'histoire* no. 83 (July–September 2004): 145–160; Todd Shepard, *The Invention of Decolonization: The Algerian War and the Remaking of France* (Ithaca: Cornell University Press, 2006), 2.

15 See Marie-Antoinette Hily and Michel Poinard, "Portuguese Associations in France," in John Rex, et al., eds., *Immigrant Associations in Europe* (Aldershot: Gower, 1987), 126–160.

16 See Philippe Dewitte, *Les mouvements nègres en France, 1919–1939*, preface Juliette Bessis (Paris: L'Harmattan, 1985). Africans residing in France in the twentieth century also founded organizations, ranging from the intellectual and workers' groups formed during the interwar period to the *Fédération des*

étudiants d'Afrique noire en France (Federation of Black African Students in France or FEANF) created in the 1950s.

17 The UTN published the journal *Cri des Nègres.*

18 Dewitte, *Les mouvements nègres en France*, 99–100.

19 Ibid., 102.

20 Ibid., 115. Original French: "Surtout, au-delà de ses faibles effectifs, l'UIC aura servi de baptême militant à toute une génération d'Antillais et d'Africains."

21 Frederick Cooper, *Decolonization and African Society: The Labor Question in French and British Africa* (Cambridge: Cambridge University Press, 1996), 407–408.

22 Ibid.

23 Ibid., 408.

24 Ibid., 413–414.

25 Ibid., 414.

26 Ibid., 411.

27 ANC 19850087 art. 159 159 M 26755 26756 Préfecture de police, "Objet: A/S de l'Association des travailleurs de l'Afrique noire de la région parisienne," 15 April 1958.

28 Castles and Miller discuss this issue of self-definition versus other-definition. See Castles and Miller, *The Age of Migration*, 27.

29 Christophe Daum discusses Malian immigrant organizations in France and Catherine Quiminal touches on the associational activism of Soninké immigrants as well. See Christophe Daum, *Les associations de Maliens en France: Migrations, développement, et citoyenneté* (Paris: Éditions Karthala, 1998); Quiminal, *Gens d'ici, gens d'ailleurs.*

30 Castles and Miller, *The Age of Migration*, 41.

31 Shepard, *The Invention of Decolonization*, 12.

32 Ibid., 12.

33 N'Dongo appeared on television and radio programs in the 1970s and also published several books. See for example: Sally N'Dongo, *La "coopération" franco-africaine* (Paris: François Maspero, 1972); Sally N'Dongo, *Voyage forcé: Itinéraire d'un militant* (Paris: François Maspero, 1975); Sally N'Dongo, *"Cooperation" et néocolonialisme* (Paris: François Maspero, 1976).

34 Association of Senegalese Workers in the Paris Region.

35 For further discussion of the French colonial administration's citizenship policies in AOF, see C. Magbaily Fyle, *Introduction to the History of African Civilization Volume 2 Colonial and Post-Colonial Africa* (Lanham; New York; and Oxford: University Press of America, 2001), 27–31.

36 With the formal political rights that accompanied his citizenship status, N'Dongo could officially create organizations recognized by the police and the Ministry of the Interior, which regulated and oversaw immigration. See Frederick Cooper "From Imperial Inclusion to Republican Exclusion? France's Ambiguous Postwar Trajectory," in Charles Tshimanga, Didier Gondola, and Peter J. Bloom, eds., *Frenchness and the African Diaspora: Identity and Uprising in Contemporary France* (Bloomington; Indianapolis: Indiana University Press, 2009), 91–119; Catherine Wihtol de Wenden, *Les immigrés et la politique: Cent cinquante ans d'evolution* (Paris: Presses de la Fondation Nationale des Sciences Politiques, 1988).

37 Manchuelle, "Background to Black African Emigration to France," 528–529.

38 CANC 19850087 art. 158/159 MI 26755/26766 Préfecture de police, "Une tentative de réunification de l''Union générale des travailleurs sénégalais en France' (UGTSF) et de l''Amicale des travailleurs sénégalais de la région parisienne' (ATSRP) n'a donné aucun résultat" (20 September 1969); 19870799 art. 25 Service départemental des renseignements généraux des Hauts-de-Seine 92, "Demande de renseignements concernant l'association dite: 'Union générale des travailleurs sénégalais en France'" September 1976.

39 CANC 19850097 art. 158/159 MI26755/26756 Amicale des travailleurs sénégalais de la région parisienne, "Mise au point" 9 September 1965; 19870799 art. 25 Service départemental des renseignements généraux des Hauts-de-Seine 92, "Demande de renseignements concernant l'association dite: 'Union générale des travailleurs sénégalais en France'" September 1976. Original French: "Sally N'Dongo ne nous a jamais présenté la comptabilité de l'association."

40 CANC 19850087 art. 158/159 MI 26755/26766 Préfecture de police, "Une tentative de réunification de l''Union générale des travailleurs sénégalais en France' (UGTSF) et de l''Amicale des travailleurs sénégalais de la région parisienne' (ATSRP) n'a donné aucun résultat" (20 September 1969).

41 CANC 19850087 art. 158/159 MI 26755/26766 Préfecture de police, "Une tentative de réunification de l''Union générale des travailleurs sénégalais en France' (UGTSF) et de l' 'Amicale des travailleurs sénégalais de la région parisienne' (ATSRP) n'a donné aucun résultat" (20 September 1969).

42 UGTSF, *Le livre des travailleurs africains en France*, preface Albert Memmi (Paris: François Maspero, 1970), 180–181 ; CAN F1a 5136 "Police Report" 1965.

43 Part of the UGTSF's emphasis on assisting all Africans and not just Senegalese nationals emerged from Sally N'Dongo's own beliefs that he was charged with fostering such solidarity among this immigrant group. His personal dedication to assisting African immigrants in finding decent housing and steady jobs was woven into the UGTSF's same commitment. See CAN F1a 5136 "Police Report" 1965; François Manchuelle, *Willing Migrants: Soninké Labor Diasporas, 1848–1960* (Athens: Ohio University Press, 1997), 179–201.

44 CANC 19870799 art. 25 UGTSF, "Buts de l'association: UGTSF" (Puteaux, 1976). Original French: "Cette association a pour but de resserrer les liens d'amitié existant entre les travailleurs sénégalais en France et d'améliorer leurs conditions de vie par l'aide sociale et professionnelle."

45 UGTSF, *Le livre des travailleurs africains*, 31–50.

46 CIEMI Madeleine Trébous, "Les noirs en France" *Esprit* (April 1966), 738. Original French: "De petites caisses de solidarité se sont ainsi constituées depuis des années dans les '*foyers*', caves ou greniers, caisses qui ont été la base de la création de l'Union générale des travailleurs sénégalais en France."

47 CANC 19870799 art. 25 Service départemental des renseignements généraux des Hauts-de-Seine 92, "Demande de renseignements concernant l'association dite: 'Union générale des travailleurs sénégalais en France'" September 1976. For an analysis of policing and surveillance in AOF, see Kathleen Keller, "Colonial Suspects: Suspicious Persons and Police Surveillance in French West Africa, 1914–1945" (PhD diss., Rutgers University, 2006).

48 For more on the impact of decolonization on citizenship status, see Frederick Cooper, "From Imperial to Republican Exclusion? France's Ambiguous Postwar Trajectory" in Charles Tshimanga, Didier Gondola, and Peter J. Blooms, eds., *Frenchness and the African Diaspora: Identity and Uprising in Contemporary France* (Bloomington; Indianapolis: Indiana University Press, 2009), 105–117. See also Frederick Cooper, *Citizenship between Empire and Nation: Remaking France and French Africa, 1945–1960* (Princeton: Princeton University Press, 2014).

49 The ONI was created in 1945 to facilitate labor migration after World War Two. Martin Schain, *The Politics of Immigration in France, Britain, and the United States: A Comparative Study* (New York: Palgrave Macmillan, 2008), 41, 46; ANC F1a 5136 Direction des Renseignements Généraux, 8éme section no 61, "Les travailleurs originaires d'Afrique noire en France" 12 February 1964; M. Legru, Préfecture de la Seine, "Problème noire région parisienne Annexe 4."

50 In contrast, Portuguese immigrant associations did not emphasize worker status. See Hily and Poinard in Rex, et al., eds., *Immigrant Associations in Europe*, 126–160.

51 CANC 19870799 art. 25 "Objet: A.S. du déjeuner anniversaire de l'Union générale des travailleurs sénégalais de la région parisienne" 6 January 1964; P.M.A. (75), Direction de la réglementation 6é bureau no. 1671 "Gala organisé par l'Union générale des travailleurs sénégalais en France en faveur des peuples africains victimes de la sécheresse" 27 November 1973.
52 Branches in Puteaux, Le Havre, and Rouen, along with their members' abilities to vote for national offices, provided important connections between members.
53 CAN Fla 5135 Michel Massenet, "L'immigration des travailleurs noirs en France: leur adaptation à la communauté française" Marseille, 17 November 1964. Original French: "Mais devant l'urgence que présentaient certains problèmes comme celui de l'hébergement ou de l'amélioration de la situation sanitaire, chaque association a pris des initiatives pour arracher à la misère les groupes africains avec lesquels elle était particulièrement en rapport. Un mot doit être dit des associations africaines en France. Elles on a certainement un rôle à jouer auprès de leurs ressortissants, un rôle d'ordre moral; en particuliér c'est à elles qu'incombe le soin de maintenir un lien vivant entre les migrants et leur pays d'origine. Je ne crois pas cependant qu'elles puissent sans péril intervenir dans un domaine qui est la responsabilité propre de l'administration française, celui du logement les ressortissants des pays africains."
54 Robert Putnam provides an extensive discussion of social connections and social capital. See Putnam, *Bowling Alone*: *The Collapse and Revival of the American Community* (New York: Simon and Schuster, 2001). Quiminal reveals the rural nature of the Soninké migration pattern. See Quiminal, *Gens d'ici, gens d'ailleurs*; Manchuelle, *Willing Migrants*, 215.
55 ADVM 6J 105/106 Letter by Sally N'Dongo, President, UGTSF 1966.
56 UGTSF, *Le livre des travailleurs africains en France*, 180.
57 CAN Fla 5136 Ministre de l'Intérieur, "Les travailleurs d'Afrique noire en France: IV associations." Paris, May 1963; "Immigration et conditions des travailleurs africains noirs en France: Ch. III La vie des africains noirs en France" 15 February 1964; J. David to M le Ministère de l'Intérieur, Paris, 4 March 1966.
58 CIEMI, *Journal officiel: Avis et rapports du conseil économique et social*, "Problèmes posés par l'immigration des travailleurs africains en France." no. 15, 23 June 1964, 554.
59 UGTSF, *Le livre des travailleurs africains*, 180–181.
60 Manchuelle, "Background to Black African Emigration to France," 530.
61 For an exploration of French policy toward Muslims in the late nineteenth century, see David Robinson, "French 'Islamic' Policy and Practice in Late Nineteenth-Century Senegal," *The Journal of African History* 29, no. 3 (1988): 415–435. For the role of missionaries in the French colonial empire, see Elizabeth Foster, *Faith in Empire: Religion, Politics, and Colonial Rule in French Senegal, 1880–1940* (Stanford: Stanford University Press, 2013).
62 CANC 19870799 art. 25 UGTSF, "Les responsables des travailleurs réunis à Rouen les 21 et 22 Mars 1964 décident de se grouper au sein d'une fédération dite 'Union générale des travailleurs sénégalais en France'" Rouen, 21–22 March, 1964.
63 Cooper, *Decolonization and African Society*, 408.
64 For more on *Négritude* and Pan-Africanism, see Dewitte, *Les mouvements nègres en France*; Boittin, *Colonial Metropolis*; Hayes Edwards, *The Practice of Diaspora*; Abiola Irele, "What Is Négritude?" in *African Literature: An Anthology of Criticism and Theory* Tejumola Olaniyan and Ato Quayson, eds., (Malden: Blackwell, 2007); Léopold Sèdar Senghor, "Négritude: A Humanism of the Twentieth Century," in *African Literature*, eds., Olaniyan and Quayson (Hoboken: Wiley-Blackwell, 2007), 195–202.
65 For more on the migration of the Soninké, see Quiminal, *Gens dici, gens d'ailleurs*; Manchuelle, *Willing Migrants*.

66 UGTSF, *Le livre des travailleurs africains en France*, 180–181; ADVM 6J 105/106 "Compte rendu des activités 65–67—UGTSF."
67 Manchuelle, "Background to Black African Emigration to France," 528.
68 Ibid., 528.
69 "Jeunes agriculteurs, décembre 1966" in UGTSF, *Le livre des travailleurs africains en France*, 152.
70 CANC F1a 5136 Ministry of the Interior, "Les travailleurs d'Afrique noire en France" Paris, May 1963. Original French: "Les travailleurs d'Afrique Noire en France demeurent attachés à leurs traditions et coutumes africaines. Ils sont pour l'instant peu perméables aux propagandes politiques ou autres et se montrent en général réticents devant les tentatives faites pour pénétrer leurs milieux."
71 "Compte rendu des activités 65–67" in UGTSF, *Le livre des travailleurs africains en France*, 152.
72 Castles and Davidson use the example of the *Amicale des Algériens en Europe* (AAE), a pro-Algerian independence organization, to illustrate the point that domestic political movements and governments in North and West Africa use organizations in France to advance their agendas. See Castles and Davidson, *Citizenship and Migration*.
73 For more on the life of Léopold Senghor, see Janet Vaillant, *Black, French, and African: A Life of Léopold Sédar Senghor* (Cambridge: Harvard University Press, 1991).
74 ADVM 6J 105/106 "Compte rendu des activités 1965–1967."
75 UGTSF, *Le livre des travailleurs africains en France*, 180–181, 185.
76 "Résumé du rapport de ce congrès (25/26) décembre 1965): Bilan." in UGTSF, *Le livre des travailleurs africains in France*, 185.
77 ADVM 6J 105/106 Letter by Sally N'Dongo, President, UGTSF 1966.
78 CANC 19770317 art. 1 Noel Monier, "Prix du lit augmente dans un foyer d'Ivry: les 700 Africains font la grève du loyer république du gérant: eau, electricité coupées." (Travailleurs noirs en France) *France soir*, Paris, 1969; CAN F1a 5136 "Logement des travailleurs d'Afrique noire en France." CAN F1a 5135 "Logement des travailleurs d'Afrique noire en France." (Paris: Direction générale des affaires politiques et d'administration du territoire/service des affaires musulmanes, 1964). AMSD 18 ACW 22/23 Noël Copin "L'Afrique noire au couer de Paris." *Études sociales nord-africains/ESNA* 14 (22 June 1963): 526–533. (1963), 526. CAN F1a 5136 Conseil économique et social et M Gérard Espéret, "Deuxième partie: conditions de vie (des immigrants africains)." *Journal officiel de la republique française: Avis et rapports du conseil économique et social*, session de 1964 Séance du 23 Juin 1964, "Problèmes posés par l'immigration africaine en France" 24 (1964): 549–566. CIEMI Pierre Bollinger, "Les Africains noirs parmi nous: étude psycho-sociale des migrations d'Afrique noire" *Hommes et migrations* (1966): 663. Claude Lecomte, "Au 3 de la rue Riquet (Paris–19ème) ils sont 500 condamnés." *L'Humanité*, Paris, May 1971.
79 CAN F1a 5136 M Legru, "Étude: problème noir région parisienne."
80 CIEMI Pierre Claver Mvele Ndango'o, "Africains dans la région parisienne," *Hommes et migrations—Documents sur les travailleurs étrangers* 887 (1975): 16. CAN F1a 5136 Conseil économique et social et M Gérard Espéret, "Deuxième partie: conditions de vie (des immigrants africains) *Journal officiel de la république française: Avis et rapports du conseil économique et social*, session de 1964 séance du 23 juin 1964, "Problèmes posés par l'immigration africaine en France." (1964): 549–566. ADSSD 1801 W art 226 "Logement du taudis au foyer-case." *Étincelle* 10.
81 AMSD 18 ACW 22/23 Questions écrits *Bulletin municipal officiel* (Ville de Paris): no 312, 282, Paris, July 1963. CAN F1a 5136 Conseil économique et social et M Gérard Espéret "Deuxième partie: conditions de vie (des immigrants

africains)." *Journal officiel de la république française: Avis et rapports du conseil économique et social*, session de 1964 séance du 23 juin 1964, "Problèmes posés par l'immigration africaine en France." CANC 19770317 art. 1 G. Brottes, "Note pour M le Préfet Directeur du Cabinet Objet: Logement des travailleurs africains." (Paris: Préfecture de la Seine, 1966).

82 CAN Fla 5136 "Projet de la création d'un foyer pour les travailleurs sénégalais," March 1963. These locales continue to serve as the geographical center of the African community in the Paris region today.

83 For more on the republican idea of integration, especially in the postwar and post-colonial contexts, see for example Erik Bleich, "The Legacies of History? Colonization and Immigrant Integration in Britain and France," *Theory and Society* 34, no. 2 (April 2005): 171–195.

84 CAN Fla 5136 Ministry of the Interior, "Les travailleurs d'Afrique noire en France" Paris, May 1963. Original French: "La colonie d'Afrique Noire a rapidement essaimé dans les quartiers de Paris et les communes de banlieue où les musulmans d'Afrique du Nord les avaient devancés, principalement dans les 19ème, 20ème, 18ème, 11ème et 13ème *arrondissements*, et à St. Denis, Clichy et Aubervilliers. A l'heure actuelle, rares sont les noirs logés dans des locaux individuels. Dans les cas les plus favorables, ils vivent à huit ou dix dans des chambres d'hôtels qui abritaient auparavant un nombre moitié moindre d'Algériens"

85 CAN Fla 5136 M. Legru, "Étude problème noire région parisienne" (Paris, Préfecture de la Seine, 1965). Original French: "Les Africains se regroupent à Paris par communautés villageoises."

86 CIEMI "Problèmes posés par l'immigration des travailleurs africains en France" *Journal officiel de la république française: Avis et rapports du conseil économique et social*, session de 1964 séance du 23 juin 1964, 550.

87 Ibid., 547.

88 Ibid., 554; CANC 19940023 art. 20 "L'association dite 'SOUNDIATA' a transféré son siège" 28 March 1966.

89 Ibid.

90 CANC 19850087 art 158/159 MI 26755/26756 AFP Spécial: Outre Mer 12/12/1963, no. 5247 Reports on Buron – President of SOUNDIATA.

91 Manchuelle, "Background to Black African Emigration to France," 531. CANC 19850087 art. 158 159 MI 26755 26756 "AFP Spécial: Outre Mer" no. 5247 12 December 1963; "SOUNDIATA: Association pour le soutien, l'union et la dignité de l'accueil aux travailleurs africains" May 1963.

92 CANC 19850087 art. 158/159 MI 26755/26756 "Objet: Activité de l'"Association pour formation technique de base des Africains et Malgaches résidant en France"" 12 January, 1963.

93 CANC 19770317 art. 1 "Objet: Logement des travailleurs africains."

94 CIEMI Trébous, "Les noirs en France," 732–743; CAN Fla 5136 J. David to Ministère de l'Intérieur Paris, 4 March 1966.

95 UGTSF, *Le livre des travailleurs africains en France*, 53–55; Manchuelle, "Background to Black African Emigration to France," 529; CANC 19940023 art. 20 "Les Travailleurs africains de la région parisienne protestent," Paris, 7 July 1969.

96 UGTSF, *Le livre des travailleurs africains en France*, 49.

97 Mercier, "La mort de cinq travailleurs africains à Aubervilliers—Qui est responsable?" *Le Monde*, Paris, 4–5 January 1970.

98 CANC 19960134 art. 17 "Le 'Front des mouvements des travailleurs africains' entend poursuivre la mobilisation des africains de race noire en utilisant le thème: 'la carte de séjour c'est le contrôle avant l'esclavage." Paris, 26 March 1975.

99 CAN Fla5136 "Les travailleurs d'Afrique noire en France III: Conditions et mode de vie … Situation de l'emploi et chômage" Ministère de l'Intérieur, May 1963.

100 ADVM 6J 105/106 "Note: A l'áttention des jeunes agriculteurs sénégalais de la part de l'UTGSF Article paru dans 'L'Écho de la mode,' no. 24, 12 June 1966. The delegation described farm women's lives prior to the commune's creation as laborious and tiresome, with family, household, and agricultural obligations taking up the majority of their time. It was also noted that the role of rural women was more vast and important than that of their urban counterparts because of their important domestic responsibilities. See also "Chapitre 6: L'alphabétisation et la formation professionnelle, Part III" in UGTSF, *Le livre des travailleurs africains en France*; Manchuelle, "Background to Black African Emigration to France," 531.
101 Sally N'Dongo, *"Coopération" et néo-colonialisme* (Paris: François Maspero, 1976), 37–96.
102 UGTSF, *Le livre des travailleurs africains en France*, 135.
103 ADVM 6J 105/106, "À l'attention des jeunes agriculteurs sénégalais de la part de l'UGTSF" in 'l'Écho de la mode' no. 24 du 12 juin 1966; UGTSF, *Le livre des travailleurs africains en France*, 150–151.
104 Sally N'Dongo, "L'école de la vie" *International Review of Education/Internationale Zeitschrift für Erziehungswissenschraft/Revue internationale de l'éducation* 40, no. 3/5 (1994): 322. Original French: "Nous avons été agréablement surpris tout au début par l'accueil chaleureux de ces familles, car nous nous étions préparés à une certaine hostilité, cette population étant moins en contact avec la peau noire que les citadins. Le contraire s'est produit, beaucoup ont tout de suite sympathisé et la coopération a été fructueuse."
105 UGTSF, *Le livre des travailleurs africains en France*, 152. ADVM 6J 105/106 "Compte-rendu de stage présenté par Diambele Diao, 6, rue des Graviers, Maison-Lafitte."
106 UGTSF, *Le livre des travailleurs africains en France*, 152.
107 N'Dongo, *"Coopération" et néocolonialisme*, 102. Original French: "Loin de rationaliser l'émigration, le système actuel permet à toute une faune de trafiquants sans scrupules …"
108 N'Dongo, *"Cooperation" et néocolonialisme*, 102. Original French: "Il est bien connu que les travailleurs africains ne viennent pas en France avec l'intention de s'y fixer de façon définitive. Ils séjournent deux à trois ans, au maximum, le temps d'économiser l'argent qui leur permettra de prendre au retour un petit commerce et de payer le voyage en France d'un autre membre de la famille ainsi que la dot pour leur mariage. L'instauration d'une *libre* circulation des personnes inciterait certainement le travailleur à réduire à une année sa présence en France."
109 See, for example, N'Dongo, *"Coopération" et néo-colonialisme.*
110 N'Dongo, *"Coopération" et néo-colonialisme*, 87–89.
111 N'Dongo, *"Coopération" et néo-colonialisme*, 87. Original French: "Le Sénégal 'indépendant' ne peut donc être mis en valeur que par les capitaux étrangers. Les richesses du Sénégal, et en premier lieu la main d'œuvre, sont bradées au profit du capital étranger."
112 N'Dongo, *"Coopération" et néo-colonialisme*, 86–88.
113 Quoted in N'Dongo, *La "coopération" franco-africaine*, 22. Original French: "La coopération a également des raisons économiques et politiques … La France n'a aucune raison de cacher qu'elle souhaite maintenir une certaine influence, une certaine présence politique, morale et culturelle."
114 N'Dongo, *"Coopération" et néo-colonialisme*, 13. Original French: "Mais les conséquences de ce pillage ne doivent pas être considérées du seul point de vue démographique. En effet les destructions, l'insécurité permanente consécutive à la traite ont complètement désorganisé les sociétés qui en ont été victimes …

La pénétration coloniale a grandement été facilitée par la saignée due à la traite des noirs."

115 N'Dongo, *"Coopération"et néo-colonialisme*, 14–15.

116 N'Dongo, *"Coopération" et néo-colonialisme*, 15. Original French: "Curieuse indépendance qui 'permet' aux Africains d'être de plus en plus exploités, que cela soit en Afrique ou bien en France."

117 N'Dongo, *La "coopération" franco-africaine*, 20–22.

118 See, for example, N'Dongo, *La "coopération" franco-africaine.*

119 CANC 19850799 art. 25 Direction de la réglementation 6é bureau no. 563, "L'Union générale des travailleurs sénégalais en France (UGTSF) et l'Union générale des étudiants, élèves et stagiaires sénégalais (UGEESS), organisent un meeting vendredi 6 avril, à 20 h. 30, à la salle Lèo Lagrange, 7 rue de Tretaigne (18èmè)," 5 April 1973.

120 ANC 19850799 art. 25 Direction de la Réglementation 6é Bureau no. 563, "L'Union générale des travailleurs sénégalais en France (UGTSF) et l'Union générale des étudiants, élèves et stagiaires sénégalais (UGEESS), organisent un meeting vendredi 6 avril, à 20 h. 30, à la salle Léo Lagrange, 7 rue de Tretaigne (18ème)" 5 April 1973. Original French: "Ces deux organisations invitent 'tous les démocrates, les hommes épris de paix, de justice et de liberté à manifester leur solidarité à la lutte du peuple sénégalais pour sauver la vie des enseignants sénégalais en danger, exiger leur libération immédiate et dénoncer la suppression des libertés politiques et syndicales au Sénégal'."

121 CANC 19870799 art. 25 Direction de la réglementation et du contentieux, Ministre d'État Ministère de l'Intérieur, "Note Objet: A/S. de l'Union générale des travailleurs sénégalais en France" Paris, 18 March 1977.

122 CANC 19870799 art. 25 M Cantan, Directeur de la réglementation et du contentieux, Ministère de l'Intérieur à M le Préfet des Hauts de Seine, Direction de l'administration générale 2ème bureau, 4 August 1978. See Catherine Wihtol de Wenden and Rémy Leveau, *La beurgeoisie: Les trois âges de la vie associative issue de l'immigration* (Paris: 2001), 7–13.

123 For more on 1968 in France, see Kristin Ross, *May 1968 and its Afterlives* (Chicago: University of Chicago, 2002).

124 CANC 19870799 art. 25 Direction générale de la police nationale direction départementale des renseignements généraux de l'Oise à Beauvais, "Membres: Regroupement des Sénégalais de l'Oise" 22 August 1977.

125 CANC 19870799 art. 25 Charles Barbeau, le Préfet, Directeur de la réglementation et du contentieux, le Ministre de l'Intérieur, "Arrêté: portant autorisation d'une association étrangère (ATMF)" 13 February 1978.

126 Castles and Miller discuss the importance of pre-migratory symbols and culture. See Castles and Miller, *The Age of Migration*, 222. CANC 19960311 art. 6 Association des travailleurs maliens en France, "Ultime appel aux Maliens." 1971. CAN 19960311 art. 5 Ambassadeur de France au Mali to Ministre des Affaires Étrangères, 12 July 1977.

127 CANC 19870799 art. 25 Direction de la réglementation et du contentieux, Ministre d'État Ministre de l'Intérieur, "Note objet: A/S. de l'Union générale des travailleurs sénégalais en France" Paris, 18 March 1977.

128 Cooper, *Decolonization and African Society*, 408.

2 Political mobilization and collective action

The Ivry rent strike

While the UGTSF emphasized the provision of housing for African immigrants as part of its social welfare program, by 1969, it was becoming clear that a crisis was mounting throughout the Paris region. The dormitories emphasized by municipal councils, the ATM-SSD, the UGTSF, and other organizations as a way of assisting African immigrants were not succeeding in addressing the housing challenges that African immigrants faced. Writing to the *Préfet* of the Val-de-Marne department in November of 1969, Mamadou Diandouma, a Malian immigrant, described the living conditions of a group of residents in a dormitory on the rue Gabriel Péri in Ivry-sur-Seine, just outside of Paris. In working to help his audience understand his plight and that of hundreds of other African workers, he explained:

> we have the honor of confirming that the water in the dormitory where 550 men live has been cut off. Without electricity for quite some time, this new provocation has totally deprived us of running water and is, in our eyes, a link in a well-established plan.[1]

The author was one of hundreds of Malian immigrants struggling to survive in an over-crowded dormitory outside of Paris. By that point, Diandouma and his fellow residents had sustained a rent strike for six months. Diandouma was one of its primary leaders. Residents demanded better housing and improvements to accommodate their social, cultural, and religious practices. As Diandouma was sending the letter, however, the situation turned desperate. Several violent altercations occurred between the protesters and the landlords, leading to a near constant police presence outside of the dormitory. Diandouma decided to reach out to a French official, hoping that the regional government of the Val-du-Marne, where the Ivry dormitory was located, could help.

Six years after the Saint-Denis riot and less than a decade after decolonization in Sub-Saharan Africa, African immigrants continued to struggle with housing problems. Dormitories such as the one on the rue Gabriel Péri became a nexus for political activism within the African community. By the late 1960s and early 1970s and in an attempt to draw attention to increasingly deplorable conditions, residents staged rent strikes, using political tactics employed in the era of decolonization. They also drew inspiration from the politically charged atmosphere of Paris and other French cities in the late 1960s and in the wake of the upheaval of 1968 as well as from the long-standing tradition within French society of striking. By that point, as historian Daniel Gordon argues, what he refers to as "politicized minorities" were part of the political landscape of Paris.[2] In looking to France and the colonies for inspiration, African workers also engaged with the emerging postwar rhetoric on human rights, individual dignity, and social justice as a way of framing their plight to the surrounding French society. They turned to the strike as a political tactic. As Gordon's work indicates, throughout the events of 1968, striking provided an important means of political participation for immigrant groups, which then became a key tactic in the struggle over housing in the late 1960s and early 1970s.[3]

The year 1969 was thus an important turning point for this growing political movement among African workers and other immigrant communities. That spring, hundreds of Malian residents of a run-down dormitory in Ivry-sur-Seine outside of Paris staged a rent strike and joined the burgeoning African political movement emerging on a variety of fronts. Residents established a committee to administer the strike's daily operations, circulated petitions, held demonstrations on the dormitory's steps, clashed with police, and, at one point, took their landlords hostage. Yet in scholarly accounts of African immigration, the Ivry rent strike, its impact, and its consequences rarely garner more than a brief mention. This chapter seeks to better understand how ethnic minorities mobilize politically through the lens of the Ivry strike in order to explore how it is that immigrant groups become engaged in civic and political life. As Mireille Rosello shows in *Postcolonial Hospitality: The Immigrant as Guest*, immigrants who choose to openly demonstrate, regardless of their legal status, forego their anonymity while challenging "the myth of their clandestinity."[4] Those residents who went on strike in Ivry did just that. As Charles Tshimanga, Didier Gondola, and Peter J. Bloom argue in *Frenchness and the African Diaspora*, "minority consciousness and activism are perceived as a threat to France's long-proclaimed international humanitarianism precisely because they reveal racial inequalities in a country that purports to be the standard bearer of the universal rights of man."[5] Participants in the Ivry rent strike undertook the kind of political activism deemed threatening by authorities because, as Tshimanga, Gondola, and Bloom explain, they drew attention to severe and significant inequalities from a racial and material standpoint.

Instead of factories, a locale frequently associated with strikes, dormitories across the Paris region served as the center of political activism for African workers by 1969, including the one on the rue Gabriel Péri.[6] Sociologist Riva Kastoryano argues that the housing projects located in the *banlieues* became key areas of upheaval.[7] The upheaval to which Kastoryano refers, however, is not a recent phenomenon and dates back to at least the early postcolonial era and the decade of the 1960s, if not earlier. The Ivry rent strike reveals that the political activism that scholars Pap Ndiaye and Abdoulaye Guéye identify as starting or peaking in 1972 in fact began a few years earlier. While residents did protest in response to the closing of certain dormitories and the relocation of residents, as Ndiaye and Guéye argue, other issues prompted this politicization as well, including disputes over rent and the conditions of the dormitories themselves.[8] Guéye, for example, dates African political activism to the late 1970s onwards.[9] Yet political engagement in various areas across the Paris region suggest that African-immigrant led collective actions occurred across the 1960s and shaped the political and social debates around immigration to a much greater extent than previously acknowledged.

Strikes in France remained an important component of the postwar political landscape, and immigrants, including African workers, became part of this broader trend.[10] Kastoryano explains that politicized identities provide an outlet for long-standing problems.[11] As residents at the rue Gabriel Péri struggled to endure deplorable housing conditions while sustaining a rent strike, they were not alone. Hundreds of Portuguese immigrants, for example, lived in a notorious dormitory in Champigny.[12] Algerian workers continued to struggle with housing problems as well.[13] Rent strikes swept through SONACOTRA-controlled *foyers* in the 1970s, which, at that point, were still home to a large number of Algerians.[14] During this same period, hundreds of African immigrants around the Paris region went on strike in response to their housing conditions as part of this broader trajectory of immigrant political protest.

The Ivry rent strike was a central event in the history of postcolonial African political activism and serves as an important moment through which to evaluate the political responses of this immigrant community to the challenges of life in postcolonial Paris. The collective action undertaken in Ivry revealed the critical political tactics developed by African workers. By the late 1960s, African immigrants were using strikes and other forms of protest as platforms to publicly criticize of French immigration policy and the conditions in which they found themselves living in France.[15] They did so even though many remained undocumented with their legal residency status in flux. These kinds of political tactics provided African workers with the means by which to protest, regardless of their legal status. This approach, in fact, transcended residency status, reflecting the global nature of political protest by the late 1960s. The situations that African immigrants confronted on a daily basis helped to foment the collective action expressed through the Ivry rent strike and countless others around the Paris region.

Some of the primary political activists within the African immigrant community at this point were workers themselves, including N'Dongo of the UGTSF, and the leaders of the Ivry strike, including Diandouma. This both resembled and differed from the interwar context in important ways. During the postwar era, African student activists from organizations such as FEANF (*Fédération des étudiants d'Afrique noire en France* [Black African Student Federation of France]), an organization serving African students in France, played an important political role. Yet many of the community's key intellectual leaders from the interwar period, including Senegal's first president, Léopold Senghor, had returned to Sub-Saharan Africa by 1960. This altered the political landscape in France, leaving more space for labor activists such as those who led the strikes in Ivry and elsewhere throughout the Paris region. Independence from the colonizer had been achieved—the focus now shifted to the plight of African immigrants in France and the neocolonial relationship between France and countries in Sub-Saharan Africa from a political, social, and economic perspective.

Rarely, though, is the broader twentieth-century history of the African diaspora's political activities taken into consideration when discussing more recent developments, including postcolonial rent strikes. Scholars such as Ndiaye argue that it was events such as the 1996 *sans-papiers* movement in the Église Saint-Bernard that generated empathy from the surrounding French society. The *sans-papiers* movement also demonstrated the capacity for collective action among African immigrants. The Ivry rent strike reveals that, in fact, this kind of collective mobilization that in turn elicited broader public support occurred decades earlier than previously acknowledged.[16]

Beyond the strike on the rue Gabriel Péri, the year 1969 saw African-led rent strikes occur throughout the Paris region, including one on the rue Bisson and another on the rue Léon Gaumont, both in the 20th *arrondissement*.[17] The latter dormitory was managed by one of the landlords, Traoré, responsible for the dormitory on the rue Gabriel Péri.[18] In another one of his dormitories—on the rue d'Orgemont in Paris—the landlord struggled with his tenants. An established pattern of conflict emerged between immigrant tenants and landlords, one that sparked everything from riots such as that in Saint-Denis to the strikes that engulfed the Paris region in the late 1960s.[19] Authorities identified several more all-African dormitories that they considered to be on the verge of a strike, including a *foyer* at 216 rue du Faubourg-Saint-Denis in the 10th *arrondissement* of Paris, another at 214 rue Raymond-Losserrand in the 14th *arrondissement*, and a third at 43 rue Pinel in Saint-Denis, which was home to more than 600 residents.[20] By that summer, the Senegalese residents of the dormitory on the rue Pinel had started rent strikes as well.[21] Each strike shared a common theme. As one report explained, "Housed in deplorable conditions, African workers in the Paris region are protesting against the abuses they suffer."[22]

No other immigrant-led rent strike, though, caught the attention of the media, government officials, or the broader public quite like the Ivry rent strike, due in large part to its length and visibility. After five immigrant workers died of asphyxiation in a dormitory in Aubervilliers a few months after the start of the Ivry strike, the two events became inextricably linked in the media and in the popular imagination, further spotlighting the challenges faced by African workers and other immigrant groups in France. Nearly a decade after the beginning of postcolonial labor migration, African workers vigorously protested their living conditions. Despite the risks, they drew attention to their plight within the politically charged atmosphere of the late 1960s while incorporating the tactics used to oppose colonial regimes in French West Africa.

The strike's origins and course

Within this context of immigrant political activism, what prompted African immigrants in Ivry to go on strike in the spring of 1969? The strike's origins lay in a relocation effort aimed at improving the housing conditions of a single group of African immigrants. On June 12, 1965 the *Service d'assistance technique de la préfecture de police* (Technical Support Service of the Préfecture de Police or SAT) relocated 150 Malian workers via police cars from slums in the 18th and 19th *arrondissements* of Paris to an old chocolate factory left vacant on the rue Gabriel Péri in Ivry-sur-Seine, outside of the capital city.[23] Rent strikes did not normally follow a relocation—usually they preceded one.[24] This case proved different, though. The residents were thrown out of their former dwelling by a court decision, rendering them nearly homeless with few options but to relocate to a new suburban community. Without first consulting officials in Ivry, the SAT decided to move 150 Malian residents there.[25] A local Ivry official later explained that, "the municipal council and the municipality of Ivry-sur-Seine bear no responsibility in the installation of workers at 45, rue Gabriel Péri. The installation of Malians in the buildings of an old factory occurred on the 13th of June 1965 in scandalous conditions, without consultation with the municipality."[26] One report argued that many dormitories were, "created or abandoned by the whims of the moment."[27] Connecting the rent strike of 1969 to the year 1965 and the moment at which the dormitory opened its doors to its Malian residents, a journalist claimed that, "this scandal has been ongoing since Sunday the 13th of June 1965."[28] The relocation to Ivry points to the ad hoc nature of some of the government initiatives in response to the growing number of African immigrants residing in the Paris region by the late 1960s. Policies associated with immigration emerged in response to particular situations, such as overcrowded living conditions and the perceived threat that they posed from the official perspective, rather than through a planned approach. Often, initiatives developed for the Algerian community served as models for policies designed to assist African workers, including the creation of SONACOTRA(L) [*Société nationale de construction de logements pour les travailleurs (algériens)* or National society for the construction of (Algerian) immigrant housing], an organization originally focused on providing housing for Algerian immigrant families.[29]

Once in Ivry, the relocated African workers found themselves living in a dormitory not unlike others in the Paris region, with a few caveats. The establishment was run by a French woman, Madeleine Morael, and a Malian man, Garba Traoré, which was not necessarily the norm.[30] Most

Figure 2.1 45 rue Gabriel Péri. Image courtesy of the Ivry Municipal Archives, Ivry, France.

dormitories were operated either by French property managers or immigrants from North or Sub-Saharan Africa. Rarely did these various constituencies oversee properties together. State-run and private management organizations also managed dormitories. By 1969, organizations such as SOUNDIATA and AFTAM had opened dormitories that exclusively housed African immigrants throughout the Paris region. Early reports placed the rent in line with those charged at other *foyers*. The landlords, however, operated as "*marchands du sommeil*" or "sleep merchants," renting each bed to at least two individuals, one of whom slept in it at night and the other of whom used it during the day, which was also a common practice. In double renting the beds in their facility, Madame Morael and Monsieur Traoré contributed to the rapid increase in the dormitory's population from an initial figure of 150 residents to over 500.[31]

Despite these practices or perhaps because of them, the dormitory's demographics followed the established pattern of most African dormitories and dwellings, with a few exceptions. Most residents were of a single nationality—Malian in this case—and of a single ethnicity, Soninké.[32]

Several hailed from the same villages in Mali's Kayes region. They were slightly more diverse in age and in profession, though, than other, comparable housing units. While most worked in the industrial sector, some inhabitants were students.[33] This proved to be somewhat of an anomaly, as African workers and students rarely lived in the same places.[34] A handful of residents came from French-controlled Guadeloupe and Martinique, which was uncommon, as Antillean workers often lived in separate dormitories from their Sub-Saharan African counterparts.[35]

By 1969, several sources estimated the dormitory's population at 541 inhabitants, quickly increasing from the 150 residents who initially moved to Ivry through the SAT's relocation effort.[36] Two key factors explain this growth. Like other immigrant groups, African workers sought to re-create a sense of community within urban spaces, neighborhoods, and *banlieues*, much as they did in the months leading up to the 1963 Saint-Denis riot.[37] The landlords' tendency to double-rent rooms contributed to overcrowding because it facilitated and even accelerated this process of reconnecting within the dormitories. Second, the more diverse nature of the *foyer*'s residents also added to its population.[38] As more and more Malians came to Paris to find work, they sought out friends, relatives, and neighbors from common villages in Mali and elsewhere. The Mauritanians who eventually rioted in Saint-Denis followed a similar trajectory, as did other immigrant groups throughout the Paris region and around France. The dormitory's challenges came to symbolize many of the housing problems faced by African workers and other immigrant communities.[39] For the rue Gabriel Péri, the problem of overcrowding presented the most pressing issue. These worsening conditions contributed directly to the burgeoning politicization and the decision to strike in the spring of 1969.[40] One of the most important components of any strike action—the availability of workers to initiate and sustain it—was therefore met and exceeded in dormitories such as that on the rue Gabriel Péri and elsewhere throughout the Paris region. The crowded living conditions with hundreds and hundreds of immigrant workers living together in dormitories were one of the main catalysts not only of the Ivry rent strike, but also of those that occurred through the Paris region in the late 1960s and early 1970s.[41]

Other factors prompted the strike as well. Not unlike the Saint-Denis riot, the Ivry rent strike was a product of the frustrations that developed between 1965, when the residents arrived, and 1969 and the strike's start. Only this time, the friction was internal and specific to the dormitory itself rather than emerging from a conflict with another immigrant group, as in the Saint-Denis riot. The tenants became increasingly alarmed at the *foyer*'s overcrowded conditions and the lack of basic amenities. Ventilation was poor, bedding was scarce, and there was little in the way of kitchen facilities.[42] Although ethnologist Michel Leiris observed an atmosphere of what he labeled camaraderie at the time, the severity of the problems within the dormitory caused continual frustration until the strike's outbreak in the spring of 1969.[43] The conditions themselves contributed to the residents' politicization. One of the strike's major catalysts was the landlords' refusal to make improvements and finally, their decision to cut access to water and electricity, intercept the mail, and coordinate an ongoing police presence in and around the neighborhood.[44] Residents later explained that they felt justified in their actions because of these developments, demonstrating that they were politicized by the problems that they encountered on a daily basis. In a letter to city officials, they argued that the strike was, "justified by the totally inhuman living conditions."[45] Living conditions contributed significantly to the strike's outbreak while politicizing the dormitory's residents.

One of the final factors leading to the strike's outbreak, though, was Traoré's decision to raise the rent from 40 to 60 francs per month. By contrast, the riot in Saint-Denis was provoked by accusations of theft. Residents in Ivry expressed anger and frustration over this increase, arguing that they could not absorb increased rent payments, contend with other living expenses, and send as much money as possible home, a primary goal that influenced the decision to emigrate in search of employment.[46] Based on previous patterns, they saw it as a manifestation of the landlord's greed and not a reflection of his desire to improve conditions in the dormitory, which by May of 1970 residents still described as "totally inhumane," a theme that ran through the strike's rhetoric.[47]

From the residents' perspective, despite the burgeoning associational movement and the visibility of advocacy organizations such as the UGTSF, there was no other option but to refuse to pay the rent. They did just that and in retaliation, the landlords cut off the dormitory's power. This proved to be the final provocation that pushed the residents into action. While rent increases proved challenging, a power outage deliberately enacted by the landlords was disastrous and affected the residents' ability to function on a daily basis and reinforced in their minds the "barbaric" nature of their living conditions. Short of rioting and with a history of strikes in the colonial and French contexts to draw on for inspiration, a rent strike presented an effective, public, and sustained means to protest these rent augmentations, power outages, and the precarious living conditions overall.[48]

The strike's objectives

The residents' objectives were twofold. Organizers wanted to secure better living conditions and create decent and safe spaces in which to carry out their daily lives. These demands were largely social in nature. For example, those on strike sought the "right to use the telephone, the right to receive visitors."[49] They wanted "adequate hygienic and sanitary conditions, and then, secondly, to be housed in dormitories that meticulously meet the conditions specified by regulations."[50] It was true that the refusal to pay a rent increase reflected their desire to hold down housing costs in the short run. Yet the strike in Ivry was multifaceted in its objectives and retained a long-term vision for the African community in France, reflecting the ideas of

Figure 2.2 45 rue Gabriel Péri. Image courtesy of the Ivry Municipal Archives, Ivry, France.

independence, freedom, and liberation embedded within the political movements challenging colonial regimes throughout the world in the postwar era and the growing transnational emphasis on human rights.[51]

In addition to refusing any increases in rent, organizers hoped for improved amenities overall within the dormitory while emphasizing the dangerous, dilapidated condition in which the residents lived.[52] They wanted better bedding, improved ventilation, and less crowded conditions.[53] One journalist argued that in undertaking a rent strike, participants were publicly denouncing "the hygenic conditions: rooms without windows, beds right next to each other, neither cupboards nor shelves, four water faucets for the entire building."[54] Their demands challenge the assumption that economically driven postcolonial migrants were preoccupied only with repatriation and events in their home countries and had little interest in community development in their host country. Scholarship on immigration frequently delineates between economically driven labor migrants as temporary and uninterested in permanent community development. They place emphasis on other sorts of migratory patterns—including family reunification and asylum—as those that prioritize community formation within the host country because of the "permanent" nature of their migration. But the Africans who rioted, went on strike, and formed associations exhibited many of the same attributes as other types of migrants, despite their supposedly temporary position within French society. Their dedication to building networks of sociability and the foundations of a postcolonial immigrant community reveals that the lines that scholars draw between different types of migration might be less rigid than originally thought.[55]

The structured nature of these demands and the strike's overall objectives suggests that it, like those occurring simultaneously across the Paris region, constituted a highly organized, internally driven form of immigrant activism. Outside groups or individuals did not instigate it, as local authorities hypothesized. Leading the strike was the residents' committee.[56] This group assumed the critical role of handling daily operations, preparing the residents' demands, and transmitting them to the landlords and the surrounding community, just as other committees would do in later immigrant-led rent strikes, including those that swept across the Paris region in 1972.[57] In doing so, they followed the pattern identified by scholars such as Alec Hargreaves in terms of ethnic mobilization and identification: they represented the activists "who (were) strongly committed to particular goals," not unlike Sally N'Dongo's role as the UGTSF's leader.[58] Observers, including the Ministry of the Interior, argued that the committees that emerged in countless dormitories across the Paris region caused restlessness and instability by inciting residents to take action against landlords and management organizations. Inside the Ivry dormitory and others, though, they were not necessarily a disruptive force. The committee and its members provided the leadership necessary to sustain an ongoing rent strike. Strike leaders worked as representatives for residents who often had little say in management-related issues and had few outlets through which to lodge their complaints. This gave residents the political voice that they lacked elsewhere in French society while also signaling the diversification of African political activism and its multifaceted nature over the course of the 1960s.

Political and ethnic mobilization

This and other rent strikes in the late 1960s and early 1970s, then, were important examples of ethnic mobilization, but not in the traditional sense. They challenge some of the earlier interpretations of how it is and why it is that ethnic mobilization occurs within a given nation-state or ethnic group. For example, scholars have argued that the prevalence of organizations assisting immigrants in countries such as France, West Germany before unification, and Switzerland helps to explain why it is that "conflict has been more contained and routinized" than in countries where they are less common, including Britain.[59] In the French context, though, the Ivry rent strike, the Saint-Denis riot, and the increasingly politicized nature of organizations such as the UGTSF suggest that, even with the increased number of immigrant groups and French organizations such as AFTAM, whose aim was to assist African immigrants, ethnic tension, violence, and collective actions still occurred in the early postcolonial era and beyond. Just as the Algerian immigrant community was particularly visible before, during, and after the Algerian War in terms of political mobilization amidst decolonization, the Sub-Saharan African community also made important contributions to the vibrant immigrant political sphere emerging throughout France in the postwar and postcolonial eras.

This political mobilization also follows some of the key patterns of ethnic mobilization, identity politics, and racial advocacy. African workers who went on strike found themselves connected to other workers from the same regions in Sub-Saharan Africa. Such activism comprised a key factor in ethnic mobilization: proximity to other members of the same immigrant group. The urban setting also facilitated the ways in which immigrants got jobs and found other opportunities: primarily through their connections with other African immigrants and the ethnic networks that they created. This landscape fostered the kind of political response seen through the Ivry rent strike: urban political movements replicated in dormitories across the Paris region and developed through the same networks that facilitated colonial and postcolonial labor migration.[60]

The strike resembled other forms of political mobilization as well. As with N'Dongo's central role with the UGTSF, the strike's leaders—including Mamadou Diandouma, Amadou Diarra, and Ali Diallo—became critical social and political actors even if they did not have full political rights due to their residency status.[61] These leaders represented the residents in most matters, calling upon them in large numbers only when necessary and, most often, for planned protests. The large rallies that occasionally took place outside of the dormitory, such as that in response to the deaths in Aubervilliers in January of 1970, represented collective actions undertaken during the strike, as the leaders who planned them viewed them as a means of promoting the strike as a means of political protest undertaken and supported by the residents.[62]

The Ivry rent strike also constituted an important form of protest with an ethnic dimension. Couching their protests in universalist language regarding individual rights and human dignity together with a critique of the capitalist system, the African immigrants who went on strike argued that they were discriminated against by their landlords because of their position as black African immigrant workers. Their approach—a rent strike—allowed them to circumnavigate laws that restricted immigrant political activism through formal associations while also drawing heavy scrutiny from authorities, all key features of an ethnic protest. The Ivry dormitory's residents leveled claims of discrimination throughout the strike, also reflecting the ways in which the Ivry strike embodied more broadly an ethnic protest. As Susan Olzak argues, the hallmarks of ethnic protest include accusations of discrimination as well as demands made to governmental authorities.[63] The rhetoric of the Ivry strike and the stance taken by the dormitory's residents reflects these markers, demonstrating the ways in which ethnic protest shaped the political rhetoric of immigrant communities in the early postcolonial era.

While fitting into the broader narrative of strikes in France in the early postwar era, this particular strike and those staged by African workers throughout the Paris region also deviated from some of the political tendencies of that decade. The number of residents—541—reflected the trend within French society of hundreds or even thousands of workers participating in any given strike action. The duration, though, was quite different. While strikes staged by French workers at this time lasted about one day, the Ivry rent strike, like other immigrant-led strikes, lasted for months and months. African residents by this point were regularly staging strikes—as were French workers—but they were doing so with the intention of sustaining the protest for weeks and months rather than a single day.[64]

The Left and African immigrant political activism

By arguing that they deserved dignity and respect, the African immigrants who staged the Ivry strike transcended the boundaries of national citizenship in the postcolonial era and made the case that all individuals, regardless of legal status, should have access to decent housing and other basic amenities. Certain rights, such as basic housing, constituted fundamental rights regardless of national citizenship. Africans who participated in the Ivry strike and other forms of political activism connected their plight to the postwar emphasis on human rights and the ongoing international dialogue in this realm.[65] The immigrants on strike in Ivry reinforced the notion that postwar documents such as the "Universal Declaration of Human Rights" applied to all peoples, including immigrants originating from colonies and former colonies.[66]

In the fall of 1969, the members of Ivry's Municipal Council echoed these sentiments, demonstrating how the strike's message and fallout reached and affected local officials. One representative on the council argued that those involved should "take action to bring about their proposals to compel the state and employers to take their responsibilities seriously and to find a solution to this problem that reflects the human dignity of our country."[67] Ivry, as a left-leaning municipality, was perhaps better positioned than more conservative areas to listen to and respond to the strike's key points. Members could then formulate policies at the local level to assist African workers and other immigrant communities, showing how strikes influenced government officials and policy making at the local level and beyond, with far-reaching effects.

Leftist groups supported the Ivry rent strike in part because the strike's message fit into the broader Marxist critique of the capitalist exploitation of labor, including that of immigrant workers. The relationship that developed between leftist groups and African immigrants demonstrates that, in fact, the Left was not as ambiguous about immigrant labor as previously thought. Trade unions, the PCF, and the Marxist-Leninist critique of colonialism itself played important roles in anti-colonial movement in French West Africa before and after World War Two.[68] In fitting with the Communist Party's support of anti-colonial movements worldwide, the Left in

France supported various political struggles waged by African immigrants, including the Ivry strike.[69] Yet in the postwar and postcolonial periods, the relationship between left-leaning organizations and immigrant communities remained complicated.

Scholars tend to argue that that the Left in France remained ambiguous at best toward immigrant groups, including African workers. While the Right's position on immigration remained consistent in terms of its opposition, relatively few accounts detail the relationship between immigrant communities and the left side of the French political spectrum. Most analyses of the relationship between French political parties and immigrant groups concentrated on the extreme Right's response to immigration and, most notably, on the rise of the National Front in the postwar era.[70] Gary Freeman, for example, argues that by 1963, the PCF had acknowledged the centrality of immigrant workers not only in the communist vision of class struggle but also in the economy itself.[71] He explains that prior to 1964, there was no position on immigration within organized labor.[72] In contrast, Catherine Wihtol de Wenden explains that trade unions played an important role in shaping immigration policy just after World War Two.[73] By 1966, trade unions were beginning to shift their position on immigration, Wihtol de Wenden argues. Five years later, in 1971, the CGT and CFDT started a joint campaign against racism and xenophobia.[74]

In the mid-1960s, though, it was becoming evident to parties and organizations on the left side of the political spectrum that immigrant communities—including African workers—could become a central component of leftist politics.[75] Guéye, for example, maintains that both the PCF and the PS (*Parti socialiste* or Socialist Party) remained skeptical about immigration and argued above all for the republican ideal of social cohesion. At various times, he explains, each party either responded tepidly to events such as the bulldozing of a Malian dormitory or edged toward an anti-immigrant stance, in the case of the PS. In other instances, trade unions and political parties shied away from what they considered the non-traditional approaches immigrants took to political protests, including rent strikes, hunger strikes, and support committees.[76] Yet both the Left's involvement in the Ivry rent strike and its response to the immigrant deaths in Aubervilliers suggest a more nuanced and complicated relationship, one in which political parties such as the PS and the PCF became publicly involved with the plight of African workers.[77]

The neocolonial critique based on social justice presented by the African workers on strike attracted the attention of several different organizations and, most notably, those on the left side of the political spectrum. In many ways, the response by African immigrants to the situation in which they found themselves reflected the commentary offered by leftists concerning social justice, humanitarianism, capitalism, and neocolonialism in France. By this point, the Left in France was more actively involved with the African immigrant community and immigrant groups in general. For example, by 1969, *L'Humanité*, the PCF's official daily publication, sponsored posters depicting

French and immigrant workers in alliance against capitalism.[78] The Left's interaction with and support of this rent strike presents a new way of understanding the relationship between the Left in France and immigrant communities in the early postcolonial era. A wide array of organizations participated in and supported the strike from beginning to end and ranging from the CGT to the *Gauche prolétarienne* (GP or Proletarian Left), a Maoist organization.[79]

By contrast, the Left barely acknowledged the Saint-Denis riot of 1963. Reacting to the riot were journalists working for newspapers on the left side of the political spectrum, including *L'Humanité*; leftist organizations had little to say in response. A demographer dating back to the 1930s who specialized in immigration policy, Georges Mauco, cast the Left as reserved toward immigrants and immigration-related issues.[80] While historians such as Frederick Cooper have evaluated the role of trade unions, for example, in postwar independence movements in French West Africa, there is no equivalent study entirely dedicated to the question of how it is that leftist organizations did or did not address African workers and other immigrant communities in France. One of the prevailing assumptions is that trade unions and other organizations on the left side of the political spectrum that supported workers' rights opposed immigration because it fostered competition with domestic workers. Archival evidence, though, suggests that groups ranging from the PCF to the *Gauche prolétarienne* took a strong interest in the political activities of African workers, much to the chagrin of French authorities, who worried about the Left's influence and its potential to incite unrest or even revolution.

In the rhetoric and political outlook of African workers and that of other immigrant groups, the Left found an important critique of capitalism, colonialism, and neocolonialism imbued within the collective experiences of African workers and other immigrant groups. Questions remained, however, in terms of the Left's ability to address systemic issues of racism amidst the focus on social class and class-based relations and power dynamics in a political culture rooted in republicanism in which it proved difficult to discuss race and racism explicitly. The Left's relationship with immigrant communities, including African workers, and events such as the Ivry rent strike are important because they demonstrate that these political movements shaped the French political sphere as well as the public discourse over immigration throughout the 1960s and 1970s from a variety of political perspectives. While leftist groups saw in African political movements, including rent strikes, the opportunity to critique the capitalist system, African workers found in leftist politics a message that described their experiences as immigrant workers in France.

The Left's response to and support of the Ivry rent strike was part of a broader critique leveled against the French state in terms of neocolonial policies toward former colonies in French West Africa. The PCF, among other organizations, associated immigration from Mali, Senegal, and Mauritania with the exploitive neocolonial economic policies pursued by France in the years after independence. One report concluded that, "Successive French governments have been guided by the same imperatives in regard to immigration: increasing monopolies by the overexploitation of a workforce that is malleable and exploitable."[81] These policies rendered the economies in those nation-states underdeveloped industrially and dependent not only on agriculture, but also on world markets, demand, and, specifically, French economic support.[82] In contrast to French authorities in the early 1960s—who constructed African immigrants as apolitical—the PCF viewed members of this immigrant community as, "... more receptive to the policies of the French Communist Party, which shares its fight and encourages more and more people to join the party ..."[83] The policies pursued by the French government in AOF combined with the challenges they experienced in France created from the PCF's perspective "fertile ground" for recruitment among African immigrants.

Even before the Ivry rent strike and those that occurred throughout the Paris region in 1969, then, leftist organizations were already supporting foreign workers' rights. By 1963, the CGT was working with African associations. Authorities hypothesized that the group was angling for influence in order to create satellite groups in Sub-Saharan African countries.[84] As early as 1966, *Le Monde* reported that the CFDT (*Confédération française démocratique du travail* or French Democratic Confederation of Labor) was advocating for centers through which to receive newly arriving immigrants as well as "the use of social welfare for immigrants, professional training, the fight against illiteracy, (and) decent housing."[85] According to one report, the CFDT and the CGT had argued that foreign labor was necessary to sustain the economic expansion that had drawn many immigrant workers in the first place.[86] The CGT prioritized its activities among this constituency, releasing bulletins and publications in several foreign languages, and disseminated information to local unions and syndicates.[87] From the standpoint of working with immigrant communities themselves, the CGT organized educational internships, night courses, and conferences for foreign workers, focusing specifically on the issue of literacy.[88] That same report, though, pointed to the ambivalence with which other trade unions received immigrant workers, arguing that, "most unions dispute that immigration policy in France is mainly determined by economic and demographic conditions."[89] Leftist groups, then, remained conflicted over the presence of foreign workers. At critical moments such as the Ivry rent strike, though, they supported immigrant political activism in large part because of the opportunity they afforded to critique the capitalist system, neocolonialism, and their consequences.

The PCF and other left-leaning political organizations also provided advocacy and publicity for the rent strike. For example, one high-ranking official within the local branch of the Ivry Communist Party argued that:

> the existence of this dormitory is a scandal ... this situation must be ended immediately, and in particular the minimum standards of liveability

> and hygiene must be respected, acceptable rent prices determined, [and] a real representation of African workers in the management of this dormitory accepted.[90]

Together with MRAP, FASTI, and *Accueil et promotion* (Reception and Promotion), the PCF and its affiliates organized a press conference in mid-July of 1969 to publicize the plight of the Malians living on the rue Gabriel Péri.[91] A variety of officials participated, including the communist mayor of Saint-Denis, the president of FASTI, and the president of the UGTSF, Sally N'Dongo.[92] French authorities observing this publicity later argued that, "encouraged by this press campaign, African workers in the Paris region are particularly agitated."[93] This press conference and the support of organizations such as the PCF touched off protests throughout the Paris region at *foyer*s in the 10th, the 14th, and the 20th *arrondissements* as well as in Montreuil, Saint-Denis, and Clichy.[94]

What exactly drew these organizations to the strike in the first place? The *Préfecture de police* argued that their involvement was purely ideological in nature.[95] One could suggest that after years of political ambivalence to immigrant communities in general, the attraction to rent strikes was multifaceted in nature. First, left-leaning groups were more likely to support rent strikes than other types of immigrant activism because they were familiar, tangible entities with a degree of political and social credibility. Second, despite the seemingly tenuous nature of their relationship with African immigrants, by the late 1960s leftist groups were looking for the opportunity to make inroads into this immigrant community. In 1969, though, left-leaning political parties and unions paid attention to this strike and to other African-led political protests throughout the entire Paris region as an extension of work already done on behalf of immigrant communities throughout the 1960s. Their involvement with this type of immigrant activism challenges the notion that left-leaning groups remained uninterested in the unrest experienced by Africans and other migrant groups in the housing realm during the late 1960s and early 1970s.[96] Despite direct clashes between the PCF and the GP during the course of this strike, leftist groups involved in the strike viewed it in a similar way.[97] They saw it as symbolic of the national government's failure in the realm of immigrant policy and the inability of the surrounding society to provide access to lodging, social services, medical care, and other measures that would have substantially improved immigrants' basic standard of living.[98] The involvement of groups from the PCF to the GP was a continuation of a relationship developed between African workers and leftist groups dating back to the interwar and early postwar periods in both France and AOF.

So, it was not a stretch to imagine that organizations on the Left might work to extend its influence to the African Diaspora, including that in France. Rent strikes offered an appealing means through which to achieve this goal. Concrete issues such as rent increases, landlord-tenant disputes,

Figure 2.3 Newspaper headline: "The City Council's report on Immigration and its impact on Ivry." Image courtesy of the Archives municipales d'Ivry-sur-Seine.

and other housing problems provided a platform from which these groups could ingratiate themselves with immigrant communities. As early as 1964, the PCF and the CGT were developing a base of influence among African workers in the Paris region. That year, the *Service des affaires musulmanes* (Muslim Affairs Service) within the Ministry of the Interior reported that "the Communist Party and the CGT have, for some time, taken concerted actions to ensure predominant influence amongst African workers, particularly in the Paris region."[99] The PCF designed a campaign specifically to denounce the inhumane living conditions endured by Africans in order to bolster its relationship with this group. By 1967, the CGT, FO (*Force ouvrière* or Workers' Force), the CFDT, and the CFTC (*Confédération française des travailleurs chrétiens* or French Confederation of Christian Workers) declared that they would provide advocacy on behalf of all categories of workers, including immigrants, to improve their conditions.[100]

For the CGT, working at the ground level through the Ivry rent strike lent the organization credibility amongst immigrant populations.[101] The organization released publications throughout Ivry pledging its support for the strike and its participants while taking the opportunity to criticize the government's immigration policy. One of the CGT's pamphlets argued that "government policy on immigration is geared toward meeting the sole interests of capitalist monopolies. It aggravates the over-exploitation of immigrant workers, puts them at the mercy of the greed of the employers, while forcing them toward slums or infected dormitories such as that on the rue Gabriel Péri."[102] That same publication also personified the Malians in Ivry as, "victims of brutal expulsions, taking place in a residence under surveillance, with police pressure."[103] By supporting the Malians on strike, these organizations worked at the grassroots level and could claim actual involvement with an immigrant-driven rent strike. At the same time, the CGT served as an intermediary between the striking tenants and local officials in asking for assistance to rectify the situation at the *foyer* and end the strife.

The strike's specific message proved intriguing because it created a common language for leftist groups and the African immigrant community. Various organizations on the Left previously deemed this group too different in terms of its experiences and traditions to become involved in political actions.[104] As the 1960s continued, however, leftist involvement in immigrant-driven forms of political activism signaled a greater society-wide acceptance of the African immigrant community's growing presence in France. African rent strikes earned recognition as a legitimate political cause while the Left's views toward immigrant communities changed over the course of the 1960s.

When faced with rent strikes and other forms of protest, some officials began to make the connection between labor migration, problematic living conditions, and the resulting politicization of African immigrants. Authorities accused left-leaning groups of "political agitation" among the Ivry dormitory's residents, exacerbating an already precarious situation.[105] As we have seen, this was not a purely theoretical observation. From the official standpoint, however, politicization was imposed from the outside and could not be internally driven. Authorities assumed that over the course of the Ivry rent strike, unions such as the CGT and extreme-leftist organizations including the *Gauche prolétarienne*, incited and created the desire to protest among residents; they did not believe that such a highly organized effort could come from the residents themselves.[106] One official argued that African psychological and social behaviors were influenced by "exterior elements," and that political activities such as a rent strike could not be undertaken solely on their own initiative.[107]

The Ivry rent strike comprised an important moment in the history of postwar immigrant political activism. As part of a wider phenomenon of rent strikes throughout the Paris region staged by various immigrant communities, it garnered considerable attention from the media and piqued the interest of leftist political organizations and authorities all at the same time.

The strike demonstrates that visible, sustained political activism by African workers occurred much earlier in the postcolonial era than previously acknowledged. The messages woven into the rhetoric revealed the ways in which certain rights—including the right to decent housing—transcended nationality and ethnicity by the late 1960s. The ideas embedded in documents such as the "Universal Declaration of Human Rights" were now part of grassroots political movements carried out by groups that did not typically have a voice within the formal French political system. By January of 1970, with the deaths of five Malian workers in a dormitory in Aubervilliers, the Ivry rent strike became inextricably linked not only with those deaths, but also with the political fallout in their aftermath.

Notes

1 ADVM 2018W art. 20 Mamadou Diandouma to M le Préfet du Val-de-Marne, Ivry, 11 November 1969. Original French: "nous avons l'honneur de vous confirmer la coupure d'eau dans le foyer où vivent 550 hommes. Sans électricité depuis fort longtemps, la nouvelle provocation nous privant totalement d'eau courante, est à nos yeux, un maillon d'une chaine d'un plan bien établi."
2 Daniel A. Gordon, *Immigrants and Intellectuals: May '68 and the Rise of Anti-Racism in France* (Pontypool: Merlin Press, 2012), 83.
3 Ibid., 87.
4 Mireille Rosello, *Postcolonial Hospitality: The Immigrant as Guest* (Stanford: Stanford University Press, 2001), 149–50.
5 Charles Tshimanga, Didier Gondola, and Bloom, Peter J., eds., *Frenchness and the African Diaspora: Identity and Uprising in Contemporary France* (Bloomington; Indianapolis: Indiana University Press, 2009), 6.
6 Edward Shorter and Charles Tilly, *Strikes in France 1830–1968* (Cambridge: Cambridge University Press, 1974), 16–18.
7 Riva Kastoryano, *Negotiating Identities: States and Immigrants in France and Immigrants in France and Germany* trans. Barbara Harshav (Princeton: Princeton University Press, 2002), 64.
8 Pap Ndiaye, *La condition noire: Essai sur une minorité française* (Paris: Éditions Calmann-Levy, 2008), 334; Abdoulaye Guéye, "The Colony Strikes Back: African Protest Movements in Postcolonial France," *Comparative Studies of South Asia, Africa and the Middle East*, no. 2 (2006): 227–228.
9 Guéye, "The Colony Strikes Back," 231.
10 Shorter and Tilly, *Strikes in France*, 47–48; Guéye, "The Colony Strikes Back," 225–242.
11 Kastoryano, *Negotiating Identities*, 115.
12 The *bidonville* in Champigny by 1960 was the largest shantytown in France, with 14,025 residents. For an engaging graphic concerning *bidonvilles* around Paris and throughout France, see Bernard Granotier, *Les travailleurs immigrés en France* (Paris: François Maspero, 1970).
13 For further discussion of immigrant housing, see Jacques Barou, ed., *L'habitat des immigrés et de leurs familles* (Paris: La Documentation française, 2002); Michel Pinçon, *Cohabiter: groupes sociaux et modes de vie dans une cité H.L.M.* (Paris: Ministère de l'urbanisme et du logement, Plan construction, 1982); Jean-Claude Toubon, *Les conditions de logement des étrangers en région d'Île-de-France* (Paris: INSEE, Direction régionale de Paris, 1979). For a discussion of the period between 1970—after the end of the Ivry strike—and 1992,

see Roselyne de Villanova, *Immigration et espaces habités: bilan bibliographique des travaux en France, 1970–1992* (Paris: L'Harmattan and CIEMI, 1994). See also Catherine Wihtol de Wenden and Zakya Daoud, eds., *Banlieues: intégration ou explosion?* (Courbevoie: Éditions Corlet-Éditions Arléa, 1993).

14 CANC 19960134 art. 17 "Le mécontentement des milieux africains de la région parisienne est exploité à des fins subversives, par les gauchistes." Paris, 25 March 1975. See Marc Bernardot's Ph.D. dissertation concerning the development of SONACOTRA. Marc Bernardot, *Une politique de logement: la SONACOTRA (1956–1992)* (PhD diss., Université de Paris I—Panthéon—Sorbonne, 1997), 143–209.

15 CANC 1996031 art. 6 P. Fournier to M le Ministre d'État, M le Ministre de l'Intérieur, 25 July 1975. ADVM 2018W art. 20 Mamadou Diandouma to M le Préfet du Val de Marne, 11 November 1969. "Pétition: les travailleurs africains en grève demandent leur soutien aux habitants d'Ivry." 30 September 1969. Christophe Daum provides an intriguing discussion of the transition immigrants can make to become social and political actors within their host country. See Daum, *Les associations de Maliens en France: Migrations, développement, et citoyenneté* (Paris: Éditions Karthala, 1998).

16 Pap Ndiaye, *La condition noire*, 312, 334–335.

17 ADVM 2018W art. 20 Maurice Grimaud to M le Ministre de l'Intérieur, 22 August 1969.

18 CANC 19960311 art. 6 Maurice Grimaud to M le Ministre de l'Intérieur, 22 August 1969.

19 CANC 19770317 art. 1 Préfecture de police, "Note à M le Préfet: Agitation dans les foyers d'hébergement de ressortissants africains de la région parisienne." Paris, 8 October 1969.

20 CANC 19940023 art. 20 Préfecture de police, "Une certaine tension se manifeste toujours dans les principaux foyers où locaux dans lesquels sont hébergés des travailleurs africains." Paris, 8 July 1969. APP GaA7 "Rapport d'activité." January 1970.

21 CANC 19770317 art. 1 Noel Monier, "Prix du lit augmente dans un foyer d'Ivry: les 700 Africains font la grève du loyer République du gérant: eau, électricité coupées." *France Soir*, Paris, 17–18 August 1969.

22 CANC 19940023 art. 20 "Les travailleurs africains de la région parisienne protestent." Paris, 7 July 1969. Original French: "Logés dans des conditions déplorables, les travailleurs africains de la région parisienne protestent contre les abus dont ils sont victimes."

23 CANC 19960311 art. 6 Préfecture de police, "Le délabrement du local dans lequel sont logés plus de 500 travailleurs africains dans un foyer sis 45 rue Gabriel Péri." 13 June 1969. ADVM 2018W art. 20 "Ivry-sur-Seine: 600 Africains évacués du dortoir-taudis." *La Croix*, Paris, October 1970. Service de Liaison et de Promotion des Migrants, "La disparation du dortoir africain de la rue Gabriel Péri à Ivry." Créteil, December 1970. Préfecture du Val-de-Marne, "Communiqué: Evacuation du dortoir pour travailleurs africains situé 45 rue Gabriel Péri à Ivry-sur-Seine." Créteil, 5 December 1970.

24 Guéye, "The Colony Strikes Back," 227–228.

25 ADVM 2018W art. 20 Claude Lecomte, "Les travailleurs africains d'Ivry ont quitté l'usine-dortoire pour vivre dans les foyers." *L'Humanité*, Paris, 10 December 1970. "Intervention de M Jacques Laloe, Maire d'Ivry-sur-Seine, sur le problème de l'immigration," Municipal council of Ivry-sur-Seine, 16 October 1969. "Ivry-sur-Seine: 600 Africains évacués du dortoir-taudis," *La Croix*, Paris, October 1970.

26 ADVM 2018W art. 20 "Ce que '*Le Monde*' appelle le scandale d'Ivry," *Le Travailleur*, 11 December 1970. Original French: "le conseil municipal et la

municipalité d'Ivry-sur-Seine ne portent aucune responsabilité dans l'installation de travailleurs africains au 45, rue Gabriel Péri. L'installation de Maliens dans des bâtiments d'une usine désaffectée s'est fait le 13 juin 1965 dans des conditions scandaleuses, sans consultation de la municipalité."

27 CAN Fla 5136 Préfecture de police, "Nombre et implantation dans le département de la Seine des travailleurs originaires des États d'Afrique noire." Paris, 5 September 1963. Original French: "crées ou abandonnés selon les impératifs du moment."

28 ADVM 2018W art. 20 Claude Lecompte, "Les travailleurs africains d'Ivry ont quitté l'usine-dortoir pour vivre dans des foyers." *L'Humanité*, Paris, 10 December 1970. Original French: "ce scandale durait depuis le dimanche 13 juin 1965."

29 Marc Bernardot, "Chronique d'une institution: La 'Sonacotra' (1956–1976)," *Sociétés Contemporaines* 33, no. 33–34 (1999): 39–40; Marie-Claude Blanc-Chaléard, "Old and New Migrants in France: Italians and Algerians," in Leo Lucassen, David Feldman, and Jochen Oltmer, eds., *Paths of Integration: Migrants in Western Europe (1880–2004)* (Amsterdam: Amsterdam University Press, 2006), 52.

30 ADVM 2018W art. 20 André Maguer to M le Directeur Général de la police municipal, Ivry 29 September 1969. CANC 19940023 art. 20 Préfecture de police, "Le délabrement du local dans lequel sont logés plus de 500 travailleurs africains." Paris 13 June 1969.

31 CANC 19960311 art. 6 Préfecture de police, "Le délabrement du local dans lequel sont logés plus de 500 travailleurs africains dans un foyer sis 45 rue Gabriel Péri à Ivry-sur-Seine vient d'être dénoncé dans un tract émanant du 'Comité de soutien aux travailleurs du foyer,'" 13 June 1969. ADVM 2018W art. 20 André Maguer to M le Directeur général de la Police municipale Ivry, 29 September 1969. ADVM 2018W art. 20 Jacques Laloe, "Intervention de M Jacques Laloe sur le problème de l'immigration," Ivry, 16 October 1969. For information on "sleep merchants," see Mahfoud Bennoune, "Maghribin Workers in France," *MERIP Reports* no. 34 (Jan., 1975): 6; Jean-Pierre N'Diaye, *Négriers modernes: Les travailleurs noirs en France* (Paris: Présence Africaine, 1970), 26.

32 APP GaA7 "Rapport d'activité" Paris, January 1970.

33 Michel Leiris, "Un témoignage: chez les Maliens d'Ivry-sur-Seine," *Le Monde*, Paris, 13 January 1970.

34 Fabienne Guimont also details the housing patterns of African students in her work. See Guimont, *Les étudiants africains en France, 1950–1965* (Paris: L'Harmattan, 1997), 269–298.

35 Michel Leiris, "Un témoignage: chez les maliens d'Ivry-sur-Seine," *Le Monde*, Paris, 13 January 1970; ADVM 2018W art. 20 Préfecture de police, "L'insuffisance extrême des conditions d'accueil du foyer pour travailleurs africains, 45 rue Gabriel Péri," 27 August 1969. For more on the relationship between France and the French West Indies see Félix-Hilaire Fortuné, *La France et l'Outre-Mer antillais: quatre siècles d'histoire économique et sociale* (Paris: L'Harmattan, 2001). Patrick Karam discusses immigrants from the Caribbean in France. See Karam, *Français d'Outre-Mer: Dossier d'une discrimination occulteé: sommes-nous à part entière ou entièrement à part?* (Paris: L'Harmattan, 2004).

36 CANC 19960311 art. 6 "Le délabrement du local dans lequel sont logés plus de 500 travailleurs africains dans un foyer 45 rue Gabriel Péri."

37 Quiminal, Daum, and Timera each discuss about the tendency to regroup in different ways. This is not a purely immigrant-related phenomenon, however. Immigrants often took over neighborhoods formerly dominated by the working classes. See Tyler Stovall, *The Rise of the Paris Red Belt* (Berkeley: The University of California Press, 1990).

38 For a structural approach to immigrant housing, see Jacques Barou, *Travailleurs africains en France: Rôle des cultures d'origine* (Grenoble: Presses Universitaires de Grenoble, 1978).
39 ADVM 2018W art. 20. Service de liaison et de promotion des migrants, "La disparition du dortoir africain de la rue Gabriel Péri à Ivry," *Créteil*, December 1970. J. B. "Le logement," *Le Monde*, Paris, 10 December 1970. CAN F1a 5136 Préfecture de police, "Nombre et implantation dans le département de la Seine des travailleurs originaires des États d'Afrique noire," Paris, 5 September 1963.
40 ADVM 2018W art. 20. "La disparition du dortoir africain de la rue Gabriel Péri à Ivry." J. Laloe, "Ce que 'Le Monde' appelle le scandale d'Ivry," 11 December 1970. "Le Logement." *Le Monde*, 10 December 1970. ADSSD 1801W art. 226 "Logement du taudis au foyer" *Étincelle* (no. 10). CANC 19960311 art. 6 Maurice Grimaud to M le Ministre de l'Intérieur, Paris, 22 August 1969.
41 David E. Gardinier, "Strike Movements as Part of the Anticolonial Struggle in French West Africa" in Gregory Maddox and Timothy K. Welliver, eds., *Colonialism and Nationalism in Africa: African Nationalism and Independence*, vol. 3. (New York; London: Garland Publishing, Inc., 1993), 106.
42 ADVM 2018W art. 20 "La disparition du dortoir africain de la rue Gabriel Péri à Ivry," *Créteil*, December 1970. "Communiqué: Evacuation du dortoir pour travailleurs africains situé 45, rue Gabriel Péri à Ivry-sur-Seine." J. Laloe, "Ce que 'Le Monde' appelle le scandale d'Ivry," *Le Travailleur*, Ivry-sur-Seine, 11 December, 1970. CANC 19960311 art. 6 M. Grimaud to M le Ministre de l'Intérieur – Cabinet Paris 22 August 1969.
43 BN MICR D-66 1970/01 L.15 MFM Michel Leiris, "Un témoignage: chez les maliens d'Ivry sur Seine," *Le Monde*, Paris, 13 January 1970.
44 ADVM 2018W art. 20 André Maguer to M le Directeur Général de la police, Ivry, 29 September 1969.
45 ADVM 2018W art. 20 "Note à l'intention du Cabinet de Monsieur Chaban Delmas, prèpare le 25 mai par les travailleurs de ce 'foyer'" Original French: "justifiée par les conditions de vie totalement inhumaines."
46 VDM 2018 W art. 20 M.D., "Ivry: Les 400 travailleurs maliens du foyer d'Ivry ont été relogés dans des locaux neufs" *Le Courrier du Val-de-Marne*, no. 67, Val-du-Marne, 15 December 1970; Mancheulle, *Willing Migrants*, 179–211.
47 VDM 2018 W art. 20 Les travailleurs de ce 'foyer' (le foyer d'Ivry 45 rue Gabriel Péri), "Note à l'intention du Cabinet de Monsieur Chaban Delmas, préparée le 25 mai par les travailleurs de ce 'foyer'," Ivry, May 1970.
48 Castles and Davidson cite other types of strikes undertaken by African immigrants, such as those that occurred in the automobile industry. See Stephen Castles and Alastair Davidson, *Citizenship and Migration: Globalization and the Politics of Belonging* (New York: Routledge, 2000), 143.
49 APP GaA7 Préfecture de police, "Mode d'intervention et d'action des mouvements gauchistes dans les foyers de travailleurs immigrés de la région parisienne," Paris, 13 February 1970. Original French: "droit d'user du téléphone, droit de recevoir des visites."
50 CANC 19940023 art. 20 "Les travailleurs africains de la région parisienne protestant," Paris, 15 July 1969. Original French: "des conditions d'hygiène et de salubrité convenables, puis dans un second temps d'être logés dans des foyers remplissant les conditions prévues par la réglementation en vigueur."
51 Guéye, "The Colony Strikes Back," 225–242; For a history of Pan-Africanism, see Tony Martin, *The Pan-African Connection: From Slavery to Garvey and Beyond* (Dover: Majority Press, 1984) and Ras Makonnen, *Pan-Africanism from Within*, ed. Kenneth King (Nairobi; London; New York: Oxford University Press, 1973).

52 ADVM 2018W art. 20 "Pétition: les travailleurs africains en grève demandent leur soutien aux habitants d'Ivry," 30 September 1969. M. Brames to M le Préfet, 29 September 1969. CANC 19940023 art. 20. M.D. pour les travailleurs du foyer, "Tribune libre: au foyer clandestin d'Ivry." *Afrique nouvelle*, 28 August–2 September 1969. Section syndicale CGT to M le Ministre de l'Intérieur, 16 July 1969. Most of the literature concerning alternative forms of citizenship centers on the discussion of immigrant associations as well as the ways in which rejection and conflict mobilize immigrant communities. For example, see Zig Layton-Henry, "Immigrant Associations," in Zig Layton-Henry, ed., *The Political Rights of Migrant Workers in Western Europe* (London: Sage Publishers, 1990).
53 CANC 19960311 art. 6 Préfecture de police, "Mode d'intervention et d'action des mouvements gauchistes dans les foyers de travailleurs immigrés de la région parisienne," Paris 13 February 1970.
54 CANC 19770317 art. 1 Noel Monier, "Prix du lit augmente dans foyer d'Ivry." *France Soir*, Paris, 17–18 August 1969. Original French: "les conditions d'hygiène: dortoirs sans fenêtres, lits serrés les uns contre les autres, ni placards, ni rayonnages, quatre robinets d'eau pour l'ensemble du bâtiment."
55 For further discussion, see Vincent Viet, *La France immigrée: construction d'une politique, 1914–1997* (Paris: Fayard, 1998); Catherine Wihtol de Wenden, *Les immigrés et la politique: Cent cinquante ans d'évolution* (Paris: Presses de la Fondation nationale des sciences politiques, 1988); Patrick Weil, *La France et ses étrangers: L'aventure d'une politique de l'immigration 1938–1991* (Paris: Calmann-Lévy, 1991). For a discussion of Jewish asylum seekers in France during the interwar period, see Vicki Caron, *Uneasy Asylum: France and the Jewish Refugee Crisis, 1933–1942* (Stanford: Stanford University Press, 1999).
56 CANC 19960311 art. 6 P. Fournier to M. le Ministre d'État, Ministre de l'Intérieur, Direction générale de la police nationale, Paris, 25 July 1975. ADVM 2018W art. 20 Maurice Grimaud to M le Ministre de l'Intérieur, 16 October 1969. "L'insuffisance extrême des conditions d'accueil du foyer pour travailleurs africains, 45 rue Gabriel Péri, a accentué le mouvement de protestation des résidents de ce foyer." 27 August 1969.
57 Guéye, "The Colony Strikes Back," 228.
58 Alec G. Hargreaves, *Immigration, "Race," and Ethnicity in Contemporary France* (New York: Routledge, 1995), 98.
59 Susan Olzak, "Contemporary Ethnic Mobilization," *Annual Review of Sociology* 9 (1983): 361.
60 Ibid., 367.
61 ADVM 2018W art. 20 Maurice Grimaud to M le Ministre de l'Intérieur, Paris, 16 October 1969. Préfecture de police, "L'insuffisance extrême des conditions d'accueil du foyer pour travailleurs africains, 45 rue Gabriel Péri, accentué le mouvement de protestations des résidents de ce foyer." Ivry, 27 August 1969.
62 ADVM 2018W art. 20 "Mécontents des conditions d'accueil qui leur sont faites, des résidents du foyer pour travailleurs africains se sont livres à quelques déprédations." Préfecture de police. 20 August 1969. André Maguer, Commissaire principal du 24ème arrondissement to M le Directeur général de la Police municipale, 29 September 1969. CANC 19960311 art. 6 M. Grimaud to M le Ministre de l'Intérieur, 16 October 1969.
63 Susan Olzak, *The Global Dynamics of Racial and Ethnic Mobilization* (Stanford: Stanford University Press, 2006), 94–95.
64 Shorter and Tilly, *Strikes in France*, 52.
65 For an assessment of the history of human rights, see Paul Gordon Lauren, *The Evolution of International Human Rights: Visions Seen* 2nd ed. (Philadelphia: University of Pennsylvania Press, 2003).

66 ADVM 2018W art. 20 "Pétition: les travailleurs africains en grève demandent leur soutien aux habitants d'Ivry," 30 September 1969. M. Brames to M le Préfet, 29 September 1969. CANC 19940023 art. 20 M. D. pour les travailleurs du foyer, "Tribune libre: au foyer clandestin d'Ivry." *Afrique nouvelle*, 28 August–2 September 1969. Section syndicale CGT to M le Ministre de l'Intérieur, 16 July 1969. Most of the literature concerning alternative forms of citizenship centers on the discussion of immigrant associations as well as the ways in which rejection and conflict mobilize immigrant communities. For example, see Zig Layton-Henry, "Immigrant Associations," in Zig Layton-Henry, ed., *The Political Rights of Migrant Workers in Western Europe* (London: Sage Publishers, 1990); Robert J. C. Young, "Preface," in Jean-Paul Sartre, *Colonialism and Neocolonialism* trans. Azzedine Haddour, Steve Brewer, and Terry McWilliams (London; New York: Routledge, 2001), xiv–xv.

67 ADVM 2018W art. 20 "Extrait du registre des délibérations du Conseil municipal," Ivry, 16 October 1969. Original French: "agir pour faire aboutir ses propositions afin de contraindre l'état et le patronat à prendre toutes leurs responsabilités pour donner à ce problème une solution humaine digne de notre pays."

68 Hans Kohn and Wallace Sokolsky, *African Nationalism in the Twentieth Century* (Princeton: D. Van Nostrand Company, Inc., 1965), 80–81.

69 For the PCF's support of political parties in AOF prior to decolonization, see Tony Chafer, *The End of Empire in French West Africa: France's Successful Decolonization?* (Oxford; New York: Berg, 2002), 104–110.

70 For more on the National Front and its anti-immigration stance, see Peter Davies, *The National Front: Ideology, Discourse, and Power* (New York: Routledge, 1999), especially chapter 3.

71 Gary P. Freeman, *Immigrant Labor and Racial Conflict in Industrial Societies: The French and British Experience, 1945–1975* (New Jersey: Princeton University Press, 1979), 90.

72 Ibid.

73 Catherine Wihtol de Wenden, *Les immigres et la politique: Cent cinquante ans d'évolution* (Paris: Presses de la fondation nationale des sciences politiques, 1988), 89. Original French: "Quant aux syndicats ouvriers, qui ont tenu un rôle non négligeable dans l'élaboration de la politique migratoire de 1945 à 1948, ils ont été très affectés, de 1948 à 1961, par les divisions résultant de la guerre froide qui se sont répercutées en matière d'immigration par des attitudes assez restrictives."

74 Wihtol de Wenden, *Les immigrés et la politique*, 89.

75 Freeman, *Immigrant Labor and Racial Conflict in Industrial Societies*, 91.

76 Wihtol de Wenden, *Les immigrés et la politique*, 89.

77 Guéye, "The Colony Strikes Back," 232.

78 François Lionnet, "Immigration, Poster Art, and Transgressive Citizenship: France 1968–1988," *SubStance* 24, no. 1/2, issue 76/77 (1995): 97.

79 ADVM 2018W art. 20 CGT Union locale des syndicats d'Ivry, "Solidarité avec les travailleurs immigrés," 18 June 1969. "Tracts/des militants de la Gauche Prolétarienne ont distribué un tract au foyer pour travailleurs africains d'Ivry." 14 January 1970. CANC 19960311 art. 6 M Flerchinger to M le Ministre de l'Intérieur, 29 September 1969. 19940023 art. 20 Section syndicale CGT to M le Ministre de l'Intérieur, 16 July 1969. APP GaA7 "Mode d'intervention et d'action des mouvements gauchistes dans les foyers de travailleurs immigrés de la région parisienne," 13 February 1970. "Implantation du mouvement maoïste de la Gauche Prolétarienne dans les bidonvilles et les foyers de travailleurs d'Outre Mer de la région parisienne," 31 October 1970. CANC 19960311 art. 6

Préfecture de police "Constitué fin novembre 1969, à 'l'initiative des résponsables de la 'Gauche Prolétarienne' … bulletin 'Le Paria.'" 20 January 1970.

80 Patrick Weil, "Georges Mauco, expert en immigration: ethno-racisme pratique et antisémitisme filleux" in *L'antisémitisme de plume 1940–1944, études et documents* dir. Pierre-André Taguieff (Paris: Berg International Éditeurs, 1999), 267–276; Georges Mauco, *Les étrangers en France et le problème du racisme* (Paris: La Pénsée universelle, 1984), 76.

81 CIEMI PCF 62/1/11 Parti communiste français, "L'immigration d'Afrique noire en France," 8. Original French: "Les gouvernements français qui se sont succédés ont été guidés par les mêmes impératifs en matière d'immigration: accroître les monopolistes par la surexploitation d'une main d'œuvre taillable et corvéable."

82 CIEMI PCF 62/1/11 Parti communiste français, "L'immigration d'Afrique noire en France," 3–5, 16.

83 CIEMI PCF 62/1/11 Parti communiste français, "L'immigration d'Afrique noire en France," 17. Original French: "plus réceptifs à la politiques de la Parti Communiste Français, qui se partagent son combat et d'engagent plus nombreux par leur adhésion au parti …"

84 CAN F1a 5136 Ministère de l'Intérieur, "Les travailleurs d'Afrique noire en France: IV Influences politiques, syndicales, ou religieuses." Paris, May 1963.

85 CAN F1a 5052 "Le CFDT s'élevé contre l'exploitation des travailleurs étrangers." *Le Monde*, Paris, 1 April 1966. Original French: "l'utilisation des prestations sociales en faveur des immigrés, leur formation professionnelle, la lutte contre l'analphabétisme, le logement décent."

86 CAN F1a 5052 "Étude sur l'implantation de la main d'oeuvre étrangère." Paris, 1967.

87 Ibid.

88 Ibid.

89 CAN F1a 5052 "Étude sur l'implantation de la main d'oeuvre étrangère." Paris, 1967. Original French: "la plupart des syndicats contestent que la politique de l'immigration en France soit essentiellement déterminée par des considérations économiques et démographiques."

90 CANC 19960311 art. 6 Georges Gosnat, député d'Ivry, les sections communistes d'Ivry, July 1969. Original French: "l'existence de ce foyer est un scandale … Il faut en finir immédiatement avec cette situation et notamment respecter les conditions minimum d'habitabilité et d'hygiène, déterminer des prix acceptables de location, accepter une véritable représentation des travailleurs africains dans la gestion de ce foyer."

91 CANC 19940023 art. 20 "Les travailleurs africains de la région parisienne." 15 July 1969. Direction centrale des renseignements généraux, "Immigrés africains en France." Paris, 15 July 1969.

92 CANC 19940023 art. 20 "Les travailleurs africains de la région parisienne protestant." Paris, 15 July 1970.

93 CANC 19940023 art. 20 Direction centrale des renseignements généraux, "Immigrés africains en France." Paris, 15 July 1969. Original French: "encouragés par toute cette campagne de presse, les travailleurs africains de la région parisienne se montrent particulièrement agités."

94 CANC 19940023 art. 20 Direction centrale des renseignements généraux, "Immigrés africains en France." Paris, 15 July 1969.

95 ADVM 2018W art. 20 Maurice Grimaud to M le Ministre de l'Intérieur, Paris, 16 October 1969.

96 For example, scholarship looking at the Left in France during the 1960s and 1970s rarely mentions immigration or the involvement of leftist groups in

immigration-related issues. See Frank L. Wilson, *The French Democratic Left 1963–1969: Toward a Modern Party System*. (Stanford: Stanford University Press, 1971); Ronald Tiersky, *French Communism, 1920–1972* (New York and London: Columbia University Press, 1974).

97 The *Gauche prolétarienne* criticized the PCF repeatedly during its involvement with the Ivry rent strike, arguing that the PCF isolated workers and collaborated with police to suppress their protests. ADVM 2018W art. 20 "Des militants de la Gauche Prolétarienne ont distribué un tract au foyer pour travailleurs africains d'Ivry sur Seine." 14 January 1970.

98 For more on the Left's relationship with immigrant communities during the 1960s and 1970s, see Gary P. Freeman, *Immigrant Labor and Racial Conflict in Industrial Societies: The French and British Experience, 1945–1975* (Princeton, NJ: Princeton University Press, 1979); Mauco, *Les étrangers en France et le problème du racisme*; Castles and Davidson, *Citizenship and Migration*; Jan Vranken, "Industrial Rights," in Zig Layton-Henry, *The Political Rights of Migrant Workers in Western Europe* (London: Sage Publications, 1990). Giovanna Campani, Maurizio Catani and Salvatore Palidda, "Italian Immigrant Associations in France," in John Rex, et al., eds., *Immigrant Associations in Europe* (Aldershot: Gower, 1987).

99 CAN Fla 5136 J. David, Service des Affaires Musulmanes, Ministre de l'Intérieur, "Bordereau d'envoi concernant les communistes et les travailleurs noirs en France: les communistes et les travailleurs noirs en France." Paris, 2 December 1964. Original French: "le Parti Communiste et la CGT ont entrepris depuis quelques temps déjà, des actions concertées pour s'assurer une influence prépondérante dans les milieux de travailleurs noirs, particulièrement dans la région parisienne."

100 CANC 19940023 art. 20 Section syndicale CGT to M le Ministre de l'Intérieur, 16 July 1970. CANC 19960311 art. 6 M Flerchinger to M le Ministre de l'Intérieur, 29 September 1969. ADVM 2018W art. 20 M Flerchinger to M le Préfet du Val-de-Marne, 16 January 1970.

101 Chafer, *The End of Empire in French West Africa*, 121–125.

102 ADVM 2018W art. 20 CGT Union locale des syndicats, "Solidarité avec les travailleurs immigrés." Ivry, 18 June 1969. Original French: "la politique gouvernementale en matière d'immigration est orientée vers la satisfaction des seuls intérêts des monopoles capitalistes. Elle aggrave la sur-exploitation des travailleurs immigrés, les met à la merci de la rapacité patronale, les rejette vers les bidonvilles ou les foyers infectés comme celui de la rue Gabriel Péri à Ivry."

103 ADVM 2018W art. 20 CGT Union locale des syndicats, "Solidarité avec les travailleurs immigrés." Ivry, 18 June 1969. Original French: "… victimes d'expulsions brutales, de mise en résidence surveillées, de pressions policières. . ."

104 See Castles and Davidson, *Citizenship and Migration*, 144.

105 ADVM 2018W art. 20 Maurice Grimaud to M le Préfet de Paris, 6 August 1970.

106 APP GaA7 "Mode d'intervention et d'action des mouvements gauchistes dans les foyers de travailleurs de la région parisienne." Paris, 13 February 1970.

107 CANC 19960311 art. 6 Maurice Grimaud to M le Ministre de l'Intérieur, Paris, 22 August 1969.

3 From private tragedy to *cause célèbre*

Five deaths in Aubervilliers

In another corner of the Île-de-France, as the Ivry rent strike continued, a tragedy unfolded in a dormitory not all that different from the one on the rue Gabriel Péri. On the morning of January 2, 1970, four Senegalese immigrants and one Mauritanian lay dead in a dormitory inhabited by African workers on the rue des Postes. They had asphyxiated after making a fire to avoid freezing to death as the temperature outside plunged on a cold January night. Two more victims were rushed to the *Hôpital Raymond-Poincaré* in Garches (Hauts-de-Seine), where, after regaining consciousness, they remained in a critical condition for several days.[1] The victims included Sow Bocar Thialel, 29, Kamara Samba Hamady, 34, Kamara Hamady, 28, and Konte Alloui, 37, all of Senegal, as well as one Mauritanian immigrant, Camara Amara Sidi, 30. Boulo Sow, 29, of Senegal and Abdourakmane Diani Faba, 40, also of Mauritania, recovered in the hospital.[2]

As the African community mourned, the Ivry rent strike and the deaths in Aubervilliers became inextricably linked in the media and the public discourse surrounding immigration to France. These two events also shaped the trajectory of French immigration policy, surveillance tactics, and social welfare for immigrant communities in the coming years and decades. The vocal response from several sectors of French society, including groups on the left side of the political spectrum, marked an important shift in the continuing debate over the place of African workers and non-western immigrants more broadly in France. As anthropologist Katherine Verdery argues, "The political consequences of such events depend on variations in the numbers and kinds of nameless dead and the causes of their deaths."[3] The deaths of five African immigrants on a cold winter night in January penetrated the public sphere. This event pointed to the problems confronted by immigrants because of shortcomings in French immigration policy in terms of housing, education, and employment in an era marked by postwar economic prosperity.[4] In an instant, the African immigrant community acquired the symbolic capital, as Verdery argues, associated with dead bodies, which could then be used, in addition to rent strikes, riots, and formal associational activism, to draw national and international attention to the plight of African immigrants in France in the hopes of bringing about marked improvements.[5] These deaths also called into question the extent to which the foundational ideas of French republicanism—liberty, equality, and fraternity—applied to all residents, including non-citizens and former colonial inhabitants.

After a decade of increasingly violent incidents involving immigrant communities throughout France, including those from the former colonies, public debate intensified over why African workers and other immigrant groups found themselves living in poverty in the very place where they thought they would find financial stability and prosperity. The Aubervilliers deaths underscored the dangers that dilapidated dormitories and decrepit housing posed to Africans and other immigrants. In doing so, this fire and the ensuing deaths fostered public debate on the question of race and ethnic minorities in France. Questions arose about what this tragedy meant for French republicanism and national identity, whether the policies pursued by the state in the realm of immigration were working, and the impact on the future of French immigration policies. What were the implications for human rights in postwar and postcolonial France, a country with its own checkered past in terms of advocating for individual rights while struggling to uphold them, if immigrants residing there struggled to survive?

The deaths in Aubervilliers also established a precedent for public support of immigrant communities. By the time the *sans-papiers* movement gained national and international prominence in 1996, an estimated 100 intellectuals had created a civil disobedience campaign, voicing their support for asylum and for the repeal of the controversial Pasqua laws of 1986, which limited access to French citizenship, while also launching a petition signed by Pierre Bourdieu and Etienne Balibar, two prominent contemporary intellectuals. The rapport between intellectuals and immigrant political movements had its roots not only in the upheaval of 1968 but also in the participation of key intellectuals in demonstrations following the deaths in Aubervilliers in 1970, which paved the way for the public support shown by Bourdieu, Balibar, and other prominent public figures for immigrant communities, including the *sans-papiers* movement.[6]

Yet few studies make the connection between the Aubervilliers deaths in 1970 and those later developments. The event itself and its broader implications are not well understood, an issue that this chapter addresses. In his book, *The Death of Luigi Trastulli*, literary scholar Alessandro Portelli explains that a seemingly insignificant event can have major consequences.[7] Portelli's assessment provides an important framework for understanding the immigrant deaths in Aubervilliers and their aftermath. This chapter considers the deaths at Aubervilliers from several perspectives, looking at the bereavement experienced by the African immigrant community as well as the responses of advocacy groups, leftist political organizations that advocated for immigrants, public intellectuals, and the media. These deaths galvanized a diverse coalition of groups from various sectors of French society. The dynamic debate that rippled throughout French society in response to these deaths signaled an important turning point in the postwar history of immigration to France as outrage replaced indifference to the plight of immigrants across the early postwar period. Whereas parties on both the Left and the Right ignored immigration beyond the policy realm across the early years of the postwar era, the issue now came to the forefront of the political sphere at the end of a tumultuous decade and the dawn of a new one. As public outcry increased, the Left advocated more visibly for immigrants in France.[8] Other French groups became much more closely involved as well, creating a foundation for immigrant advocacy seen throughout the 1980s and 1990s.[9]

With public and political engagement as the backdrop, French policy makers began reconsidering French immigration policy, including the laws governing labor migration. Four years after the deaths in Aubervilliers and amidst a global economy spiraling into recession, open migration to France came to an end. While economic and political forces often directed immigration policies, the five deaths in Aubervilliers also shaped the state's initiatives because they highlighted in a very public way the challenges facing African immigrants and other immigrant groups, marking a watershed moment in French immigration history. If, to this point, the public was less engaged in the plight of immigrants in France, the deaths in Aubervilliers, together with other publicly visible political moments such as the Ivry rent strike, heightened awareness while fostering a public will to address these challenges.[10]

These deaths at Aubervilliers and their aftermath also provide an important opportunity to explore the cultural side of immigrant life in France through an examination of the responses they provoked, the funerals that were held, and the rituals of mourning that were carried out. The complex context involving religious practices, state regulations, and cultural differences in mourning and burial played a significant role in shaping the trajectory of the mourning process, the funeral and burial, and the ways in which this moment became politicized within and beyond the African immigrant community.[11] Rarely has scholarship on modern immigration to France examined the ways in which immigrant groups process the deaths of community members while in the host country. Nor have there been extensive studies of the logistics that non-western, Muslim groups confront in burying fellow migrants while adhering to religious and cultural traditions. In the aftermath of the deaths in Aubervilliers, we see the ways in which Sub-Saharan African and Muslim burial practices were sometimes at odds with one another and how those customs clashed with the French regulations. More broadly, through the deaths in Aubervilliers and their aftermath, we come to have a more complete understanding of black Islam in France. The struggle to mourn the five deaths at Aubervilliers highlighted questions about the place of Muslim immigrants within French society while revealing important tensions over the spaces that they inhabited both in life and in death.

The attention that the Aubervilliers deaths received also points to their unique and dramatic position within the twentieth-century history of immigration to France. This event garnered national media attention, contributed to the ongoing debate over how best to house immigrant communities, and involved organizations as far-ranging as *Gauche prolétarienne* (GP) on the far left side of the political spectrum and the *Mouvement contre le racisme, l'antisémitisme et pour la paix* (Movement against Racism and Anti-Semitism and for Peace or MRAP), an anti-discrimination and racial advocacy group created after World War Two. While postcolonial immigrant advocacy was still in its early phases, this event solidified the commitment of organizations such as MRAP to spotlighting the plight and position of immigrant communities in France. Aubervilliers also attracted the interest and involvement of public intellectuals such as Jean-Paul Sartre and Marguerite Duras and became a symbol of the suffering endured by immigrants throughout France. Advocacy on behalf of immigrant organizations increased throughout the 1970s. Rights-based organizations working on behalf of immigrant groups also became more vocal within the public sphere, moving from a "behind the scenes" approach in the 1960s to a more visible form of advocacy across the 1970s and into the 1980s. Coming out of the protests of 1968, organizations on the Left became stronger advocates for immigrant rights and anti-racism through events such as the Ivry rent strike and the deaths in Aubervilliers.[12]

Becoming a *cause célèbre*

How and why, though, did the deaths in Aubervilliers become a *cause célèbre* throughout French society? Why was there such a strong interest—public, political, intellectual, and otherwise—in the Aubervilliers deaths? In other words, how did a news story become a symbol of immigrant suffering? Until this point, events such as the Saint-Denis riot, the strike in Ivry, and other rent strikes throughout the Paris region had drawn national—and even international—attention, but not to the same degree as what happened in Aubervilliers. The five deaths in Aubervilliers marked an important moment when the deadly nature of immigrant living conditions penetrated the national consciousness and public discourse.

Yet other immigrant communities struggled with similar issues without drawing this kind of national attention. Several deaths preceded those in Aubervilliers. In 1966, for example, Malian worker Gagara Camara died in a fire in a *foyer* in the 20th *arrondissement* of Paris. Three children perished in a fire in a *bidonville* in Nanterre.[13] Every year, immigrants found themselves struggling to avoid death due to the makeshift use of heating sources and carbon monoxide poisoning in the winter, worrying about the risk of fire due to an absence of ventilation, and securing safe housing, leaving them vulnerable to the effects of precarious living conditions.

What was different, then, about the deaths in Aubervilliers? First and foremost, the story morphed into something larger within the popular imagination because it involved multiple deaths in a single night. The narrative's dramatic trajectory represented the challenges in formulating a postwar immigration policy that worked for all constituents: recruiters, employers, and immigrants alike.[14] The failure to do so, as Aubervilliers underscored, had dire consequences. What started as a news story became a symbol because it prompted people in and beyond the African immigrant community to take action and protest on the ground in a grassroots manner.

Another critical factor was that this scandal overlapped with the Ivry rent strike, which attracted considerable media attention and engendered public reflection on the lives led by immigrant workers in France. The fact that five immigrants died in Aubervilliers in the midst of a major immigrant strike that was already attracting national media attention indicated that the situation in Ivry was not unique. Perhaps the dire circumstances faced by immigrants in Ivry were more widespread than officials, observers, and ordinary citizens wanted to admit. Coming at the peak of the Ivry rent strike, the deaths in Aubervilliers marked the culmination of protests and riots across the 1960s, capping off a tumultuous decade, one that included significant immigrant political activism and protest throughout France. As the response to Aubervilliers grew more visible, vocal, and politicized, officials harked back to the turmoil of the 1960s while hoping to avoid another round of political and social upheaval like that of 1968. Whether the Aubervilliers protests would spark another round of protest was not known. Yet the potential was there. The timing of the protests around the Aubervilliers deaths was also not coincidental. As Verdery argues, "corpses lend themselves particularly well to politics in times of major upheaval."[15] These deaths came in the aftermath of the global uprisings of 1968 and the close of a tumultuous decade.

Within the turmoil of the late 1960s, immigrant participation in the May, 1968 protests was evident, which made authorities nervous.[16] They had not necessarily foreseen that a group of student protesters in Nanterre outside of Paris could start a movement that threatened, at one point, to bring down the French government. Nor had they anticipated the widespread participation of immigrant groups in the protests of that year. Might the situation in Aubervilliers spark another round of national protests? What would come of growing social and political strife over the plight of immigrants in France, from Saint-Denis to Ivry and Aubervilliers?[17] If authorities worried about the potential for upheaval once again, activists in the wake of 1968 took note of what happened in Aubervilliers and helped to elevate it within the national dialogue around immigration in France. In fact, as Gordon argues, 1968 heightened public awareness of the plight of immigrants in France even as the memory of immigrant participation in the protests of that year faded over time.[18]

The timing of the deaths also contributed to their visibility and the public's response. As they came at the start of a new decade, the challenges associated with postcolonial immigration once again vaulted into the national consciousness. From the perspective of ordinary citizens, including well-known intellectuals, writers, and filmmakers such as Sartre, Duras, and Claude Lanzmann, it seemed that the French government had not done enough at this point to address the challenges faced by African workers. Broader questions swirled around French immigration policy in the wake of these deaths. Was France capable of providing a decent standard of living for members of this and other immigrant communities? Were the mechanisms of *accueil* ("welcoming" or "reception") set up to integrate other immigrant communities insufficient, failing to meet the needs of Sub-Saharan Africans and potentially other immigrant groups in France? How could one reconcile the ideas of integration embedded within French citizenship with the realities faced by African workers and other immigrant groups? Rather than emphasize the inability of non-western, postcolonial immigrants to assimilate or focus solely on their impoverishment, discussion drifted toward French society's ability to help them integrate and while addressing the dire circumstances in which they found themselves living. It was these deaths in Aubervilliers together with the other crises within this and other immigrant communities that pushed this issue of reception to the forefront of the national immigration debate.

What was it, though, that precipitated the events that would prompt none other than Jean-Paul Sartre to protest publicly on behalf of immigrant communities? Just as the Ivry *foyer*'s residents and landlords maintained a rocky, sometimes confrontational relationship, a tenant–landlord dispute contributed to these deaths, not unlike those which prompted the Ivry rent strike and the Saint-Denis riot. As with the Ivry dormitory and others before, the conflict centered on a dispute in rent payments when seven tenants failed to turn over 70 francs for the month of January. As a result, the landlords cut the dormitory's heat and electricity, the same response seen in Ivry and throughout the Paris region. This time, however, the decision proved deadly as the loss of power came during early January—one of the coldest months of the year in northern France.[19]

Conditions on the rue des Postes

So what was the state of the living conditions in the dormitory on the rue des Postes where the five Malian workers died? In fact, it resembled many of the dwellings inhabited by immigrant workers across the Paris region. Monsieur Messaoud Prosper Benghozi, an Algerian-born tailor, owned the property. The dormitory's managers, including Oumar Dia, a former employee of the Senegalese consulate, Senegalese immigrant M N'Dao Abdoulaye, and Bernard Salleron of Martinique, opened it on October 13, 1968, more than a year prior to the tenants' deaths, and handled its daily operations. The *foyer*'s management organization, *Centre d'hébergement d'Afrique noire* (Center for Black African Housing), was declared to the *Préfecture de police* on 22 August 1968 under the 1901 law regulating associations. On September 9, 1968, the association *Solidarité franco-africaine* (Franco-African Solidarity) was declared to the *Préfecture de police*. That same day, 41 African tenants moved into the dormitory.[20]

In less than two years, tragedy struck and five Malian immigrants died in their dormitory. Surviving residents faced a number of challenges in this regard, highlighting key issues facing diasporic communities in addressing death while residing thousands of miles from home. They grappled with important questions such as whether to bury fellow workers in France or repatriate their bodies and whether and how to have a Muslim funeral and burial. These deaths also spotlighted the limitations for a Muslim and African burial in a country that constructed itself as secular and Catholic simultaneously. As revealed by the deaths in Aubervilliers, Muslim immigrants encountered challenges in dealing with the deaths of fellow community members in a host country that struggled to accommodate their religious preferences in terms of burial. A pressing question emerged. Where would the deceased person's friends and family bury the bodies: in a local cemetery or in the country of origin, which was home not only to immediate family but also to the ancestors? One study found that although complex and based on factors such as gender, age at migration, and age at the time of the interviews, many immigrants hoped to be buried in their home countries.[21] African spiritual traditions around death and burial emphasized the importance of both occurring in the home country and home town.[22] Yet several issues often prevented deceased immigrants from being buried at home and death itself was unpredictable. Ostensibly immigrants were younger and could expect someday to return home. But the dicey living conditions in France together with challenging demographics in terms of lifespan meant that this was not a certainty. If a death did occur, the deceased's country of origin was many thousands of miles away and repatriating the body proved difficult and costly.[23] Alternative arrangements became necessary and in this instance, those who died in Aubervilliers were buried in a French cemetery, far from their homes and families.

Mourning the dead in an immigrant community

Another challenge facing the African immigrant community at this moment was this: it was uncommon for African workers to publicly mourn the death of another immigrant. A lack of financial resources often prohibited formal recognition of a death as expected within Soninké, Mande, and West African cultural traditions more broadly.[24] The fear of arousing suspicion from authorities also dissuaded public mourning, as unwanted attention might result in an investigation of legal status resulting in deportation proceedings. Publicity was not always a positive development. For these reasons, recognition of a death within the African immigrant community took place privately. This matches up with practices within the Islamic faith, which was the religion of the majority of African immigrants in France in the 1960s.[25] Although Muslim immigrants from Sub-Saharan Africa participated in political protests throughout the 1960s, they did not necessarily do so with their religious beliefs at the forefront of their activism. For the African community in particular, political activism was not necessarily religiously based. In this case, though, what was intended as a private religious ceremony and burial became a highly publicized and politicized event, a development that was uncommon for African immigrants. While other immigrant burials occurred anonymously throughout the Paris region in cemeteries from Bobigny to Père Lachaise in Paris, this funeral proved to be one of the most unique events to occur in the 14-year period between the start of postcolonial African immigration and the end of labor migration in 1974.[26]

The victims' bodies themselves would soon become the focal point of one of the most politicized, publicized immigrant funerals in modern French history. The funeral took place on January 10, outside of Aubervilliers at the *Institut médico-légal* (Medical-Legal Institute) in the 12th *arrondissement* of Paris. The event began at approximately 1:45 in the afternoon with the interment held afterward at the Thiais cemetery outside of Paris. Dozens of associations, unions, political groups, and representatives from African embassies participated in the funeral, the burial, and the tragedy's aftermath. An estimated 1,500 people attended the ceremonies—including between 200 and 400 West African immigrants—while hundreds more came to the inhumation.[27]

Religious and political elements were woven throughout that day. During the funeral, the first imam of the Paris Mosque recited traditional prayers while the attendees from Senegal, Mauritanian, and Mali waited to view the bodies of their fellow immigrants in line with the tradition in African culture of spending time with the deceased person's body. Following the ceremony, the victims' coffins and those mourning their loss traveled to the cemetery in Thiais. The imam once again said ritual prayers, repeated by those present, after which the coffins were placed in the area of the cemetery reserved specifically for Muslims. As those gathered mourned, political activists protested. The political organization *Humanité rouge* (Red Humanity) distributed pamphlets after the burial entitled "Aubervilliers, five African workers assassinated by capital the proletariat will 'avenge' them."[28] Young French and African workers staged demonstrations, carrying red flags and calling for improved housing conditions for all workers residing in France. Their presence at the cemetery reflected the politicized nature of the funeral and its aftermath as well as the ways in which various organizations not only negotiated but also in some ways appropriated the deaths in Aubervilliers within their own political sphere.[29] The participation in the funeral, the burial, and the ensuing protests also suggest a political position shifting more toward advocacy for organizations on the left side of the political spectrum in regard to immigration than previously accounted for.

By 1970, there was already a precedent set for combining high-profile funerals with political protests. On February 8, 1962, police beat and killed nine protesters demonstrating against the Algerian war in front of the metro stop Charonne in Paris. The violence against these protesters came just four months after the murder by French forces of hundreds of Algerians who were demonstrating in the streets of Paris in support of the *Front de libération nationale* (FLN or the National Liberation Front) on October 17, 1961. Combined, the two events became symbolic of police repression and anti-immigrant violence in France.[30] Literary scholar Kristen Ross has called them, "... the two most disastrous of the police altercations presided over by Prefect of Police Maurice Papon in the early 1960s ..."[31] Although the bodies of the Algerians killed by police lay in the streets and in the Seine, and most did not receive a proper funeral, those of the Charonne victims were formally buried during funerals accompanied by between 500,000 and one million people marching in protest at their deaths and the police violence that precipitated them.[32] Ross argues that this moment constituted an important series of leftist funeral rituals that would include the funeral of Jean-Paul Sartre in 1980 and those of other luminaries, including that of Gilles Tautin, a young Maoist who died in June of 1968.[33] Although absent from Ross' list of important leftist funeral rituals between the late 1960s and Sartre's death in 1980, the funeral and accompanying protests following the Aubervilliers deaths constituted another important moment of public mourning and fits into this trajectory of funerary rituals used by the political Left in France. A key difference, however, was that rather than focusing on the death and lifelong contributions of an intellectual such as Sartre, the funeral and protests in Aubervilliers marked the passing of individual immigrants who were largely anonymous within the public sphere. Their names were nowhere near as well-known as that of Sartre, but their deaths nonetheless became the focus of public demonstrations held by leftist groups.

Several immigrant and advocacy organizations together with community leaders and African embassies also played a prominent role in the funeral and the public discourse more broadly. The UGTSF and other African associations, including the *Association général des travailleurs sénégalais en France* (General Association of Senegalese Workers in France AGTSF) and the *Union des travailleurs mauritaniens en France* (Union of Mauritanian Workers in France or UTMF), denounced the deaths in Aubervilliers. The UTMF contributed to immigrant participation in the funeral and associated protests that day by transporting African workers living in cities such as Reims, Le Havre, Rouen, Lille, and Marseilles to the funeral. The UGTSF's N'Dongo—who was by 1970 one of the most prominent leaders of the African immigrant community—attended, representing his organization as well as his fellow migrants more broadly. He declared that:

> Owners and managers of dormitories are not the only ones responsible ... It is inaccurate to say that African labor is not qualified. Africans

> may not know how to read or write, but they have skills as mechanics, drivers, cooks ... But we refuse to utilize them at the level of their qualification by trapping them in work that French workers will not do.[34]

N'Dongo argued that culpability in these deaths lay beyond simply the property managers who ran dormitories such as that in Aubervilliers and ascribed it to those who hired them to do the jobs that French citizens preferred not to do while overlooking the important skills that they did bring to the French economy. Beyond N'Dongo's critique, the national consulates of Senegal and Mauritania became involved, sending their consuls Thomas Seck of Senegal and Kamara Ali of Mauritania to assist directly with the ceremonies. Representatives from the anti-racism group MRAP also attended, demonstrating the ways in which these deaths transcended the challenges faced by the African immigrant community and became part of a broader dialogue about anti-racism, anti-discrimination, and human rights.

Links between sending and receiving countries

As part of the broader trajectory of postwar political mourning, the Aubervilliers funeral and burial connected the sending and receiving countries and reaffirmed social ties within the postcolonial African immigrant community.[35] These ceremonies linked that community to French society in a way that immigrant cultural and social rituals have done across the nineteenth and twentieth centuries in and beyond France, dating back to the interwar period and even earlier. In this case, the deaths of five African workers in Aubervilliers brought together Islamic, Senegalese, Mauritanian, and Soninké rituals surrounding death and responses to mortality, creating an overlap of different religious faiths, social and cultural practices, and political elements within the host society. Although the Aubervilliers deaths and funeral generated significant political interest, this was still an important cultural and social event that underscored the hybrid nature of immigrant responses to death within a host society and the ways in which multiple social and cultural rituals shaped the mourning within this and other immigrant communities.

While linking the two regions together by introducing elements of their own cultures and societies when responding to events such as the deaths of fellow migrants, immigrants also incorporated elements of the host society's cultural and social norms.[36] Funerals often involved the intersection of social, political, and religious elements, not only in African cultures but also across geographical divides.[37] Just as immigrant communities throughout the world have combined aspects of their own culture and that of the host society in their responses to death, so too did African immigrants grappling with this situation in France.[38] From the perspectives of various ethnic groups, including that of the Mandinga from Guinea-Bissau in West Africa, death was seen as part of an individual's life trajectory as determined at the time of birth.[39] Death, as with key moments in life, was commemorated and publicly marked across African societies and cultures throughout the world. The immigrants mourning their fellow residents in Aubervilliers felt the same imperative to commemorate these losses. This then combined with the experience of separation and travel, which was also woven into attitudes toward death and burial within the African immigrant community. For members of the African ethnic groups who migrated to France, including the Mandinga and the Soninké, migration, travel, and diaspora are critical components of their collective identity. Separation was expected and found its way into responses to death and rituals surrounding it, especially with the burial of African immigrants.[40]

The funeral's impact

This was the case with the Aubervilliers funeral, as it simultaneously represented a Muslim, African, and immigrant funeral while morphing into a highly volatile political protest involving organizations from throughout the French political sphere.[41] As a ritual performed within the African immigrant community, the Aubervilliers funeral did what funerals do across cultures: it assisted in community building and formation.[42] The cultural significance of funerals, as anthropologist Peter Geschiere explains, is that they reinforce social connections.[43] In doing so, the ceremonies also served an important political function, drawing outside constituencies and individuals into the struggle over human rights percolating within a growing discourse over immigration to France and the lives of immigrant communities in France.

These deaths also underscored the tensions surrounding Muslim burial rituals and French legal standards. The ritual responses following the deaths became contested spaces in which the acts of mourning and burial themselves became highly politicized. The *Code générale des collectivités territoriales* (General Code of Territorial Collectives) (CGCT) guides burial in France, which is secular, mandatory, and public in nature in accordance with the 1905 law regulating the separation of church and state. In accordance with the law, only individual plots intended for private use can include religious symbols—the cemetery as a whole was to remain secular in nature.[44] Rosemarie Van Den Breemer and Marcel Maussen define Muslim burial as one that occurs "without a coffin and within twenty four hours."[45] This kind of approach clashed with state prohibitions on confessional parcels (burial plots), which, as the authors argue, "forced Muslims to choose between repatriation to the land of origin or their parents' origin, or non-Islamic burial on a common public graveyard."[46] Overtly Muslim parcels were not allowed in French cemeteries and yet Muslim immigrants needed a proper burial in France that met both religious and state regulations. There were also tensions between Islamic requirements and African customs, which dictated that mourners spend up to three days washing and caring for the body before burial, thereby contradicting the twenty-four-hour rule within Islamic customs.[47] The choice, then, of how to proceed proved difficult, given conflicting customs and the precarious financial situation in which many African immigrants found themselves. Burial in France was a more viable but perhaps less desirable option from the standpoint of properly carrying out Muslim and African rituals in regards to death and burial, such as washing the body and properly dressing it.[48]

One of the biggest challenges for African and, in this case Muslim, immigrants, though, was in locating a cemetery that would legally allow the burial of the victims. A few cemeteries close to Aubervilliers could accommodate the burial, including that in Thiais. This cemetery provided burial plots for Jews and Muslims in addition to Catholics and Protestants, starting in 1957. Other cemeteries also allowed Muslim burials, including Père Lachaise in Paris, which permitted Muslim burial as early as 1857, and the Muslim cemetery in Bobigny, which opened in 1934.[49] Because of its proximity, though, those who died in Aubervilliers were buried in Thiais in the Val-de-Marne department. This became an important cemetery for African immigrants who died while in France because it provided space for Muslims to be buried there. By this point, cemeteries had become contested spaces that reaffirmed the secular nature of French national identity while conceding individual spaces to Muslim immigrants, reflecting the complicated relationship between French national identity and immigration. Who belonged within the French nation-state and why became an important question in death as in life. The politics of burial remained visible in the aftermath of the deaths in Aubervilliers.[50]

Muslim immigrants and French immigration policy

While surviving tenants in Aubervilliers grappled with how and where to bury those who died, French officials continued to struggle with the cultural implications of a growing immigrant population that, in terms of religious beliefs, was mostly Muslim in composition. Historian Naomi Davidson explains that it was in the 1970s that the French state began to realize that "a unitary vision of religious identity and practice was not tenable."[51] Davidson argues further that:

> The rationale for this segregation was corporeal: the French belief in the centrality of embodied practices in the lives of Muslims meant that the kinds of services that were designed to assist North African immigrants took for granted that Muslim bodies had different demands than non-Muslim ones.[52]

As with housing and other aspects of state policies towards non-western and former colonial immigrant populations, North Africans served as the main community for which postwar officials constructed immigration policies as part of the developing postwar welfare state. Social welfare initiatives implemented for North Africans became an important model for those created for their West African counterparts.[53]

In comparing state policy for North African immigrants with that designed for Sub-Saharan Africans, however, we see that there was less of a unitary vision of Islam and Muslim immigrants in the postcolonial era and especially those from Sub-Saharan Africa. French officials saw Sub-Saharan African immigrants as less ardently Muslim than their North African counterparts, a holdover perception from the colonial era. AOF was home to multiple religious faiths: Islam, indigenous belief systems, and Catholicism, making it a multifaceted religious space.[54] Because of the dynamics surrounding decolonization in Algeria and the war that ensued, Muslim immigrants became associated with anti-colonial activism within the official imagination. While concern over the place of Muslim immigrants in France continued to grow, the state made provisions for the practice of Islam within state-run dormitories and in other social welfare-affiliated institutions such as the *Centre médico-social Bossuet*, a health clinic that opened in the early 1960s in Paris designed for immigrants from Sub-Saharan Africa.

Political protests and politicization

While these shifting understandings of Islam in France helped to define the response to the deaths in Aubervilliers, understandings of political radicalization also factored in. By the time the deaths occurred in Aubervilliers, and as the Ivry rent strike and other rent strikes continued thorughout the Paris region, officials interpreted Africans as much more likely to engage politically than previously thought. From the official perspective, however, the source of radicalization for West Africans, unlike their North African counterparts, was not religious—it was political. Authorities honed in on the relationships between African immigrants and radical leftist organizations to explain what seemed to be an uptick in African political activism by the late 1960s and early 1970s, just as the Left in France was starting to take a more serious interest in immigrant-related issues.

While highlighting some of the key issues confronting the African immigrant community and policy makers alike, particularly around issues of mortality, the deaths touched off protests and debates that went beyond the African immigrant community itself and involved organizations and individuals ranging from the UGTSF to Sartre. Well-known intellectuals and writers joined the discourse over the fate of immigrant workers in France, prompted, in large part, by the deaths in Aubervilliers. Multiple protests across the Paris region followed. Already carrying out a prolonged strike, African workers in Ivry staged a demonstration in solidarity on the day of the funeral for the Aubervilliers workers.[55] Observers worried that those immigrants might meet a similar fate. One political tract, building on this concern, warned that the residents of Ivry could be next: "RESIDENTS OF IVRY do not allow a murder like that in Aubervilliers to happen in our city. Residents of Ivry do not wait for new deaths to react."[56] Would they survive or would they also perish in a run-down dormitory, just as their counterparts in Aubervilliers had?

That the political protests following the deaths in Aubervilliers happened as they did also reflected the coalition that immigrants and their French supporters created through the protests of 1968. The multiethnic and multinational nature of the protests of 1968 helps explain why a broad constituency across French society responded to the deaths at Aubervilliers.[57] As the Left extended its relationship with immigrant communities throughout France by the late 1960s, students and workers became more conscious of the plight of immigrant workers through and because of 1968, and key intellectuals came to see the struggles of immigrants in France as reflective of the problems that plagued France. Coming in the aftermath of 1968, the Ivry rent strike helped to draw national attention to the struggles faced by African immigrants. The deaths in Aubervilliers reawakened and revitalized the important relationships formed on the streets and in the occupied buildings of Paris in May of 1968. One can trace a direct line, then, between the complex protests of that year and the public response to Aubervilliers less than two years later.

The deaths at Aubervilliers and the subsequent funeral and political demonstrations also connected the social and political upheaval of the 1960s to the state's response in terms of surveillance and social welfare. Protests staged by African immigrants themselves together with the increasingly visible involvement from the Left seemingly confirmed authorities' worst fears: that the African community was in danger of becoming a "hotbed" of leftist political action. Similar concerns had circulated around the Ivry rent strike. Yet the deaths in Aubervilliers and the public response marked a turning point. As public outrage grew, authorities started to take a more direct approach with policies addressing African workers and other immigrant groups. The combination of a perceived threat to the political sphere and the precarious conditions in which immigrants lived contributed to the tightening of immigration policies by the early 1970s, culminating in the government's decision to suspend labor migration in 1974.

What happened in Aubervilliers and the protests that followed connected the political activism undertaken by African immigrants across the 1970s to those carried out by and on behalf of immigrant communities into the 1980s, 1990s, and 2000s. Because of the wide-ranging political participation seen that day and in the days and weeks after, the funeral and burial were also labeled by authorities as a "political meeting" of sorts. Following these deaths, African immigrant organizations became more vocal in their demands for improved conditions and more critical of the role that African workers played in the French economy, shifting their advocacy from one that was based in social welfare to one that was rights based and more specifically focused on racial advocacy.[58] As a result, the surveillance of immigrant communities, including African workers, ramped up in the years following and became more concerned with politicization and interactions with leftist groups. Something else, though, emerged out of the Aubervilliers deaths: an increased focus on social welfare initiatives intended for African immigrants within the broader spectrum of services offered to immigrant groups.[59] The deaths in Aubervilliers, then, serve as the lynchpin between the political activism undertaken in the 1960s, the surveillance carried out in the 1960s and 1970s, and the ways in which it informed the social welfare programs and advocacy initiatives undertaken in response, which continued throughout the 1980s and into the contemporary period.

While the UGSTF and other immigrant groups actively participated that day, leftist organizations also weighed in on the situation. By this point, the relationship between the African immigrant community and politically left-leaning groups in France had solidified as a variety of organizations participated as a means of showing solidarity. Although support from the Left for the African immigrant community and other immigrant groups was apparent by January of 1970, it reached a new level with the deaths in Aubervilliers. The critique rendered by organizations such as the PCF (*Parti communiste français*) and the CGT (*Confédération générale du travail*) regarding the plight of immigrants in France generally and the situation they faced in Aubervilliers specifically reflected a broader twentieth-century socialist and communist critique of colonialism as an extension of capitalism. From this perspective, the exploitation of colonial labor continued into the postcolonial era through immigration to the former colonies, which maintained neocolonial influence in Sub-Saharan Africa through policies collectively referred to as Franceafrique.[60] The leftist critique of colonialism shifted in the postcolonial Cold War era to one that focused not only on France's neocolonial relationship with Sub-Saharan Africa but also on the plight of immigrants in France and the ways in which the French government and French enterprises continued to exploit African workers.

Leftist participation on the day of the funerals proved multifaceted and wide-ranging. While members of groups such as *Gauche prolétarienne* attended the funeral and burial, political groups made their presence felt more in the protests and pamphlet distributions staged outside each event and throughout the Paris region. The *Comité d'action de la région parisienne* (Committee for Action in the Paris Region), for example, distributed tracts, including one entitled "Aubervilliers is not an accident, it's an assassination," which posed the question of "who (was) responsible?"[61] In total, at least 137 different demonstrations took place on the day of the funeral, most of which were organized by the *Gauche prolétarienne*. One of the organization's pamphlets called for a mass demonstration at the *Institut médico-légal* on the day of the funeral. Beyond this particular demonstration, the organization encouraged students to protest at educational institutions throughout Paris. The *Humanité rouge* called on students in the 5th *arrondissement* of Paris, where the Sorbonne and other universities are located, to protest on the day of the funeral. This was one of the centers of protest during May of 1968. In another corner of the city, protesters staged demonstrations at the *Centre national du patronat français* (National Center of French Employers or CNPF).[62] Africans who attended the funeral also took the opportunity to speak out. One attendee seized a microphone in the lobby of the *Institut médico-légal* and accused the capitalist system in general of ending the lives of the five African workers who lived on the rue des Postes.[63]

The language comparing the deaths in Aubervilliers to a capitalist conspiracy reveals the ways in which the Cold War and the clash of ideologies within it influenced perceptions of the deaths in Aubervilliers and the aftermath. Organizations on the Left ascribed the deaths of these workers to the exploitive nature of capitalism, demonstrating the ways in which the Marxist critique of capitalism influenced debates about immigration within the Cold War context. One of the strongest responses to the deaths in Aubervilliers came from the *Gauche prolétarienne*, which published *La Cause du peuple* (Cause of the People).[64] Together with other organizations, the *Gauche prolétarienne* positioned the Aubervilliers tragedy within a broader analysis of class struggle, which reveals the important focus placed on immigration by leftist organizations by the late 1960s and early 1970s. From the GP's perspective, while immigrant workers suffered in dilapidated dormitories, the industries that employed them benefitted from using an inexpensive labor source for which they provided little in the way of housing or social services. This, together with other analyses, revealed the way in which the Marxist critique of capitalism was woven into assessments not only of the Aubervilliers deaths but also of the plight of immigrants in France more broadly.

Important tensions emerged between various organizations on the left side of the political spectrum, as revealed by the GP's criticism of the PCF. This friction also highlighted the diversity and lack of uniformity in the Left's response to immigration, including that from former French colonies where the PCF and other organizations had gained a strong political foothold by the end of the colonial era. Rather than remaining aloof from immigration policy or universally critical of it, the GP and other organizations weighed in while also using these events to criticize the French capitalist system that they blamed for exploiting immigrant workers.

These responses show a much more nuanced position in regard to immigration and one that focused specifically on human rights through the intersection of immigration and the Marxist critique of capitalism in the postcolonial era. Here, various organizations on the left side of the political spectrum advocated for immigrant groups such as African workers in a way that mirrored what occurred in Ivry and marked an important turning point for the Left in France regarding immigration. Where previously ambivalent or perhaps even anti-immigration, leftist groups came to support African workers and other immigrant groups not only in the midst of strikes such as that in Ivry but also during moments of crisis, including in the aftermath of the deaths in Aubervilliers. At the same time, the GP and other leftist groups saw an opportunity through this event to increase their outreach efforts among immigrant groups. In particular, they focused on the African community, portraying African workers as more receptive to their message in the wake of the Aubervilliers tragedy.[65]

The Left's response to the deaths in Aubervilliers, though, went beyond that of the *Comité d'action de la région parisienne* or the *Gauche prolétarienne*. The CGT, for example, took a similar stance when it argued that the Aubervilliers tragedy was the direct consequence of collusion between industry and government to provide an inexpensive, expendable labor force in the form of African workers. For their part, the *Sections communistes d'Ivry* (Communist Divisions of Ivry) of the PCF took a similar position, holding those in power—both in industry and government—responsible for creating the conditions that many West Africans found themselves confronting throughout France. The Aubervilliers deaths ushered in a new era of political involvement and visibility for the political Left in France within France's immigrant communities.

The Ivry connection

The protests around the Aubervilliers deaths dovetailed with others occurring throughout the Paris region. On the same day as the funeral, a near riot occurred at the former chocolate factory turned *foyer* on the rue Gabriel Péri in Ivry, indelibly linking these two dormitories and the tragedies that occurred within their walls. Amidst the protests staged by leftist groups and the individual participation of noted writers, intellectuals, and politicians, this demonstration in particular stands out. The protest held at the dormitory in Ivry on the day of the Aubervilliers funeral reveals the ways in which these two places and the events that took place there remained connected while defining, in some ways, the African immigrant experience in France. Not only was one appropriated to understand the other, but they also remained uniquely lodged together in the imaginations of authorities and organizations invested in the issues and events surrounding African immigration to France. The rent strike staged by residents of the rue Gabriel Péri dormitory was viewed in the context of this most recent tragedy in Aubervilliers. Leftist organizations shifted their focus to the Ivry rent strike, wondering aloud if these residents might share the same fate as their counterparts in Aubervilliers.

That the two events were so quickly cast together in the public mind was reflected on the day of the Aubervilliers funeral, when a large rally occurred outside of the Ivry dormitory. A wide range of organizations from the UGTSF to the *Gauche prolétarienne* and MRAP spent days promoting the demonstration and went so far as to invite attendants of the victims' burial at the Thiais cemetery as they departed the grounds. They labeled it an expression of solidarity for those "assassinated" in Aubervilliers as well as an opportunity to begin seeking vengeance for those who perished.[66] The language used to describe the deaths and the pending demonstrations took on a violent tone. The terminology of non-violent resistance, which appeared in civil rights and anti-colonial movements throughout the world was notably absent.[67] Participating organizations and individuals adopted a more militaristic approach, infusing their announcements with terminology that pointed to not only the violent nature of these deaths but also to the possibility of violence arising in the protests that followed. Media attention was an important component of the rally, as various organizations—including the *Sections communistes d'Ivry*—planned for radio, television, and newspaper coverage of the event in order to disseminate the message underscoring the exploitation endured by African immigrants while publicly revealing the plight of the African community.[68] Writers Michel Leiris, Jérôme Peignot, and Jean-Pierre Faye participated and were arrested in conjunction with the protests.[69]

What was described by media outlets and local officials alike as an "occupation" of the Ivry *foyer* began the morning of January 10. Influenced by the massive demonstrations in May of 1968 and the tactics employed, several groups—including members of the *Comités d'action* and the *Gauche prolétarienne*—organized and carried out the rally. Residents of the *foyer* joined in. As with the funeral and burial in Aubervilliers, several literary and political figures participated, including Leiris from the *Union des écrivains* (Writers' Union), Peignot, Faye, and attorneys and representatives of the *Ligue des droits de l'homme* (League of the Rights of Man). Protesters carried signs decrying the dangerous living conditions that immigrants confronted, comparing *foyers* and factories to prisons, accusing the capitalist system of perpetrating the deaths of immigrants, and implicating the bourgeoisie in the neocolonialist policies they deemed responsible for the deaths in Aubervilliers and the rent strike in Ivry. Tracts circulated through the crowd bearing similar messages.[70] Beyond the events of May 1968, this was one of the first times that non-immigrants participated publicly in advocating for immigrant rights, foreshadowing the movement of second-generation North Africans born in France, referred to as *beurs*, and the "*touche pas à mon pote*" ("hands off my buddy") campaign, both of which developed in the 1980s. This moment also highlighted the grassroots nature of political activism on behalf of immigrant communities by the late 1960s and early 1970s.[71]

The rally quickly drew a police response. Authorities halted the distribution of tracts and dispersed the demonstration's participants. By 6 p.m., the *foyer*'s doors were closed and its residents returned inside. Later, the *Gauche prolétarienne* accused police of invading and occupying the *foyer* just as the rally's participants had attempted to do earlier that day. Reports on the number of arrests made varied, with some placing the number at 21 and others claiming that upwards of 116 people were taken into custody. Some of the demonstration's more famous participants were among those arrested, including the writers Maurice Clavel and Marguerite Duras.[72]

The correlation between the Ivry rent strike and the Aubervilliers deaths rested in part on the fear that the residents of the rue Gabriel Péri could suffer the same fate as the Africans who perished on the rue des Postes. One tract recovered by the *Préfecture de police* in Aubervilliers asked whether, after the tragedy in Aubervilliers, there would be similar deaths in Ivry. By January of 1970, reports placed the Ivry *foyer*'s population at 700. The thought of hundreds of African immigrants dying in one *foyer* troubled city council members, human rights activists, public intellectuals, and members of political organizations alike, bringing together sometimes divergent constituencies to discuss, debate, and address the challenges facing African workers and other immigrant communities. The deaths provided a united force of concern, as the fate of the five Africans in Aubervilliers was one that could befall any of the over 20,000 immigrants from Sub-Saharan Africa living in the Paris region—the majority of whom endured similarly precarious living conditions.[73]

Linguistic descriptions

The situation was further magnified by the language that organizations such as the *Gauche prolétarienne* chose to apply to the Aubervilliers and Ivry situations. Linguistically and descriptively, Aubervilliers was depicted in numerous ways. In one vein, it became a cautionary tale, one whose lessons could be applied to other dormitories, such as that in Ivry. In another, though, it elicited comparisons to the German occupation of World War Two, concentration camps, and mass violence. This was not the first time that the events of World War Two had surfaced as a metaphor. In response to the killings of Algerian protesters by police on October 17, 1961, writers Jacques Lanzmann and Simone de Beauvoir compared French bystanders' failure to respond to the killing of Algerian protesters to Germans who did not try to stop the Holocaust.[74] The *foyer* under scrutiny due to the rent strike in Ivry was referred to by a journalist for the radio network Europe 1 as "Auschwitz at the port of Paris."[75] Aubervilliers was also associated with large-scale violence, whether imagined, symbolic, or real, inflicted upon immigrant communities residing in France. Terms such as "genocide" and "concentration camp" surfaced as a means to discuss the Ivry and Aubervilliers, directly linking them with the crimes against humanity perpetrated throughout Europe during World War Two. Residents, however, could be "liberated" and relocated to more suitable housing, invoking another term with important resonance among the French population almost 26 years after the liberation of France from German occupation.[76] Descriptions of World War Two and the liberation of camps became a means through which to understand the plight of African immigrants in France, its implications for human rights, and the pressing need for improved housing conditions in the wake of the Ivry strike and the deaths in Aubervilliers.

The Ivry rent strike, though, was not the only instance in which the Aubervilliers tragedy became a means through which to understand the challenges endured by West African workers. This incident intensified the debate concerning the dearth of housing options available to most immigrants. Pierre Lanier—the President of *Accueil et rencontres, région lyonnaise* (Welcome and Meet, Lyon Region)—described lodging as the most pressing problem facing Africans and their host society. Public opinion, he explained, was particularly swayed by the deaths in Aubervilliers. He also situated the struggle over immigrant housing more broadly within what he characterized as the French national housing drama. As Leiris argued in an article in *Le Monde* exploring the lives of Malians in Ivry, the "dangers that threaten Malian workers, such as the risks of a catastrophe are on a par with that of Aubervilliers."[77] The Malians in Ivry risked a similar fate to their counterparts in Aubervilliers, as did the majority of Africans residing in France due to the shortcomings of their housing.[78]

Public figures, public responses

Several noteworthy individuals, including public officials, political leaders, activists, and intellectuals responded to the deaths and attended the funeral, revealing its impact within the broader public sphere and to the public debate over immigration. Among them, Maurice Grimaud, the *Préfet de Police*, Michel Rocart, the national secretary of the *Parti socialiste unifié* (Unified Socialist Party or PSU), Algerian writer Kateb Yacine, Sartre, and Duras publicly denounced the treatment of African immigrants within French society.[79] As Gordon argues, between May of 1968 and May of 1981:

> ... (French) society was impatient for change. This was an era in which the Left sought to challenge at last the inequalities of French society. It was a time when famous intellectuals from Jean-Paul Sartre to Michel Foucault marched in the street alongside immigrant workers.[80]

The involvement of Sartre and others in the protests undertaken in the aftermath of the Aubervilliers deaths reflects the convergence of intellectuals and immigrants after 1968 to which Gordon points. The idea of "impatience for change" that he identifies in the 13 years between the upheaval of 1968 and the election of socialist François Mitterrand in 1981 played out in the public's response to the bleak situation facing African immigrants and other immigrant groups, as highlighted by the deaths in Aubervilliers. As Gordon himself points out, though, Sartre's activism on behalf of immigrant communities pre-dated the Aubervilliers deaths. On November 1, 1961, Sartre gave a speech following the October 17 massacre of Algerian protesters while also signing a petition along with de Beauvoir, Duras, Claude Lanzmann, Aimé Césaire, and others.[81] While leftist intellectuals over the course of the 1960s may have focused more on the developing world as *tiermondistes* or "thirdworldists," an important focus remained on France's immigrant communities not only from an activist perspective but also from an intellectual one. The deaths in Aubervilliers, though, brought this advocacy back into the national spotlight.[82]

Authorities took note of the involvement of intellectuals and activists such as Sartre. Officials labeled Rocart and Sartre in particular as "*personnalités de gauche*" or the "leftist personalities" present during the funeral. Long committed to anti-colonialism in his writings and political affiliations, Sartre observed in this situation the ways in which the Marxist critique of French neocolonialism played out in real time.[83] In his speech that day, Sartre explained that:

> The deaths of African workers illustrate the scandal of French society, which uses underpaid workers to its profit. It is critical to awaken public opinion against a certain racism that breeds indifference. The use of African labor is a form of internal colonialism, and we hope that a better situation results from this catastrophe and that public opinion is finally made aware of this scandal that must come to an end.[84]

His argument that the use of African labor constituted a form of internal colonialism fit his broader critique of French colonial and neocolonial policies. In the postwar era, Sartre grew increasingly critical of French colonialism and neocolonialism in line with his existentialist version of Marxism by the late 1960s and early 1970s.[85] At this point, he had become involved in the public debate over French immigration policies and their correlation with French neocolonial initiatives in the former African colonies.[86] At the same time, Sartre's influence among Francophone writers continued to grow and his contact with and stature among the African intellectual community in and beyond France was unrivaled by 1970. Given this ongoing involvement and the way that it shaped his postwar philosophical and political outlook, it was not surprising that Sartre attended and participated in the funeral. He and others argued that Africans residing in France endured many of the same humiliations as their counterparts in AOF under colonialism. The social injustices leveled by the French colonial regime against African subjects became a way to understand the plight of postcolonial African immigrants and, more specifically, the deaths in Aubervilliers.[87] Sartre's involvement on behalf of immigrant communities in France, though seldom discussed, reflected the shift encapsulated by de Beauvoir: "With the war Sartre had to renounce *being* and resolve to *do*."[88] Sartre's protest and advocacy on behalf of the Malian immigrants who died in Aubervilliers reflected this change while also representing his critique of the bourgeois capitalist order as the primary explanation for these deaths. In this way, Sartre wove together existentialism and Marxism, as he did throughout the postwar era, to critique neocolonialism through an analysis of African immigration and the lives of immigrant workers in France. Although Sartre was not a Marxist in a traditional sense and never joined the PCF, the combination of existentialism and Marxist philosophy espoused by him and other French intellectuals in the postwar era remained attractive to African immigrant political activists in France, just as it was in AOF prior to decolonization.[89] In *Between Existentialism and Marxism*, Sartre notes:

> In order that there should be *consciousness* and *struggle*, it is necessary that somebody should be fighting ... Consciousness is only born in struggle: the class struggle only exists insofar as there exist places where an actual struggle is going on.[90]

Sartre's visions of freedom, consciousness, and struggle help explain his attraction to immigrant-related causes as he saw these elements within the political demonstrations surrounding the deaths in Aubervilliers, the rent strike in Ivry, and elsewhere. While Sartre saw in the African immigrant community an agent through which to challenge the capitalist and neocolonial order, African political activists found in Sartre a philosophical outlook that supported their political goals.[91]

Sartre, though, was not the only writer present at the protests, demonstrations, and occupations that occurred on the same day as the funeral. Several other intellectuals became involved as well, signaling the investment of public intellectuals in the aftermath and the broader debate over immigration. Duras, together with 150 others, participated in the occupation of the CNPF headquarters the day of the funeral, declaring herself and her fellow participants, "against the conditions of life and death of immigrant workers."[92] She and others placed the Aubervilliers tragedy within a broader framework that focused on the lives and experiences of immigrants residing in France and the ways in which they were treated by their host society. The *Union des écrivains* became involved as well. Three of the organization's members—Jean-Pierre Faye, Michel Leiris, and Jérôme Peignot—were arrested for protesting on the day of the funeral. In a press release following their arrests, they demanded "the immediate halt to the proceedings against the participants for an action whose sole purpose was to expose a long-running scandal fostered by the established political power" and added that they would continue "to support the struggle that they have undertaken, with others, against Ivry and elsewhere."[93]

The deaths, the funeral, and the political protests that accompanied them in and beyond Aubervilliers brought together a wide range of constituencies, from immigrant groups to advocacy organizations and diplomatic representatives, establishing an important template for contemporary immigrant activists. The political Left also became a vocal advocate for immigrant communities and immigrant rights while filtering a discussion of human rights from the perspective of a Marxist analysis. By the 1980s, immigrant organizations and advocacy groups would increasingly work together to highlight immigrant-related issues in the national media and the public consciousness using anti-racism and anti-discrimination as a key framework. The deaths in Aubervilliers together with rent strikes, riots, and other incidents involving African workers and other immigrant groups established a space within which these varied groups could work together in a public, grassroots way. This diverse coalition disseminated their responses to the deaths through the media and public discourse while shaping public opinion and reaction to the situation and around the issue of immigration more broadly.[94]

The kind of widespread political protests seen in the wake of the Aubervilliers deaths also helped to shape French immigration policy in the 1970s. As protests such as these mounted and the economy slowed, immigration policy tightened, harking back to the more restrictive measures taken in the interwar period.[95] Against a background of increased politicization and concerns about the effects of political unrest on the sometimes fragile Fifth Republic in the wake of Charles De Gaulle's resignation and only two years after the protests of 1968, authorities sought to clamp down on immigration as a way of guaranteeing social and political order. The theory was that a net immigration rate of zero combined with repatriation efforts would stabilize the public sphere and temper the growth of immigrant political movements. Surveillance tactics and social welfare programs undertaken throughout the 1960s and into the 1970s emerged as a response to the political activism undertaken by West African immigrants throughout the early postcolonial era while also serving as a foundation for more contemporary policies in regards to immigration and immigrant groups in France.

Notes

1 Bibliothèque nationale MICR D-66 1970/01 MFM J. M. Mercier, "La mort de cinq travailleurs africains à Aubervilliers—qui est responsable?" *Le Monde*, Paris, 4–5 January. CANC 19960311 art. 6 Préfet de Police, Aubervilliers, 9 January 1970.
2 Ibid.
3 Catherine Verdery, *The Political Lives of Dead Bodies: Reburial and Postsocialist Change* (New York: Columbia University Press, 1999), 20.
4 Gérard Noiriel, *Immigration, antisémitisme et racisme en France (XIXe–XXe Siècle)* (Paris: Fayard, 2007), 562–565.
5 Verdery, *The Political Lives of Dead Bodies*, 33.
6 Catherine Raissiguier, *Reinventing the Republic: Gender, Migration, and Citizenship in France* (Stanford: Stanford University Press, 2010), 21–23.
7 Alessandro Portelli, *The Death of Luigi Trastulli and Other Stories: Form and Meaning in Oral History* (Albany: State University of New York Press, 1991), viii.
8 Noiriel, *Immigration, antisémitisme et racisme en France*, 562–565.
9 Daniel Gordon, "Reaching Out to Immigrants in May 68: Specific or Universal Appeals?" in Julian Jackson, Anna-Louise Milne, and James S. Williams, eds., *May 68: Rethinking France's Last Revolution* (Houndmills; Basingstoke; Hampshire; New York: Palgrave Macmillan, 2011), 93–106.
10 Gordon in Jackson et al., eds., *May 68*, 105.
11 Verdery, *The Political Lives of Dead Bodies*, 23–25.
12 Daniel A. Gordon, *Immigrants and Intellectuals: May '68 and the Rise of Anti-Racism in France*, (Pontypool: Merlin Press, 2012), 1–18.

13 Préfecture de police Archives GaA7 Jean-Marc Theolleyre "Mort d'un Malien" 11 February 1970; VDM 2018W art. 20 Comité d'action de la région parisienne (Préfecture de police), "Tract: 'Aubervilliers n'est pas un accident! C'est un assassinat!'" Aubervilliers, January 1970; Gordon, *Immigrants and Intellectuals*, 39.
14 Portelli, *The Death of Luigi Trastulli and Other Stories*, 1–28.
15 Verdery, *The Political Lives of Dead Bodies*, 31.
16 Gordon, *Immigrants and Intellectuals*, 1–18; Félix F. Germain, *Decolonizing the Republic: African and Caribbean Migrants in Postwar Paris (1946–1974)* (East Lansing: Michigan State University Press, 2016), 141–157.
17 For recent scholarship on May of 1968 and the participation of immigrant communities, see Gordon, *Immigrants and Intellectuals* and Shepard, "Reaching out to Immigrants in May 68: Specific or Universal Appeals?" in Jackson, et al., eds., *May 68*, 76–92.
18 Gordon, *Immigrants and Intellectuals*, 39.
19 CANC 19960311 art. 6 Préfet de police, Aubervilliers, 9 January 1970. BN MICR D-13 1970/01 L 1.15 MFM Robert Bruyers, "À Aubervilliers, dans un foyer d'hébergement pour travailleurs africains: sept locataires intoxiqués par les émanations d'un feu de charbon de bois cinq d'entre eux ont succombé." *Le Figaro*, Paris, 3–4 January 1970. BN MICR D-95 1970/01 L 1.15 D.R., "Dans un foyer pour africains à Aubervilliers cinq travailleurs meurent asphyxiés." *Combat*, Paris, 3–4 January 1970. BN MICR D-66 1970/01 MFM J. M. Mercier, "La mort de cinq travailleurs africains à Aubervilliers—qui est responsable?" *Le Monde*, Paris, 4–5 January. ADVM 2018W art. 20 Gauche prolétarienne maoïste, "Tract: Halte aux assassinats d'ouvriers! Justice!" Aubervilliers, January 1970. ADVM 2018W art. 20 Le Collectif marxiste-leniniste martinique de liaison étudiants-travailleurs, "Les travailleurs antillais dans la lutte des travailleurs émigrés en France." January 1970.
20 CANC 19960311 art. 6 Préfet de Police, Aubervilliers, 9 January 1970.
21 Claudine Attias-Donfut, Francois-Charles Wolff, and Catriona Dutreuilh, "The Preferred Burial Location of Persons Born Outside France," *Population* 60, no. 5/6 (December 2005): 699.
22 Adama Doumbia and Naomi Doumbia, *The Way of the Elders: West African Spirituality and Tradition* (Saint Paul, MN: Llewellyn Publications, 2004), 151.
23 Peter Geschiere, "Funerals and Belonging: Different Patterns in South Cameroon," *African Studies Association* 48, no. 2 (September 2005): 47.
24 Doumbia and Doumbia, *The Way of the Elders*, 149–153.
25 Carolyn M. Warner and Manifred W. Wenner, "Religion and the Political Organization of Muslims in Europe," *Perspectives on Politics* 4, no. 3 (September 2006): 461.
26 Catherine Quiminal, *Gens d'ici, gens d'ailleurs: Migrations soninké et transformations villageoises* (Paris: Bourgois, 1991), 20.
27 2018W art. 20 VDM "Des manifestations ont marqué les obsèques des victimes: Cent trente-sept personnes interpellées" January, 1970.
28 19960311 art. 6 Political tract signed by Humanité rouge, Préfet de Police, Aubervilliers, 10 January 1970. Original French: "Aubervilliers, cinq ouvriers africains assassinés par le capital, le proletariat les 'vengera.'"
29 CANC 19960311 art. 6 Préfecture de police (P.M.A.), "La levée des corps des cinq travailleurs africains (quatre sénégalais et un mauritanien) victimes d'une intoxication par oxyde de carbone à Aubervilliers, aura lieu le samedi 10 janvier à 13h 45, à l'Institut Médico-Légal, 2 place Mazas (12ème)." Paris; Préfecture de police, 7 January 1970. CANC 19960311 art. 6 Préfet de Police, Aubervilliers, 9 January 1970. Préfet de Police, Aubervilliers, 10 January 1970. Préfecture de police (P.M.A.), "Divers groupements et associations de travailleurs africains appellent leurs adhérents et sympathisants de province à se rendre aux obsèques des cinq

Africains, décédés accidentellement le 2 janvier dans un grandi clandestin d'Aubervilliers qui auront lieu au cimetière de Thiais, le samedi 10 janvier, à 14 heures." Paris: Préfecture de police, 8 January 1970. BN MICR D-66 1970/01 J. M. Mercier, "La mort de cinq travailleurs africains à Aubervilliers—Qui est responsable?" *Le Monde*, Paris, 4–5 January 1970. BN MICR D-95 1970/01 L 1.15 MFM "Manifestations de solidarité aux cinq morts d'Aubervilliers: samedi, l'heure des obsèques, le siège du CNPF et l'usine dortoir d'Ivry ont été occupés par des manifestants." *Combat*, Paris, 12 January 1970. ADVM 2018W art. 20 "Des manifestations ont marqué les obsèques des victimes: cent trente-sept personnes interpellées." January 1970. ADVM 2018W art. 20 Préfecture de police, "Les obsèques des cinq travailleurs africains décédés accidentellement à Aubervilliers (Seine-Saint-Denis), dans la nuit du lère au 2 janvier, se sont déroulées le 10 janvier dans l'après-midi et ont été marqués par quelques incidents provoqués par des jeunes gauchistes." 10 January 1970. BN MICR D-66 1970/01 "Après le drame du 'foyer' d'Aubervilliers: Des manifestations ont marqué les obsèques des victimes. Cent trente-sept personnes interpellées." *Le Monde*, Paris, 13 January 1970.

30 Kristin Ross, *May '68 and its Afterlives* (Chicago and London: University of Chicago Press, 2002), 41.
31 Ibid.
32 Gordon, *Immigrants and Intellectuals*, 10; Ross, *May '68 and its Afterlives*, 42.
33 Ross, *May '68 and its Afterlives*, 41; Philippe Buton, "Inventing a Memory on the Extreme Left" in Jackson, et al., eds., *May 68*, 61–63, 70.
34 BN MICR D-66 1970/01 "Après le drame du 'foyer' d'Aubervilliers: Des manifestations ont marqué les obsèques des victimes: cent trente-sept personnes interpellées." *Le Monde*, Paris, 13 January 1970. Original French: "Les prorietaires gérants de foyers ne sont pas les seuls responsables ... Il est inexact de dire que la main d'oeuvre africaine n'est pas qualifiée. Les Africains ne savent souvent ni lire ni écrire, mais ils ont une qualification de mécanicien chauffeur, électricien, cuisinier ... Mais on se refuse à les utiliser au niveau de leur qualification pour les enfermer dans un travail que les Français ne veulent plus faire."
35 Michelle C. Johnson, "Death and the Left Hand: Islam, Gender, and 'Proper' Mandinga Funerary Custom in Guinea-Bissau and Portugal," *African Studies Association* 52, no. 2 (September 2009): 97–98.
36 Johnson, "Death and the Left Hand," 97–98.
37 Sjaak Van der Geest, "Between Death and Funeral: Mortuaries and the Exploitation of Liminality in Kwahu, Ghana," *Africa: Journal of the International African Institute* 76, no. 4 (2006): 487.
38 Linda Sun Crowder, "Chinese Funerals in San Francisco Chinatown: American Chinese Expressions in Mortuary Ritual Performance," *The Journal of American Folklore* 113, no. 450 (Autumn 2000): 451–463.
39 Johnson, "Death and the Left Hand," 103–104.
40 Johnson, "Death and the Left Hand," 104; Manchuelle, *Willing Migrants*, 118–145.
41 Geschiere, "Funerals and Belonging," 48–50.
42 Verdery, *The Political Lives of Dead Bodies*, 42.
43 Geschiere, "Funerals and Belonging," 47.
44 Rosemarie Van Den Breemer, "The French and Dutch Muslim Parcel Compared: An Institutionalist Account of Religious Governance and Secularism on the Cemetery," Politicologen Etmaal, Leuven, 27–28 May 2010.
45 Rosemarie Van Den Breemer and Marcel Maussen, "On the Viability of State-Church Models: Muslim Burial and Mosque-Building in France and the Netherlands," *Journal of Immigrant and Refugee Studies* (11 September 2012): 284.
46 Ibid.

47 Doumbia and Doumbia. *The Way of the Elders*, 149–153.
48 Ibid.
49 A. J. Shermen, “Insider Outsiders,” *New England Review* 24, no. 3 (Summer 2003): 171; Juliette Nunez, “La gestion publique des espaces confessionnels des cimetières de la Ville de Paris: l’exemple du culte musulman (1857–1957),” *Le mouvement social* no. 237 (December 2011): 13–14; Soraya El Alaoui, “L’espace funéraire de Bobigny: du cimetière aux carrés musulmans (1934–2006),” *Revue européenne des migrations internationales* 28, no. 3 (1 September 2012): 27–49.
50 Quiminal, *Gens d’ici, gens*, 20; Verdery, *The Political Lives of Dead Bodies*, 41–43.
51 Naomi Davidson, *Only Muslim: Embodying Islam in Twentieth-Century France* (Ithaca: Cornell University Press, 2012), 63.
52 Ibid.
53 For the Algerian case, see Amelia Lyons, *The Civilizing Mission in the Metropole: Algerian Families and the French Welfare State during Decolonization* (Stanford: Stanford University Press, 2013), especially pages 1–16 and 81–114.
54 For perhaps the most famous example of state violence against Algerian immigrants, see Jim House and Neil MacMaster, *Paris 1961: Algerians, State Terror, and Memory* (Oxford; New York: Oxford University Press, 2006). For a look at the impact of the Algerian war in France, see Linda Amiri, *La bataille de France: La guerre d’Algérie en metropole* (Paris: R. Laffont, 2004).
55 2018W art. 20 VDM “Des manifestations ont marqué les obsèques des victimes: Cent trente-sept personnes interpellées” January, 1970.
56 2018W art. 20 VDM “Tract: Des morts à Ivry?” Ivry, January 1970. Original French: “HABITANTS d’IVRY ne laissons pas un assassinat comme celui d’Aubervilliers se produire dans notre ville. Habitants d’Ivry n’attendons pas de nouveaux morts pour réagir!”
57 For discussion of the multiethnic and multiracial dimensions of the May ’68 protests in France and global perceptions of the Civil Rights Movement in the U.S., see Gordon, *Immigrants and Intellectuals* and Mary L. Dudziak, *Cold War Civil Rights: Race and the Image of American Democracy* (Princeton: Princeton University Press, 2000).
58 For more on racial advocacy, see Erik Bleich, “Anti-Racism without Races: Politics and Policy in a ‘Color Blind’ State,” in Herrick Chapman and Laura Levine Frader, eds., *Race in France: Interdisciplinary Perspectives on the Politics of Difference* (New York; Oxford: Berghahn Books, 2004), 162–188; Erik Bleich, *Race Politics in Britain and France: Ideas and Policymaking since the 1960s* (Cambridge: Cambridge University Press, 2003); Jeremy Jennings, “Citizenship, Republicanism and Multiculturalism in Contemporary France,” *British Journal of Political Science* 30, no. 4 (2000): 575–598; Michel Wieviorka, “Contextualizing French Multiculturalism and Racism,” *Theory, Culture & Society* 17, no. 1 (2000): 157–162.
59 Gordon, *Immigrants and Intellectuals*, 39.
60 Ruth Ginio, *The French Army and its Africa Soldiers: The Years of Decolonization* (Lincoln: University of Nebraska Press, 2017), xvii.
61 VDM 2018W art. 20 Comité d’action de la région parisienne, “Aubervilliers n’est pas un accident! C’est un assassinat!” January 1970. Original French: “Aubervilliers n’est pas un accident, c’est un assassinat” and “Qui est responsable?”
62 CANC 19960311 art. 6 Préfet de Police, Aubervilliers, 9 January 1970. Préfet de Police, Aubervilliers, 10 January 1970. BN MICR D-95 1970/01 L 1.15 MFM “Manifestations de solidarité aux cinq morts d’Aubervilliers: samedi, l’heure des obsèques par des manifestants.” *Combat*, Paris, 12 January 1970. ADVM 2018W art. 20 “Des manifestations ont marqué les obsèques des victimes: cent trente-sept personnes interpellées.” January 1970. ADVM 2018W art. 20 Gauche Prolétarienne maoïste, “Tract: Halte aux assassinats d’ouvriers! Justice!”

Aubervilliers, January 1970. ADVM 2018W art. 20 Préfecture de police, "Des éléments d'extrême gauche de tendance pro-chinoise, ont tenté une action, hier, 10 janvier, en faveur des travailleurs africains ..." 11 January 1970. ADVM 2018W art. 20 Préfecture de police, "Les obsèques des cinq travailleurs africains décédés accidentellement à Aubervilliers (Seine-Saint-Denis), dans la nuit du 1er au 2 janvier, se sont déroulées le 10 janvier dans l'après-midi et ont été marquées par quelques incidents provoqués par des jeunes gauchistes." 10 January 1970. BN MICR D-66 L 1.15 MFM Jean Pierre Quelin, "De la mort de cinq Maliens à l'occupation du CNPF: une peine de prison ferme est requise contre un architecte inculpé de violence et rébellion." *Le Monde*, Paris, 25 February 1970.

63 ANC 19960311 art. 6 Préfet de Police, Aubervilliers, 10 January 1970.

64 Philippe Buton defines Maoists as "the political groups formed after the open breach between the Soviet Union and China in 1963." Philippe Buton, "Inventing a Memory on the Extreme Left," 59.

65 CANC 19960311 art. 6 Préfecture de police, "Un tract émanant de la Gauche Prolétarienne maoïste et concernant les problèmes des foyers africains d'Aubervilliers et d'Ivry, a été distribue, hier 20 janvier, a 6h55, a l'entree des établissements Danone au Plesissis-Robinson (Hauts-de-Seine)." Paris, 21 January 1971.

66 CAN 19960311 art. 6 Préfet de Police, Aubervilliers, 10 janvier 1970.

67 Dudziak, *Cold War Civil Rights*, 3–17.

68 ADVM 2018W art. 20 "Tract: Des morts à Ivry?" Ivry, January 1970. CANC 19960311 art. 6 Préfet de Police, Aubervilliers, 10 January 1970. ADVM 2018W art. 20 Comité d'action de la région parisienne, "Tract: Aubervilliers n'est pas un accident! C'est un assassinat!" Aubervilliers, January 1970. ADVM 2018W art. 20 Gauche Prolétarienne maoïste, "Tract: Halte aux assassinats d'ouvriers! Justice!" Aubervilliers, January 1970. CANC 19960311 art. 6 "Tract 2: Après la mort de cinq travailleurs africains immigrés à Ivry une diversion policière et gauchiste pour esquiver les responsables du pouvoir et du patronat." Aubervilliers, January 1970.

69 Jean-Pierre N' Diaye, *Négriers modernes: les travailleurs noirs en France* (Paris: Présence Africaine, 1970), 122.

70 BN MICR D-95 1970/01 L 1.15 "Manifestations de solidarité aux cinq morts d'Aubervilliers: samedi, l'heure des obsèques, le siège du CNPF et l'usine dortoir d'Ivry ont été occupés par des manifestants." *Combat*, Paris, 12 January 1970. BN MICR D-66 1970/01 "Après le drame du 'foyer' d'Aubervilliers: des manifestations ont marqué les obsèques des victimes cent trente-sept personnes interpellées." *Le Monde*, Paris, 13 January 1970. ADVM 2018W art. 20 Préfecture de police, "Des éléments d'extrême gauche de tendance pro-chinoise, ont tenté une action, hier, 10 janvier, en faveur des travailleurs africains ..." Ivry, 11 January 1970. ADVM 2018W art. 20 C.G.T. du Val-de-Marne, "Face à la honteuse et criminelle exploitation des travailleurs africains il faut dénoncer les responsables et cesser les manœuvres de diversion et de provocation." Ivry sur Seine, January 1970. ADVM 2018W art. 20 Municipalité les séctions communistes d'Ivry, "Tract: Après la mort de cinq travailleurs africains immigrés à Ivry ... une diversion policière et gauchiste pour esquiver les responsabilités du pouvoir et du patronat." Ivry, January 1970.

71 Belinda Davis, "What's Left?: Popular Political Participation in Postwar Europe," *American Historical Review* 113, no. 2 (April 2008): 363–390. Peter Bloom, "Beur Cinema and the Politics of Location: French Immigration Politics and the Naming of a Film Movement," in Ella Shohat and Robert Stam, eds., *Multiculturalism, Postcoloniality, and Transnational Media* (New Brunswick: Rutgers University Press, 2003), 44–62.

72 ADVM 2018W art. 20 André Maguer, Commissariat principal du 24ème arrondissement to Monsieur le Directeur général de la police municipal Ivry sur

Seine, 10 January 1970. "Des manifestations ont marqué les obsèques des victimes: cent trente-sept personnes interpellées." January 1970. Préfecture de police, "Tracts + des militants de la Gauche Prolétarienne ont distribué un tract au foyer pour travailleurs africains d'Ivry sur Seine (Val-de-Marne)." Ivry, 14 January 1970. Préfecture de police, "Des elements d'extrême gauche de tendance pro-chinoise ont tenté une action, hier, 10 janvier, en faveur des travailleurs africains …" 11 January 1970. "Dans le cadre des manifestations organisées par la 'Gauche Prolétarienne' à l'occasion des funérailles des cinq ouvriers africains décédés …" 12 January 1970. BN MICR D-66 L 1.15 O "Dans la presse française." *Le Monde*, Paris, 13 January 1970. BN MICR D-95 1970/01 L 1.15 "Manifestations de solidarité aux cinq morts d'Aubervilliers: samedi, l'heure des obsèques, le siège du CNPF et l'usine dortoir d'Ivry ont été occupés par des manifestants." *Combat*, Paris, 12 January 1970. BN MICR D-66 1970/01 "Après le drame du 'foyer' d'Aubervilliers: des manifestations ont marqué les obsèques des victimes cent trente-sept personnes interpellées." *Le Monde*, Paris, 13 January 1970.

73 CANC 19960311 art. 6 Préfet de Police, Aubervilliers, 9 January 1970. Préfecture de police, Tract from the Gauche prolétarienne, January 1970. ADVM 2018W art. 20 "Des manifestations ont marqué les obsèques des victimes: cent trente-sept personnes interpellées." January, 1970. Comité d'Action de la Région parisienne, "Tract: Aubervilliers n'est pas un accident! C'est un assassinat!' Aubervilliers, January 1970. CANC 19960311 art. 6 Préfecture de police, "Un tract, émanant de la Gauche Prolétarienne maoïste et concernant les problèmes des foyers africains d'Aubervilliers et d'Ivry, a été distribué, hier 20 janvier, à l'entrée des établissements Danone au Pleissis-Robinson (Hauts-de-Seine)." Paris: Préfecture de police, 21 January 1970. ADVM 2018W art. 20 Préfecture de police, "Tracts + Des militants de la Gauche Prolétarienne ont distribué un tract au foyer pour travailleurs africains d'Ivry sur Seine (Val-de-Marne), dans lequel il est annoncé la tenu d'une permanence, tous les jours, de 18 heures à 20 heures, devant la porte de l'établissement." Ivry, 14 January 1970. Gauche prolétarienne, "Tract: Halt aux assassinats d'ouvriers! Justice!" Aubervilliers, January 1970. Claude Lecompte, "Les travailleurs africains d'Ivry ont quitté l'usine-dortoir pour vivre dans des foyers." *L'Humanité*, Paris, 10 December 1970. "Après Aubervilliers. Faut-il des morts à Ivry?" 19960311 art. 6 Gauche prolétarienne, supplément à *La Cause du peuple*, Tract, Aubervilliers, 14 January 1970.

74 Gordon, *Immigrants and Intellectuals*, 26.

75 Centre d'études anti-impérialistes, *Les immigrés: contribution à l'histoire politique de l'immigration en France* (Paris: Stock, 1975), 237.

76 CANC 19960311 art. 6 Préfet de Police, Aubervilliers, 9 January 1970. Préfecture de police, tract from the Gauche Prolétarienne, January 1970. ADVM 2018W art. 20 "Des manifestations ont marqué les obsèques des victimes: cent trente-sept personnes interpellées." January, 1970. Comité d'action de la région parisienne, "Tract: Aubervilliers n'est pas un accident! C'est un assassinat!' Aubervilliers, January 1970. CANC 19960311 art. 6 Préfecture de police, "Un tract, émanant de la Gauche Prolétarienne maoïste et concernant les problèmes des foyers africains d'Aubervilliers et d'Ivry, a été distribué, hier 20 janvier, à l'entrée des établissements Danone au Pleissis-Robinson (Hauts-de-Seine)." Paris: Préfecture de police, 21 January 1970. ADVM 2018W art. 20 Préfecture de police, "Tracts + Des militants de la Gauche Prolétarienne ont distribué un tract au foyer pour travailleurs africains d'Ivry sur Seine (Val-de-Marne), dans lequel il est annoncé la tenu d'une permanence, tous les jours, de 18 heures à 20 heures, devant la porte de l'établissement." Ivry, 14 January 1970. Gauche prolétarienne, "Tract: Halt aux assassinats d'ouvriers! Justice!" Aubervilliers, January 1970. Claude Lecompte, "Les travailleurs africains d'Ivry ont quitté l'usine-dortoir pour vivre

dans des foyers." *L'Humanité*, Paris, 10 December 1970. "Après Aubervilliers Faut-il des morts à Ivry." 19960311 art. 6 Gauche prolétarienne, supplément à *La Cause du peuple*, Tract, Aubervilliers, 14 January 1970.

77 BN MICR D-66 1970/01 L.15 Michel Leiris, "Un témoignage: Chez les maliens d'Ivry sur Seine." *Le Monde*, Paris, 13 January 1970. Original French: "dangers qui menacent les travailleurs maliens, autrement dit des risques d'une catastrophe analogue à celle d'Aubervilliers."

78 CANC 19810221 art. 4 Pierre Lanier, Président d'accueil et rencontres secrétariat social de la région lyonnaise/Chronique sociale de France, "Travailleurs étrangers et responsabilités collectives." Lyon: Accueil et rencontres, 1970. BN MICR D-66 1970/01 L.15 Michel Leiris, "Un témoignage: Chez les Maliens d'Ivry sur Seine." *Le Monde*, Paris, 13 January 1970.

79 ADVM 2018W art. 20 "Des manifestations ont marqué les obsèques des victimes: cent trente-sept personnes interpellées." January, 1970. BN MICR D-66 1970/01 "Après le drame du 'foyer' d'Aubervilliers: des manifestations ont marqué les obsèques des victimes: cent trente-sept personnes interpellées." *Le Monde*, Paris, 13 January 1970. ADVM 2018W art. 20 Préfecture de police, "Les obsèques des cinq travailleurs africains décédés accidentellement à Aubervilliers (Seine-Saint-Denis), dans la nuit du 1er au 2 janvier, se sont déroulées le 10 janvier dans l'après-midi et ont été marquées par quelques incidents provoqués par des jeunes gauchistes." 10 January 1970.

80 Gordon, *Immigrants and Intellectuals*, 6.

81 Ibid., 28.

82 Ibid., 32–33.

83 Robert J. C. Young, "Preface" in Jean-Paul Sartre, *Colonialism and Neocolonialism* trans. Azzedine Haddour, Steve Brewer, and Terry McWilliams (London and New York: Routledge, 2001), xvi–xvii. For one of his most famous analyses of colonialism, see Sartre's preface to Frantz Fanon, *The Wretched of the Earth* (Paris: Présence Africaine, 1963).

84 BN MICR D-95 1970/01 L 1.15 MFM "Manifestations de solidarité aux cinq morts d'Aubervilliers: samedi, l'heure des obsèques, le siège du CNPF et l'usine dortoir d'Ivry ont été occupés par des manifestants." *Combat*, Paris, 12 January 1970. Original French: "La mort des travailleurs africains illustre le scandale de la société française qui utilise à son profit une main d'œuvre sous payée. Il faut réveiller l'opinion publique contre un certain racisme qui conduit à l'indifférence. L'utilisation de la main d'œuvre africaine est une forme de colonialisme interne, souhaitons que du malheur sort une situation meilleure et que l'opinion publique soit enfin alertée sur un scandale qui doit finir."

85 For scholarship on the relationship between Jean-Paul Sartre, existentialism, and Marxism, see Jean-Paul Sartre, *Between Existentialism and Marxism* trans. John Mathews (New York: Pantheon Books, 1974); Thomas R. Flynn, *Sartre and Marxist Existentialism: The Test Case of Collective Responsibility* (Chicago and London: The University of Chicago Press, 1984); Tony Judt, *Past Imperfect: French Intellectuals, 1944–1956* (Berkeley: University of California Press), 1992; Frederic Jameson, *Marxism and Form: Twentieth-Century Dialectical Theories of Literature* (Princeton: Princeton University Press, 1971); Raymond Williams, *Marxism and Literature* (Oxford; New York: Oxford University Press, 1977); Pietro Chiodi, *Sartre and Marxism* trans. Kate Soper (New Jersey, NJ: Humanities Press, 1976).

86 Young in Sartre, *Colonialism and Neocolonialism*, viii–x, xx; Gordon, *Immigrants and Intellectuals*, 28.

87 Young, "Preface" in Sartre, *Colonialism and Neocolonialism*, viii–x, xx.

88 Chiodi, *Sartre and Marxism*, 1. Simone de Beauvoir, *Force of Circumstance* (New York: G.P. Putnum's Sons, 1965), 5.

89 Chiodi, *Sartre and Marxism*, 1
90 Sartre, *Between Existentialism and Marxism*, 123.
91 Young, "Preface" in Sartre, *Colonialism and Neocolonialism*, viii–x, xx.
92 BN MICR D-66 L1.15 0 MFM "Dans la presse française." *Le Monde*, Paris, 13 January 1970. Bibliothèque nationale MICR D-95 1970/01 L 1.15 Maurice Clavel, "Les conditions de vie et de mort." *Combat*, Paris, 12 January 1970. Original French : "contre les conditions de vie et de mort des travailleurs immigrés."
93 BN MICR D-66 1970/01 "Après le drame du 'foyer' d'Aubervilliers: Des manifestations ont marqué les obsèques des victimes: cent trent-sept personnes interpellés." *Le Monde*, Paris, 13 January 1970. Original French: "l'arrêt immédiat des poursuites engagées contre les participants à une action dont l'unique but était de dénoncer avec éclat un scandale entretenu depuis longtemps par le pouvoir" and "elle continuera à soutenir la lutte qu'ils ont entreprise, avec d'autres, pour y mettre un terme, à Ivry, comme ailleurs."
94 CANC 19960311 art. 6 Préfet de Police, Aubervilliers, 10 January 1970. CANC 19960311 art. 6 Préfecture de police (P.M.A.), "Divers groupements et associations de travailleurs africains appellent leurs adhérents et sympathisants de province à se rendre aux obsèques des cinq Africains, décédés accidentellement le 2 janvier dans un garni clandestin d'Aubervilliers qui auront lieu au cimetière de Thiais, le samedi 10 janvier, à 14 heures." Paris: Préfecture de police, 8 January 1970. BN MICR D-95 1970/01 L 1.15 MFM "Manifestations de solidarité aux cinq morts d'Aubervilliers: samedi, l'heure des obsèques, le siège du CNPF et l'usine dortoir d'Ivry ont été occupés par des manifestants." *Combat*, Paris, 12 January 1970. "Après le drame du 'foyer' d'Aubervilliers: Des manifestations ont marqué les obsèques des victimes cent trente-sept personnes interpellées." *Le Monde*, Paris, 13 January 1970. CANC19960311 art. 6 Préfet de Police, Aubervilliers, 9 January 1970. Centre des archives nationales contemporaines. Préfecture de police (P.M.A.), "La levée des corps des cinq travailleurs africains (quatre sénégalais et un mauritanien) victimes d'une intoxication par oxyde de carbone à Aubervilliers, à l'Institut Médico-Légal, 2 place Mazas (12ème)." Paris: Préfecture de police, January 1970.
95 See for example, Clifford Rosenberg, *Policing Paris: The Origins of Modern Immigration Control between the Wars* (Ithaca and London: Cornell University Press, 2006).

4 Policing the postcolonial order

In light of the African immigrant community's increasingly visible politicization across the 1960s and into the 1970s, it is not surprising that the Fifth Republic's surveillance apparatus turned its attention to this group.[1] African workers were under surveillance in France dating back to the interwar period, as were immigrant groups from Europe and the colonies. Yet the policing of African immigrants across the 1960s looked different than in the colonies or for other immigrant groups across the twentieth century. This was not necessarily the repressive surveillance found in AOF.[2] Nor was this surveillance intended specifically to prevent crime, as we see detailed by Clifford Rosenberg in his book on the interwar period.[3] There was an important social welfare element to the state's surveillance of this immigrant group, one that shaped policies on health, housing, education, and other programs into the 1970s and beyond.

Yet police surveillance reveals the level of anxiety caused by the idea of politically active African immigrants after decolonization. Much of the French state's surveillance focused on understanding, tracking, and eventually slowing the arrival of African workers after 1960, while grappling with the consequences of what was referred to by officials as the "*problème noir*" or "black problem," a racially charged term used to refer to the challenges presented African immigration overall. Analyzing how the French surveyed, observed, and monitored the postcolonial African immigrant community makes evident the ways in which practices within the colonial and postcolonial contexts overlapped.[4]

After 1960, the French state blended colonial and metropolitan surveillance tactics to monitor African immigrants, making them understandable, visible, and ultimately, as Michel Foucault argues, controllable.[5] Styles of surveillance shifted as well, from more of an ethnographic approach in the early 1960s, motivated in part by a desire to better know this population, to one that was much more alarmist by the late 1960s and early 1970s, focusing on gauging politicization and political influences, particularly from the Left. Surveillance was also done with an eye toward informing social welfare initiatives, including the opening of the *Centre Bossuet* and the implementation of the anti-slum campaign. This meant that there were multiple forms of surveillance occurring simulteanously: repressive political surveillance and surveillance designed to support and bolster social welfare services. Policies based on this surveillance sought to contain African workers spatially, geographically, and physically within the urban realm. Enacting control over immigrant communities proved vitally important to French immigration policy across the twentieth century and often dovetailed with the development of the colonial state abroad, as scholars such as Rosenberg and Martin Thomas have shown.[6]

This chapter examines how the French state watched African immigrants and the ways in which this monitoring was influenced by factors such as immigrant political activism, the Cold War, discourse on international human rights, and decolonization and independence. The surveillance of African immigrants reflected a shift in French immigration policy as the state incorporated new and existing approaches from the colonial and metropolitan contexts to monitoring and tracking immigrant populations. Surveillance changed over the course of the 1960s, from an effort to examine the African immigrant population to one increasingly focused on thwarting potential politicization. Officials paid more and more attention to the probability of leftist political influence and its potentially destabilizing effects, not only on the African immigrant community but also on the surrounding political and social sphere, especially in the wake of protests in Ivry and Aubervilliers. Yet the surveillance of African immigrants went beyond political repression. It shaped the social welfare policies enacted by the French state, which surveyed the social and political spheres navigated by African workers. These developments have implications for contemporary debates about surveillance, police monitoring, and the relationship between police, the state and various communities, including from the standpoint of racial profiling.

History of surveillance and policing

The tracking of African immigrant populations after decolonization continued an important nineteenth- and twentieth-century trend toward the meticulous codification of populations within nation-states and empires. The precedent for tracking colonial subjects and foreign nationals living and working in metropolitan France emerged during the colonial era and this approach to surveillance continued well into the postwar period. With the introduction of the Nationality Code of November 2, 1945, just after World War Two's end, and the categories that accompanied it, the Ministry of the Interior continued its role as the dominant force in the surveillance of foreign populations, determining who belonged within the postwar nation-state, which was still in control of a colonial empire.[7] By 1950, as Gérard Noiriel argues, "the suspicion in regard to immigrants had become systematic."[8] The postwar era's system of surveillance was built upon that established during the interwar period. Throughout the 1920s and 1930s, the Ministry of the Interior monitored African workers, nationalists, artists, and intellectuals, just as they did residents from all over the world. These various impulses converged after decolonization as the same agency carefully watched, surveyed, monitored, and even infiltrated African immigrant associations, including the UGTSF, while putting grassroots political activists such as Sally N'Dongo under close police observation. Yet officials declined to acknowledge the long-standing tradition of African migration to France following independence. Maurice Grimaud, writing for the *Préfet de Police* in 1969, compared African to Algerian immigrants: "in contrast to Algerian immigration, which began before the war of 1914–1918, the establishment of populations originating from black Africa in the former Seine department is a relatively recent development."[9] Although the two groups circulated to and from France throughout the first half of the twentieth century, the historical origins of African immigration remained inconspicuous.

Other historical forces shaped the state's surveillance of immigrant populations as well. As the Fourth Republic gave way to the Fifth Republic, French society continued to distance itself from and grapple with the legacy of the Vichy regime. One could detect, though, important continuities between how authorities tracked and monitored immigrants and other "suspicious populations" under the Third Republic and during World War Two and the approaches taken by the Fourth and Fifth Republics in the postwar era. Tactics used in the nineteenth century—from identifying and tracking "problematic" individuals to opening and reading mail—continued well into the twentieth century and across political regimes.[10] In regard to African immigrant workers in particular, the core of the French state's surveillance efforts focused not only on slowing their arrival but also on containing their presence geographically within urban areas. Across regimes with vastly different political orientations, the control of immigration and of immigrants themselves remained an important continuity. In the era of decolonization and within the context of postwar, Cold War tensions, this kind of control became even more urgent within state policy. As early as 1962, one official in a letter to the *Préfet du Seine* emphasized the need to "put in place a system of immigration control."[11] Controlling African immigration remained an important goal within official surveillance early on after decolonization.

Postcolonial surveillance: continuities with colonial tactics

In postwar AOF, the context of colonial governance changed significantly following the Brazzaville Conference of 1944 and the introduction of the "French Union" in 1946.[12] The extension of citizenship and the rights and privileges that accompanied it was an important aspect of this reorientation. Alongside these reforms, though, Frederick Cooper explains that colonial authorities carried into the postwar era their propensity for monitoring and surveying African colonial residents. As "objects of surveillance and objectified knowledge," Cooper reveals that officials actually increased their surveillance practices in order to amass the kind of understanding instrumental in implementing postwar reforms, including the extension of citizenship for colonial subjects together with the abolition of forced labor through the Lamine Guèye Law.[13] By 1960 and independence in AOF, the out-going colonial regime was experienced in the area of collecting information on African groups.

The surveillance carried out on African immigrants in France after 1960 constituted an important continuation of colonial surveillance in AOF as well as in interwar France of workers and activists from AOF.[14] The surveillance of organizations such as the UGTSF looked much as it did for African organizations during the 1920s and 1930s in France and AOF. Authorities recruited informants who fed information to the police regarding meetings, individuals, and activities. A 1934 report on the *Union des travailleurs nègres* (Union of Black Workers or UTN) in Paris, for example, detailed a November 3 meeting on 57 rue de Charlot with extensive notes on the topics covered, including the group's grave financial situation.[15] In interwar AOF, colonial officials recruited similar kinds of informants while closely monitoring the movements and activities of people deemed "suspicious."[16] Meetings that took place during the 1960s and 1970s attracted similar attention, with informants recruited to relay information about what kinds of topics were covered and who attended.

As the African immigrant community continued to grow in size across the 1960s, it attracted the interest of authorities perplexed by the expanding presence of African workers. What Gary Freeman labels an "unpredictable" postwar and postcolonial migration pattern concerned officials, especially in regard to the arrival of former colonial residents.[17] Between 1963 and 1964, France signed bilateral treaties with Mali, Mauritania, and Senegal, which initiated the regulation of labor migration from these three former colonies.[18] One report on African citizenship following decolonization also intimated that labor migrants from Sub-Saharan Africa posed "social, sanitary, and public order problems."[19]

Several gatherings and events piqued official interest. One in particular took place on October 13, 1964 and involved the communist municipality of Saint-Denis and a meeting that it hosted to "win the sympathy" of several African immigrants residing in the town.[20] The interplay between communist officials and African workers left authorities within the Ministry of the Interior wondering what this might mean more broadly for the Paris region. Earlier that year, officials took note of a meeting held by the *Association des travailleurs maliens en France* (Association of Malian Workers in France or ATMF), documenting its location and the number of people who might attend (estimated at 20) without any reference to political motives or influence.[21] A dinner party hosted by the UGTSF and N'Dongo in January of 1964 also attracted scrutiny, with the *Direction de la réglementation 6e bureau* documenting who attended, for how long, and where. In a speech that night, N'Dongo discussed the difficulties facing African immigrants, from housing to hygiene and illness while highlighting the efforts of *Secours catholique* (Catholic Relief) and other groups in assisting with these challenges. The tone of the surveillance remained measured, while taking a particular interest in the social welfare initiatives undertaken by private French organizations and the UGTSF on behalf of the African community.[22] Authorities went to great lengths to collect documentation produced by various African organizations in France, dating back to the interwar era. A tract produced by the *Union des travailleurs nègres* from the 1930s found its way into police files. Citing the repression of the African diaspora in places such as the U.S. and Germany, the UTN challenged black Africans to "organize ourselves to defend ourselves."[23] Officials continued to collect tracts throughout the 1960s and into the 1970s produced by various African organizations, from the UGTSF to tenants on strike in Ivry, and especially those, like this one, that demonstrated overt politicization and political objectives.

The influence of the civil rights and anti-apartheid movements

Global developments shaped surveillance as well. In their notes and observations, officials wondered whether the U.S. Civil Rights Movement and the struggle to end segregation would have a far-reaching effect. The question remained of whether France's growing black population could be prone to radicalization through the U.S. example. Officials worried about how such a movement might impact African workers in France. One police report from 1964 expressed anxiety that "black American communists have, in effect, the intention to visit various dormitories throughout the Paris region where Africans live ..."[24] This alarm over the potential influence of black Americans who were supposedly communist and the Civil Rights Movement more broadly intersected with a growing global concern over apartheid, resistance to the regime in South Africa carried out by organizations such as the African National Congress (ANC), growing international protest over the regime's treatment of the black population there, and the increasingly violent clashes that ensued.[25]

Concerns over these movements percolated in France. A 1965 report, for example, documented the participation of several different groups in an event intended to raise awareness around apartheid. In attendance were members of several different organizations, including the *Association pour la coopération franco-africaine* (Association for Franco-African Cooperation), the *Comité anti-apartheid* (Anti-Apartheid Committee), the *Ligue des droits de l'homme* (League for the Rights of Man), the *Ligue internationale contre l'antisémitisme et le racisme* (International League against Anti-Semitism and Racism), and the *Mouvement contre le racisme, l'antisémitisme et pour la paix* (Movement against Racism and Anti-Semitism and for Peace or MRAP). Several representatives from religious organizations as well as the PCF and the CGT were also in attendance. Information was distributed concerning racially discriminatory legislation in South Africa. Participants unanimously adopted a resolution condemning all forms of discrimination and planned to participate in a worldwide protest on behalf of political prisoners in Africa. A day of prayer would also be held in various churches in opposition to the apartheid regime.[26] While this meeting remained focused on peaceful means of demonstration and protest, the question remained of whether African workers might mobilize themselves politically based on the models presented by the Civil Rights and anti-apartheid movements. What would be the consequences of this radicalization? Could this heightened political consciousness and activism spill over into postcolonial France and inspire political activism among African workers, who were already organizing themselves into unions? These concerns pushed officials to more intensely monitor and track African workers generally and the organizations and individuals that advocated for them.[27]

The rationale for surveillance

While expressing concerns about the local impact of what was seen as an increasingly globalized movement for civil rights, another key factor fueling increasing levels of surveillance was the sense that authorities claimed to know very little about African workers and had no real policies, protocols, or programs in place to assist this population. A 1964 report in the *Journal Officiel* explained that, "... the problem of African workers in France is not well understood (number, origin, working conditions) and the authorities have not given it a specific character."[28] This was, in part, because various organizations within the French state were more wholly focused on Algerian workers and their families. As Amelia Lyons has shown, postwar social welfare policies enacted to address the arrival of Algerian workers and their families were built upon the scaffolding of French colonialism and the "civilizing mission" embedded within it. Much the same could be said for state policies designed to address the housing, health care, and educational needs of workers from Sub-Saharan Africa. Yet by 1964, one official noted that in regard to African immigrants, "The organization of reception is currently insufficient."[29] The resources and programs necessary to address the needs of the growing African population were not in place or were based on those intended for other immigrant groups. While non-western immigration is often presented as a challenge to French republicanism, the state itself put little in the way of resources toward integrating African workers. Often, they labeled them "unassimilable" and questioned their ability to integrate into French society. In a 1962 letter to the Préfet du Seine, J. P. Dennaud categorized African workers as "an inassimilable sub-proletariat."[30] In 1963, a Ministry of the Interior report explained that:

> [a] minority of Africans is integrated into the metropolitan population. This minority has been a fixed presence in France for several years and they have found suitable employment and are often married. But a large

> proportion of black workers residing in our country maintain a completely communitarian lifestyle. Whether housed in hotels, in apartment buildings or in 'dormitories', this essentially male population is grouped by ethnic affinity, forming nuclei of the same nationality, and religion, belonging to the same tribe, often the same village ... The life of these groups is organized in a closed circuit, with few established relationships with the outside world or with other groups.[31]

Officials deemed the "communitarian lifestyle" that they observed among African immigrants an impediment to integration into French society.

This phrase was part of a long-standing tradition of not only "othering" minority groups and subordinating them racially, ethnically, and culturally but of also deeming them a "problem" in various countries throughout the world. Nation-states under non-democratic and democratic regimes conceptualized minority groups as "problems" for the state to solve through various measures, including relocation, segregation, assimilation, integration, or in the case of the Third Reich during World War Two, extermination. In the French case, it was African immigration that posed a "black problem." A report entitled "A Study of the Black Problem in the Paris Region," written by a French sociologist and commissioned by the *Préfecture de la Seine* in the mid-1960s, explained that "from the French point of view, the (black) problem is three-fold: the problem of public order, the problem of public health, (and) the problem of public morality."[32] This language reveals the ways in which racialized conceptualizations of African colonial subjects, and the emphasis placed on assimilation within colonial citizenship laws prior to World War Two shaped postcolonial views of this immigrant group within the context of long-standing international conceptualizations of race and ethnicity.

The effort to better understand African immigrants played a key role in driving the surveillance of African immigrants, just as it did for that of colonial populations throughout the French empire. As Martin Thomas argues, surveillance and information gathering played key roles in colonial policy formation.[33] In asking how it was the colonial governments made the decisions that they did in terms of policy making, Thomas explains that it was not only politics, racial assumptions, and intellectual formation that played a role but also "the intelligence available to those in authority."[34] This was also the case in the early 1960s as officials scrambled to learn more about a migratory pattern that seemingly caught them by surprise. The surveillance of African workers residing throughout France in the postcolonial era helped to decipher this immigrant population for authorities. What initially remained a puzzling migratory pattern became knowable and understandable and therefore controllable through extensive monitoring and observation.[35] Administrators working within the Ministry of the Interior tried to grasp just how many African workers were living in the Paris region and other urban areas throughout France. In commissioning reports referencing the "*problème noir*," officials grappled with what, exactly, this meant for France, a country that has historically received immigrants without much of an identity or collective memory of doing so. The colonial origins of this migration pattern seemed elusive to those observing it.[36]

Surveillance tactics and policing

With these concerns in mind, several divisions within the Ministry of the Interior, including the *Préfecture de police*, the *Sûreté nationale* (National Security), and the *Service des affaires musulmanes* (Department of Muslim Affairs) monitored and observed African workers with increasing intensity. In AOF and other areas of the French empire, scholars interpret even the seemingly inconspicuous collection of data as a more distant and insidious form of surveillance done in support of policies to create physical, racial, and sexual separation between colonial subjects and Europeans living in the colonies and in colonial cities such as Dakar.[37] Built upon assumptions of inferiority, colonial empires required systems through which to monitor populations that were not part of a participatory democracy and had not agreed to European subjugation. With that developed, as Thomas argues, "a violent and self-destructive dynamic to colonial empire."[38]

Sometimes, though, surveillance became personal. The Ministry of the Interior and the police apparatus within it targeted particular members of the African immigrant community who seemed to hold outsized influence over others politically, socially, and even religiously. N'Dongo, for example, was monitored throughout the 1960s and into the 1970s, especially after he rose to prominence through the UGTSF. Officials knew where he lived, to whom he was married, and the places that he visited on a daily, weekly, and monthly basis. As early as 1964, when the UGTSF was in the process of opening an all-African dormitory, officials debated denying official permission for the project. In a letter, an official within the Muslim Affairs Service reasoned that "the decision was made not to grant official funds to dormitories created and managed by foreign nationals as they might raise problems related to public order that would be difficult to solve."[39] Beyond initiatives in France, they also monitored N'Dongo's trips to Senegal. In September of 1965, for example, N'Dongo took a well-documented trip to Dakar, the purpose of which kept officials speculating in their correspondence. The French embassy in Senegal took note of his arrival as well.[40] Officials hoped that in better knowing individuals such as N'Dongo and their political and social connections, they could control or at least contain them. In N'Dongo's case, though, his influence only seemed to grow. By 1973, the Swiss Section of the *Ligue marxiste révolutionnaire* (Marxist Revolutionary League or LMR) invited N'Dongo to attend a conference titled "Immigration in France." His pending visit to Switzerland captivated authorities. N'Dongo's interactions with the LMR caused alarm for officials monitoring him and who, by this point, also noted his affiliation with syndicalist organizations and leftist political parties in France.[41]

Yet early studies of the African community focused more on the general characteristics of postcolonial migration to France, providing statistics concerning the overall population, its composition, and its location. Rarely did officials include individual names or details regarding specific immigrants, as they focused on the migratory group as a whole. This early postcolonial monitoring set out, as one 1963 report by the *Préfecture de police* indicated, to determine "the number and division in the Paris region of workers originating from our former colonial possessions in black Africa."[42] As a result, the information collected seemed distant in tone and often represented African immigration as a uniform phenomenon lacking in individual nuances, stories, or perspectives, continuing a colonial tendency to portray Africans as such. Authorities watched African workers' residences and workplaces as well the associations that assisted them and the bars and restaurants where they congregated. They also perused academic journals—including *Cahiers nord-africains*, later known as *Études sociales nord-africains* (North African Social Studies or ESNA)—trolling for information. One edition of ESNA, titled "Approaches to the problems posed by black migration in France," included articles looking at issues such as disease, unemployment, and social welfare and provided the kind of data and analysis that officials often looked for in scholarly journals. It wound up in the Ministry of the Interior's classified documentation on African immigration.[43] At times, articles debating the origins of this migration pattern appeared in publications such as *France-Eurafrique*. Robert Canton, the president of AFTAM (*Association pour la formation technique de base des Africains et Malgaches résident en France*), discussed the internal migrations undertaken by Soninké, which he referred to using the colonial term ("Sarakolé"), as a means of explaining what he deemed the "massive arrival" of African workers from that same region after 1959.[44] His contribution and that of others struck a concerned tone, pointing to the idea of African migration as a "problem" posed to the French state and to French society more broadly.

The idea of politically connected African visitors exposing elements of this problem, especially in the realm of housing, proved especially concerning. As early as 1964, the Ministry of the Interior reported on a visit to France by a nephew of Senegalese President Léopold Senghor. The nephew "visited several African dormitories and was extremely surprised by the precarious living conditions of Senegalese workers."[45] In reporting on this visit via official correspondence, Jacques Aubert of the *Services des statuts des étrangers et des groupements étrangers* (Legal Status Service for Foreigners and Groups of Foreigners) indicated that he understood the potential political ramifications for Franco-Senegalese relations should the Senegalese government hear directly of the problematic living conditions of its citizens residing in France. In a 1964 letter from the Ministry of the Interior to the Prime Minister, Roger Frey concluded that "immediate action proves essential, particularly with regard to citizens from black African states."[46] Surveillance, social welfare policy, political concerns, and the idea of a "*problème noir*" remained intertwined, even early on in postcolonial migration.

Throughout the early 1960s, officials focused on housing and the issues outlined in ESNA, using them as a lens through which to study and monitor the growing African immigrant community. Areas of inquiry included geographical location, professional qualifications, nationality and ethnic composition, and propensity for politicization. The total number of Africans residing in France and where they lived also became a source of intense interest in the first few years after 1960. As they attempted to measure the overall African population residing in France, authorities within and beyond the Ministry of the Interior evaluated its geographic distribution and population density in provinces and cities throughout France. Observations also indicated the types of housing inhabited by African immigrants, which remained a major source of anxiety for officials throughout the 1960s and into the 1970s. By 1963, the *Sûreté nationale* branch of the Ministry of the Interior indicated that 25,000 Africans were living in the Paris region alone.[47] Many officials expressed concern at the rate at which African immigration to France grew during the early 1960s and hoped to control and contain it. Dating back to the nineteenth century, government officials investigating groups deemed problematic or unruly initially determined where and how they lived. This pattern continued into the early 1960s as reports commissioned by the *Préfecture de police* pinpointed the exact location of African immigrants in Paris and in cities throughout France. Regionally, officials identified the principal provinces of residence as the Seine, the Seine-Maritime, the Bouches-de-Rhône, and Normandy.[48] Cities with the largest population of African residents included Paris, Marseille, Bordeaux, and Rouen.[49]

A key question early on that shaped much of subsequent surveillance efforts was that of how African workers arrived in France in the first place. A sociological report from the mid-1960s attempted to answer this query. Starting with an investigation in Africa, the study found that the railway from Bamako to Dakar played an important role, while migrants also made their way from Bamako to Abidjan, often by truck and without the assistance of the train, the costlier of the two options. Most immigrants passed through Dakar at some point, while others visited, in addition to Abidjan, Konakry, Douala, and other ports, including Monrovia. The possibility of purchasing falsified identity papers often presented itself in port towns. From there, migrants took ferries from Dakar and Abidjan to Marseille and Bordeaux. Several companies ran these ferries, from the *Compagnie Paquet* to the *Compagnie Fraissinet et Fabre*. Most African workers arriving in France passed through Marseille first and by the mid-1960s, records indicated that there might have been as many as 354 passengers arriving from Sub-Saharan Africa on a single ship. By 1962, the sociologist writing the report noted that, "it is not uncommon that the emigrant spends time in Marseille, earning money before leaving for Paris."[50] Marseille became an important stopping point for African immigrants as they entered France, so much so that just a few years later, "the labor force is completely saturated for Africans in this city."[51]

Yet the community in Paris was even bigger. Because it was home to the largest African population in France, authorities focused intensely on Paris and the *banlieues*. Officials within the Ministry of the Interior looked carefully at the *arrondissements* or neighborhoods with the highest concentration of African immigrants and identified several important locales throughout the city. Continuing a demographic trend dating back to the nineteenth century, authorities discovered that many African immigrants lived in neighborhoods and *banlieues* already associated with working-class and immigrant populations, from Italians and Poles to Algerian, Spanish, and Portuguese workers.[52] By 1964, the *arrondissements* with the largest populations of Africans immigrants included the 11th, 13th, 18th, 19th, and 20th.[53] African workers also settled beyond the city's limits in several *banlieues* surrounding the city, including Aubervilliers, Saint-Denis, Clichy, and Montreuil-sous-Bois, which are still home to important African populations.[54] The French state's focus on locale reflected long-standing efforts by police to investigate and control urban populations, perpetuating colonial and metropolitan concerns over problematic groups within the urban realm into the postcolonial era.

Yet even as authorities gathered information spatially and otherwise, colonially influenced ideas about former African "subjects" also became an important tool for undertaking the surveillance of African workers in the Paris region while reconfiguring state policies to address the needs of this immigrant group. As Alice Conklin argues, colonial governors debated, "… the best means to bring about the desired progress in Africans' social mores."[55] Yet many of the goals remained the same between the colonial and postcolonial contexts. Just as colonial officials hoped to initiate and foster "progress" among African societies, French authorities attempted to redirect what they viewed as the problematic presence of African immigrants and its consequences through planned relocations, educational opportunities including language classes, job training, and medical care.[56] In doing so, they monitored organizations offering language classes and other services to African workers, from AFTAM to SOUNDIATA and *Accueil et promotion*, which enrolled an estimated 750 African immigrants per year in language courses in the mid-1960s. Officials kept track of where the language classes were held, how many students attended, the capacity of each course, which organizations offered them, and how much funding they received from the *Fonds d'action sociale pour les travailleurs étrangers* (Social Action Fund for Immigrant Workers or FAS).[57]

In another parallel with earlier perceptions, French officials initially characterized Sub-Saharan African immigrants as docile and as less violent than their Algerian counterparts. As the 1960s wore on, the international emphasis on human rights, the aftermath of the Algerian war of independence, the turmoil over civil rights in the United States, and violent clashes over apartheid in South Africa rendered French authorities reticent to use violent tactics against Africans or other immigrant groups. In a 1970 letter to the Associate Director of the Air and Borders Police, Jean Gouaze, Director of Regulations, cautioned that, while directives concerning immigration control and enforcement required strict application, they should be undertaken with "much humanity and with care to avoid all appearances of any overt discrimination."[58] Yet in several instances, including the Saint-Denis riot of 1963, violence between and among immigrant groups attracted increased surveillance and monitoring of those involved in the fracas. After 1961, immigrant populations in France were often monitored because of concerns—real or imagined—over the potential for interethnic violence. However, violence against African immigrants rarely resulted from official surveillance in the postcolonial metropolitan context.

Perceived penchant for political involvement

Officials attempted to gauge politicization and the propensity for political involvement among African immigrants. As the 1960s continued, the question of politicization and political orientation of African workers became one of the biggest sources of anxiety and concern for officials monitoring this immigrant group. At the onset of African labor migration in the early 1960s, representatives of the *Préfecture de police* and other entities within the Ministry of the Interior constructed this immigrant group as largely apolitical and incapable of complex political activities.[59] Officials expressed contradictory views of the potential for politicization among African immigrants. As early as 1963, one report commissioned by the *Préfecture de police* argued that, "African workers appear indifferent to political propaganda."[60] That same year, an official from the Ministry of the Interior argued that African immigrants "show in general a reticence toward attempts to penetrate their circles."[61] This tendency to see African immigrants remained disengaged from and uninterested in politics reflected an inclination in AOF to see colonial "subjects" as apolitical. A 1964 report characterized Africans as non-threatening "large children" incapable of engagement with the political sphere.[62] In discussions of this perceived lack of interest in politics, the language used borrowed from a long-standing racially charged view of Africans as primitive and in need of assistance within the colonial context.[63] That same assessment, however, also personified African workers as politically malleable by organizations such as AFTAM, which was accused of steering its clients toward Marxism.[64]

Beyond the realm of immigrant organizations, police surveillance surmised that other organizations such as the *Confédération générale du travail* (General Confederation of Labor or CGT) found little success in recruiting African immigrants.[65] A 1964 report suggested:

> We have observed that AFTAM has attempted to steer blacks toward Marxism. The CGT Metal Federation has, for its part, attempted to indoctrinate certain black workers, without much success. In effect,

> living amongst themselves, imbued with their own doctrines, blacks remain not very permeable to political or syndicalist propaganda. If they have a well-developed social outlook, and their communitarian lifestyle demonstrates this, nevertheless, they do not yet have the necessary training to carry out industrial action on the trade union level. [66]

Early on, officials seemed convinced that African immigrants harbored few political ambitions in metropolitan France despite the role that political organizations such as the PCF played in decolonization in French West Africa. This view stemmed from colonial conceptualizations of Africans and the French insistence that colonialism could bring civilization, culture, politics, and society to Africans living under French authority in AOF.[67] The architects and purveyors of the colonial administration viewed Africans in this way because they wanted to believe that colonial subjects and citizens could not or would not resist French colonialism. They learned otherwise. In the aftermath of decolonization, surveillance of this immigrant community continued at levels that rivalled those of the interwar period.[68] Within the growing immigrant surveillance structure, officials could not ignore the signs of growing politicization and yet, they struggled to come to terms with it. As late as 1969 and the Ivry rent strike, officials remained convinced that left-leaning and extreme left groups had manipulated the dormitory's Malian residents for their own political objectives and ends. That authorities initially constructed the Malians on strike in Ivry as devoid of interest in politics demonstrates the ways in which colonial conceptualizations of an apolitical African subject spilled into postcolonial French society and politics.

Yet the growing visibility of African political activism in various forms, from organizations to riots and rent strikes, forced officials to see the political side of the African immigrant community. The reason for this shift lay partly in the leftist movement's willingness to work with immigrants on strike as well as the continued perception of the presence of an African immigrant community as a threat to the order and stability of the surrounding community.[69] Despite other statements to the contrary, authorities predicted this potential as early as 1963, when one report from the Ministry of the Interior argued that:

> black African workers are not suited at present to any political agitation. But they are already subjected to diverse forms of propaganda and it is feared that these settings will end up providing a breeding ground for the propagation of revolutionary theories and for the development of certain enterprises and subversions.[70]

Some regional officials went so far as to argue that political agitation within the *foyers* had become an effective means of political recruitment for outside parties and trade unions. Leftist organizations such as *Gauche prolétarienne* were accused of developing "a campaign of agitation in the shantytowns and dormitories of African workers in the Parisian *banlieues*."[71] Frequently, they singled out two nationalities deemed susceptible to outside influence: Malian immigrants and their Senegalese counterparts. Both of these immigrant groups had access to active and influential associations as well as embassies that authorities suspected of supporting their political activism.[72]

Embassies themselves and their officials also became a target for surveillance efforts. In 1964, officials from the Senegalese embassy visited several African dormitories during a visit to Paris, accompanied by representatives of *Secours catholique* and the president of the *Association des travailleurs maliens* (Association of Malian Workers or ATM).[73] At the end of the visit, a Senegalese official confirmed that "his government would study in the coming months the situation of African workers, in conjunction with other governments interested in this question."[74] This left French officials feeling uneasy, while worrying about what the living conditions of African immigrants might do not only for France's international reputation but also for diplomatic relations with former colonies.

Politicization and surveillance efforts

Building over the course of the 1960s, official concerns over increasing politicization amongst African immigrants solidified alongside tangible evidence that their worries were playing out in real time. Across the 1960s, the Ministry of the Interior expanded its efforts to detect individuals and groups within the African immigrant community that they believed to be radical, politically engaged, and dangerous. Other groups attracted attention as well—including the *Union des travailleurs mauritaniens en France* (Union of Mauritanian Workers in France or UTMF) and the *Association des travailleurs maliens en France* (Association of Malian Workers in France or ATMF), as did their leaders.[75] The *Service des affaires musulmanes*, for example, noted that one leader of the UTMF had a previous police record in France for offences of vagrancy, theft, and smuggling in 1948 and 1950.[76] By 1964, officials monitoring African workers began to detect "… currently a certain amount of politicization among this movement …"[77] Ongoing surveillance of organizations such as FEANF and the UGTSF and individuals such as Sally N'Dongo continued and intensified. The Ministry of the Interior also placed new constituencies under observation as well, including student dwellings such as the *Maison des étudiants de Côte d'Ivoire* (Ivory Coast Student House), whose residents were suspected of inciting radical, anti-social, and revolutionary behavior among African students and workers.[78] At this point, officials also introduced new surveillance tactics beyond monitoring groups, individuals, and meetings, while shifting away from the ethnographic techniques of the early 1960s. To detect political attitudes and sentiments, authorities collected tracts, including two from 1969 entitled "Residents and Workers of Ivry" and "General Association of Malian

Workers in France: Barakela."[79] Officials also monitored the specific interactions of well-known "leftists" in France with African workers, kept lists of names of "persons of interest," intercepted letters from African workers to family members, and even collected a play they considered to be politically subversive entitled "*Le commencement de la fin*" or "The Beginning of the End."[80] While the surveillance undertaken in the early 1960s was more observational in nature, that which officials conducted later in the decade and into the 1970s became more intimate, more paranoid and suspicious, and in many ways, more insidious.

Officials also used other approaches in tracking immigrant organizations. One key tactic included requiring them not only to register annually with the *Préfecture de police*, but also to provide a list of members along with their ages, home addresses, and locations in France. Failure to do so could result in the loss of an association's charter. Only French citizens could establish and oversee officially recognized organizations registered with the *Préfecture*, which meant that immigrants without French citizenship were not allowed to create organizations legally until 1981.[81] The UGSTF and other similar organizations also had to prove that they were not conducting any sort of political activities in France while detailing the type of organization that they constructed themselves to be in conjunction with the French state's requirement that they remain apolitical.[82] To meet this requirement, N'Dongo and the UGTSF, for example, focused on social welfare programs such as the construction of an all-African dormitory. The group's advocacy initiatives and its work within the media drew attention to the plight of African workers residing in France and the challenges that they faced, from impoverishment to unemployment, disease, racism, and dilapidated housing. Yet officials came to associate the unions that emerged in France after 1960 with those found in AOF and France prior to decolonization. While the UGTSF and other organizations took pains to avoid the kind of overt political activism banned for immigrants, the advocacy it provided was construed as political by state authorities. By the 1970s, leaders such as N'Dongo had become more outspoken and overtly political, as evidenced by the publication of several books focused on French neocolonialism, including *"Coopération" et néo-colonialisme,* (*Cooperation and Neocolonialism*) and increased contact with leftist groups, as evidenced by his trip to Switzerland in 1973.[83] Surveillance and monitoring increased, as revealed by the heightened interest in rent strikes and the aftermath of the Aubervilliers deaths, as officials became more and more worried over the potential for radicalization.

French officials were also familiar with and informed by the impact of African political activism in the colonial realm, which contributed to decolonization by putting pressure on French colonial officials through popular mobilization and participation in the colonial political sphere. A 1957 report detailed the relationship between the PCF, the CGT, and African syndicalist groups, explaining that:

> [the] principle of solidarity between the metropolitan CGT and African syndicalist groups of the same persuasion is expressed by the Resolution adopted by the '3rd point of order of the day' (Development of a Syndicalist Movement in all of the Colonial and Semi-Colonial Countries) of the 4th Worldwide Syndicalist Congress (Vienna—October 1953).[84]

Even before the Vienna meeting of 1953, AOF officials viewed the African syndicalist movement as a creation of metropolitan unions, arguing that "The communist-affiliated syndicalist movement in AOF is a metropolitan creation. From 1945 to 1950, there were metropolitan residents who created the first African syndicalist organizations and gave them their impetus to start. They assisted the first militants."[85] This tendency to see external influence shaping the trajectory of African politicization continued after decolonization in the metropolitan context, as authorities observing rent strikes such as that in Ivry maintained that external influence shaped and guided the strike. As Cooper has argued, labor unions in particular played a big role in protesting and mobilizing against postwar French policies in AOF, calling strikes among railway workers and in other key areas of the economy.[86] French political organizations and labor unions, from the PCF to the CGT, became involved, supporting African labor unions while also confronting the French state directly in the colonies. Officials understood the power of these movements because they had played a critical role in independence in AOF.

African immigrant political activism after decolonization reflected a long-standing tradition linking African immigrants in France to political activities, dating back to the interwar period and the various political engagements undertaken by African intellectuals living in France at the time.[87] The founding of African labor unions in France after independence drew out an interesting contradiction within the French political imagination and underscored an important reading of African workers residing within the metropolitan context. French officials viewed African workers as apolitical in the early 1960s despite extensive surveillance of African syndicalist groups and their affiliation with the PCF, the CGT, and others. According to this interpretation, they were uninterested in politics and incapable of political activism. By the late 1960s, authorities had started to view African immigrants as highly capable of political activism while remaining susceptible to leftist influence.

At this point, the African associational sphere was thriving with dozens of organizations emerging throughout the 1960s. These groups represented the interests of African immigrants through trade unions while providing for their needs socially through the establishment, for example, of an all-African dormitory in Le Havre, as French welfare initiatives and private industries continued to struggle to provide basic housing to African workers. When organizations such as the UGTSF focused more on social welfare initiatives, such as language courses and housing, in the early to mid-1960s, they attracted more distant and data-driven surveillance. Not surprisingly, the more politically engaged African workers, organizations, and community leaders such as N'Dongo seemed, the more alarmed French officials became. By the late 1960s, officials scrutinized N'Dongo's relationships, for example, with other prominent leaders of the African immigrant community. A 1969 meeting between N'Dongo and one of his rivals, Abdoulaye N'Dao, secretary general of the *Amicale des travailleurs sénégalais de la région parisienne* (Association of Senegalese Workers in the Paris Region or ATSRP) attracted the attention of authorities. According to an informant present that day, the two became angry with one another and:

> they accused one another of wanting to maintain the divisiveness among Senegalese workers for reasons of personal prestige and interest; M N'DAO in particular blamed his opponent for deriving most of his resources from "indelicacies" committed at the expense of his salaried fellow countrymen.[88]

Tensions between leaders added anxiety to the already heightened level of politicization and could, from an official standpoint, destabilize the urban order, which was already showing signs of strain by the late 1960s.

From the mid-1960s to the mid-1970s, political surveillance of the African immigrant community picked up substantially as officials grew increasingly alarmed over what they observed as increased politicization. While officials continued to characterize African immigration as "massive" and "anarchic," officials grew more suspicious and skeptical as they believed that African workers were growing more radical by the day.[89] In the colonial context, Kathleen Keller refers to this as a "culture of suspicion."[90] By 1966, authorities were monitoring gatherings of African immigrants—including the "Anti-Colonialism Conference" held on February 21 of that year—and detected what they labeled as Marxist-Leninist leanings as well as pro-Chinese sentiments.[91] In this particular instance, officials identified what they characterized as "virulence with regard to the French government" among those participating in the conference.[92] Over the course of the 1960s, Africans overall became disenchanted with what they perceived as a neocolonial relationship between France and its former colonies.[93] This manifested itself in publications by N'Dongo and the UGTSF by the late 1960s and early 1970s, including the aforementioned *'Coopération' et néo-colonialism* as well as *La coopération franco-africaine*, as the organization and its leader critiqued the "neocolonial" influence of France within Senegal.[94] N'Dongo wrote that "For direct colonial exploitation, made ever more unpredictable and costly by the liberation struggles, French imperialism has substituted neo-colonial exploitation, more subdued, more subtle, but equally effective."[95] At the same time, officials monitoring African immigrants in France grew more paranoid that political critiques rendered by the UGTSF and N'Dongo regarding neocolonialism could morph into a more radical and dangerous movement.

The Cold War also shaped the kinds of surveillance undertaken by the French state in regards to African immigrants. The concerns inherent within state surveillance, however, shifted as early as the first years of the 1960s, fixating on the political orientation of African workers and their potential for radicalization and politicization. Authorities identified what they perceived as increasing interest in African immigrants from the left side of the political spectrum. The *Sûreté nationale*, for example, reported in 1964 that "[t]he Communist Party and the CGT have for some time already undertaken concerted efforts to ensure significant influence among African workers, particularly in the Paris region."[96] These perceptions echoed those in AOF during the 1950s. While officials closely monitored the situation in Paris, concerns over a political partnership between the French Communist Party, the CGT, and African immigrants manifested themselves in Marseille. An official with the *Sûreté nationale* noted that leftist propaganda dispersed among African immigrants showed signs of "bearing fruit" in that city as individuals from Mali, Senegal, and even Guinea held meetings in dormitories on behalf of leftist and African organizations.[97] One individual representing the *Fédération régionale afro-malgache et d'Outre Mer* (Afro-Malagasy and Overseas Regional Federation or FRAMOM) was labeled especially problematic in Marseille as he held "Francophone and modern ideas ..."[98] From the official perspective, these ideas could prove potentially destabilizing and threatening to the status quo among the growing population of African immigrants in Marseille and other cities.

The political Left itself did become more involved with immigrant communities, including African workers, just as public support for immigration-related issues increased and as advocacy for social justice and human rights continued across the postwar era. By the late 1960s and in the wake of the rent strike in Ivry and the deaths in Aubervilliers, organizations such as the CGT and even the PCF that were previously ambivalent or opposed to immigration seemed much more interested in working on behalf of immigration-related causes. As the anti-racism movement expanded through the work of the MRAP and others, public awareness around and support for immigrant communities increased as well.[99] This shift can be explained in part by the global dialogue about human rights and the Left's ongoing support of independence movements throughout the postwar era and, more generally, the anti-colonial stance of the PCF, the CGT, and the communist movement overall. By the mid-1950s, the *Direction des services de sécurité de l'AOF* (Security Services Directorate of the AOF) made the following argument about the CGT's activities there:

> And indeed the metropolitan CGT, which originated the constitution of syndicates of communist allegiance in the Federation, never ceased to assist them financially, oriented them morally and technically on the

> way to separatism, and pushed in this direction to eventually mask its own decisive action in the matter of a simple demonstration of proletarian solidarity.[100]

The history of activism in AOF together with the dual emphases on rights and independence shaped how it was that leftist organizations interacted with the African immigrant community and how it was that this community received them. Yet this emerging rapport between the Left and immigrant communities, including African workers, concerned authorities. French officials worried about the influence of Maoist groups and whether or not contact between the two could result in radicalization amongst this population. As Mao had theorized about the possibilities of a Marxist-style revolution amongst a predominantly agrarian population, French authorities worried that Maoism might have particular resonance for a population viewed as rural, even if in reality African workers moved from cities such as Dakar and worked in the industrial sector. Maoists supported the idea of just war, violent resistance, the use of volunteers, and the support of popular will and opinion. None of this pleased officials, who cringed at the idea of organizations such as the *Gauche prolétarienne*, which was often accused of Maoism, recruiting amongst African workers who might then undertake violent resistance to authorities in France.[101] Encounters with Maoism were possible for immigrants throughout the 1960s. In 1963, Jacques Verges created the first Maoist magazine.[102] As early as 1964, African workers in the Citroën automobile factory worked alongside Robert Linhart, a well-known Maoist.[103] In part because immigrants were viewed as more politicized overall after 1968, it was in the late 1960s and early 1970s that perceptions of Maoist political intervention in the African immigrant community increased because of concerns over how Maoists constructed 1968 in the first place: as a moment of action and will.[104] In 1969, one police report observed the following about a demonstration by Maoists:

> At 6:15 p.m., Place de la République, in Ivry, a group of 20 Maoists, including a half dozen blacks, suddenly started demonstrating, with red flags, placards, and the distributing tracts, with the goal of attracting the attention of the general population to the situation at the Malian dormitory. They made speeches at the exit for the metro stop Marie d'Ivry.[105]

By 1974, officials believed that the president of the *Union générale des travaillieurs maliens en France* (General Union of Malian Workers in France or UGTMF), Toure Camara, was affiliated with Maoists via the GP.[106]

Officials argued that leftist groups were actively campaigning for violent action among African workers throughout the Paris region, including in Ivry amongst African residents on strike on the rue Gabriel Péri. In observing this strike and the Left's involvement, the *Préfecture de police* and other entities differentiated between left-leaning trade unions and political parties—such as the CGT and the PCF—and the more extreme "leftist movement." Authorities asserted that the extreme Left's tactics, including those of *Gauche prolétarienne* and *Force ouvrière* (Workers' Force or FO), remained suspicious and that these organizations attempted to exploit existing ethnic tensions by continually emphasizing the ways in which industrial societies took advantage of migrant laborers. These groups, though, used rather mainstream tactics to participate in the strike itself, holding meetings and distributing literature in and around the dormitory itself. The language they used in this literature was however extremely critical of capitalism, industrial employers, and the system that had brought Africans to France. For example, one of the organization's pamphlets argued that the, "dormitory is a symbol of the misery wrought by French imperialist capitalism ..."[107] This approach, so closely aligned with the leftist critique of capitalism overall and coming so soon after the events of 1968, convinced authorities that further radicalization amidst the rent strike was possible.[108]

The dormitory in Aubervilliers in which five African immigrants died in January of 1970 was another location that received significant police attention. From its inception, local police scrutinized this dormitory, just as they did those throughout the Paris region, including Ivry. The police worried about the dormitory's substandard and potentially dangerous housing conditions. In fact, the *Service d'assistance technique de la préfecture de police* (Technical Assistance Service of Police Headquarters) and the city of Aubervilliers repeatedly warned the establishment's landlords regarding their management practices and the dilapidated state of this dormitory, urging them to undertake steps to rectify the situation and improve living standards. Concerns about the dormitory's potential for political ferment permeated police scrutiny, given the decrepit living conditions, the already tense situation surrounding housing, the increasingly vocal involvement of organizations such as the UGTSF, and the tumult at other dormitories, such as that in Ivry.[109] As anxieties over the potential for politicization increased, perhaps outpacing safety fears, so too did police scrutiny.

From the 1960s to the 1970s

What explains this shift to an increasingly heightened concern over politicization and anxiety over leftist involvement in Ivry, Aubervilliers, and elsewhere? Part of it was timing. The Ivry rent strike and the deaths at Aubervilliers came in the aftermath of 1968's upheavals. Following the turmoil of that year, authorities read African immigrants in terms of politicization levels, demonstrating that domestic events influenced perceptions of immigrant workers. This pivotal year became a turning point for surveillance of immigrant communities, including those from Sub-Saharan Africa. At this point, the state stepped up surveillance while viewing African workers as much more viable and politically active, in large part because of their participation in the May, 1968 events and as illustrated by the expulsion of 147 immigrants in June of 1968.[110] The Ministry of the Interior justified the expulsions by claiming the right to expel any foreigner deemed dangerous to public safety while suspending the right to appeal.[111] In the aftermath of 1968, authorities undertook several initiatives. Police closely monitored dormitories and other dwellings inhabited by Africans. Instead of recording their location and their state of disrepair, as they did earlier in the decade, authorities watched closely for signs of left-leaning political activity or radicalization.

Fears about the potential for violence also drove surveillance efforts in the late 1960s and early 1970s. It seemed that the trend in the postwar era, beyond the colonies, was toward less rather than more violent forms of political protest.[112] Yet immigrant political activism seemed not only to be on the increase but also held, from the official standpoint, the capacity for violence. The possibility for violence between immigrant groups, as demonstrated by the Saint-Denis riot, remained palpable, while rent strikes such as that at Ivry and the demonstrations in the aftermath of the deaths in Aubervilliers reminded authorities of the precarious nature of the public sphere and the delicate balance between public demonstration and public order. At the same time that the New Left identified students as a possible agent for revolutionary change, leftist organizations were also taking a greater interest in the political possibilities offered by immigrant communities. This concerned authorities, who conducted extensive surveillance to determine if, in fact, this potential for political activism really did exist and whether African immigrants might pose a real threat to public order and stability in the neighborhoods and *banlieues* in which they lived.

As revealed by the Saint-Denis riot, interethnic tension premised on the power dynamics inherent within a tenant–landlord relationship could sometimes explode into violent altercations. Rent strikes also held the capacity for violence. Concern over the potential for violence during the course of the strike in Ivry, for example, was not entirely unfounded or rooted in abstract notions concerning the influence of left-leaning groups on potentially receptive yet supposedly naïve Malian immigrants. Over the strike's course, residents took their landlords hostage at least twice, holding them captive until local police arrived, dispersed the residents, and negotiated for the landlords' release.[113] Rumors of proposed lynchings and other forms of violence against the landlords circulated as well—even before the strike's official start—revealing the extreme and personal nature of the residents' frustrations.[114] One report from January of 1969 detailed an attempted attack on one of the landlords: "at 4:35 p.m. through the police station I was informed of an emergency call for help by Madame Moreal, who declared that Monsieur Garba was in the process of being lynched."[115] In late September, the situation between the landlords and the residents again became heated, with death threats against the landlord circulating from the strike's leaders. Traoré Garba was chased from the premises on more than one occasion and at least twice turned up at a local hospital wounded from confrontations with residents.[116] In January of 1970, residents protested as the foyer was evacuated by the SAT.[117]

Local officials monitored the threats circulating among the Ivry *foyer*'s residents against the landlord, which contributed to the imagined and real potential for violence. One official described the foyer as a "tribal environment where the sociological connections are closer than in our society."[118] The police believed that the strike could turn violent at any moment, that the *foyer*'s landlords were in real and constant danger, and that organizations such as the GP were directly responsible for the actual and perceived potential for violence. If the Malian residents on the rue Gabriel Péri were capable of taking their landlords hostage and threatening their lives, authorities asked whether this violence could spread to other African-dominated *foyers* throughout the Paris region whose residents were also on strike. Such rampant speculation only fueled authorities' gravest concerns about the presence of non-western immigrants in France. The memory of the Saint-Denis riot and other moments of violence permeated official understandings of African immigrants and other groups, even six years later.[119] Concern ran high among local and regional officials, resulting in a near-constant police presence at the foyer for the duration of the strike. This development in turn reinforced the idea that immigrant communities required constant monitoring and surveillance, whether or not they were involved in highly visible political activities.

With the mid-1970s and a world-wide economic recession came important changes in French migration policy. Officials exacted the control they sought throughout the 1960s and early 1970s over a migratory pattern deemed from its inception "unruly" and "out of control." Doubting whether African workers could integrate into French society, they made entry requirements into France more stringent in an effort to deter immigrants. And officials, who viewed African workers as the "*problème noir*" very early in the 1960s, had not ever been sure they could assimilate in the first place. Although the French state attempted to provide the same housing, educational, and health programs that it offered to other immigrant groups and French citizens, officials remained skeptical concerning the compatibility of African immigrants with French society. As officials grew increasingly suspicious of African workers, their perceived leftist political orientation, and their radicalism, they became convinced that this immigrant group posed a threat to the French political and social order. By tightening the rules regarding Sub-Saharan African migration to France in the early 1970s, officials hoped to enact the kind of control over this immigrant group that they had envisioned dating back to the early 1960s and even earlier.[120] This policy shift emerged as a direct consequence of the French state's surveillance of African immigrants throughout the 1960s and 1970s, its use of colonial and French tactics, worldwide political protest in the mid-to-late 1960s, and the fears and anxieties provoked by postcolonial African migration to France.

The growth of the postwar and postcolonial surveillance state in France was tied to several important themes, from Cold War tensions to social welfare. African immigration itself contributed significantly to the crafting of surveillance as officials drew on long-standing surveillance tactics in AOF and applied them to the metropolitan context during and after decolonization. This reflected an important continuity across different French regimes of the twentieth century, from the Third Republic through Vichy and the occupation to the Fourth and Fifth Republics, all of which surveyed, tracked, and monitored immigrant communities and other groups. The focus on African immigrants in particular reflected growing concerns about the stability of the urban social and political order and how it was that politically active populations of black workers might challenge it. Much of the surveillance was infused with colonial understandings of African subjects dating back to the era of French colonialism, even as officials complained that they knew nothing of this population. The status of immigrants in France also mattered to this story, as authorities were now tracking, for the most part, foreign citizens rather than colonial subjects, which they might have interpreted as less threatening because they were perceived to be under French authority. This, combined with heightened concern over possible politicization, especially from the communist perspective, meant that French authorities increasingly spent time watching a growing immigrant community. Increased surveillance led not only to the development of social welfare policies directed at African workers but also to important changes to immigration policy by the 1970s, including the end of labor migration in 1974 and the shift to family reunification. In undertaking these policies and practices, officials in the 1960s and 1970s established a template for the contemporary surveillance of immigrant populations while reinforcing the culture of suspicion that grew up around immigration over the course of the twentieth century in France and beyond.

Notes

1 Portions of this chapter appeared as "Policing the Post-Colonial Order: Surveillance and the African Immigrant Community in France, 1960–1979," *Historical Reflections/Réflexions historiques* 36, no. 2 (2010): 108–126.
2 Kathleen Keller, "Colonial Suspects: Suspicious Persons and Police Surveillance in French West Africa, 1914–1945" (PhD diss., Rutgers University, 2006); Martin Thomas, *Empires of Intelligence: Security Services and Colonial Disorder After 1914* (Berkeley; Los Angeles: University of California Press, 2008).
3 Clifford Rosenberg, *Policing Paris: The Origins of Modern Immigration Control between the Wars* (Ithaca; London: Cornell University Press, 2006).
4 Gary Wilder, *The French Imperial Nation-State: Négritude and Colonial Humanism between the Two World Wars* (Chicago; London: University of Chicago Press, 2005) 14, 19; Keller, "Colonial Suspects," 35–38. See also Gregory Mann, "Locating Colonial Histories: Between France and West Africa," *The American Historical Review* 110 (2005): 409–434.
5 Michel Foucault, *Discipline and Punish: The Birth of the Prison* 2nd ed. (New York: Vintage Books, 1995); Keller, "Colonial Suspects," 24. Jennifer

Sessions, "An Empire under Observation: French Colonial and Post-Colonial Surveillance in Metropole and Colony, 1918–1970" panel commentary at the Society for French Historical Studies annual meeting, New Brunswick, NJ, 5 April 2008.

6 See Rosenberg, *Policing Paris*; Thomas, *Empires of Intelligence*. For a now-classic and transformational take on surveillance and the state, see Foucault, *Discipline and Punish*.

7 Gérard Noiriel, *Immigration, antisémitisme et racisme en France (XIXe–XXe Siècle)* (Paris: Fayard, 2007), 503; Alexis Spire, *Étrangers à la carte: l'administration de l'immigration en France (1945–1975)* (Paris: Bernard Grasset, 2005), 30.

8 Noiriel, *Immigration, antisémitisme et racisme en France*, 503. Original French: "la suspicion à l'égard de ces immigrants devient systématique."

9 VDM 2018W Maurice Grimaud, Préfet de Police, to the Ministry of the Interior, "OBJET: Agitation dans les foyers d'hébergement des ressortissants africains de la région parisienne" Paris, 22 August 1969. Original French: "[c]ontrairement à l'immigration algérienne, bien antérieure à la guerre de 1914–1918, l'implantation dans l'ancien département de la Seine populations originaires d'Afrique Noire est un fait relativement récent."

10 John Merriman, *Police Stories: Building the French State, 1815–1851* (Oxford: Oxford University Press, 2005), 89–117; Shannon L. Fogg, *The Politics of Everyday Life in Vichy France: Foreigners, Undesirables, and Strangers* (Cambridge: Cambridge University Press, 2009), 1.

11 F1a 5136 J. P. Dannaud to the Préfet du Seine, Paris, 15 February 1962. Original French: "mise en place d'un système de contrôle de l'immigration."

12 Martin Thomas, Bob Moore, and L. J. Butler, *Crises of Empire: Decolonization and Europe's Imperial States, 1918–1975* (London: Hodder Education, 2008), 139, 146.

13 Frederick Cooper, *Decolonization and African Society: The Labor Question in French and British Africa* (Cambridge: Cambridge University Press, 1996), 16; Frederick Cooper, *Citizenship between Empire and Nation: Remaking France and French Africa, 1945–1960* (Princeton: Princeton University Press, 2014), 8.

14 Both Keller in her dissertation "Colonial Suspects" and Rosenberg in *Policing Paris* discuss policing tactics during the colonial era in French West Africa and metropolitan France, respectively. See also the SLOTFOM files in the Archives Nationales d'Outre Mer in Aix-en-Provence, France, which contained declassified surveillance documents from the interwar period in AOF.

15 ANOM 3 SLOTFOM 136.

16 Keller, "Political Surveillance and Colonial Urban Rule: 'Suspicious' Politics and Urban Space in Dakar, Senegal, 1918–1939," *French Historical Studies* 35, no. 4 (2012): 736.

17 Gary P. Freeman, *Immigrant Labor and Racial Conflict in Industrial Societies: The French and British Experience, 1945–1975* (New Jersey: Princeton University Press, 1979), 77–78.

18 Ibid.; Maxim Silverman, *Deconstructing the Nation: Immigration, Racism and Citizenship in Modern France* (London: Routledge, 2002), 43.

19 CAN F1a 5135 J. Trillat, Sous-Directeur du Peuplement au Ministère de la population, "Aspects généraux de l'immigration des travailleurs africains en France" in *L'immigration des travailleurs noirs en France: Leur adaptation à la communauté française* (Marseille: Centre de Conjoncture Africaine et Malgache de la Chambre de Commerce et d'Industrie de Marseille, 17 November 1964). Original French: "des problèmes sociaux, sanitaires et d'ordre public."

20 CANC 19850087 art. 10 mi 26607 "Objet: Réunion de travailleurs africains de la région parisienne, organisée par la municipalité de Saint-Denis" 13 October 1964.

21 CANC 19850087 art. 10 mi 26607 "Objet: Réunion organisée par l'Association des travailleurs maliens en France" 15 May 1964.
22 CANC 19870799 art. 25 Direction de la réglementation 6e bureau "Objet: A.S. du déjeuner anniversaire de l'Union générale des travailleurs sénégalais de la région parisienne" 6 January 1964.
23 3 SLOTFOM 136 Union des travailleurs nègres, Paris. Original French: "s'organiser pour se défendre."
24 CANC 19850087 art. 10 mi 26607 Préfecture de police, Direction des renseignements généraux et des jeux, "Objet: Propagande extrémiste de gauche parmi les Africains résidant dans la région parisienne" 26 February 1964. Original French: "[d]es Américains communistes de race noire ont, en effet, l'intention de se rendre dans divers foyers de la région parisienne où logent des Africains ..."
25 For analyses of the anti-apartheid movement globally, including in Britain, see Håkan Thörn, *Anti-Apartheid and the Emergence of a Global Civil Society* (Basingstoke: Palgrave Macmillan, 2009); Genevieve Klein, "The British Anti-Apartheid Movement and Political Prisoner Campaigns," *Journal of Southern African Studies* 35, no. 2 (June 2009): 455–470; Håkan Thörn, "Solidarity Across Borders: The Transnational Anti-Apartheid Movement," *Voluntas: International Journal of Voluntary and Nonprofit Organizations* 17, no. 4 (December 2006): 285–301; Håkan Thörn, "The Meaning(s) of Solidarity: Narratives of Anti-Apartheid Activism," *The Journal of Southern African Studies* 35, no. 2 (June 2009): 417–436.
26 CANC 19850250 art. 4 liasse 417 "Divers moyens de lutte contre l''apartheid' ont été envisagés au cours des journées d'étude organisées à Paris" Paris 3 March 1965.
27 For more on the Civil Rights Movement in the U.S. from a global perspective, see Mary L. Dudziak, *Cold War Civil Rights:* Race and the Image of American Democracy (Princeton: Princeton University Press, 2000).; Jonathan Rosenberg, *How Far the Promised Land: World Affairs and the American Civil Rights Movement from the First World War to Vietnam* (Princeton: Princeton University Press, 2005); Michael Wayne, *Imagining Black America* (New Haven: Yale University Press, 2014).
28 Gérard Espéret, "Avis et rapport du Conseil économique et social: L'immigration des travailleurs africains dans le cadre de l'immigration étrangère." *Journal officiel de la république française* 23 June 1964: 552. Original French: "le problème des travailleurs africains en France est demeuré mal connu (nombre, origine, conditions de travail) et les pouvoirs publics ne lui ont pas accordé un caractère spécifique ..."
29 CAN Fla 5136 "Les travailleurs originaires d'Afrique noire en France" Note No. 5, 12 February 1964. Original French: "L'organisation de l'accueil est actuellement insuffisante."
30 CAN Fla 5136 J.P. DANNAUD, Ministre et par délégation, le Directeur de la Coopération culturelle et technique to le Préfet du Seine, Paris, 15 February 1962. Original French: "un sous-proletariat inassimilable."
31 CAN Fla 5136 Ministère de l'Intérieur, Direction générale de la sûreté nationale, Direction des renseignements généraux, Sous-direction de l'information, "Les Travailleurs d'Afrique Noire en France." Original French: "[u]ne minorité d'Africains s'est intégrée à la population métropolitaine. Il s'agit d'éléments fixes en France depuis plusieurs années qui ont trouvé un emploi convenable et sont souvent mariés. Mais la grande masse des travailleurs noirs mène sur notre territoire une vie absolument communautaire. Qu'elle soit logée en hôtels, en immeubles collectifs ou dans des 'foyers', cette population essentiellement masculine s'est regroupée par affinité ethnique, formant des noyaux de même nationalité, de même religion, appartenant à la même tribu, souvent au même village ... La vie de ces groupes s'organise de la sorte en circuit fermé, peu de rapports s'établissant avec le milieu extérieur, pas même avec les autres groupes."
32 CAN Fla 5136 "Étude problème noir région parisienne." Préfecture de Seine, 1965.

33 Thomas, *Empires of Intelligence*, 2. On the relationship between knowledge, information gathering, and colonial policies and states, see also George R. Trumbull IV, *An Empire of Facts: Colonial Power, Cultural Knowledge, and Islam in Algeria, 1870–1914* (Cambridge: Cambridge University Press, 2009).
34 Thomas, *Empires of Intelligence*, 1.
35 Foucault, *Discipline and Punish*, 170–171.
36 Fla 5136 M. Legru, "Étude problème noir région parisienne," (Paris: Préfecture de la Seine, 1965).
37 Thomas, *Empires of Intelligence*, 4, 296; Keller, "Colonial Suspects," 21; Ann Stoler, "Sexual Affronts and Racial Frontiers: European Identities and the Cultural Politics of Exclusion in Colonial Southeast Asia," *Comparative Studies in Society and History* 34, no. 3 (July 1992): 514–515. For a look at Dakar and the experiences of people of mixed racial backgrounds there, see Hilary Jones, *The Métis of Senegal: Urban Life and Politics in French West Africa* (Bloomington; Indianapolis: Indiana University Press, 2013).
38 Thomas, *Empires of Intelligence*, 4.
39 CAN Fla 5136 C. Charbonniaud, le Préfet Chef du services des affaires musulmanes à M le Directeur général d'affaires politiques et de l'Administration du territoire, Paris, 20 August 1964. Original French: "[i]l avait été convenu de ne pas accorder d'appui officiel, des foyers créés et gérés par des ressortissants étrangers pouvant soulever des problèmes d'ordre public difficiles à résoudre."
40 CANC 19960023 art. 20 SDECE/SCTIP, "Objet: Travailleurs africains en France Accords franco sénégalais Activités de l'UGTSF (N'Dongo)" 23 October 1965.
41 CANC 19960311 art. 7 Direction de la réglementation, "M N'DONGO Sally, Président de l'Union générale des travailleurs sénégalais en France ..." Paris, 17 October 1973.
42 CAN Fla 5136 Préfet de Police, "Nombre et implantation dans le département de la Seine des travailleurs originaires des États d'Afrique noire" Paris, 5 September 1963.
43 CAN Fla 5136 ESNA, "Approches des problèmes de la migration noire en France" no. 104 (1965).
44 Robert Cantan, "Le problème des travailleurs noirs en France: transformer des migrations anarchiques en facteur de développement," *France-Eurafrique* no. 148: 10–11.
45 CAN Fla 5136 Jacques Aubert, Services des statuts des étrangers et des groupements étrangers 5ème Bureau to M le Premier Ministre à l'attention de M Journiac, Paris, 23 March 1964. Original French: "a visité quelques dortoirs africains et a été vivement surpris par les conditions de vie très précaires des travailleurs sénégalais."
46 CAN Fla 5136 Roger Frey, Ministère de l'Intérieur/Cabinet du Ministre to M le Premier Ministre, Paris, 18 June 1963. Original French: "[u]ne action immédiate s'avère indispensable, particulièrement à l'égard des ressortissants des États d'Afrique noire."
47 CAN Fla 5136 Ministère de l'Intérieur Direction générale de la Sûreté nationale, "Les Travailleurs d'Afrique noire en France" May 1963.
48 CAN Fla 5135 "Immigration et condition des travailleurs d'Afrique noire en France" 15 February 1964. J. P. Rosier, "Africains noirs présents et au travail en France" *Cahiers Nord-Africain* 86 (October–November 1961), 9–20.
49 CAN Fla 5136 Ministère de l'Intérieur Direction générale de la Sûreté nationale, "Les Travailleurs d'Afrique Noire en France" Paris, May 1963. CAN Fla 5135 "Immigration et condition des travailleurs d'Afrique noire en France" 15 February 1964.
50 CAN Fla 5136 Préfecture Seine, "Étude problème noir région parisienne." Original French: "il n'était pas rare que l'émigrant fasse étape à Marseille, le temps de gagner un peu d'argent avant de monter à Paris."

51 CAN Fla 5136 Préfecture Seine, "Étude problème noir région parisienne." Original French: "[l]e marché du travail est complètement saturé pour les Africains dans cette ville."

52 For an examination of the Parisian *banlieues* and particularly that of Bobigny, see Tyler Stovall, *The Rise of the Paris Red Belt* (Berkeley: University of California Press, 1990). For a discussion of urban planning and migration, see "Spatializing Practices: Migration, Domesticity, Urban Planning" in Paul A. Silverstein, *Algeria in France: Transpolitics, Race, and Nation* (Bloomington; Indianapolis: Indiana University Press, 2004), 76–120.

53 CAN Fla 5136 Ministère de l'Intérieur, Direction générale de la sûreté nationale, "Les travailleurs d'Afrique noire en France" May 1963. Ministère de l'Intérieur Service des affaires musulmanes "Objet: La situation des travailleurs africains dans le département de la Seine" Paris, 25 August 1964. Fla 5135 "Immigration et condition des travailleurs africains noirs en France" 15 February 1964. J. P. Rosier, "Africains noirs présents et au travail en France," 9–20. Service des affaires musulmanes, "Logement des travailleurs d'Afrique noire en France" 1964. CANC 19770317 art. 1 G. Brottes, le Secrétaire Général Préfecture de la Seine, "Note pour M le Préfet Directeur du Cabinet Objet: logement des travailleurs africains" Paris, 26 October 1966.

54 CAN Fla 5135 Service des affaires musulmanes, "Logement des travailleurs d'Afrique noire en France," 1964.

55 Alice Conklin, *A Mission to Civilize: The Republican Idea of Empire in France and West Africa, 1895–1930*. (Stanford: Stanford University Press, 1997), 129.

56 Ibid., 129, 141.

57 CANC 19770391 art. 2 "Cours aux jeunes musulmanes" Paris, 1967.

58 Ibid. CANC 19960134 art. 15 Jean Gouaze, le Directeur de la Réglementation à M le Sous-Directeur de la police de l'air et des frontières 1 April 1970. Original French: "être exécutées avec la plus grande humanité et avec le souci d'éviter toutes dispositions qui revêtiraient un caractère ouvertement discriminatoire."

59 CAN Fla 5136 Ministère de l'Intérieur, "Les travailleurs d'Afrique noire en France: Influences politiques syndicales" May 1963. Préfecture de police, "Nombre et implantation dans le département de la Seine des travailleurs originaires des États d'Afrique noire." 5 September 1963.

60 CAN Fla 5136 Préfecture de police, "Nombre et implantation dans le département de la Seine des travailleurs originaires des États d'Afrique noire." Paris, 5 September 1963. Original French: "les travailleurs africains apparaissaient peu perméables aux propagandes politiques."

61 CAN Fla 5136 Ministère de l'Intérieur, "Les travailleurs d'Afrique noire en France." Paris, May 1963. Original French: "se montrent en général réticents devant les tentatives faites pour pénétrer leurs milieux."

62 CAN Fla 5135 "Immigration et condition des travailleurs africains noirs en France" 15 February 1964.

63 Conklin, *A Mission to Civilize*, 2.

64 CAN Fla 5135 "Immigration et condition des travailleurs africains noirs en France" 15 February 1964.

65 Ibid.

66 Ibid. Original French: "On a vu que l'AFTAM tente d'orienter les Noirs vers le marxisme. La Fédération CGT des Métaux a, de son côté, tente d'endoctriner certains travailleurs Noirs, sans grand succès d'ailleurs. En effet, vivant entre eux, imbus de leurs propres doctrines, les Noirs demeurent assez peu perméables à la propagande politique ou syndicale. S'ils ont un sens social très développé et leur mode de vie communautaire en apporte la preuve, ils n'ont cependant pas encore la formation suffisante pour mener une action revendicative sur le plan syndical."

67 CAN Fla 5052 "Étude sur l'immigration de la main d'œuvre étrangère." Paris, 1962. Fla 5136 Ministère de l'Intérieur, "Les travailleurs d'Afrique noire."

68 For example, Philippe Dewitte bases his book examining the interwar African diaspora in France, *Les mouvements nègres en France*, largely on the SLOTFOM files housed at the Overseas Archives in Aix-en-Provence. Surveillance of immigrant communities continued throughout the twentieth century. See Philippe Dewitte, *Les mouvements nègres en France, 1919–1939* (Paris: Éditions L'Harmattan, 1985).

69 CANC 19960311 art. 6 "Mode d'intervention." CANC 19870623 art. 1 "Les activités subversives dans la colonie africaine francophone en France." 2 March 1974.

70 CAN Fla 5136. Ministère de l'Intérieur, "Les tavailleurs d'Afrique noire en France: conclusions et suggestions." Paris, May 1963. Original French: "les travailleurs d'Afrique Noire ne sont prêtés jusqu'au présent à aucune agitation politique. Mais ils sont soumis d'ores et déjà des propagandes diverses et il est à craindre que ces milieux ne finissent par devenir un terrain favorable à la propagation des théories révolutionnaires et au développement de certaines entreprises et aux subversions."

71 CANC 19960311 art. 6 Préfecture de police, "Mode d'intervention et d'action des mouvements gauchistes dans les foyers de travailleurs immigrés de la région parisienne." Paris 13 February 1970. Original French: "une campagne d'agitation dans les bidonvilles et les foyers de travailleurs africains immigrés de la banlieue parisienne."

72 The *Préfecture de police* and the Ministry of the Interior identified embassies as a potential source of political involvement in a 1963 report entitled, "Les travailleurs d'Afrique noire en France." The Malian embassy was directly involved in the rent strike in Ivry. What is interesting, however, is that the Malian tenants approached the embassy and not the other way around. Furthermore, the Malians who visited the embassy were tenants who disagreed with the tactics taken by the strike's leaders and claimed to be on the side of the landlords. ADVM 2018W art. 20 "Les locataires du foyer d'Ivry, favorables au gérant T.G. … ont envoyé une délégation auprès du Consul général du Mali en France …" 1 October 1969.

73 CAN Fla 5136 Ministère de l'Intérieur, Direction générale des affaires politiques et de l'administration du territoire, "Objet: visite des foyers africains par un représentant du gouvernement sénégalais."

74 CAN Fla 5136 Ministère de l'Intérieur, Direction générale des affaires politiques et de l'administration du territoire, "Objet: visite des foyers africains par un représentant du gouvernement sénégalais." Original French: "son gouvernement étudierait dans les mois à venir la situation des travailleurs africains, en liaison avec les autres gouvernements intéressés par cette question."

75 CAN Fla 5136 Ministère de l'Intérieur, Service des affaires musulmanes, "Objet: La situation des travailleurs africains dans le département de la Seine" 25 August 1964.

76 Ibid.

77 CAN Fla 5136 Ministère de l'Intérieur, Service des affaires musulmanes, "Objet: La situation des travailleurs africains dans le département de la Seine" 25 August 1964. Original French: "une certaine politisation de ce mouvement se manifeste actuellement."

78 CANC 19870623 art. 1 "Opposition africaine se fait plus virulent et prend en France des forms clandestines ce qui la rend de plus en plus dangereuses" 9 June 1973.

79 CANC 19940023 art. 20 Préfecture de police, "Le délabrement du local dans lequel sont logés plus de 500 travailleurs africains" 13 June 1969. Préfecture

de police, "Des tracts mettant en cause la gestion des responsables actuels de l'Association Générale des Travailleurs Maliens en France ont été distribués dans un foyer de Montreuil" 8 April 1969.

80 CANC 19870623 art. 1 "Recrudescence de l'agitation dans les foyers des travailleurs de l'Afrique noire francophone" 29 September 1973. 19870623 art. 1 Letters from African workers to their brother and mother respectively dated 1964 and 1969. 19960134 art. 18 Union nationale des étudiants centra-africains, "Le commencement de la fin."

81 Catherine Wihtol de Wenden and Rémy Leveau, *La beurgeoisie: Les trois âges de la vie associative issue de l'immigration* (Paris: CNRS Éditions, 2001).

82 For more on the 1901 law of associations and its impact on immigrant organizations, see Wihtol de Wenden and Leveau, *La beurgeoisie.*

83 Sally N'Dongo, *"Coopération" et néo-colonialisme* (Paris: François Maspero, 1976).

84 CANC 19960325 art. 8 Direction des d'ores et de la Sécurité de l'AOF, "Synthèse sur l''Action Communiste en A.O.F.: Première Partie L'Action Communiste sur les Syndicats" December 1957. Original French: "Le principe de la solidarité entre la CGT métropolitaine et les syndicats africains de même obédience est exprimé par la Résolution adoptée sur le '3ème point de l'ordre du jour' (Développement du Mouvement Syndical dans l'ensemble des Pays coloniaux et semi-coloniaux) du IIIe Congres Syndical Mondial Vienna—October 1953."

85 Ibid. Original French: "Le syndicalisme d'obédience communiste est en AOF une création métropolitaine. De 1945 à 1950 ce sont des métropolitaines qui ont créé les premiers syndicats cégétistes ou leur ont donné l'impulsion nécessaire à leur démarrage. Ils ont aidé les premiers militants."

86 See Cooper, *Decolonization and African Society.*

87 See Dewitte, *Les mouvements nègres en France, 1919–1939.*

88 CANC 19850087 art. 158/159 MI 26755/26756 Préfecture de police, "Une tentative de réunification de l''Union générale des travailleurs sénégalais en France' (UGTSF) et de l''Amicale des travailleurs sénégalais de la région parisienne' (ATSRP) n'a donné aucun résultat" 20 September 1969. Original French: "ils se sont accusés mutuellement de vouloir maintenir la division parmi les travailleurs sénégalais pour des raisons de prestige et d'intérêts personnels, M N'DAO a particulièrement reproché à son adversaire de tirer le plus clair de ses ressources d''indélicatesses' commises aux dépenses de ses compatriotes salariés."

89 AN F1a 5052 Directeur général des affaires politiques, Service de liaison et de promotion des migrants to M le Ministre des Affaires sociales, Direction de la population et des migrations "Note d'information concernant le Débat sur les étrangers en France (*Combat* du 28 fevrier 1968)" 1968. CANC 19770317 art. 1 Préfecture de Paris, "Note à Monsieur le Préfet: Agitation dans les foyers d'hébergement de ressortissants africains de la région parisienne" Paris, 8 October 1969.

90 For more on this idea of the "culture of suspicion," see Keller, "Colonial Suspects"; Keller, "Political Surveillance and Colonial Urban Rule," 727–749.

91 CAN F7 16108 Police nationale, "Note No. 7: La journée anticolonialistes du 21 février 1966" Paris, 16 March 1966.

92 Ibid.

93 Wilder, *The French Imperial Nation-State*, 295–302.

94 See for example Sally N'Dongo, *La "coopération" franco-africaine* (Paris: Maspero, 1972).

95 N'Dongo, *"Coopération" et néo-colonialisme*, 7. Original French: "A une exploitation coloniale directe, rendue chaque jour plus aléatoire et plus coûteuse

par la montée des luttes de libération, l'impérialisme français a substitué l'exploitation néo-coloniale, plus feutrée, plus subtile, mais tout aussi efficace."

96 CAN F1a 5136 Ministère de l'Intérieur, Direction de la sûreté nationale to M le Ministre de l'Intérieur, Service des affaires musulmanes, "Les communistes et les travailleurs noirs en France" 2 December 1964. Original French: "Le Parti communiste et la CGT ont entrepris depuis quelques temps déjà, des actions concertées pour s'assurer une influence prépondérante dans les milieux de travailleurs noirs, particulièrement dans la région parisienne."

97 CAN F1a 5136 Ministère de l'Intérieur, Direction de la Sûreté nationale to M le Ministre de l'Intérieur, Service des Affaires Musulmanes, "Les communistes et les travailleurs noirs en France" 2 December 1964. Original French: "cette propagande commence à porter ses fruits."

98 CAN F1a 5136 Ministère de l'Intérieur, Direction de la sûreté nationale to M le Ministre de l'Intérieur, Service des affaires musulmanes, "Les communistes et les travailleurs noirs en France" 2 December 1964. Original French: "les sentiments francophiles et modernes."

99 Noiriel, *Immigration, antisémitisme et racisme en*, 586–587.

100 CANC 19960325 art. 8 Direction des Services de sécurité de l'A.O.F., "Synthèse sur l'action communiste en A.O.F.: Première partie L'Action communiste sur les syndicats" December 1957. Original French: "Et en effet la CGT métropolitaine, qui est à l'origine de la constitution des syndicats d'obédience communiste dans la Fédération n'a cessé de les aider financièrement, moralement et techniquement les a orientés sur la voie du séparatisme et a abondé dans ce sens pour en fin de compte masquer sa propre action qui fut décisive en la matière en simple manifestation de solidarité prolétarienne."

101 Philippe Buton, "Inventing a Memory on the Extreme Left: The Example of the Maoists after 1968" in Jackson, et al., eds., *May 1968: Rethinking France's Last Revolution*, (Houndsmills; Basingstoke; Hampshire; New York: Palgrave Macmillan, 2011), 61–63.

102 Daniel A. Gordon, *Immigrants and Intellectuals: May '68 and the Rise of Anti-Racism in France* (Pontypool: Marlin Press, 2012), 55.

103 Ibid., 33.

104 Ibid., 53; Buton in Jackson et al., eds., *May 1968*, 63.

105 ADVM 2018W art. 20 André Maguer, Commissaire Principal du 24ème arrondissement à M le Directeur général de la Police municipale, Ivry-sur-Seine, 29 Septembre 1969. Original French: "A 18h15, Place de la République, à Ivry, une groupe d'une vingtaine de maoïstes, parmi lesquels une demi-douzaine de noirs, manifestaient brusquement, avec drapeaux rouges, pancartes et distribution de tracts, dans le but d'attirer l'attention de la population sur la situation dans le Foyer Malien. Des prises de paroles s'esquissaient, à la sortie de la situation de métro Mairie d'Ivry."

106 CANC 19870623 art. 1 "Les activités subversives dans la colonie africaine francophone en France" 2 March 1974.

107 ADVM 2018W art. 20 Gauche prolétarienne, "Pour des conditions de vie décentes travailleurs, tous unis, en avant!" September 1969. Original French: "foyer est un symbole de la misère engendrée par le capitalisme impérialiste française."

108 APP GaA7 "Mode d'intervention et d'action des mouvements gauchistes ..." CANC 19960134 art. 17 M Cantan, "Le mécontentement des milieux africains de la région parisienne est exploité à des fins subversives, par les gauchistes." 25 March 1975. CANC 19770317 art. 1 Préfecture de police, "Note à M le Préfet: Agitation dans les foyers d'hébergement de ressortissants africains de la région parisienne." 8 October 1969. CANC 19960311 art. 6 "Constitué fin du novembre

1969, à l'initiative des responsables de la 'Gauche Prolétarienne.'" 20 January 1970. CANC 19870623 art. 1 "Les activités subversives dans la colonie africaine francophone en France." 2 March 1974. ADVM 2018W art. 20 M. Grimaud to M le Préfet, 6 August 1970. "Intervention de M Jacques Laloe, Maire d'Ivry sur Seine, sur le problème de l'immigration." 16 October 1969.

109 CANC 19960311 art. 6 Préfet de Police, Aubervilliers, 9 January 1970.

110 Freeman, *Immigrant Labor and Racial Conflict*, 86.

111 Ibid., 85.

112 Buton in Jackson et al., eds., *May 1968*, 58–59.

113 ADVM 2018W art. 20 "T. G., gérant du foyer malien, 45 rue Gabriel Péri vient de déposer plainte au commissariat de police de la localité." 21 January 1970 A. Maguer to M le Directeur général de la Police municipale, 10 January 1970.

114 ADVM 2018W art. 20 André Maguer, Commissaire principal du 24ème arrondissement to M le Directeur général de la Police municipale, Ivry-sur-Seine, 29 September 1969. "Objet: A/S de la plainte deposée par le gérant du foyer des travailleurs maliens – 45 rue Gabriel Péri à Ivry-sur-Seine (94)." 30 September 1969 P. Derousseau to M le Directeur général de la Police municipale, Ivry 15 January 1969. Bramens to M le Préfet 29 September 1969.

115 ADVM 2018W art. 20 P. Derousseau, Le Commissaire Principal de Voie publique du 24ème arrondissement à M le Directeur général de la Police municipale s/c de M le Sous-Directeur Chef du 5ème district, Ivry sur Seine, 15 January 1969. Original French: "A 16h35 au commissariat d'Ivry j'ai été informé d'un appel à l'aide de M MORAEL déclarant que le sieur GARBA était en train de se faire lyncher."

116 ADVM 2018W art. 20 Préfecture de police, "Les locataires du Foyer d'Ivry ont envoyé une délégation auprès du Consul Général du Mali en France." Ivry 1 October 1969. "M Traorè Garba, gérant du foyer malien, 45 rue Gabriel Péri à Ivry, vient de déposer plainte au commissariat de police de la localité." Ivry 21 January 1970.

117 ADVM 2018W art. 20 Préfecture de police, "Depuis quelques jours, le Centre d'hébergement pour travailleurs africains … est le théâtre d'une nouvelle série d'incidents." Ivry, 1 October 1969. "M Traorè Garba, gérant du foyer malien, 45 rue Gabriel Péri à Ivry vient de déposer plainte au commissariat de police de la localité." Ivry, 21 January 1970.

118 CANC 19960311 art. 6 Préfecture de police, "Mode d'intervention d'action des mouvements gauchistes dans les foyers de travailleurs immigrés de la région parisienne." Paris, February 1970. Original French: "milieu tribal où les liens sociologiques sont beaucoup plus étroits que dans notre société."

119 For a discussion of the 1961 massacre of Algerians in Paris, see Jean-Luc Einaudi, *Octobre 1961: un massacre à Paris* (Paris: Fayard, 2001).

120 Spire, *Étrangers à la carte*, 328–330.

5 Tuberculosis, disease, social welfare initiatives, and the *Centre Bossuet*

"It has been three years since I came [to France]. Within eighteen months, I had fallen ill. Tuberculosis .... In the spring, I left [for home]," explained Moussa, a Malian immigrant.[1] He came to France in 1961 as a temporary worker from Mali. During his stay, he sent money back to missionaries in Kayes for safekeeping and expected, as many African workers did, to one day return home. That day came sooner than planned when Moussa fell ill with tuberculosis. He decided that heading back to Mali was an easier solution to his health problems than staying in France.[2]

His plight was not uncommon in the 1960s and 1970s, as thousands of African workers along with members of other immigrant groups contracted tuberculosis and other diseases during their stay in France. In searching for answers as to why healthy immigrants such as Moussa fell ill, many doctors and journalists blamed the migrants themselves, arguing that they came to France diseased. In 1963, just three years after decolonization in French West Africa and in an attempt to address tuberculosis within the African community, a medical center designed exclusively for African immigrants—the *Centre médico-social Bossuet* (CMSB or *Centre Bossuet*)—opened its doors in Paris to assist workers such as Moussa.[3] As Professor of Medicine L. Brumpt explained in the *Revue des sciences médicales* (Medical Sciences Review):

> Illness represents a catastrophe for these subjects: attracted by high salaries, they came not to care for themselves but also to earn money, create a nest egg or assist their African families with living expenses. Time spent in the hospital is time lost and they understand even less the necessity of convalescence or a cure pursued through a sanatorium.[4]

The medical challenges experienced by immigrant groups and the solutions undertaken by both those communities and their host countries remain an important part of the story and experience of migration. The ways in which a society addresses health care for documented and undocumented immigrants reveals much about their attitudes overall toward the immigrant communities living in their midst. Over the course of the twentieth century, medical centers in France and in the colonies became sites of interaction, treatment, surveillance, social welfare, and even, in some instances, community interactions. The *Centre Bossuet*'s opening symbolized the state's recognition of and concern over the growing African immigrant population, as well as its desire to become more intimately acquainted with this group. While representing an attempt to address perceived problems and challenges within this community, the center continued a long-standing tradition of providing social welfare services for colonial subjects and citizens residing in France dating back to the interwar period and the establishment in 1935 in Bobigny of the *Hôpital franco-musulman* (Franco-Muslim Hospital), which served North Africans. That facility established a template for providing colonial and postcolonial immigrants with separate medical facilities from French citizens and other immigrant groups.[5] The CMSB then became a site of negotiation between the state and African immigrants, as they appropriated it as their own. Because its focus was the Sub-Saharan African immigrant population, the clinic also revealed important demographic changes over time within the community, especially by the 1970s with the arrival of women and children, who joined their husbands through the French government's family reunification program as it was ending labor migration.[6] According to the 1945 immigration law, "undocumented immigrants who faced severe health problems and who had no access to effective treatment at home might obtain a residence permit 'for humanitarian reasons.'"[7] The clinic continued the practice of providing medical care to a variety of populations for varying reasons, from those that tended toward humanitarian aid to those that established a basis for surveillance and infiltration. Its emphasis on categorization and tracking also reflected the perpetuation of racialized thinking into the postcolonial era, especially as it related to the intersection of scientific thinking on and social constructions of race dating back to the nineteenth century.[8]

Connections to the *Hôpital franco-musulman* and the colonial administration

When the *Centre Bossuet* opened its doors in the 10th *arrondissement*, it did so with a complicated past traced back to World War Two. Between 1942 and 1943, the General Government of AOF purchased the building with credits made available through the Ministry of France Overseas. The Chief of the Colonial Service of Bordeaux signed off on the purchase. At that time, the General Government provided the center to the Ministry of France Overseas on the condition that a residential center would be made available for Africans returning from Germany. Eventually, though, the residents were evacuated and the building became a hotel. Between 1947 and 1948, the Social Affairs Service of France Overseas (*Service des affaires sociales de la France d'Outre-Mer*) transformed the hotel into a medical-social center for colonial workers. By 1953, the center was lent to the Ministry of France Overseas in order to develop social services for colonial personnel. Under an April 1, 1949 agreement, the space was loaned to the Social

Affairs Service of the Ministry of France Overseas on the condition that it provided services to French citizens who resided in the colonies. In 1958, the *Secrétariat d'état à la France d'Outre-Mer* (State Secretariat to France Overseas) created a management committee one year before the Ministry of France Overseas was dissolved in 1959. At that point, the Ministry of Public Health assumed oversight of the center. In 1963, shortly after independence in AOF, the *Centre Bossuet* opened its doors to African patients.[9]

When it opened, the *Centre Bossuet* was only the most recent in a long line of private and public entities that conducted outreach efforts in the realm of health care to immigrants from the colonies. As Clifford Rosenberg points out, during the interwar period, there were no special provisions made in terms of social welfare services for European immigrants. Yet amidst the turmoil of the Great Depression, the French government opened the *Hôpital franco-musulman* to provide medical care and social assistance to Algerians residing in Paris and the surrounding area.[10] While extending important medical services, the *Hôpital franco-musulman*, together with other social services, allowed the state to "monitor North African immigrants much more intensely, with less violence, than any of their counterparts in the colonies."[11] Following World War Two and the advent of postwar economic migration, the *Hôpital franco-musulman* provided a template for the kinds of services and surveillance undertaken by the *Centre Bossuet*.

One of the major focal points in addressing the prevalence of tuberculosis among African immigrants was the experience of migration itself and the extent to which the French state could control the entry of African immigrants and regulate their health as a result. There was historical and legal precedent for controlling immigrants' health by literally checking their physical condition during the process of migration. The Third Republic's law of April 5, 1884 regulated public health and hygiene, stipulating that the Ministry of Public Health should work to avoid the contamination of the French population through illnesses and epidemics.[12] This legislation laid the foundation for state regulation of health and behavior for French citizens and immigrants alike. From the standpoint of policy making, labor migrants' health proved easier to regulate than other areas of their lives in France—including housing—because legislation included provisions for its control. For example, the provisional government's law of November 2, 1945 created major changes in France's citizenship law by liberalizing procedures for migration and opening the way for the Plan Monnet and the immigration policies ushered in by the French state after World War Two.[13] According to Article 5, immigrants seeking to work legally in France had to:

> … present not only the documents specified … but also work contracts authorised by the Minister of Labor or authorization provided by the Minister of Labor, complying with art. 7 … It is also necessary to bring a medical certificate provided by a doctor approved by the administration.[14]

The law increased the duration of residence before naturalization from three to five years, unless an immigrant married a French person, received a diploma from a French institution, or performed important scientific, industrial, or literary services in France.[15] This same law also established other requirements for naturalization, including attaining the legal age of eighteen, exhibiting morality and assimilation, and maintaining good health.[16]

Building on the 1945 statute, wellness itself became a prerequisite for citizenship in the postwar era. Decree 46–1574 of June 30, 1946 and the Fifth Republic's ruling of April 21, 1959 mandated that all workers who legally migrated to France through the *Office national de l'immigration* (ONI) submit to a medical exam prior to their arrival in France.[17] The regulation of African immigrants' medical status began in 1959. Exams administered to incoming immigrants measured two important criteria: their health status and the extent to which they were physically able to work in France.[18] Immigration officials automatically refused entry to those diagnosed with tuberculosis because of concerns that they could infect the French population, echoing colonial sentiments about disease and long-standing notions of immigrants as harbingers of disease in and beyond France.

After independence, immigration authorities communicated these requirements to French consulates. For immigrants who arrived legally, officials distributed work permits only after confirming the results from their medical exams or following their examination at one of the ONI's regional centers; the state could deny the right to work in France to those found to be ill.[19] Anxieties over public order, security, and health provided the rationale behind this regulation and gave officials the sense that they could control the medical status of incoming migratory workers.[20] Free circulation agreements negotiated between France and Senegal, Mali, and Mauritania required that the citizens of those three countries show proof that they had submitted to medical testing prior to their arrival.[21] Initially, officials and doctors emphasized the need for screening in the countries of origin and continued to do so throughout the 1960s. Professor Marc Gentilini, for example, argued that "strict medical surveillance is required, especially for tuberculosis. Screening prior to departure from the country of origin or by default upon arrival in France is indispensable."[22]

The prevalence of tuberculosis among African immigrants in the Paris region, however, suggested that regulating African immigrants' health at the point of entry was not necessarily the most efficient way to ensure that they were disease-free. Tensions emerged between implementing an ambitious medical screening initiative within French immigration policy and the need for labor within a growing economy. The state struggled to reconcile the desire to control immigration from the standpoint of health and disease and the need to address the ongoing shortage of workers in the expanding French economy. A member of the Academy of Medicine observed that "African workers are now arriving in France without having submitted to a medical examination."[23] By 1966, one doctor argued that there was a total lack of screening at the point of departure in Africa, which meant that the medical testing requirement in France's immigration policies was not realized within the actual experience of immigration.[24] Yet these kinds of screenings proved nearly impossible to enforce and regulate, despite the provision for such procedures in France's immigration policy.

The problems encountered in regulating screening policies reflected the challenge of undocumented migration, which put pressure on the state's ability effectively regulate immigration through policy initiatives and laws, especially within the realm of public health. From the state's standpoint, the inability to control the disease among this immigrant population contributed to the notion that this was an "anarchic" and chaotic migration in need of state control.[25] With the growing sense that external controls were failing to contain tuberculosis among African immigrants, the emphasis on health care for them changed over the course of the 1960s and the 1970s. Officials came to understand that the state could not successfully regulate the disease from the exterior. The emphasis within the realm of immigration policy gradually shifted over the course of the 1960s from one of regulation and control at the point of departure to broader initiatives regarding the diagnosis, screening, prevention, and provision of medical care for non-French residents.[26] Instead of relying on the screening process prior to departure, various organizations undertook a series of related initiatives to address the challenges of tuberculosis within the African community in France. A consensus emerged that French officials, policy makers, and related government and private organizations needed to diagnose, treat, and prevent tuberculosis in the host country instead of relying on policies within the countries of origin.

This approach to health care for the African immigrant community was not a new idea, however. As Rosenberg points out, there were resources available to assist the North African community in France during the colonial period, just as the state put resources toward aiding Africans after decolonization through organizations such as the *Centre Bossuet*.[27] Through the *Centre Bossuet*, we see the same emphasis on "social control and exceptional forms of assistance" that Rosenberg identifies during the interwar era.[28] While French officials did not embrace African immigrants as "part of the nation," as Amelia Lyons argues they did for Algerians in France after World War Two, the intersection of social welfare, surveillance, and social control reveals that they not only recognized their presence but also saw it as important enough to create space for medical treatment and social welfare programs.[29]

Although the overall needs of each community, from housing to health care, remained different, officials turned to social welfare initiatives for Algerians as a template when creating those for African immigrants after decolonization. In addressing these challenges, as Lyons argues for Algerian immigrants, social welfare programs and their providers often reinforced, whether intentionally or not, negative racial stereotypes associated with

African workers, including those that suggested that they were illiterate, unprepared for urban life, and unassimilable. Riva Kastoryano argues that, "This is one of the contradictions of the initiatives of the welfare state, whose concern for equal treatment produces an identity classification that becomes a new source of inequality."[30] Yet postcolonial social welfare policies aimed at immigrants were not just focused on integration. They were also intended to monitor, survey, and control an immigrant population that the state neither fully understood nor accepted. Long-term integration was, from many officials' perspectives, not possible.

The scourge of tuberculosis

Why was there such a focus on tuberculosis in the first place? In the first decade after decolonization, Paris became the geographical center of the tuberculosis crisis among African immigrants as their population in the French capital increased from several thousand to tens of thousands in just a few short years. This was, in part, because it was also the region in which the majority of African immigrants settled. As one report indicated, "[African workers] have a tendency to cluster themselves in urban centers, with a large concentration in Paris and its *banlieues*."[31] The association between immigrants and disease, however, was not new. Officials associated Algerian and other North African immigrants, for example, with both tuberculosis and syphilis during the interwar period.[32] Policy makers and medical professionals alike debated the reasons for which this disease proved so challenging for African immigrants. They considered several possibilities, from malnutrition and a lack of hygiene to problematic housing conditions, an inherent susceptibility or weakness to the disease, eating habits considered "foreign" and "communitarian," and promiscuous sexual practices. The foreword to the October 1964 edition of *Revue des sciences médicales* asked readers to:

> … consider relations with Black Africa, which are more and more important, and from where the continual influx into France is something new. Physiologically and socially maladjusted, weakened by difficult and even miserable living conditions, often overburdened by the strenuous tasks of manual labor to which their complete lack of professional training destines them, they are, and often from the start, sick or helpless.[33]

Officials wondered whether African immigrants contracted tuberculosis in Africa and brought it to France or whether they caught it after their arrival. Professor of Medicine L. Brumpt argued that "… the pathology of North Africans is somewhat close to our own, while African workers give us access to tropical medicine."[34] Illness and disease also received considerable attention. The June 23, 1964 edition of *Journal Officiel*, for example, explained that, "the medical community draws the attention of the Government to the health problem posed by the arrival of Africans who are often already sick, or who become sick after their arrival in France."[35] Officials agreed that steps had to be taken not only to protect French health, but also to address the crisis of tuberculosis within the African community. Death rates among African immigrants from this disease were at 1.87 percent compared to 0.05 percent of the French population and 0.15 percent of the overall immigrant population. These statistics alarmed authorities, who recognized that they needed to respond with some sort of policy initiative or adjustment.[36]

Initially, in addressing tuberculosis amongst this immigrant group, the emphasis remained on medical screenings within the immigration process. The bilateral treaties governing immigration signed between France and the new nation-states of Mali, Mauritania, and Senegal in the early 1960s required workers to undergo a medical examination before departure to receive legal authorization to work in France.[37] These agreements required "a sanitary control certificate" in addition to a written work contract and a visa.[38] A 1965 report on the *Centre Bossuet*'s activities explained that "[t]he conventions signed between the French Republic and the Republics of Mali, Mauritania, and Senegal, intended for all African Workers to bring with them a medical certificate when arriving in France."[39] Officials realized, though, that immigration policy alone might not be the only area in which to effectively regulate and improve the community's overall health.

For its part, the *Centre Bossuet* not only provided medical care to African immigrants but also coordinated efforts between immigrant associations, employers, social welfare services, and hospitals.[40] Authorities recognized that, despite challenges, ambulatory and site-specific treatments at dormitories throughout the Paris region and in other urban areas could reduce the prevalence of tuberculosis and preserve public health in France. Medical personnel started visiting dormitories to screen and treat residents. As early as November of 1963, the *Préfecture de la Seine* sponsored a screening and vaccination event at an African dormitory at the passage de l'Epargne and the rue Petit in the 19th *arrondissement* of Paris. One police report detailing the event predicted that up to 200 people could attend.[41] In December of that same year, mobile X-ray units under the direction of the *Préfecture de la Seine* screened African workers at 3 rue Riquet et 73 quai de Seine.[42] Across the 1960s and into the 1970s, these kinds of screening and treatment efforts became more common and reflected an effort to provide medical care amidst rising concern about the threat of tuberculosis and to better understand where African workers lived and in what conditions.

There was also considerable discussion over the frequency with which African workers fell ill with diseases such as tuberculosis in Paris, the *banlieues*, and other cities throughout France. A variety of political organizations—from the far-left *Gauche prolétarienne* to the government organization *Direction des mouvements de population* (Bureau of Population Movements)—argued that between 80 percent and 90 percent of all African immigrants fell ill with this disease at some point during their time in France.[43] While it was perhaps an exaggerated figure, this statistic points to the fact that several organizations with different political and social agendas interpreted tuberculosis as a significant problem for African immigrants. Statistical information also suggests that the rate of illness was higher for African workers than for their French counterparts. As the population of Africans residing in France and in the Paris region grew from 1960 on, the number of tuberculosis cases among the African community increased as well.[44] In 1960, for example, there were only a few Africans who sought treatment for the illness at the *Hôpital Tenon* in Saint-Denis, a facility with a considerable number of African patients on its rosters. The number increased with each passing year.[45] In the winter months of 1962–1963, the Saint-Denis hospital admitted between 15 and 20 African workers with full-blown cases of tuberculosis, demonstrating a significant increase in the span of a few years.[46] Among the hardest hit were workers between the ages of 21 and 30, which corresponded to the demographics of African immigration overall.[47]

The health problems that plagued African workers posed problems for other immigrant groups as well. A study group formed by the *Comité national de défense contre la tuberculose* (National Tuberculosis Defense Committee or CNDCT) found that as early as 1965, the rate of tuberculosis was much higher among immigrant workers than their French counterparts. For workers between the ages of 20 and 29, 304 workers fell ill per 100,000 in comparison to the figure of 81 for French laborers in the same age group.[48] By 1972 in the Paris region, for every 100 new cases of tuberculosis, between 35 and 40 were immigrant workers.[49] These statistics suggest a rather high incidence of tuberculosis, given that immigrants overall made up less than 10 percent of the total population.[50]

A study commissioned by the CNDCT found that by 1968, African immigrants had some of the highest instances of tuberculosis of any immigrant group admitted to sanatoriums and hospitals throughout France.[51] Only North Africans, and Algerians in particular, had higher rates of this illness.[52] However, the disease proved deadlier for African immigrants, as they were 40 times more likely to die from the disease than patients within the general French population were. In comparison, Portuguese workers were more than twice as likely to die as French patients were; Polish, Yugoslavian, and Tunisian workers three to four times more likely; and Algerians and Moroccans were seven to eight times more likely to die from this illness.[53] Death rates for Africans appeared to be increasing over the course of the 1960s while declining for the French population.[54]

Because the Paris region was the area with the largest population of immigrants in France, it was also the place with the highest tuberculosis rate in the country. By 1968, 56.4 percent of all cases of this disease among immigrants occurred in Paris and the *banlieues*.[55] In 1966, one official characterized the situation among Sub-Saharan African and North African immigrants in the Parisian *banlieue* of Montreuil as a "veritable explosion of tuberculosis cases."[56] Among the African community, most cases occurred in the 11th, 18th, 19th, and 20th *arrondissements*, which directly corresponded to the community's settlement.[57] *Banlieues* outside of Paris such as Saint-Denis, Aubervilliers, and Montreuil housed a significant number of African immigrants. Correspondingly, they endured higher instances of tuberculosis among this population in comparison to the French population residing there, as did Ivry.[58] In the Seine-Saint-Denis department, Africans accounted for 21 percent of all tuberculosis cases in 1972.[59] While only a small percentage (0.27 percent) of the Parisian population originated from former French colonies, this group comprised 16 percent of the cases reported in the city.[60] The African community comprised only 0.13 percent of the total population of the Val-de-Marne department but made up 11 percent of the total tuberculosis cases seen there by 1972.[61] This health crisis among immigrant groups and especially African workers was an urban phenomenon centered in Paris and the surrounding banlieues.

The *Centre Bossuet* (CMSB)

The *Centre Bossuet* provides an example of the ways in which government officials and medical experts created treatment options for African immigrants while African immigrants made the most of the opportunities afforded through the Center. In the midst of the tuberculosis crisis, the CMSB opened its doors in 1963. The CMSB was created under the auspices of the 1901 law regulating associations on October 22, 1963 and was reported to the *Journal Officiel* on November 15 of that same year. The organization continued to serve patients until it closed in 1979 due largely to budgetary problems and the changing nature of the African immigrant community following shifts in legislation regulating labor migration to France.[62] Not only did the CMSB succeed in treating tuberculosis and other illnesses, but the center also built an important following among the African immigrant community, while providing an intriguing window into the group's development from the 1960s into the 1970s. The clinic's opening was part of an effort to eliminate tuberculosis among the African community and among other migrant groups as well as actions undertaken by organizations such as the CNDCT.[63] Under the control of the Ministry of Health and Population, the center was designed to serve African workers and, eventually, their families arriving in the Paris region.[64] Yet it carried with it traces of colonialism, as its first two directors worked in AOF prior to independence.[65] Several of its doctors and nurses, for example, had previously worked in former French colonies before returning to France.

The *Centre Bossuet* was part of a larger structure for community-specific clinics and hospitals for immigrants living in France. After decolonization, the Ministry of Health and Population took control of the center and then placed it under the guidance of the *Service de la coopération sociale* (Social Cooperation Service). At this point, the center provided medical and social assistance for French nationals and their families returning from AOF.[66]

While Bobigny's *Hôpital franco-musulman* provided medical services for non-western and western immigrants, the Centre was the first health clinic oriented to immigrants from Sub-Saharan Africa to open in the postcolonial era.[67]

Financially, the CMSB drew support from a variety of sources. In addition to support from the Ministry for Public Health and Population, the *Fonds d'action sociale* (FAS) provided between 70 percent and 80 percent of its financial resources. The *Préfecture de Paris* and the *Préfecture de la Seine* contributed to the organization's operating budget, as did the *Comité national contre la tuberculose*, the *Lutte anti-tuberculose de la région parisienne* (Paris Region Anti-Tuberculosis Campaign), and the Ministry for Cooperation. By 1973, the center's budget reached 680,000 francs.[68]

The CMSB's mission was dual in nature. Its overarching objective was to assist African immigrants with their physical and mental health.[69] From a medical standpoint, one of its primary objectives was to provide a wide range of health services—including tuberculosis screenings—free of charge to African immigrants. These services included dental and eye exams. The center also supplied African workers with certificates outlining their fitness for work.[70] It offered an infirmary for sick patients, medical consultations, lung treatments, dental screenings, laboratory tests, and social services.[71] After 1963, the organization focused extensively on preventative medicine.[72] While the debate over where Africans contracted tuberculosis continued, doctors and medical staff working on the ground focused on its prevention and treatment in the African community. It was well positioned to carry out its mission, as it was located in the 10th *arrondissement* and in close geographical proximity to many of the dormitories inhabited by African workers.[73]

The center's patient roster continued to grow. Between April of 1964 and December of 1973, the staff opened 26,521 new cases.[74] In that same timeframe, the center diagnosed 1,574 new cases of tuberculosis, assisted 2,235 patients in entering sanatoriums, and coordinated 936 outpatient and mobile treatments.[75] By the mid-1960s, the organization saw an average of 60 patients per day. Many visitors reported frequenting the center several times per year and checking in during their second and third stays in France after temporarily returning home.[76] Not only did the CMSB accept new patients, but it also created a loyal following among already established clients, who frequently sought out the center and its resources. The medical services offered to the African patrons allowed the staff to observe and survey the population seeking treatment while working to better understand the dynamics of this immigrant community.[77] The center regularly reported its findings among the African community in terms of their struggles with tuberculosis and other diseases.[78]

The CMSB was also part of an attempt to change how French medical institutions responded to the disease among the African population. Between the mid-1960s and the mid-1970s, tuberculosis treatment for immigrants moved away from the exclusive domain of hospitals to mobile treatment in *foyers*, at specialized clinics such as the CMSB, and in the workplace.[79] Mobile treatment became an effective means of diagnosing tuberculosis. Health care workers could go to *foyers* throughout the Paris region and work directly with residents.[80] Medical personnel traveled throughout the Val-de-Marne and the Seine-Saint-Denis departments, visiting *foyers*, performing screenings, dispensing vaccinations, and providing treatment. In 1966, the CMSB reported a decrease in the number of tuberculosis cases overall among its African patients, which can be linked to the multifaceted approach to diagnosis and treatment undertaken by the organization to address the illness within this community.[81]

The *Centre Bossuet* also worked closely with French organizations focused on providing social aid to immigrant groups to foster ambulatory anti-tuberculosis efforts, including the diagnosis and treatment of this and other diseases among residents of the *foyers*. For example, AFTAM —one of the largest organizations that provided housing and social services for African immigrants—sent ill residents from its *foyers* directly to the CMSB for treatment.[82] Staff members from the center visited AFTAM-run *foyers*. These kinds of relationships increasingly became common throughout the 1960s and into the 1970s, representing a cooperative inter-agency approach to providing assistance to immigrant groups. Groups such as SONACOTRA, SOUNDIATA, and *Accueil et promotion* worked with the *Centre Bossuet* to coordinate ambulatory visits and treatments within their *foyers*. The CMSB also coordinated efforts with various embassies representing sending countries and with employers in several different industries, addressing some of the challenges identified in screening immigrant workers in their countries of origin.[83]

Not every patient expressed enthusiasm about tuberculosis treatment, however, reflecting the challenges of addressing the prevalence of this disease. At times, treatment could serve as an opportunity for resistance on the part of patients. In September of 1969, medical professionals visited the *foyer* on the rue Gabriel Péri. They arrived at the height of the rent strike, treating 55 of 540 residents. One of the strike's leaders—Mamadou Diandoumba—urged his fellow tenants to refuse medical care as a means of protest.[84] Mobile treatment sites could become contested spaces and provoke protests amongst residents of the dormitories visited by CMSB personnel. Police often accompanied medical professionals to each *foyer*, signaling the perceived possibility of violence. The police presence also served as a reminder of the French government's authority over immigrant communities in and beyond the realm of medical treatment.[85] With law enforcement officials waiting in the background, residents frequently refused to see visiting medical professionals and proved as reluctant to accept treatment in their *foyers* as they were in visiting hospitals. They feared that interacting with medical professionals could lead to deportation, especially if they arrived in France without legal documentation.

Despite resistance, ambulatory efforts carried the message of treatment and prevention to each locale visited. Although many officials believed that Africans arrived in France already carrying the disease, there was an increased emphasis on preventative and early treatments over the course of the decade.[86] Educational initiatives also focused on treatment and preventative efforts were also undertaken within clinics and *foyers*.[87] By 1969, the CNDTC announced at its annual National Assembly that it would undertake "... all the effort necessary for prevention, early detection and treatment of tuberculosis among foreign workers, prioritizing black Africans and Algerians."[88] The same report detailed decreases in tuberculosis cases throughout the Paris region, attributed to the CMSB's treatment and prevention campaign.[89]

African immigrants not only paid attention to this emphasis on prevention but also took it one step further, seeking out the *Centre Bossuet* in preparation for return trips to Africa. Prior to the end of labor migration in 1974, the Center's patients frequently went home for several months at a time and sought care at the center prior to their departure. After 1974, the change in immigration status and the downturn in the economy forced most workers to return home only for short vacations and holidays. Regardless of the length of time spent at home, however, vaccinations moved to the top of the list of tasks to accomplish before leaving France. To make such a trip less risky, African workers often employed the *Centre Bossuet*'s free vaccination services. Patients obtained shots against yellow fever and other diseases. By 1975, for example, the center provided vaccines to 892 immigrants. While ambulatory diagnosis and treatment campaigns reminded African immigrants of similar types of colonial initiatives, the *Centre Bossuet* itself was increasingly viewed by members of the community as an important resource, as reflected in their use of it in preparation for trips home.

While many African workers used the CMSB prior to going home, some decided to return permanently of their own accord.[90] This decision was especially difficult for those who struggled with tuberculosis. Some migrants believed that going home was the most viable option for surviving the disease.[91] Some officials opposed medical repatriation, however, because they argued that "medical repatriation could be a source of contamination for those around the patient on return to their country."[92] The CMSB, however, assisted its African tuberculosis patients who chose to return home rather than face the disease on their own. On their behalf, the center contacted regional branches of the *Lutte contre la tuberculose* in Sub-Saharan Africa to coordinate treatment options. Yet other officials argued that returning home interrupted treatment, making it more difficult for patients to recover. Staying in France for the duration of the recovery posed its own challenges, however. As one official pointed out, "[f]or all of the departments, it seems that convalescence at home is problematic because of several adverse social factors: housing, nutrition, promiscuity."[93]

While grappling with the issue of repatriation versus recovery in France, the *Centre Bossuet* established an ongoing partnership with the *Service de lutte contre la tuberculose de Kayes au Mali* (Tuberculosis Service of Kayes in Mali or SLCTKM).[94] These two organizations cooperated to facilitate treatment for patients who returned, reflecting the transnational and global nature of medical treatment and the ongoing relationship between African and French organizations in the postcolonial era. By coordinating treatment options with SLCTKM and branches of this organization in other African countries, the *Centre Bossuet* and its staff fostered a smoother transition for repatriating immigrants while also working to contain the spread of tuberculosis in Sub-Saharan Africa. The center also ensured that future immigrants from countries such as Mali knew of the services it offered as well as its capacity to provide services for immigrants residing in France before they even left Africa. Medical repatriation comprised an important part of the organization's services while also affording the opportunity to wage a broader, multi-continent campaign against tuberculosis, reflecting the increasingly global nature of the center's mission.[95]

Yet social services remained a core component of the *Centre Bossuet*'s mission. Beginning in 1965, its offerings in this area were almost as wide-ranging as its medical care. Gravely ill patients in need of hospitalization, for example, could request the assistance of interpreters paid by the center. Most of the time, bilingual immigrants from the Soninké ethnic group worked in this role and assisted patients in navigating check-in procedures and other bureaucratic aspects of hospitalization. This approach to overcoming language barriers reflected the long-standing practice of using interpreters in the colonial context to navigate communication between various ethnic groups and colonial officials throughout AOF. As Benjamin L. Lawrance, Emily Lynn Osborn, and Richard L. Roberts explain, in French West Africa, "[t]he Africans who rendered crucial services to Europeans also acquired skills, knowledge, and situated authority with which they furthered their own strategies of accumulation."[96] The same could be argued for postcolonial African immigrants who worked at the *Centre Bossuet* as interpreters and provided a critical service while gaining contacts and insider knowledge to ease their acculturation. By 1967, for example, the center employed three Malian interpreters: Abdoulaye-Malick Sy, M'Boullé Gassama, and Malali Bathily. Additionally, two women from the Congo and Cameroon, respectively—Catherine Matsocota and Faustine Mgouat—worked as social assistants.[97] A report published the following year called for the center to employ even more interpreters.[98] This echoed directives from Paris to use African medical personnel to staff ambulatory medical units within the colonial administration.[99]

In its metropolitan form, this approach called for the use of African and often specifically Soninké immigrants to assist the clinic's clientele, with staff members serving as advocates for their patients. Yet the call for more interpreters and the presence of interpreters also reflected conceptualizations of Africans that reflected aspects of the center's approach to medical treatment, especially in the 1960s. One of the center's reports from the late 1960s explained that, "most of the clinics recognize themselves their dismay at their black clients, the quasi-insurmountable obstacles in terms of the language barrier, and, it must also be recognized, the very particular mentality of the black African."[100] The latent racism behind the idea of a particular "black African mentality" intersected with the idea of quasi-insurmountable linguistic barriers. This reflected a concern over a lack of fluency in French as well as concerns over the continued use of African languages such as Bambara and Soninké in both France and Sub-Saharan Africa.

Yet the center's employees recognized that West Africans confronted a plethora of problems when they needed to leave their jobs to pursue treatment. Accordingly, the *Centre Bossuet* informed employers of their employees' conditions, worked to ensure that they were treated decently during treatment, and relayed information to the *Sécurité Sociale* (Social Security). The staff assisted patients whose treatment required travel to hospitals and sanatoriums. Staff members also accompanied patients to train stations, helping them with their transport and assisting them in purchasing train tickets.[101] This reflected the ways in which the Centre became a site of mutual cooperation in which African immigrants procured assistance and services not readily available in other parts of French society.

Beyond medical treatment and advocacy, however, the *Centre Bossuet* offered several training opportunities to its clients. Training seminars for the acquisition of job-related skills became an important aspect of the Centre's outreach efforts.[102] Internships often provided the necessary training to compete on the job market and the *Centre Bossuet* created such opportunities along with the UGTSF and other immigrant organizations. Each year the center extended most of its social service-oriented internships to young African immigrants. Such on-the-job experience afforded valuable contact not only with the center's staff and services, but also with other organizations that assisted African migrants, such as *Accueil et promotion*, AFTAM, and SOUNDIATA. While training its young interns in the provision of social services, the center also hoped to impress upon them the necessity of creating similar social services networks in their countries of origin. If they were to return home, these interns could assist in creating similar social service organizations for their families, communities, and sending countries.[103] This reflected a postwar, postcolonial emphasis on development in Sub-Saharan Africa that emerged through organizations such as the *Centre Bossuet* and the UGTSF while emphasizing educational, agricultural, and health-related initiatives.

The *Centre Bossuet* also offered other types of educational and health-oriented programs. Literacy courses proved popular, as some of the African immigrants who arrived in France during the 1960s and 1970s lacked proficiency in the French language.[104] The dual emphasis on social and medical services quickly attracted the attention of the African community. In this context, the *Centre Bossuet* became an important source of social welfare in providing both health and educational programs. While language and professional training courses remained central to the CMSB's social welfare mission, the clinic also worked to improve the health of African immigrants through educational seminars. Yet it could not provide these types of courses alone and often worked with AFTAM and other management organizations to offer health education courses within the *foyers* to more directly serve the African community's needs. Through these courses, the center and other associations could work to prevent the spread of diseases and promote the health and welfare of these immigrants. Such partnerships reveal once again the role that the *Centre Bossuet* played as a crossroads for organizations that assisted African immigrants through Paris and the *banlieues.* The center demonstrated its willingness to work within the network of organizations creating reception and integration opportunities for the African immigrant community.[105] However, the *Centre Bossuet* was not the only medical center to offer educational opportunities. Other hospitals offered literacy courses to African immigrants undergoing in-patient treatment for tuberculosis, thereby undertaking an effort to better integrate this community through language acquisition.[106]

Although the CMSB was originally founded as a medical clinic, by the late 1960s and early 1970s its social services division became the dominant aspect of the center's mission. A 1976 report indicated that:

> [t]he African workers who frequented the *Centre Bossuet* have had, like previous years, use of the Social Service FOR ALL PROBLEMS ASSOCIATED WITH THE DISEASE, in pneumophtisiology as well as in general and tropical medicine: papers to fill out, explanations of treatments, medical supplies for those without resources, referrals for consultations with specialists in hospitals or to centers providing free examinations, relations with employers.[107]

The number of patients seeking medical treatment decreased and the number of visitors seeking social services increased. For example, in 1975, 733 patients sought medical treatment for tuberculosis; by 1976 this number had decreased to 685. Over the same time span, however, the number of visitors seeking help with socially related issues increased from 1,487 in 1975 to 2,380 in 1976—a substantial jump. The changing context of immigration following the 1974 law restricting labor-related migration and allowing for family reunification contributed to this shift. With higher numbers of women and children arriving as a result, the need for social services in addition to medical treatment increased. Furthermore, the economic downturn and competitive nature of the job market in France throughout the 1970s demanded improved job skills. Many immigrants looked to the *Centre Bossuet* to provide the necessary training to stay employed in a changing economy.[108]

The question of who patronized the center in the 1970s highlights the composition of the African community in the Paris region and the ways in which it changed over time. The impact of changes to French immigration laws and their increasingly restrictive nature affected not only who came to France—and it was increasingly women and children who did through family reunification—but also the kinds of social and medical services that they sought. The CMSB's changing client roster and services reflected these important shifts throughout the 1970s, making it an excellent locale through which to understand these shifts.

The CMSB's patrons proved to be as diverse as the African community itself. Senegalese immigrants comprised 35 percent of the center's visitors, reflecting their important position statistically within the African immigrant community more generally. In 1975, 34.8 percent of the center's visitors were Malian, while migrants from the Ivory Coast comprised another 10.8 percent. Mauritanian, Cameroonian, and Congolese immigrants also frequented the center. By the mid-1970s, a larger percentage of African immigrants originated from countries other than Senegal, Mali, and Mauritania, revealing an important demographic shift in the composition of the African community. Beyond nationality, the center kept track of its visitors' ethnicity, a practice also carried out by other institutions, including the Ministry of the Interior and the *Préfecture de police*. In 1976, for example, 572 immigrants of the Soninké ethnicity utilized the center's resources, which constituted 30 percent of the center's patronage. An additional 154 Toucouleurs frequented the center, comprising 8 percent of its visitors. The center also kept track of the patronage of members of no fewer than seventeen other African ethnic groups.[109]

The *Centre Bossuet*'s statistical use of ethnic categories reveals the institution's interest in race and ethnicity as a means through which to understand the African community. Its appropriation of the colonial term Sarakolé—which referred to the Soninké ethnicity—points directly to the *Centre Bossuet*'s colonial roots. The center appropriated colonial tendencies to track ethnicity and community composition while also categorizing its clients similarly to how colonial administrators categorized and divided Africans with the *politique des races* of the colonial administration and the "civilizing mission."[110] The center's record-keeping was not colorblind, nor was the Fifth Republic's approach to immigrant communities, surveillance, and tracking overall. The national government supported the center's interest in ethnic categorization through various government agencies and their financial contributions to the institution, including the FAS and the Ministry of Health and Population. The CMSB's use of government funds demonstrates that the FAS and the French government retained an interest in tracking ethnicity to understand developments within the African community.

The Center's patrons were young, reflecting the overall demographic trends of this immigrant group. The organization's 1975 report indicated that of the 2,006 new files opened that year, 117 patients were younger than 20. Immigrants between the ages of 20 and 30 frequented the center most often, with 1,329 visiting the center that year. Not all of the center's clients could be categorized as young, however. For example, in 1975, 413 visitors were between the ages of 30 and 40, while another 141 were older than 40 years old; six declined to specify their age. Many of the center's older patrons may have been in France since the early 1960s, when they migrated as young men. These statistics also suggest that postcolonial immigration was more diverse than previously acknowledged in terms of ethnicity, nationality, and age.[111]

Most of the center's patients lived in the Paris region. In 1976, for example, 64.8 percent of the center's total clientele lived in Paris. The departments surrounding Paris also helped in attracting patients. The Seine-Saint-Denis department was responsible for sending 379 patients to the center in 1979—almost 20 percent of the total client roster. This geographical distribution mirrors the settlement pattern that this immigrant group pursued throughout the postcolonial period.[112]

The composition of the center's clientele by the 1970s sheds light on the changing nature of African immigration, especially after 1974. As early as 1965, the Centre acknowledged that, "priority problems that we are led to consider: health, housing, adaptation to the environment, education, employment, etc., can hardly be separated."[113] The connections between housing, health, education, employment, and even adaptability became clear. This had not changed by the 1970s. Yet the African community's composition itself had, demonstrating the impact of important immigration-related legislation passed in 1974. This law fundamentally changed the nature of French immigration, cutting off labor migration while allowing for the arrival of women and children under the guise of family reunification. For example, after November, 1976, African workers could no longer obtain a *carte de séjour* (residency permit), effectively eliminating the possibility of securing legal permission to work in France. Furthermore, those who arrived in France without such documentation could no longer procure regularization of their status.[114] The 1974 law also resulted in the permanent settlement of several non-western, non-European immigrant communities, including that of African workers. Instead of returning to their countries of origin as predicted, many decided to stay in France and were joined by their families.[115]

The *Centre Bossuet*'s interaction with the African community after 1974 demonstrates the impact of this law on the ground. The number of Africans returning home diminished considerably while the consequences of this reduced migration were seen almost immediately in the *Centre Bossuet*'s services. For example, in 1974, 1,206 Africans visited the center prior to their return to Africa. By the following year, only 892 sought out the center's services prior to their departure—a 26 percent decrease. Fewer patients returned to their countries of origin, in large part because of the family reunification program, with 54 in 1975 compared to 129 in 1974, while more women and children arrived to rejoin their families. The center's staff worked less frequently to coordinate repatriations. Instead, the organization concentrated its efforts in assisting newly reunited families in easing their transition into French society and providing them with the necessary medical care and social services.[116]

As the number of documented immigrants arriving in France declined over the course of the 1970s, undocumented migrants continued to enter. Many arrived without work contracts or the proper documentation verifying their health status. While the lack of proper paperwork did necessarily not prevent them from obtaining employment, the problem lay in the types of jobs available for undocumented immigrants. Not unlike their counterparts in the early 1960s, African immigrants in the late 1970s found themselves working long hours in perilous working conditions with limited time off. These workers also experienced the constant anxiety that accompanied their undocumented status, which included the threat of deportation. Some dealt with these problems by obtaining a falsified *carte de séjour*. As many as 40 such documents were stolen and resold in one dormitory alone. The social services division of the *Centre Bossuet* tried to help undocumented immigrants who fell ill, assisting them to find suitable housing, and aiding them in obtaining proper immigration papers.[117] Despite their immigration status, the *Centre Bossuet* assisted them, acknowledging that disease did not distinguish between those with and without legal residency status. That a state-funded organization assisted undocumented workers is important, as it demonstrates the state's interest in identifying and controlling diseases such as tuberculosis among documented and undocumented immigrant populations alike, while also providing social welfare services regardless of immigration status. This also reveals a social justice dynamic to the CMSB's mission to treat patients regardless of immigration status.

The growing number of African women who frequented the center, however, revealed the full impact of the 1974 law ending labor migration and introducing family reunification on the African community and French society more broadly.[118] Women visited the center in such large numbers that their presence forced the *Centre Bossuet* to re-evaluate and expand its mission. Almost immediately, the center and its staff recognized that the face—and gender—of African immigration to France was changing as a direct result of the 1974 law. While it tailored many of its offerings to meet these new demands, the biggest shift came in its medical services. The center's social services were also impacted as well.[119] The center, however, did not always welcome the changes brought by the 1974 law. The economic crisis of 1974 took its toll on subsequent years, financially and otherwise. As one report explained:

> over the course of this year 1976 the actual demand for social interventions has manifested itself much more intensely. This increase in social demand is due in large part to the difficulties caused by the economic crisis: the suspension of immigration was applied in a much stricter

> manner to black African workers in 1976 (it became impossible for new arrivals to obtain a residency card) (and) employment losses due to lay-offs and unemployment were frequent.[120]

Staff members often regarded the arrival of African women with a mixed response. As early as 1974, officials discussed the arrival of African women, attributing the phenomenon to the fact that African workers no longer wanted to be apart from their wives. One report argued that, "African workers are less and less likely to accept living far away from their wives."[121] To provide social and medical services to this new group, the center started to adjust its programs and approach by the mid-1970s. Characterizations of African women reflected, as Lyons argues for Algerians, problematic racial stereotypes for Africans overall.[122] As a 1974 study suggested, "[t]his African female population, newly arrived in France, remains poorly understood because they frequent social services designed to welcome and orient them less often. Women remain isolated in their homes and rarely participate in language courses …"[123] It was clear that the center would have to adjust its offerings to include all-female literacy courses, while also rethinking the kinds of medical services that it offered, including an expanded focus on reproductive health. As the African population shifted demographically, the center resolved to undertake a study of the women who frequented the center to "determine their needs and, possibly, what structures would be necessary to put in place to respond to them."[124] While reinforcing stereotypes of African women as isolated and unprepared for life in an urban area, the center showed a certain willingness to get to know this population and to adjust its offerings accordingly, in line with its emphasis on serving the African community as a whole.

Although the center remained concerned about how to address the needs of female clients, demographically, the African women who visited the center closely resembled their male counterparts. The population was generally young—between the ages of 20 and 30—originated largely from the same countries, including Senegal, Mali, and the Côte d'Ivoire. Many of the women who frequented the center belonged to the Soninké ethnicity, the same ethnic group as many of the male immigrants living in Paris. These statistical similarities make sense as most women came to France during this period to reunite with their husbands, who decided to remain in France permanently after 1974. Furthermore, 65 percent of the center's female patients were married at the time of their first visit, 31 percent had children, and another 47 percent found their way to the center because of referrals from husbands or friends. This pattern reflected the Center's standing within the African immigrant community as one of the only acceptable places to seek medical assistance and social services. In terms of geographical location, 68 percent lived in Paris, while the remaining 32 percent lived in nearby towns. Most women—68 percent—visited the center within less than a year of their arrival.[125]

Finally, African women used the center for a variety of reasons. Most female patrons sought out the center to obtain assistance with family planning and motherhood, while others sought educational opportunities for their children and help with family challenges. Some clients wanted job training and assistance in finding work. By the late 1970s, the center provided gynecological exams, birth control, and abortion services.[126] Tuberculosis was no longer the main health concern among the African community, and the community's changing demographics demanded a shift in medical services as well. One issue that officials grew worried about was that of family planning and childbirth. Fear of hospitals and dislocation from family and community support were particular areas of concern. A 1977 report indicated that:

> Women who are pregnant for the first time in France dread experiencing their pregnancy alone without the support of their family or their social group. They are quite afraid of delivering in hospital, and although women who do not speak French cannot comment on the subject, they must also be anxious.[127]

Beyond birth control and other medical services, the *Centre Bossuet* also offered critical social services to its female patients, as its social services division worked closely with several immigrant women's organizations that formed after 1974. Literacy remained a key issue. The CMSB worked with several associations such as AEE (*Association Evangile et Enfance* or Evangelical and Childhood Association) ACAFOM (*Association culturelle et amicale des familles d'outre-mer et migrants* or Cultural and neighborly association of overseas and migrant families) and CIMADE (*Comité inter-mouvements auprès des évacués* or Inter-Movement Committee for Evacuees) to design language courses.[128] Women often utilized these classes as an opportunity to ask questions and seek advice concerning legal documentation, housing, and educational options for their children. Such classes provided a site for informal sociability, networking, and a common place of assembly rarely available outside of the center, while meeting the African community's definition of integration. African women enrolled in language courses offered by the *Centre Bossuet*, hoping to gain a variety of skills and opportunities.[129] By October of 1976 the CMSB "provided a haven ... a literacy course, designed for women, supported by ACAFOM and AEE."[130]

In the fall of 1979, the announcement was made by the center's director that the CMSB would shut its doors by the end of the year. Severe financial difficulties, combined with an overall decrease in the number of African workers coming to France, constrained the center's ability to provide medical and social services. Upon learning of these plans, the Africans who frequented the center reacted with a combination of outrage and sadness. They formed committees and circulated petitions, interpreting its demise as a crushing blow to their health and the social services available to them.

The center provided critical social and medical services and its closing reduced access to these sorts of resources. A petition circulated by the *Comité défense Bossuet* (Committee to Defend Bossuet) explained the CMSB's humanitarian role, arguing that:

> the immigrant without a residency permit is no longer recognized as a person with, as any human being has, the right to health. The *Centre Bossuet* has been a place where the basic right to be cared for was recognized for all without discrimination or regard to the residency permit.[131]

Another tract voicing support focused on the specific role that the CMSB played for female immigrants: "African women could meet up and discuss problems that interest them: motherhood and contraception, education, work, preparation to return home, education of their children."[132] In letters sent to the center, patients expressed their ownership and attachment, explaining that it was one of the few organizations expressly meeting the needs of their community. It also served as what was described as an African milieu, affording the opportunity to meet and converse with other immigrants from the same villages and countries of origin while also allowing patients to speak their regional languages with one another and outwardly display their cultural identities through traditional dress. The *Centre Bossue*t provided a rare space outside of the *foyers* in which African social relationships, culture, languages, and ethnic, regional, and national identities could thrive.[133] The community appropriated the center as its own and the fear and anxiety expressed over visiting hospitals, for example, was non-existent when it came to the *Centre Bossuet.*

From the perspective of health care, medical treatment, and social services, African immigrants battling tuberculosis became visible to a whole host of constituencies throughout French society, not the least of which was the *Centre Bossuet* and its staff. The CMSB and its role in treating this disease within the African community reveal several important aspects of postcolonial migration to France. The center and the battle against tuberculosis demonstrate that colonial-era policies and attitudes toward Africans returned to France after decolonization and influenced the ways in which officials understood this community. Yet the CMSB also undertook critical initiatives for a group deemed "unassimilable" by some constituents in French society. Surveillance, control, and community development were not incompatible in the realm of medical treatment. As the tuberculosis crisis among African immigrants subsided in the late 1960s and early 1970s, there was a palpable shift toward social services initiated by the center and its staff. The CMSB provides a critical window into the changing demographics of the African community in the 1970s and after 1974. There is perhaps no better way to understand the community's transformation after the end of labor migration than through the lens of the *Centre Bossuet* and its services. The crisis of tuberculosis within the African community demonstrates how immigration policies could change over time and in relation to the needs of different immigrant groups. Through the CMSB, its services, and the French government's approach to treating this illness, we not only observe surveillance and monitoring efforts, but also the ways in which Africans themselves appropriated the center become evident. The crisis of tuberculosis among African immigrants in the early postcolonial era provides important context and background for contemporary debates regarding immigration, health screening, and social services.

Notes

1 An earlier version of this chapter appeared as "Curing Patients, Connecting Lives: The *Centre Médico-Social Bossuet*, the West African Community, and the Struggle Against Tuberculosis, 1963–1979," *Proceedings of the Western Society for French History* 32 (2005). AMSD 28 ACW 22/23 Madeleine Garrigou-LaGrange, "Parce-qu'il n'y avait pas de place pour eux," *Témoignage chrétien*, 17 December 1964.
2 ADVM 2018W art. 20 Bureau de Syndicat (CGT) to M le Préfet du Val-de-Marne, Ivry, 30 January 1970.
3 CAN Fla 5136 M. Legru, "Étude: probléme noir région parisienne Ch. V – Le problème sanitaire," (Paris: Préfecture de la Seine, 1965).
4 CIEMI L. Brumpt, "Problèmes sanitaires posés par les travailleurs africains" in *Revue des sciences médicales: La pathologie du noir africain en France* 162 (October 1964): 7. Original French: "La maladie représente pour ces sujets une catastrophe: attirés par les hauts salaires, ils sont venus non pour se soigner mais pour gagner de l'argent, amasser un pécule ou aider à vivre leur famille africaine. Ce temps passé à l'hôpital est du temps perdu et ils comprennent encore moins les nécessités d'une convalescence ou d'une cure sanatoriale."
5 Clifford Rosenberg, *Policing Paris: The Origins of Modern Immigration Control between the Wars* (Ithaca; London: Cornell University Press, 2006), 168, 181, 188.
6 For more on family reunification in the context of political activism and immigration policy, see de Catherine Wihtol de Wenden, "Immigrants as Political Actors in France," *West European Politics* vol. 17, no. 2 (1994): 91–109; Michel Farge, *Le statut familial des étrangers en France de la loi nationale à la loi de la résidence habituelle* (Paris: L'Harmattan, 2003).
7 Didier Fassin, "Compassion and Repression: The Moral Economy of Immigration Policy in France," *Cultural Anthropology* 20, no. 3: 368.
8 "Introduction," in Nicholas Bancel, Pascal Blanchard, and Dominic Thomas, eds., *The Invention of Race: Scientific and Popular Representations* (New York: Routledge, 2014), 1–15; Carole Reynaud-Paligot, "Construction and Circulation of the Notion of Race in the Nineteenth Century," in Bancel, Blanchard, and Thomas, eds., *The Invention of Race: Scientific and Popular Representations*, 87–98.
9 CANC 19870009 art. 1 "Note concernant le Centre Médico-Social: Historique" 1–3.
10 Rosenberg, *Policing Paris*, 168. Clifford Rosenberg, "The Colonial Politics of Health Care Provision in Interwar Paris," *French Historical Studies* 27, no. 3 (2004): 637–688.
11 Rosenberg, "The Colonial Politics of Health Care Provision in Interwar Paris," 664.
12 CAN Fla 5136 R. Marcellin to M le Premier Ministre, 13 May 1963.
13 Patrick N'Diaye, *Négriers modernes: Les travailleurs noirs en France* (Paris: Présence Africaine, 1970), 15–16.

14 GITSI "Ordonnance n° 45–2658 du 2 novembre 1945 Relative aux conditions d'entrée et de séjour en France des étrangers et portant création de l'Office national de l'immigration" (J. O. 4 Novembre 7225; R., J. O. 7 Novembre 7351). www.gisti.org/spip.php?article3844. Original French: "... présenter non seulement les documents prévus ..., mais encore les contrats de travail régulièrement visés par le ministre chargé du travail ou l'autorisation à lui délivrée par le ministre chargé du travail, conformément à l'art. 7 .... Il doit être également porteur d'un certificat médical délivré par un médecin agréé par l'administration."

15 Patrick Weil, *Qu'est-ce qu'un Français?* (Paris: Éditions Grasset, 2004), 230.

16 Ibid., 230.

17 CANC 19810201 art. 4 "Note: dispositions en vigueur pour la prévention et le dépistage de la tuberculose chez les travailleurs migrants." 1966. For a discussion of French citizenship law, see Vincent Viet, *La France immigrée: construction d'une politique, 1914–1997* (Paris: Fayard, 1998). Weil, *La France et ses étrangers: l'aventure d'une politique de l'immigration 1938–1991* (Paris: Calmann-Levy, 1991). Wihtol de Wenden, *Les immigrés et la politique: Cent cinquante ans d'évolution* (Paris: Presses de la Fondation Nationale des Sciences Politiques, 1988).

18 CANC 19810201 art. 4 Charles Barbeau à Etienne Bernard, 12 March 1973.

19 CANC 19810201 art. 4 "Note: dispositions en vigueur pour la prévention et le dépistage de la tuberculose."

20 Ibid.

21 CANC 19810201 art. 4 Direction des mouvements de population, "Compte rendu de la réunion du 29 mai sur la tuberculose chez les migrants" 1966. CAN F1a 5136 R. Marcellin to M le Premier Ministre, 13 May 1963.

22 "Pathologie de l'immigrant" in N'Dongo, *La "coopération" franco-africaine* (Paris: Maspero, 1972), 94–95. Original French: "une surveillance médicale stricte s'impose, portant surtout sur la tuberculose. Un dépistage avant le départ dans le pays d'origine ou à défaut à l'arrivée en France est indispensable."

23 CAN F1a 5136 Legru, "Étude: problème noir." Original French: "les travailleurs originaires d'Afrique arrivent actuellement en France sans avoir été soumis à un examen médical."

24 CAN F1a 5053 Dr. Jean Brincourt, "Les Noirs africains dans un hôpital parisien," *Esprit Nouvelle série: Les Étrangers en France* (April 1966).

25 CIEMI Brumpt, "Problèmes sanitaires posés par les travailleurs africains."

26 Ibid.

27 Ibid.

28 Ibid.

29 Amelia Lyons, *The Civilizing Mission in the Metropole: Algerian Families and the French Welfare State during Decolonization* (Stanford: Stanford University Press, 2013), 2.

30 Riva Kastoryano, *Negotiating Identities: States and Immigrants in France and Germany* trans. Barbara Harshav (Princeton: Princeton University Press, 2002), 103.

31 CANC 19870009 art. 1 Bossuet 1969 6 CMSB, "Service Social" 5. Original French: "[les travailleurs Africains] ont tendance à se regrouper dans les centres urbains avec une grosse concentration à Paris et sa banlieue ..."

32 Rosenberg, *Policing Paris*, 176.

33 "Foreword" *Revue des sciences médicales: La pathologie du noir africain en France* 162 (October 1964): 3. Original French: "... considérer les rapports d'Afrique noire, de plus en plus importants, et dont l'afflux continuel en France constituè un fait nouveau. Physiologiquement et socialement inadaptés, fragilisés par des conditions de vie difficiles, voire même misérables, surmenés souvent par des tâches

pénibles de manœuvre à quoi les destine un manque complet de préparation professionnelle, ils sont, et souvent dès l'abord, des malades ou des impotents."

34 CIEMI L. Brumpt, "Problèmes sanitaires posés par les travailleurs africains," *Revue des sciences médicales: La pathologie du noir africain en France* 162 (October 1964): 5. Original French: "... la pathologie des Nord-africains diffère assez peu de la nôtre, celle des travailleurs africains nous donne un large accès à la médicale tropical."

35 CIEMI "Problèmes posés par l'immigration des travailleurs africains en France," *Journal officiel de la république française: Avis et rapports du conseil économique et social*, session de 1964 séance du 23 juin 1964: 547. Original French: "le milieu médical attire l'attention du Gouvernment sur le problème sanitaire pose par l'arrivée d'Africains souvent malades, ou le devenaient à la suite de leur transplantation en France."

36 Centre des études anti-impérialistes, *Les immigrés: contribution à l'histoire politique de l'immigration en France* (Paris: Lutter, 1975), 207.

37 CANC 19870009 art. 1 Bossuet 1965 Madame Audibert, "Rapport trimestriel d'activité du service médico-social du 1.1.1965."

38 CIEMI "Problèmes posés par l'immigration des travailleurs africains en France," *Journal officiel de la République française: Avis et rapports du conseil économique et social.* session de 1964 séance du 23 juin 1964: 548. Original French: "un certificat de control sanitaire."

39 CANC 1987009 art. 1 Bossuet 1965 Madame Audibert, "Rapport trimestriel d'activité du service médico-social du 1.1.1965" 1 January 1965, 2. Original French: "[l]es conventions signées entre la République Français et les Républiques du Mali, de la Mauritanie, du Sénégal, ayant prévue tout Travailleur Africain devait être porteur d'un certificat médical à son arrivée en France ..."

40 CANC 1987009 art. 1 Bossuet 1965 Madame Audibert, "Rapport trimestriel d'activité du service médico-social du 1.1.1965" 1 January 1965, 3.

41 CANC 19850087 art. 158/159 MI 26755/26756 "Séances de vaccination antituberculose dans des foyers de travailleurs africains." 29 November 1963.

42 CANC 19850087 art. 158/159 MI 26755/26756 "Objet: Examens radiographiques des travailleurs africains." 4 December 1963.

43 ADVM 2018W art. 20 Gauche prolétarienne, "Pour des conditions de vie décentes travailleurs, tous unis, en avant!" CANC 19810201 art. 4 Direction des mouvements de population, "Compte rendu de la réunion du 29 mai sur la tuberculose chez les migrants" 1966.

44 CAN F1a 5136 Conseil économique et social, "Problèmes posés par l'immigration des travailleurs africains en France Deuxième partie: conditions de vie," *Journal officiel de la république française: Avis et rapports* séance, 23 June 1964.

45 CAN F1a 5053 Dr. Jean Brincourt, "Les noirs africains dans un hôpital parisien," *Esprit: Nouvelle série les étrangers en France* April 1966.

46 AMSD 18 ACW 22/23 "Tract: Pour le relogement d'urgence des travailleurs noirs." 24 August 1964.

47 CAN F1a 5136 Conseil économique et social, "Problèmes posés par l'immigration des travailleurs africains en France," *Journal Officiel*, 23 June 1964.

48 CANC 19810201 art. 4 Groupe du travail réuni à l'initiative du Comité nationale de défense contre la tuberculose, "Pour un programme de lutte anti-tuberculose adapté à la situation présenté." 4–5 May, 1968.

49 CANC 19810201 art. 4 Etienne Bernard to M Barbeau, 30 August 1972.

50 CANC 19810201 art. 4 Dr. Coudreau, "Annexe 5: la lutte contre la tuberculose."

51 CANC 19810201 art. 4 E. Bernard to M Fontanet, 22 September 1969.

52 CANC 19810201 art. 4 Comité nationale de la défense contre la tuberculose, "Assemblée générale du 13 juin 1969." 13 June 1969.

53 Ibid.

54 For example, between 1948 and 1965, the death rate per 100,000 for the French population dropped from 333 to 85, while Africans and North Africans increasingly constituted the victims of tuberculosis. CAN F1a 5051 Dr. Max Fourestier and Mlle R. Robert, "Rapport sur la morbidité tuberculeuse observée chez les africains noirs et les sujets originaires d'Afrique du Nord dénombrés à Montreuil en 1964, en 1965 et les 9 premiers mois de 1966" 1966.

55 CANC 19810201 art. 4 Comité national de la défense contre la tuberculose, "Assemblée générale du 13 juin 1969." 13 June 1969.

56 CAN F1a 5051 Bernard Delaniare, "Note d'information concernant la morbidité tuberculeuse observée chez les Africains noirs et les sujets originaires d'Afrique du Nord." 9 December 1966.

57 CANC 19810201 art. 4 Préfecture de police, "Annexe 2: Lutte contre la tuberculose chez les travailleurs migrants de la région parisienne et leurs familles Table ronde du 22 mars 1972." 22 March 1972.

58 Ibid.

59 Ibid.

60 Ibid.

61 Ibid.

62 AP 1206W art. 6 "Rapport sur le Centre médico-social Bossuet." 1976.

63 CANC 19810201 art. 4 "Ouverture de la campagne anti-tuberculose: les dangers de contamination sont encore très élevés en France pour les enfants," *Le Monde*, 17–18 November 1968.

64 *Revue française des Affaires sociales* 29ème année janvier–mars 1975 in N'Dongo, *La "coopération franco-africaine,"* 132. CIEMI "Le Centre médico-social Bossuet: dix ans d'action en faveur des travailleurs migrants d'Afrique noire francophone," *Revue française des affaires sociales* 29 (January–March 1975).

65 *Revue française des Affaires sociales* 29ème année janvier–mars 1975 in N'Dongo, *La "coopération" franco-africaine*, 132.

66 *Revue française des Affaires sociales* 29ème année janvier–mars 1975 in N'Dongo, *La "coopération" franco-africaine*, 131–132. CIEMI "Le Centre médico-social Bossuet: dix ans d'action en faveur des travailleurs migrants d'Afrique noire francophone," *Revue française des affaires sociales* 29 (January–March, 1975). AP 1206W art. 9 "Rapport sur le Centre médico-social Bossuet." 1976.

67 PPA Ga7 Dr. Keita, "Rapport d'activité." January 1970.

68 *Revue française des affaires sociales* 29ème année janvier–mars 1975 in N'Dongo, *La "coopération" franco-africaine*, 132. AP 1206W art. 9 Letter to M le Directeur Général de l'URSSAF, 2 September 1979.

69 "Le Centre médico-social Bossuet: dix ans d'action en faveur des travailleurs migrants d'Afrique noire francophone," *Revue française des affaires sociales* 29 (January–March 1975).

70 CAN F1a 5136 Ministère de la santé publique et de la population aux associations qui exercent une action sociale auprès des travailleurs noires-africaines dans la région parisienne, 23 September 1963.

71 CIEMI "Le Centre médico-social Bossuet: dix ans d'action en faveur des travailleurs migrants d'Afrique noire francophone," *Revue française des affaires sociales* 29, (January–March 1975).

72 CAN F1a 5136 Bernard Lory to M le Premier Ministre, 14 June 1963.

73 CAN F1a 5136 Ministère de la santé publique et de la population aux associations qui exercent une action sociale auprès des travailleurs noirs africains dans la région parisienne, 23 September 1964.

74 *Revue française des affaires sociales* 29ème année janvier–mars 1975 in N'Dongo, *La "coopération" franco-africaine*, 133.

75 Ibid., 137, 143.

76 AP 1206W art. 6 "Note: Origine du Centre Bossuet." Association de Centre médico-social Bossuet (ACMSB), "Rapport d'activité 1977: Service social."
77 CAN F1a 5136 Secrétariat général du gouvernement, "Compte-rendu de la réunion du 4 octobre 1963: immigrants d'Afrique noire."
78 CIEMI Georges Jaeger, "L'examen de dépistage des travailleurs africains en France" *Revue des sciences médicales: La pathologie du noir africain en France*, October 1964.
79 CANC 19810201 art. 4 Dr. Chaix and Dr. Pretet, "Annexe 4: Lutte contre la tuberculose chez les travailleurs migrants de la région parisienne—Table Ronde du 22 mars 1972" 22 March 1972. Dr. Coudreau, "Annexe 5: La lutte contre la tuberculose chez les migrants de la région parisienne Table ronde du 22 March 1972."
80 CANC 19810201 art. 4 Préfecture de police, "Réunion du 22 mars 1972 Problème régional de la lutte contre la tuberculose chez les travailleurs migrants." 22 March 1972.
81 *Revue française des affaires sociales* 29ème année janvier–mars 1975 in N'Dongo, *La "coopération" franco-africaine*, 137.
82 ADVM 2252W art. 253 AFTAM, February 1967.
83 *Revue française des affaires sociales* 29ème année janvier–mars 1975 in N'Dongo, *La "coopération" franco-africaine*, 140.
84 CANC 19960311 art. 6 Préfecture de police, "Cinquante-cinq africains seulement sur 540 ont subi, le 17 septembre au soir, la visite de dépistage de la tuberculose au 'dortoir' de la rue Gabriel Péri à Ivry." 18 September 1969. Préfecture de police, "Le 'responsable' d'une des communautés africains d'Ivry invite ses compatriotes à ne pas subir la visite de dépistage de la tuberculose qui doit avoir lieu demain mercredi 17 septembre." 16 September 1969.
85 CANC 19960311 art. 6 Maurice Grimaud to M le Ministre de l'Intérieur, 16 October 1969.
86 CANC 19810201 art. 4 Bernard to Barbereau, 30 August 1972.
87 Ibid.
88 CANC 19810201 art. 4 Comité national de défense contre la tuberculose, "Assemblée générale du 13 juin 1969." Original French: "... tout l'effort qu'il faut poursuivre pour la prévention, le dépistage précoce et le traitement de la tuberculose chez les travailleurs étrangers, en priorité chez les Noirs africains et les Algériens."
89 CANC 19810201 art. 4 Comité national de défense contre la tuberculose, "Assemblée générale du 13 juin 1969."
90 Quiminal argues that illnesses forced many Soninké workers to repatriate. See Quiminal, *Gens d'ici, gens d'ailleurs: migrations soninké et transformations villageoises*, 20.
91 CANC 19810201 art. 4 Dr. Chaix and Dr. Pretet, "Annexe 4: Table Ronde du 22 mars 1972."
92 CANC 19810201 art. 4 Dr. Chaix and Dr. Pretet, "Annexe 4: Table Ronde du 22 mars 1972." Original French: "le rapatriement sanitaire peut être source de contamination de l'entourage du malade de retour dans son pays."
93 CANC 19810201 art. 4 Dr. Chaix and Dr. Pretet, "Annexe 4: Table Ronde du 22 mars 1972." Original French: "[p]our l'ensemble des départements, il apparait que la convalescence à domicile est mauvaise en raison de facteurs sociaux défavorables: logement, nutrition, promiscuité."
94 AP 1206W art. 9 ACMSB, "Rapport d'activité année 1976: Service social/ activité médico-social."
95 The African immigrant community in France continued to take an interest in health care in Africa after 1974 and the more permanent settlement of the community. In the 1980s and 1990s, various associations in France worked to build clinics in their countries of origin. The emphasis had shifted, yet the concern

over health care and medical treatment remained salient for the African community. They were now looking at it from the perspective, however, of what they could do from France to improve the situation at home. See Christophe Daum, *Les Associations de Maliens en France: Migrations, développement, et citoyenneté* (Paris: Éditions Karthala, 1998), 46–47.

96 Benjamin N. Lawrance, Emily Lynn Osborn, and Richard L. Roberts, "Introduction: African Intermediaries and the 'Bargain' of Collaboration" in Lawrance, Osborn, and Roberts, eds., *Intermediaries, Interpreters, and Clerks: African Employees in the Making of Colonial Africa* (Madison: University of Wisconsin Press, 2006), 5.

97 CAN 19870009 art. 1 1967 3 Association du Centre Médico-Social Bossuet, "Rapport d'activité Année 1967" 3.

98 CAN 19870009 art. 1 1967 3 Centre Médico-Social Bossuet, "Rapport d'activité 1967" Paris, 15 March 1968, 12.

99 Alice Conklin, *A Mission to Civilize: The Republican Idea of Empire in France and West Africa, 1895–1930* (Stanford: Stanford University Press, 1997), 221.

100 CAN 19870009 art. 1 1967 3 Centre Médico-Social Bossuet, "Rapport d'activité 1967" Paris, 15 March 1968, 14. Original French: "[p]ourtant la plupart de ces dispensaires reconnaissent d'eux-mêmes leurs désarroi devant la clientèle noire, les obstacles quasi-insurmontable que dressent la barrière linguistique, et aussi il faut bien le reconnaître, la mentalité très particulière du Noir Africain."

101 AP 1206W art. 9 ACMSB, "Rapport d'activité année 1976: Service social Activité médico-social."

102 AP 1206W art. 9 Association pour l'accueil médico-social des migrants, "Centre Bossuet: Budget Provisionnel pour 1981." CMSB, "Rapport d'activité 1976 Services sociales." CMSB, "Procès-verbal de la réunion du conseil d'administration" 1976.

103 AP 1206W, art. 9 "Questions et réponses: Etablissement d'hospitalisation, de soins et de cure." Assemblée Nationale – Questions et réponses, May 1980. Note 22335 -13, November 1979.

104 AP 1206W, art. 9 CMSB, "Rapport d'activité 1976, Services Sociaux." CMSB, "Rapport d'activité année 1975: Services Sociaux."

105 AP 1206W, art. 9 CMSB, "Rapport d'activité année 1976: Services Sociaux." CMSB, "Rapport d'activité année 1976: Activité Sociale." CMSB, "Procès-verbal de la réunion de conseil d'administration." "Rapport sur le Centre médico-social Bossuet" 1979.

106 CIEMI Roland Garrigues, "L'alphabétisation des migrants dans l'hôpital." AP 1206W art. 6 ACMSB, "Rapport d'activité 1976: Services sociaux, activité médico-social" ACMSB, "Rapport d'activité 1975: Services sociaux."

107 AP 1206W art. 9 CMSB, "Rapport d'activité année 1976: Services sociaux" Paris, 1976. Original French: "[l]es travailleurs africains fréquentant le Centre Bossuet ont eu, comme les années passées, recours au Service Social POUR TOUS LES PROBLÈMES LIES A LA MALADIE, tant en pneumophtisiologie, qu'en médecine générale et tropicale: papiers à remplir, explication des traitements, approvisionnement en médicaments pour les sans ressources, orientation vers les consultations spécialisées hospitalières ou vers les centres d'examens complémentaires, relations avec les employeurs."

108 AP 1206W art. 9 Association pour l'accueil médico-social des migrants, "Centre Bossuet: Budget Provisionnel pour 1981." CMSB, "Rapport d'activité 1976 Services sociaux." CMSB, "Procès-verbal de la réunion du conseil d'administration" 1976.

109 AP 1206W art. 9 CMSB, "Rapport d'activité année 1975: Services sociaux." CMSB, "Rapport d'activité 1976: Services sociaux."

110 Conklin, *A Mission to Civilize*, 109–119.

111 AP 1206W art. 9 CMSB, "Rapport d'activité année 1975: Services sociaux." CMSB, "Rapport d'activité 1976: Services Sociaux."
112 AP 1206W art. 9 CMSB, "Rapport d'activité année 1976: Services sociaux."
113 CANC 19870009 art. 1 1965 Madame Audibert "Rapport trimestriel d'activité du service médico-social du 1.1.1965," 10. Original French: "Les problèmes prioritaires que nous sommes amenés à examiner: santé, hébergement, adaptation au milieu, éducation, emploi, etc. peuvent difficilement être dissociés."
114 AP 1206W art. 9 CMSB, "Rapport d'activité année 1976: Services sociaux."
115 For more on the 1974 change in immigration law, see Viet, *La France immigrée*, 364–383.
116 AP 1206W art. 9 CMSB, "Rapport d'activité 1976: Services sociaux." Association du Centre social-médico Bossuet, "Rapport d'activité 1975: Services sociaux."
117 AP 1206W art. 9 CMSB, "Rapport d'activité 1976: Services sociaux." CMSB, "Rapport d'activité 1975: Service sociaux." CMSB, "Procès-verbal de la réunion du conseil d'administration." Conseil d'Administration, CMSB. "Ordre du jour de la réunion extraordinaire du Conseil d'Administration, 27 septembre 1979." Ministère du Travail to M le Président, CMSB. Paris, 22 December 1977.
118 Quiminal discusses the contemporary role of associations in mediating and facilitating African women's health issues and concerns. See Catherine Quiminal, "The Associative Movement of African Women and New Forms of Citizenship," in Jane Freedman and Carrie Tarr, eds., *Women, Immigration and Identity in France* (Oxford: Berg, 2000), 52–53.
119 AP 1206W art. 9 "Note: Origine du Centre Bossuet." CMSB, "Rapport d'activité 1976: Services Sociaux." Association du Centre médico-social Bossuet, "Rapport d'activité année 1976." CMSB, "Rapport année 1974: Services Sociaux." CMSB, "Annexe: Étude de la population féminine ayant fréquenté le Centre médico-social Bossuet au cours de l'année 1974." "Rapport sur le Centre médico-social Bossuet."
120 AP 1206 W. art. 9 "Rapport d'activité année 1976: Services sociaux." Original French: "Cependant au cours de cette année 1976 la demande en interventions sociales proprement dite s'est manifestée d'une façon beaucoup plus intensive. Cette augmentation de la demande sociale est due en large partie aux difficultés causées par la crise économique: la suspension de l'immigration fut appliquée d'une façon beaucoup plus stricte en 1976 aux travailleurs d'Afrique Noire (impossibilité aux nouveaux arrivants d'obtenir une carte de séjour) (et) les pertes d'emploi par licenciement et le chômage furent fréquents."
121 AP 1206 W art. 9 "Rapport d'activité année 1974: Annexe Étude de la population féminine ayant fréquenté le centre médico-social Bossuet au cours de l'année 1974." Original French: "Les travailleurs africains acceptent de moins en moins de vivre éloignés de leurs femmes."
122 Lyons, *The Civilizing Mission in the Metropole*, 99–113.
123 AP 1206W art. 9 "Rapport d'activité année 1974: Annexe: Étude de la population féminine ayant fréquenté le centre médico-social Bossuet au cours de l'année 1974." Original French: "[c]ette population féminine africaine, nouvellement arrivée en France, reste encore mál connue car elle fréquente très peu les services sociaux spécialisés destines á l'accueillir et á l'orienter. Les femmes restent souvent isolées chez elles et participent rarement aux cours d'alphabétisation ..."
124 AP 1206W art. 9 "Rapport d'activité année 1974: Annexe: Étude de la population féminine ayant fréquenté le centre médico-social Bossuet au cours de l'année 1974." Original French: "déterminer ses besoins et, éventuellement, quelles structures il serait nécessaire de mettre en place pour y répondre."
125 AP 1206 W art. 9 CMSB, "Rapport d'activité 1977: Activité auprès des femmes."

126 AP 1206W art. 9 CMSB, "Rapport d'activité 1977: Activité auprès des femmes." CMSB, "Rapport d'activité 1974: Annexe: Étude de la population féminine ayant fréquenté le Centre médico-social Bossuet au cours de l'année 1974." (Paris: Association médico-social Bossuet, 1974). "Note: Origine du Centre Bossuet." CMSB, "Rapport d'activité 1976: Services Sociaux." Association du Centre médico-social Bossuet, "Rapport d'activité année 1976."

127 AP 1206W art. 9 "Rapport d'activité année 1977: Planning familial et maternité." Original French: "Les femmes qui sont enceintes pour la première fois en France appréhendent beaucoup de vivre leur grossesse seule sans le soutien de leur famille ou de leur groupe social. Elles ont très peur d'accoucher à l'Hôpital, les femmes qui ne parlent pas français ne peuvent s'exprimer sur le sujet, mais doivent être aussi angoissées."

128 AP 1206W art. 9 AMSB, "Rapport d'activité 1976: Services Sociaux." CMSB, "Rapport d'activité 1976: Note de présentation." CMSB, "Rapport d'activité année 1974: Annexe étudie de la population féminine ayant fréquenté le Centre médico-social Bossuet au cours de l'année 1974." CMSB, "Procès-verbal de la réunion du conseil d'administration." (Paris: Centre médico-social Bossuet, 1976). "Rapport sur le Centre médico-social Bossuet."

129 AP 1206W art. 9 CMSB, "Rapport d'activité 1976: Services sociaux." CMSB, "Rapport d'activité 1976: Note de présentation." Centre médico-social Bossuet, "Rapport d'activité année 1974: Annexe étudie de la population féminine ayant fréquenté le Centre médico-social Bossuet au cours de l'année 1974." CMSB, "Procès-verbal de la réunion du conseil d'administration." "Rapport sur le Centre médico-social Bossuet."

130 1206 W. art. 9 "Rapport d'activité année 1976: Services sociaux" Paris, 1976. Original French: "donne asile … à un cours d'alphabétisation, s'adressent aux femmes, assuré par l'ACAFOM et l'AEE."

131 AP 1206W art. 9 Comité de défense Bossuet, "Tract: Pour la reconnaissance du droit à la santé des immigrés sans titres de séjour." Original French: "l'immigré sans titre de séjour n'est plus reconnu comme une personne ayant, comme tout être humain droit à la santé. Le Centre Bossuet était un lieu où ce droit élémentaire à être soigné était reconnu tous y étant soignés sans discrimination avec ou sans titre de séjour."

132 AP 1206W art. 9 Comité pour la survie du service médico-social rendu aux Africains à Bossuet, "Tract: Il faut sauver 'Bossuet'." Original French: "Les femmes africains pouvaient s'y rencontrer et discuter entre elles de problèmes les intéressant: maternité et contraception, formation, travail, préparation du retour au pays, éducation des enfants."

133 AP 1206W art. 9 "Note: La fermeture du Centre Bossuet—Origine du Centre Bossuet." ACMSB, "Rapport d'activité 1975: Service sociaux." "Note: La fermeture du Centre Bossuet—Origine du Centre Bossuet." "Objet: Réception des Africains Noirs." Le Comité pour la survie du service médico-social rendu aux Africains à Bossuet, "Il faut sauver 'Bossuet'." Comité défense Bossuet, "Pour la reconnaissance du droit à la santé des immigrés sans titres de séjour." Le Comité pour la survie du service médico-social Bossuet, "Motion pour la réouverture du Centre médico-social Bossuet."

6 The desire to disperse

The anti-*bidonville* campaign

Returning to the old chocolate factory in Ivry, we see the link between rent strikes, relocations, social welfare, and the anti-slum campaign of the 1960s and 1970s. One official supervising the effort to evacuate the Ivry dormitory argued that "the hygienic conditions that prevailed in the dormitory had proven disastrous."[1] In reality, though, the evacuation in Ivry was less concerned with improving residents' living and hygienic conditions and more focused on exacting control, breaking up the social and political networks linked to protests and political activism, and dispersing Africans throughout the Paris region. By December 1970, over 470 of the former chocolate factory's residents were relocated, finding themselves spread from an ASSOTRAF-run *foyer* in Ivry to housing in other municipalities such as Villejuif and Thiais.[2] Lucien Miard, writing for *Le Figaro*, explained that this was one of the largest evacuations and relocations of immigrant residents carried out to that point in Paris or the *banlieues*.[3] He pointed out that, "this relocation operation targeting dangerous housing undertaken by the *Préfecture* of the Val-de-Marne, is one of the most important that has been undertaken."[4]

By the early 1970s, official policies toward African workers and other immigrants became more aggressive, using extensive surveillance while initiating a large-scale relocation program. In what was referred to by officials as, "one of the most important (relocations) that was realized in the Paris region," representatives from the SAT—the same organization that placed the Malians there in the first place in 1965—began forcibly removing the residents from their *foyer* on the rue Gabriel Péri in December of 1969.[5] Relocations continued well into 1970.[6] Officials conducting the program decided against waiting for the construction of a new dormitory—a solution to the rent strike proposed at the local level. It was the only idea that emerged from the Ivry Municipal Council with which representatives from the *Préfecture de police* and the Ministry of the Interior agreed, arguing that it would "constitute the last opportunity to put an end to a dangerous situation from all perspectives, both in terms of security and in terms of public order."[7]

The anti-slum campaign points to the important relationship between the knowledge acquired through state surveillance and the ways in which

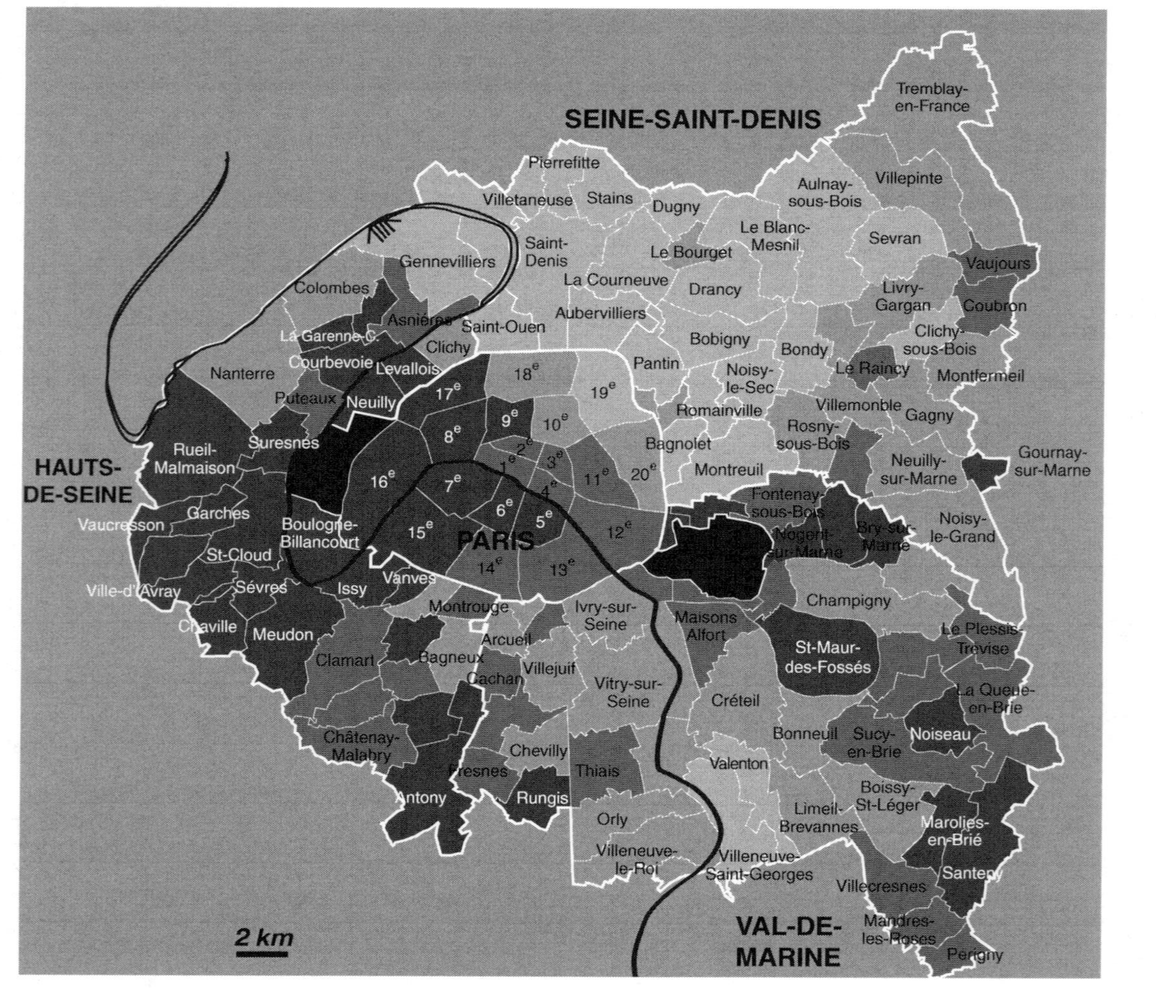

Figure 6.1 Map of Paris and the surrounding *banlieues*. Image courtesy of Wikicommons.

it influenced subsequent policy initiatives. We see how activism such as rent strikes not only attracted the state's attention but also shaped its response. More troubling, however, was the forcible removal and relocation of African immigrants, many of whom found themselves separated from their friends, relatives, and support networks. This chapter uses the relocation of African immigrants across the Paris region to understand the impact of political protest, state surveillance, and social welfare initiatives on the African immigrant community.[8] State-led relocation efforts demonstrate how immigrant political activism together with state surveillance and social welfare initiatives contributed to the policies undertaken by the French government in response to the growing African community between 1963 and 1974, the year that unrestricted labor migration to France ended. Examining the program shows how government entities used the anti-slum campaign and relocations to exert control over the African immigrant community and the urban spaces which they inhabited in the aftermath of events such as the Saint-Denis riot, the Ivry rent strike, and the deaths at Aubervilliers. The anti-*bidonville* campaign reveals how it is that the state organizes the urban landscape and its inhabitants and reflects current debates regarding segregation and what have been labeled as apartheid-like conditions in contemporary France. The residential segregation observed in urban areas by the 1990s had its origins much earlier in the twentieth century and can be traced, at least in part, to the anti-slum campaign of the late 1960s and early 1970s.[9] This means that the state itself contributed to emerging segregation policies after decolonization and in response to growing populations of non-Western immigrants, including African workers. The state's postcolonial role in organizing housing geographically contributed to a more segregated and differentiated society, impacting subsequent patterns of segregation in urban areas, including Paris and the *banlieues*.

Policies and approaches

On the surface, the campaign was shaped by the idea that anyone living in France should be entitled to decent housing conditions, a perspective that also influenced the ways in which French authorities dealt with the housing of French citizens.[10] By 1965, *Hommes et migrations*, a journal that covers migration-related issues, noted that "the fight against slums is for black workers the priority item above all others ... the solution is urgent."[11] This growing sense of urgency emerged by the mid-1960s. In an open letter to African residents living within its jurisdiction, the municipality of Saint-Denis argued that "you must be provided with the housing, work, resources, and liberties necessary to live normally."[12] This emphasis on providing basic resources was in line with a key goal of the Debré Law: to guarantee housing to residents displaced by the effort to close down slums.[13]

Several national laws guided the efforts undertaken in the anti-slum campaign. A 1945 statute governed the treatment of illegal tenants and shaped the ways in which each effort could be carried out. The sometimes chaotic nature of many of the relocation efforts was directly related to the fact that additional legislation guiding the efforts—the Debré Law of 1964—emerged four years after the beginning of postcolonial African labor migration. The law intended to "facilitate for the purposes of reconstruction or development the expropriation of land on which was built insalubrious housing beyond repair, commonly called 'slums'."[14] This law called for the elimination of all *bidonvilles* and other forms of problematic housing.[15] Architectural scholar Jacob Paskins argues that the Debré Law allowed the state to take over areas that housed slums while also guaranteeing residents' relocation to alternative housing.[16] The law also focused on the construction of at least 15,000 HLM (*Habitation à loyer modéré* or Affordable Housing) units.[17] Those residences, in addition to the 8,000 units already proposed, would provide accommodation for residents who were displaced through the campaign.[18] Beyond the directive to eliminate *bidonvilles*, several decrees defined more narrowly what constituted problematic housing conditions. For example, administrative decree 62–146 passed in April of 1962. Later legislation provided more precise guidance, including a 1964 law specifying that any inhabited yet dilapidated structure could be interpreted as problematic housing and targeted for relocation within the anti-slum campaign.[19] Authorities could ignore or address these kinds of dwellings, depending on their objectives with various neighborhoods and immigrant groups. Broad legal definitions were open to interpretation, depending on the status of each individual residence. Two unifying goals by the late 1960s and early 1970s, however, were "the total disappearance of slums"[20] and "the prevention of the creation and spread of slums."[21] The 1970 Vivienne Law created an organizational structure through which to address and eliminate this kind of housing. A decree from that same year created the permanent *Groupe interministériel permanent* (Permanent Interministerial Group or GIP) to coordinate campaigns against *bidonvilles* and ensure that programs were put in place to address problematic housing.[22] Prime Minister Jacques Chaban-Delmas proved instrumental in organizing the GIP. As Gary P. Freeman describes it, Chaban-Delmas was "visibly shaken by the sordid conditions in which thousands of foreigners were living only a few miles from the Champs Elysée."[23]

The campaign targeted a number of neighborhoods and *banlieues* throughout the Paris region. Several immigrant groups—including African, Portuguese, and Algerian workers and their families—were swept up into the program. While the plight of African immigrants within the anti-*bidonville* campaign remains the focus here, it is important to note that this was a multidimensional effort that targeted many residents—and therefore numerous immigrant groups—throughout the Paris region. The variety of immigrant communities caught up in the anti-*bidonville* campaign reflects the universal struggle to secure decent housing that affected immigrants, regardless of their country of origin. While important differences existed between immigrant groups—Algerians were more likely to arrive as families whereas African workers often came on their own or with family members that did not include their wives or children, especially prior to the 1970s—many found themselves living in slums in and beyond Paris. The multiethnic nature of the anti-*bidonville* campaign reflects this challenge, as the state recognized that numerous immigrant groups struggled to secure decent housing. To have thousands of immigrants living in these conditions alarmed officials, who understood the links between the housing conditions endured by immigrant groups and the riots, rent strikes, and political mobilization that emerged across the 1960s within and beyond the African immigrant community.

Ideas of race and the anti-*bidonville* campaign

By targeting enclaves of Africans and other immigrant groups labeled "problematic" for evacuation and relocation, officials aimed to control where and how Africans and other immigrants lived in the Paris region.[24] Through this program, officials could, as the *Préfecture de police* recommended in a 1964 report, "Maintain a relative dispersion of Africans."[25] The program relied heavily on police surveillance of specific dormitories and dwellings collected by the *Préfecture de police*, *Sûreté nationale*, and other divisions within the Ministry of the Interior. Occasionally, the relocation efforts resulted in minor arguments and scuffles, but no large-scale violence occurred between officials and those they relocated or the tenants themselves.

Conceptualizations of race and concentrations of black African immigrants proved to be two key factors that shaped the anti-slum campaign overall. In French West Africa, colonial authorities developed the *politique des races* in the first decades of the twentieth century to assert and reinforce French colonial rule and to signal, "Dakar's new interest in regulating its subjects' political and social affairs."[26] As we have seen in various instances, a similar approach influenced policy in France after decolonization. Housing was an area where officials addressed what they considered to be the *problème noir* or "black problem" emerging in Paris alongside the settlement of African workers in the Paris region. A sociological report titled *A Study of the Black Problem in the Paris Region* (*Étude problème noir région parisienne*), commissioned by the *Préfecture de la Seine* in the mid-1960s, explained that "from the French point of view, the [black] problem is three-fold: the problem of public order, the problem of public health [and] the problem of public morality."[27] That same report argued that, to effectively respond to the African presence, authorities would have to "regulate, organize, and control" this immigrant group.[28] Initiatives such as the anti-slum campaign represented the ways in which officials sorted out how and whether Africans could be included in the political and social fold of French society and in urban areas such as Paris.

Officials in France focused on breaking down the African tendency to regroup in *foyers* and other housing establishments by dispersing them throughout the Paris region. They retained a secondary interest in providing opportunities for improved access to education, training, and medical care through relocation efforts. The campaign's focus on dispersing African immigrants throughout the Paris region also stemmed from the desire to separate French and African populations within cities such as Dakar in French-controlled Africa. This resulted in, as Conklin argues, "distancing between colonizer and colonized."[29] Rigid separation was maintained neither in AOF nor in metropolitan France. Policies in metropolitan France and French West Africa before decolonization echoed the same set of assumptions about racial difference, influencing the way in which French officials understood the place of African immigrants in the metropolitan context.[30] One 1965 report argued that "it is necessary to maintain a relative dispersion of Africans."[31] In 1970, the *Conseil général* of the Seine-Saint-Denis department demanded "an equitable distribution of immigrant workers in the Paris region."[32] The emergence of hierarchies, distinctions, and differences within the contemporary French political sphere, documented by Dominic Thomas, began, in part, with policies such as the anti-slum campaign in the 1960s and early 1970s, prior to the National Front's rise and the prominence of anti-immigrant rhetoric within recent political debates.[33] Regional officials in the era just after decolonization did not want to be a repository for impoverished immigrants. Dispersal could be directly achieved and maintained through relocation efforts, which reflected an attempt to exact control over a city that was home to a larger and increasingly more diverse non-western immigrant population.[34]

Official concerns over African immigration reflected a reluctance to come to terms with the presence of former African "subjects" in metropolitan France. Phrases such as "problematic" indirectly referenced what authorities by the early 1960s identified as the *problème noir*, which reflected the core ideology of the anti-slum campaign: that concentrations of black African immigrants were viewed, literally, as a problem for urban areas. By 1963, one report argued that:

> the difficulties that arose from the influx in the Paris region of a large number of African workers who were poorly adapted to our climate and our way of life could only be overcome within a comprehensive policy focused on this immigration.[35]

Phrases such as "poorly adapted" implied that Africans arrived inadequately prepared to successfully navigate life in France and that their return to Africa would be the best solution—from both the French and African perspectives.

The relocations undertaken in peripheral Parisian neighborhoods and *banlieues* such as Ivry pointed to the extent to which the anti-slum campaign attempted to disperse immigrants.[36] At times, officials labeled *foyers* inhabited by African workers as "communitarian ghettos," viewing them as closed-off ethnic enclaves that promoted racial solidarity and stunted integration, in line with broader views regarding the challenges of integrating immigrant groups.[37] Yet there were efforts to understand why it was that African immigrants sought each other out. One report from the *Préfecture de police* argued that African immigrants sought each other out because they were:

> practically broke, naturally searching for material and moral support from their compatriots, predisposed to the communitarian lifestyle, new arrivals seek out already-formed groups who have crowded into overcrowded dormitories ... the only lodgings that their meagre resources allow them to occupy.[38]

Despite misgivings about concentrations of immigrant groups, officials acknowledged that Africans lived in dire poverty, which contributed to the state's motivation to undertake this relocation program.

From the standpoint of housing, one of the major problems identified with slums was the lack of internal cohesion and structure. With few authority figures beyond landlords to assert control, authorities worried that Africans and members of other immigrant groups could potentially threaten public order and safety.[39] Officials labeled African migration patterns as "anarchic" and "out of control" while projecting these characterizations onto their dwellings.[40] Authorities considered this perceived threat to public order grave, as immigrants without decent accommodations were perceived as unruly. The tendency to see larger concentrations of African workers in this manner only intensified in the wake of the Saint-Denis riot in 1963, which pointed to racial tensions between different immigrant communities and their French counterparts.[41] Riots, rent strikes, and urban unrest further reinforced the ways in which officials understood immigrant dwellings and their potential for danger and instability. This in turn reflected the general anxiety and unease among officials observing the growing population of African immigrants throughout the Paris region.

Many of the relocations conducted throughout the campaign rested on the assumption that African immigrants could be better controlled once they arrived in France if authorities rather than the migrants themselves determined where they lived and with whom.[42] Through relocations, the goal was to make it more difficult for migrants to riot and strike by disrupting their ability to organize and further the social networks that fostered political activism.[43] The anti-slum campaign also took place against the backdrop of a shifting debate about labor in the final decade of the postwar economic boom. While relocating African immigrants from one dwelling to the next, officials often complained about the state of African immigration in general. They questioned the entire labor migration policy sanctioned by the French government throughout the 1960s and its *laissez-faire* attitude, pointing out that it was France's largely unregulated labor migration that contributed to housing problems. One report explained that, "all of these problems (of unfit housing) are related to the definition of an immigration policy."[44] Authorities also expressed concern bordering on resentment over the growing African community's presence in France, arguing that it exacerbated the already challenging situation of securing acceptable housing for immigrant groups. They believed that this trend signaled an irreversible and alarming shift toward a non-western, non-European migration of populations deemed problematic and incompatible with French society.[45] The possibility of permanent settlement loomed and the anti-*bidonville* campaign together with other initiatives—such as the opening of the *Centre Bossuet*—reflected the state's attempt to address these developments.

The desire to disperse the growing population of African immigrants also reflected the idea within French society that ethnic enclaves and concentrations of immigrant communities prevented integration.[46] Relocations could effectively interrupt what was referred to as the communitarian impulse while distributing Africans throughout the Paris region in smaller, more manageable numbers. In part, this represented the desire among French officials to change and modify African social behaviors.[47] Yet as François Manchuelle demonstrates, the tendency to seek out members of the Soninké ethnicity once in France remained a long-standing trend over the course of the twentieth century. He argues that even in the 1930s in Dakar and Marseille, regrouping provided migrants from the same villages with the ability to assist one another by living in proximity to each other. [48] This pattern continued into the postcolonial era, but French officials viewed it as threatening rather than seeing it as an immigrant-initiated support system.

Beyond the need for control, officials often conducted evacuations and relocations because of a fear of disease among immigrant populations and their proximity to the surrounding public.[49] In France after 1960, the anti-slum campaign was guided in part by the law of February 15, 1902, which protected public health against problematic and unsanitary housing conditions.[50] Authorities perceived unregulated concentrations of African immigrants as a potential threat to the surrounding community. One of the fundamental criteria for relocating residents was the physical condition of the slums in which they lived and their associated health risks. The GIP argued that damp, poorly ventilated, unsanitary conditions combined with overcrowding created the perfect environment for the spread of disease.[51] Authorities often worried, not entirely unreasonably, that inhabitants of run-down *foyers* and slums would become more susceptible to disease—including tuberculosis—during the winter months. The fear of disease among African immigrants became a major catalyst in the anti-slum campaign.[52]

Official relocation efforts forced newly relocated tenants to re-establish social connections with fellow immigrants, while creating uncertainty, as authorities had the power to shift them from one area to another at any moment. These dispersal efforts created an inherent sense of insecurity among residents, as they never quite knew if, when, or how they might be relocated.

Because most African immigrants at this time did not own restaurants, hotels, or shops, their ability to foster social connections was centered on their residence in *foyers*, hotels, and other dwellings.[53] By shifting the social space in which African immigrants lived, authorities removed their ability to anchor themselves and form connections to the surrounding community.[54]

The campaign's scope

While criticizing the lack of initiative on housing and relocation on the part of the embassies and industrial firms, officials also looked directly to local initiatives for inspiration. The anti-slum campaign in its late-1960s incarnation grew out of local approaches that served as immigration policy laboratories. Local governments with higher concentrations of African immigrants explored and tried to enact the policies of dispersal and relocation in the years after the Saint-Denis riot. National officials appropriated and applied these local efforts as they acknowledged that they needed some sort of solution to assist African immigrants. As the campaign struggled to achieve its stated objective of providing decent accommodations for all immigrant communities in the early 1970s, the French government considered suspending labor migration altogether. Attempts to control and disperse African immigrants through the anti-slum campaign were in some ways a precursor to the end of labor immigration in 1974.

The anti-slum campaign sought to do more than eliminate *bidonvilles*, however. As Marc Roberrini, who worked for the *Service de liaison et de promotion des migrants* (Migrant Liaison and Promotion Service, part of the *Préfecture de la Seine* within the Ministry of the Interior) and coordinated the campaign at the national level, explained, by 1971 the campaign's goal was to "rehouse singles already isolated in micro-*bidonvilles* and in slums and in irregular dwellings."[55] Although focused on reshaping how it was that the French state received immigrants, those overseeing the effort also worked to assist immigrants who faced eviction or whose landlords had already forced them out.[56] Authorities deemed landlord-initiated eviction a threat to public order, even if they were essentially evicting and relocating residents in the anti-slum campaign. The difference from the official standpoint was that they, the officials, were providing alternative housing rather than forcing residents onto the streets.[57]

One of the rationales behind the campaign was the idea that the government needed to limit opportunities for politicization and political activism among African immigrants. If immigrants were allowed to create elaborate networks of sociability and successfully carve out space for themselves in neighborhoods and *banlieues*, they might be able to establish contacts with far left organizations, such as the *Gauche prolétarienne*, a group heavily involved in the Ivry rent strike. By restricting African residents' opportunities to form these connections, authorities believed that they were reducing their chances of involving themselves with elements of French society perceived to be dangerous.[58] Officials remained concerned over the interethnic tensions and tenant–landlord strife that had contributed to the Saint-Denis riot and the Ivry rent strike. Relocations could diffuse this threat and enact some semblance of control within the urban environment. In attempting to protect public safety and stability, authorities remained less concerned with the conditions confronted by the relocated groups than the overall safety of the communities surrounding them.

These relocations also revealed the fact that the government perceived concentrations of marginalized groups as undesirable for the urban social order throughout the Paris region. Despite its ambitious agenda of redistributing and re-organizing the African immigrant community, the anti-slum campaign was a piecemeal effort, coordinated one *foyer* and one slum at a time. Efforts within the program varied in approach from municipality to municipality and neighborhood to neighborhood. Officials such as Roberrini maintained that the residential marginalization experienced by African immigrants in various neighborhoods and suburbs of Paris was at the root of their problems. Yet one of the anti-slum campaign's goals was to separate African immigrants from their existing social networks. What was promoted as an attempt to rectify African immigrants' housing situation and promote integration contributed to further marginalization and exacerbated many of the problems faced by the African immigrant community throughout the Paris region.[59]

Yet the anti-slum campaign was the closest that the French government came to creating a more systematic approach to receiving African immigrants and other groups while also physically asserting control over the community in France. From the 1960s into the 1970s, officials at all levels of government argued that relocations would promote better education, training, and health for African immigrants.[60] Reformers also emphasized more subtle quality-of-life improvements. One report proposed that dormitories accepting newly relocated residents could offer access to libraries, night courses, leisure activities, and organized sports.[61] Several foyers, including those run by SOUNDIATA and other management firms, provided these opportunities, while others—including the *foyer* on the rue Gabriel Péri in Ivry—did not. The problem was that in the relocation process, officials seldom confirmed the availability or feasibility of such amenities. Some *foyers* provided them, but not in a standardized manner for all residents. There was no guarantee that relocation meant better access to educational programs, medical assistance, or so-called constructive leisure pursuits such as television viewing or soccer playing that French officials deemed important to the integration process.

Debates over the reception of immigrants

Part of the challenge implicit in developing immigration-related policies and efforts to receive and possibly integrate migrant workers was the continuing debate over who was responsible for housing African workers in the first place. Some government officials believed that the industrial firms that recruited African immigrants should bear the primary costs.[62] This argument was not without precedent. For example, the automobile manufacturer Renault provided housing and other amenities to African workers it recruited. By 1969, the company offered housing to 2,593 single immigrant workers in company-run *foyers*.[63] Renault specifically set aside places for black African employees.[64] The company's black African workforce, however, comprised only a small fraction of the estimated 30,000 African workers who lived in the Paris region by 1963.[65] Other companies such as Citroën did not usually offer company housing, even though they also employed immigrant workers. There is little evidence to suggest that construction firms and metalworking companies—two other major employers of African immigrants—offered anything in the way of housing. Industrial enterprises, however, were not the only potential source of social provisions for immigrant workers. African embassies were also called upon to aid in the provision of housing for their citizens. However, only the Congolese embassy created a *foyer* for its citizens: the *Maison du Congo*. In the 1960s, Congolese immigrants comprised only a tiny fraction of African workers from Sub-Saharan Africa who lived in the Paris region. Based on the model of Renault and the Congolese embassy, the French government argued that the various entities responsible for the presence of African immigrants in metropolitan France should bear the responsibility of providing them with acceptable housing.[66]

The role of *foyers*

While debates continued over who should bear the cost and responsibility for housing immigrant workers, *foyers* were identified both as a problem and positioned as a solution. In accordance with the Debré Law, officials orchestrating this campaign sought to eliminate all forms of sub-par housing inhabited by immigrants, including run-down, mismanaged *foyers*, hotels, slums, and *bidonvilles*.[67] Authorities guiding the anti-slum campaign posited that *foyers* could be the key to eliminating slums while also providing the housing options required by the Debré Law.[68] One official argued that "*foyers* play a necessary and normal role in the prevention of slums."[69] As Vincent Viet explains, "the massive construction of *foyers* starting in 1967 (close to 700 *foyers* in 1976) had led to making this form of housing the most visible in terms of immigrant conditions."[70]

Across the 1960s and into the 1970s, *foyers* were seen as a key problem within the realm of the immigrant housing crisis as well as a solution. Dormitories built before the establishment of the *Fonds d'action sociale pour les travailleurs étrangers* or, as Viet argues, in its earliest years, were viewed as particularly problematic because of their overcrowded and run-down state.[71] At their best, dormitories provided the supervision and structure deemed necessary by the state for single male African immigrants residing largely outside of a traditional family structure and living in France without the stabilizing effect of their families and, in particular, their wives. Authorities worked to move Africans into dormitories to facilitate direct supervision as several aspects of African private life worried the French government. Officials continued to obsess over African sexuality, for example, arguing that "the society of black workers is a uniquely masculine society."[72] Concerns emerged over "the sexual behavior of black Africans, very liberal from European perspectives."[73] From the official perspective, relocations could work as a check against perceived sexual deviancy, a concern that dated back to the earliest years of French control in AOF. At the same time, improved housing and quality of life through relocation served as a plausible public explanation for why local, regional, and national officials were shuffling African residents of foyers, slums, and hotels throughout the Paris region. Yet concrete opportunities for interaction with the surrounding community proved rare for residents relocated to new neighborhoods with unfamiliar surroundings and few contacts with other members of the African community. Even as *foyers* factored into the anti-slum campaign, dispersal rather than regrouping or integration was the primary focus.

The challenge of how to move African immigrants out of dormitories continued to plague relocation and evacuation efforts throughout the 1960s. African workers often gravitated toward *foyers* because they resembled the *chambres* in Dakar and Marseille that, as Manchuelle explains, "reflected the desire of migrants from the same village to live together and to help each other."[74] Manchuelle argues that for the Soninké ethnic group—one of the largest groups to arrive in France from Sub-Saharan Africa across the twentieth century—the *chambres* became a critical institution within the migratory experience.[75] *Foyers* in France met many of their social and cultural needs.[76] The government identified management organizations such as SOUNDIATA, SONACOTRA, and AFTAM as critical components of the relocation effort, as they could provide at least partially standardized housing for relocated African immigrants. Much like the rent strike in Ivry, several of SONACOTRA's *foyers* experienced rent strikes of their own in the 1970s. Dormitories run by individuals and management companies seemed to offer the answer for African immigrants in need of better housing, but just as frequently, they became sites of unrest through rent strikes and protests.[77] In a 1971 report on the campaign's progress, Roberrini struck a pessimistic tone, arguing that:

> it was too late TO TRANSFORM ALREADY EXISTING AFRICAN DORMITORIES and some of them rapidly had to avoid little by little the control of associations, to satisfy tribal necessities and under the pressure of external and extreme ideologies; illegals multiplied, various locations deteriorated and gave way imperceptibly to rent strikes and complete anarchy.[78]

Because the commitment to dispersal remained stronger than to creating housing opportunities with the possibility of fostering integration, the results proved mixed. Despite relocations and broader efforts within the anti-slum campaign to secure better housing for immigrant groups, African access to adequate housing remained questionable throughout the 1960s.

Surveillance and relocations

Drawing on extensive surveillance, the SAT, the *Préfecture de police*, and other government entities mapped exactly where African immigrants lived by neighborhood, nationality, and ethnicity. Using this information, it became easier to target concentrations of African workers and other immigrant groups for dispersal. Government organizations knew exactly where African immigrants lived and whether they were active politically. The Paris *Préfecture de police* together with the *Préfecture de la Seine* and the Ministry of the Interior tracked the precise locations of African immigrants and other immigrant groups throughout the Paris region.[79] Officials commissioned counts of the precise number of Africans living in neighborhoods in Paris and surrounding communities such as Montreuil, Aubervilliers, and Ivry. For example, in 1963 one report from the *Préfecture de police* noted that three establishments on the rue de l'Ourcq in the 19th *arrondissement* housed African immigrants.[80] Five housing establishments on the passage Kracher in the 18th *arrondissement* offered shelter to African tenants.[81] Officials also tabulated African groups by ethnicity and nationality while noting what type of housing they inhabited and under whose jurisdiction. A report dated 1971 by Roberrini for the *Préfecture* of the Paris region indicated how many *bidonvilles*, micro-*bidonvilles*, and substandard housing units were located in neighborhoods throughout Paris and in suburban communities surrounding the capital.[82] With such information, it became easier to target African immigrant populations for dispersal.

So how was the campaign carried out? These efforts targeted enclaves of Africans and other immigrant groups labeled "problematic" for evacuation and relocation.[83] The program was initially comprised of individualized, localized efforts to remove African immigrants from dwellings. The number of operations conducted each year varied widely, as did the volume of slums closed down by authorities and the quantity of individuals removed and relocated during the campaign. Largely under the direction of municipal governments, the campaign's earliest manifestations came in the first years of the 1960s.[84] These local initiatives later served as a template for the nationally directed program undertaken by agencies such as the *Préfecture de police*, housed in the Ministry of the Interior, by the end of the 1960s.

Directed by national agencies, local, regional, and national authorities cooperated in increasingly centralized relocation efforts. Not surprisingly, disputes arose over who was responsible for which relocations, who would supervise the new residents once they arrived, and who would finance the effort individually and collectively. Departmental budget constraints proved to be a major problem.[85] Tensions between local and national officials and entities grew as the numbers of African immigrants increased over the course of the 1960s. Some officials argued as early as 1961 that inertia at the national level contributed to the housing problem and left regional departments and municipalities with fewer resources to address the challenges of properly housing immigrant communities.[86] For instance, as early as 1961, Saint-Denis Mayor Auguste Gillot accused the *Office national de l'immigration* of purposefully directing African immigrants to communist departments and municipalities.[87] He argued that "on the one hand the government claims to apply a policy of decentralization and, on the other hand, it continues to allow many residents into our departments and, in the case that I'm highlighting, residents of Senegal."[88] Gillot asserted that local municipalities were left to figure out how to assist immigrant populations from Senegal and elsewhere with few resources provided by the state, which seemingly directed them there in the first place.

Although the scope and breadth of the campaign differed from one relocation effort to the next, overall it targeted immigrant groups in certain neighborhoods and grew increasingly ambitious in scope toward the end of the 1960s. One of the first relocations, orchestrated by the *Comité du 13ème arrondissement de défense des expulsés* (Committee of the 13th neighborhood in defense of the evicted) in 1963, evicted tenants from a slum on the boulevard de l'Hôpital in the 13th *arrondissement* of Paris.[89] Another occurred in Saint-Denis in 1964, after 70 African tenants faced for several months the prospect of eviction from a *foyer* at 189 avenue Wilson.[90] Communities such as Saint-Denis constituted "local" laboratories for later national policies regarding the housing of African and other non-western immigrant groups. These early relocations were localized efforts, undertaken by organizations such as the aforementioned *Comité* as a way to address the presence of African immigrants in different neighborhoods. While localized early on, evacuations and relocations would later gain national attention and broader momentum by the end of the decade and into the 1970s.

By the late 1960s, as the campaign expanded in scope and size, more and more African immigrants found themselves shuffled from one location to another. In 1966, authorities evacuated 150 African tenants from a *foyer* on the rue d'Orgemont in the 20th *arrondissement* of Paris.[91] By 1969, the Seine-Saint-Denis department had earned its designation as "the most 'slummed.'"[92] Thirty-one relocations occurred in the Seine-Saint-Denis department that year. The communist municipalities of Aubervilliers and Saint-Denis closed 14 slums, relocating 974 residents. Authorities also removed 160 African immigrants from the rue Léon Gaumont in the 20th *arrondissement* and sent them to Montreuil outside of Paris, which was home to a growing population of Malian immigrants. The rue Léon Gaumont housed at least two more dormitories that authorities evacuated in subsequent years. During February 1970, 1,030 individuals underwent relocation in the Paris region. Between 1965 and 1970 in the Val-de-Marne department, efforts within the anti-slum campaign closed 13 *bidonvilles* and slums over the course of 61 operations while relocating 2,869 individuals. Over a ten-month period in 1971, 16 different operations evacuated 320 tenants. That same year, 40 African residents were removed from a slum on the rue Léon Gaumont. Eighteen residents found themselves relocated from a slum in Asnières in 1971, while fourteen Africans accepted new accommodations on the rue Clairaut in the 17th *arrondissement*. Authorities relocated over 100 African residents from a *foyer* at 42 rue du Landy to a SOUNDIATA-run dormitory. Nearly 600 Africans were moved from the rue de la République in Montreuil during a single effort in 1973. During the relocations detailed here, 6,021 residents were dispersed between 1964 and 1973. Hundreds of individuals could be evacuated in a single operation, as the scale of the efforts varied widely from one evacuation to the next, depending on the local context.[93]

Yet it was local officials and communities that often provided the impetus for the relocation efforts, especially early in the 1960s. Mayors called for assistance in the housing realm from various government entities. Communist municipalities such as Montreuil, Bobigny, and Saint-Denis had a much higher stake concerning the evacuation process and the relocation of residents across the Paris region than their national counterparts, because they found themselves hosting African immigrants and other migrant groups at higher rates than non-communist municipalities.[94] Although officials such as Gillot continually requested regional and national assistance, typically it was only in the wake of events such as the Saint-Denis riot or the Ivry rent strike that interest in initiating relocation programs spiked.[95] Later in the decade, the Ministry of the Interior and other government organizations looked to the work of local municipalities such as Saint-Denis to understand how exactly to undertake large-scale relocations.

Authorities often struggled to execute the relocations in an efficient manner. Tenants were frequently moved from one *foyer* to the next without the knowledge of local officials. Few experts in the area of immigration guided policies regarding African labor migration, evidenced by the fact that most officials did not understand the nature of African migration in the first place. This area of public policy and the anti-slum campaign represented an area of French policy making not dominated by experts, knowledge, or technocracy. Instead, it was characterized by disorganization, disorder, a lack of expertise, misunderstandings, the prevalence of racial constructions and understandings of the African community, and a perception of inferiority.[96]

Whereas authorities bickered over jurisdiction and finances and officials were often guided by perceptions of the immigrants themselves, the relocations often assumed predictable rhythms and routines. Relocations themselves were ordered through an *arrêté d'inhabitabilité* or decree of uninhabitability. Each evacuation typically started early in the morning and continued throughout the day until all tenants were removed from their former dwelling. They were carried out on every day of the week, including Sundays. Relocated residents took taxis, buses, and vans to their new dwellings with their suitcases and possessions in tow.[97] Sometimes those evacuated were relocated to nearby facilities; more often, they were moved to distant neighborhoods. Police frequently assisted, compelling reluctant residents to leave their homes while preventing anyone from returning to the condemned dwelling.[98] Authorities sent the message through police participation that relocations above all emphasized orderliness, timeliness, and structure while also symbolizing the French state's power over immigrant groups and the ways in which authorities could dictate the parameters of their experience in France. The newspaper *L'Humanité* reported on a relocation in Pierrefitte and explained that "police placed the *foyer* in a state of siege. Armed police penetrated the room, ordering its occupants to evacuate and threw their suitcases out of the windows."[99]

The single biggest challenge throughout the anti-slum campaign, however, was securing accommodations for newly evacuated residents. Not only was there a housing shortage for immigrants, but also for French residents. As space was difficult to come by, authorities typically made reservations at *foyers* run by organizations such as SONACOTRA, SOUNDIATA, and other semi-private management organizations. That these establishments often housed various immigrant groups in each *foyer* often deterred those undergoing relocation from accepting these housing offers. Officials also tended to make reservations far from places of employment in an effort to achieve their goal of dispersal and distribution. This, too, was considered unacceptable from the standpoint of the African workers targeted for relocation.

As a result, residents preferred to seek assistance from friends and family members when they were evacuated or displaced rather than move to officially sanctioned housing, reinforcing the ethnic enclaves and concentrations of immigrants that officials hoped to eliminate in the first place. Occasionally, the tenants themselves proposed dormitories that they deemed acceptable.[100] In a 1970 report, one official named Orsetti noted that, during an operation, "the African workers voluntarily chose dispersal over re-lodging in 2 *foyers* that they were offered."[101] While in this particular instance, the residents who were relocated from 4 rue Labois-Rouillon in Paris had their proposal accepted, immigrant-driven suggestions for relocations were often rejected by authorities hoping to break up rather than reinforce social networks. During one effort, African residents refused authorities' initial evacuation plan because it included relocation to what they perceived to be a multiethnic, poorly maintained *foyer*. In this instance, the residents ultimately agreed to be separated from their fellow tenants, a concession that reinforced the overwhelming goals of dispersal and control. Not every evacuation and relocation went as smoothly as authorities predicted.[102]

Responses and resistance

One of the biggest challenges facing officials, then, was the resistance to relocation efforts put up by the African tenants themselves. Authorities deemed this immigrant group the most difficult to relocate, as they frequently demanded to be rehoused with fellow residents. Their tendency to resist relocations became a factor in the planning and executing of these efforts, as authorities searched for accommodations that would be well-received by the populations targeted for relocation. At times, residents undergoing the process mounted considerable protest, despite the fact that officials projected an image of the efforts as orderly, well-executed evacuations and relocations. Tenants fought relocations through a variety of means, including the formation of committees to address the relocation plans. As Gérard Noiriel explains, action committees emerged amidst broader politicization, which in turn provided a collective voice for immigrant workers.[103] Individually and collectively, residents physically resisted leaving their homes. They rejected the idea of relocating to *foyers* with members of other immigrant communities or ethnicities. Price was also an issue, with soon-to-be-relocated residents expressing concern over the rental rates charged in their prospective *foyers*. One report explained that Africans shied away from relocation because of the low rents and the proximity to work of the places where they were currently living.[104] Some groups targeted for relocation initially agreed to it but then backed out at the last minute. Often, relocated residents made their way back to the *foyer* from which they were evacuated, much to the chagrin of the officials who had carried out the relocation in the first place. In anticipation of this, authorities frequently locked evacuated dormitories in an effort to prevent former residents from returning.[105]

While residents resisted relocations, so did local municipal and political organizations. During the evacuation of a *foyer* on the boulevard de l'Hôpital in November of 1963, the *Préfecture de Police* argued that local organizations utilized and appropriated the situation for their own benefit rather than to aid the immigrants involved in the relocation. The *Comité du 13ème arrondissement de défense des expulsés* worked on behalf of these tenants. In 1973, the *Préfecture de la Seine-Saint-Denis* accused the *Comité de soutien* (Support Committee) of encouraging a group of African and North African workers to resist relocation.[106] Many other groups participated in the resistance effort as well, including several local groups affiliated with the 13th *arrondissement*, local branches of union and syndicalist organizations such as the *Union locale des syndicats* (Local Union of Trade Unions), CGT-CFTC, and CGT-FO. Human rights organizations such as *La Ligue des droits de l'homme* (the League of Human Rights) protested the relocations as well. Collectively, these organizations contended that the relocation did not provide residents with improved accommodations.[107]

This was not the only relocation effort that would attract outside opposition. Several different organizations, including the *Secours rouge*, the *Association de solidarité avec les travailleurs immigrés* (Association for Solidarity with Immigrant Workers or ASTI), and the *Groupe révolutionnaire du 15ème arrondissement* (Revolutionary Group of the 15th Neighborhood) became heavily involved in opposing a relocation effort on the rue Lecourbe in the

15th *arrondissement* during the fall of 1970. Liberal newspapers such as *Combat* also questioned the validity of relocations. In 1971, *Combat* posed several questions about the relocations' logistics. It asked whether it was prudent to "impose long commutes on workers who had lived close to their factory?" and whether it was reasonable to "disperse people belonging to the same ethnic group in accommodations in several HLMs a few kilometers apart."[108] The opposition of a range of groups within civil society constituted a real impediment when authorities attempted to carry out relocations, while also indicating growing criticism of state policy that prioritized dispersal over integration.[109]

Members of the African community held varying interpretations of the government's role in housing immigrant populations, depending on their situation. They sometimes looked to local officials for relocation, even demanding it at times when housing situations reached a crisis level or grew especially dire. Camara Galadio, president of the *Association des travailleurs maliens, section Saint-Denis,* repeatedly demanded that the city of Saint-Denis provide alternative housing arrangements for himself and his fellow migrants who lived in a run-down house. He emphasized that it was the responsibility of local municipalities to provide suitable housing for immigrant communities residing within their borders. Galadio explained:

> [i]n this case, I ask you gentlemen councillors to place at my disposition, an uninhabited house where we could create a *Foyer*, where at the end of each month, I will take responsibility for paying the rent. This is a major problem that has befallen me today, which makes it necessary to address myself to you the elected officials of the community, to the municipality and finally to the entire Dionysian population to find a solution. I count entirely on you.[110]

Galadio went so far as to propose several possibilities himself, including abandoned houses and factories that could be renovated into *foyers* for Malian immigrants. He asked for the city's help in acquiring and renovating these sites. Instead of resisting the idea of relocation, Galadio embraced it. His initiative demonstrates that African immigrants were not the passive, inwardly focused migrants that officials made them out to be. Instead, they were invested in their local communities and saw decent housing as a way to solidify and stabilize their presence in metropolitan France while using the tools available to them within the host society.[111] Galadio's initiative and his understanding of the city's obligation to provide the Malian community with improved housing coalesced with the African community's vision for itself. If they obtained suitable housing, they could achieve stability within the community and appropriate space in which to solidify their social networks and their place within local municipalities such as Saint-Denis.

In the end, the anti-slum campaign remained a piecemeal effort conducted on the local, regional, and national levels to evacuate and relocate

Africans and other immigrants from housing deemed dangerous and dilapidated. Relocations carried out on streets and in neighborhoods throughout the Paris region comprised the bulk of the campaign's efforts, relocating anywhere from a handful of residents to hundreds at a time. Early in the 1960s, local communities initiated relocations and served as laboratories for the national government. Officials who conducted them sometimes found new homes with better opportunities for tenants faced with few other alternatives. More often, however, they moved them from one run-down dwelling to another because they prioritized dispersal over French-defined opportunities for integration.

While the campaign focused almost exclusively on the housing challenges faced by immigrants, officials conducting the program often complained about the implications of the national government's immigration policy. They argued that the reception of immigrants at their point of entry into France was the single most important moment in their migratory experience. The problematic housing conditions faced by West Africans and other immigrant communities revealed that the French government and French society had failed to properly receive immigrants up to that point. Programs such as that anti-slum campaign served as corrective action, providing the kind of housing to immigrants that should have been extended to them upon their initial arrival.

Despite officials' best efforts, the tendency to regroup helped to establish the social networks upon which the contemporary African immigrant community was founded after 1974. Influenced by colonial notions of race and ethnicity and ideas of cultural, social, and racial inferiority, authorities often misconstrued the very nature of African labor migration through the tendency to regroup. Authorities remained focused on dispersal and control to the extent that they missed the role that the African community played in facilitating its own settlement through the kinds of regroupings undertaken by previous generations of African immigrants in cities such as Marseille and Dakar.

Authorities who initiated the program did not anticipate that residents of *foyers*, hotels, and slums might resist and refuse relocation. What government officials perceived as more acceptable housing could be construed by tenants as efforts to break up communities, sever individual ties, and place migrants far from their workplaces, their neighborhoods, and their social milieus. The residents were correct in their perception that officials intended to interrupt the community development undertaken by African immigrants in the early years of their postcolonial migration. Local organizations protested as well, demonstrating that the area of immigrant housing policy remained a contested political and social space within the urban milieu. Those who resisted these efforts were not entirely wrong in the way that they read them.

While the relocations were presented as a means through which to improve the housing conditions of thousands of immigrants, they also reflected a desire among local and national officials to disperse, distribute, and control Africans throughout the Paris region. Officials argued that dense outposts of the African community were unacceptable and a threat to public safety, order, and health. The French government expressed its anxieties over the presence of postcolonial African immigrants in Paris and its *banlieues* through the efforts undertaken in the anti-slum campaign. The evacuations and relocations carried out during this campaign were viewed as a way to assert control not only over African immigrants but also within the Paris urban order. Elements of control and dispersal implicit in the campaign, however, brought into play colonial notions regarding Africans and cast a shadow of implicit and unspoken racial stereotyping on French government policy.

The 1974 decision to halt labor migration to France while allowing family reunification to continue represented the culmination of over a decade's worth of efforts to find solutions to the problems of reception and welcoming inherent in French immigration policy. This decision was viewed as yet another way to "fix" the problems of immigrants living in France by reducing the numbers of newly arriving labor migrants each year. The rationale was that by stopping the arrival of new immigrants, the government could focus on the situation faced by those already in France. One of the unintended consequences of this decision, however, was the ways in which family reunification promoted permanent settlement rather than the large-scale repatriation authorities had hoped for. The anti-slum campaign was a precursor policy to this decision, as it sought to rectify the problems faced by African immigrants and other immigrant communities by addressing only their housing situation and hoping that other challenges could be addressed along the way.[112] One can trace the residential segregation observed in Paris and its suburbs today not only to historical settlement patterns that date back to the postcolonial era and even earlier but also to the anti-*bidonville* campaign and state intervention in the housing of African workers and other immigrant groups. Throughout the 1960s and 1970s, the state was deeply concerned about and active in deciding and at times dictating where it was and, at times, how it was, that African immigrants lived. The impact of these policies reverberates into the present day and is reflected in current debates about segregation and even apartheid in France.

Notes

1 CANC 19770317 art. 1 Marc Roberrini to M le Préfet, Paris 15 December 1969. Original French: "les conditions d'hygiène régnant dans ce dortoir s'étant avérées désastreuses."

2 ADVM 2018W art. 20 Lucien Helix to M le Préfet, 15 December 1970. ADVM 2018W art. 20. André Maguer to M le Directeur général de la Police municipale, Ivry-sur-Seine, 6 December 1970. Lucien Miard, "La lutte contre les bidonvilles: les six cent travailleurs noirs du dortoir-taudis d'Ivry relogés dans de nouveaux foyers d'accueil." *Le Figaro*, Paris, 9 December 1970.

3 ADVM 2018W art. 20 Lucien Miard, "La lutte contre les bidonvilles." *Le Figaro*, Paris, 9 December 1970.
4 ADVM 2018W art. 20 Lucien Miard, "La lutte contre les bidonvilles." *Le Figaro*, Paris, 9 December 1970. Original French: "cette opération de résorption de l'habitat insalubre entreprise par la Préfecture du Val-de-Marne, est l'une des plus importantes qui aient été réalisées."
5 ADVM 2018W art. 20 Préfecture du Val-de-Marne, "Communiqué: Evacuation du dortoir pour travailleurs africains situé 45, rue Gabriel Péri à Ivry-sur-Seine," Créteil, 5 December 1970. CANC 19770317 art. 1 Lucien Helix to M le Préfet, 15 December 1970. Original French: "l'une des plus importantes qui ait été réalisée en région parisienne."
6 The relocation effort started on 13 December 1969 and continued into the following spring. ADVM 2018W art. 20 M. Grimaud to M le Préfet de Paris, 6 August 1970. Service de liaison et de promotion des migrants, "La disparition du dortoir africain de la rue Gabriel Péri à Ivry." December 1970. CANC 19770317 art. 1 M. Roberrini to M le Préfet, 15 December 1969. L. Helix to M le Préfet, 15 December 1970.
7 ADVM 2018W art. 20 Maurice Grimaud to M le Préfet de Paris, 6 August 1970. Original French: "constituer la dernière occasion de mettre un terme à une situation dangereuse à tous égards, tant au point de vue de la sécurité que de l'ordre public."
8 Mauco, *Les étrangers en France et le problème du racisme* (Paris: Pensée Universelle, 1977), 87.
9 Gregory Verdugo, "Public Housing and Residential Segregation of Immigrants in France, 1968–1990," *Population* 66, no. 1 (January–March 2011): 179; Mirna Sofi, "La dimension spatiale de l'intégration: évolution de la ségrégation des populations immigrées en France entre 1968 et 1999," *Revue française de sociologie* 50, no. 3 (July–September, 2009): 521–552; Jean-Louis Pan Ké Shon, Gregory Verdugo, and Amy Jacobs, "Immigrant Segregation and Incorporation in France: Extent and Intensity from 1968 to 2007," *Revue française de la sociologie* 55, no. 2 (2014): 179–214.
10 See Manuel Castells, et al., *Crise du logement et mouvements sociaux urbains: enquête sur la région parisienne* (Paris: Mouton, 1978); Pierre Baudry, *Premiers résultats de l'enquête sur le logement en 1973 dans la région parisienne* (Paris: Institut national de la statistique et des études économiques, Direction régionale de Paris, 1974).
11 CIEMI Georges Colas "Les problèmes de l'immigration africaine noire," *Hommes et migrations* no. 625 (8 November 1965). Original French: "la lutte contre les taudis est pour les travailleurs africains noirs, le point prioritaire par excellence … la solution est urgente."
12 AMSD 18 ACW 22/23 La Municipalité to Messieurs les Immigrés Africains, Saint-Denis, 15 January 1968. Original French: "ils doivent vous assurer le logement, le travail, les ressources et les libertés indispensables pour vivre normalement."
13 Jacob Paskins, *Paris Under Construction: Building Sites and Urban Transformation in the 1960s* (New York: Routledge, 2016), 120.
14 "Loi No. 64–1229" *Journal Officiel* (15 December 1964): 11139. Original French: "faciliter aux fins de reconstruction ou d'aménagement l'expropriation des terrains sur lesquels sont édifiés des locaux d'habitation insalubres et irrécupérables, communément appelés 'bidonvilles'."
15 CAN F1a 5116 "Pour une politique." CIEMI "Problèmes posés par l'immigration." *Journal Officiel* 1964. CAN F1a 5136. Préfecture de Police, "Nombre et implantation dans le département de la Seine des travailleurs originaires des États d'Afrique noire." Paris, 5 September 1963. AMSD 18 ACW 22/23 "Questions

écrites: No. 312, 282." *Bulletin municipal officiel (Ville de Paris)*, Paris, 7 and 27 August 1963. CANC 19960311 art. 6 "Déclaration des maires communistes de la région parisienne et des élus de Paris pour la liquidation des bidonvilles et pour le relogement humain des travailleurs immigrés." 29 November 1969.

16 Paskins, *Paris Under Construction*, 120.

17 For more on mass housing in postwar France, see Nicole C. Rudolph, *At Home in Postwar France: Modern Mass Housing and the Right to Comfort* (Oxford; New York: Berghahn, 2015).

18 Paskins, *Paris Under Construction*, 121.

19 CAN F1a 5116 "Pour une politique."

20 CANC 19770317 art. 1 Roberrini, "Rapport à M le Préfet de la région parisienne sur la résorption des bidonvilles et les problèmes des migrants." 1 March 1971. Original French: "la disparition totale des bidonvilles."

21 CAN F1a 5116 "Pour une politique concertée du logement et de l'action socio-éducative appliqué à la résorption des bidonvilles." 1967. Original French: "la prévention de la création et l'extension des bidonvilles."

22 Vincent Viet, "La politique du logement des immigrés," *Vingtième siècle. Revue d'histoire* 64, no. 1 (1999): 97; Gary Freeman, *Immigrant Labor and Racial Conflict in Industrial Societies: The French and British Experience, 1945–1975* (New Jersey: Princeton University Press, 1979), 92.

23 Freeman, *Immigrant Labor and Racial Conflict in Industrial Societies*, 91.

24 CIEMI "Problèmes posés par l'immigration des travailleurs africains en France." *Journal Officiel*, séance, 23 June 1964.

25 CAN F1a 5136 Préfecture de la Seine et M. Legru, "Étude problème noir région parisienne 1963–1965" Paris, 1965.

26 Alice Conklin, *A Mission to Civilize: The Republican Idea of Empire in France and West Africa, 1895–1930* (Stanford: Stanford University Press, 1997), 129.

27 CAN F1a 5136 M. Legru, "Étude problème noir région parisienne." Préfecture de la Seine, 1965. Original French: "du point de vue français, le problème [noir] est triple: problème d'ordre public, problème de santé publique, [et] problème de moralité publique."

28 CAN F1a 5136 "Étude problème noir région parisienne." Préfecture de la Seine, 1965. Original French: "réglementée, organisée, [et] controlée."

29 Conklin, *A Mission to Civilize*, 141. This reflects the "*seuil de tolérance*" or the "threshold of tolerance" theory of immigrant housing explored by several scholars. Stephen Castles and Mark J. Miller argue that it "was introduced in both housing and education, according to which the immigrant presence should be limited to a maximum of ten to fifteen percent of residents in a housing estate or twenty-five percent of students in a class." See Stephen Castles and Mark J. Miller, *The Age of Migration: International Populations Movements in the Modern World* 2nd ed., (New York: Palgrave, 1998), 209. Neil MacMaster also explores this concept in his article in Maxim Silverman's volume. See MacMaster, "The '*seuil de tolérance*': The Uses of a 'Scientific' Racist Concept," in Maxim Silverman, ed., *Race, Discourse, and Power in France* (Aldershot: Avebury, 1991), 17–18. The anti-slum campaign incorporated this idea of the "threshold of tolerance" without actually citing percentages of African immigrants allowable in a certain neighborhood and municipality.

30 For a discussion of colonial segregation in relation to disease, see Myron Echenberg, *Black Death, White Medicine: Bubonic Plague and the Politics of Public Health in Colonial Senegal, 1914–1945* (Portsmouth, NH: Heinemann, 2002), 4.

31 CAN F1a 5136 "Étude problème noir région parisienne." 1965. Original French: "il est nécessaire de maintenir une relative dispersion des Africains."

32 CANC 19960311 art. 6 Conseil général Préfecture de la Seine-Saint-Denis, "Conseil général: 2ème session ordinaire de 1969." January 1970. Original French: "une répartition équitable des travailleurs immigrés de la région parisienne."

33 Dominic Thomas, "Fortress Europe: Identity, Race, and Surveillance," *International Journal of Francophone Studies* 17, no. 3 & 4 (2014): 451–452.
34 CAN Fla 5136 Préfecture de police, "Nombre et implantation dans le département de la Seine des travailleurs originaires des États d'Afrique noire." Paris, 5 September 1963. ADSSD 1801W art. 227 "Étude statistique des colonies étrangères du département de la Seine-Saint-Denis." March 1966. CANC 19770317 art. 1 Roberrini, "Rapport à M le Préfet de la région parisienne." 1 March 1971.
35 AMSD 18 ACW 22/23. "Questions écrites: no. 282, 312," *Bulletin municipal officiel (Ville de Paris)*, 7 August 1963 and 27 August 1963. Original French: "les difficultés qui résultent de l'afflux dans la région parisienne d'un grand nombre de travailleurs africains mal adaptés à notre climat et à nos conditions de vie ne pourront être surmontées définitivement que dans le cadre d'une politique d'ensemble concernant cette immigration."
36 Stephen Castles and Mark J. Miller discuss ethnic clustering and residential segregation in several national contexts. See Castles and Miller, *Age of Migration*. Sophie Body-Gendrot discusses immigrant ghettos in her article "Ghetto, mythes et réalités" in Dewitte, *Immigration et intégration*, 279–290.
37 Viet, "La politique du logement des immigrés," 99.
38 CAN Fla 5136 Préfecture de police, "Nombre et implantation dans le département de la Seine des travailleurs originaires des états d'Afrique noir." Paris, 5 September 1963. Original French: "pratiquement démunis d'argent, recherchant tout naturellement une assistance matériel et un soutien moral auprès de leurs compatriotes, prédisposés d'ailleurs à la vie communautaire, les nouveaux arrivants s'ajoutent aux groupes déjà formés qui se pressent dans des chambres surpeuplés ... seuls logements que leurs médiocres ressources leur permettent d'occuper."
39 AMM Immigration. M Bolloré to M le Préfet, 16 July 1973.
40 CAN Fla 5116 "Pour une politique concernée du logement et de l'action socio-éducative." Fla 5136 "Étude problème noir région parisienne." 1965.
41 CAN Fla 5136 Préfecture de police, "Nombre et implantations dans le département de la Seine des travailleurs originaires des États d'Afrique noire." 5 September 1963.
42 ADSSD 110 art. 22 "Étude statistique des colonies étrangères du département de la Seine-Saint-Denis." March 1966.
43 CAN Fla 5136 "Étude problème noir région parisienne." 1965. Préfecture de police, "Nombre et Implantation." CAN Fla 5116 "Pour une politique concernée du logement et de l'action socio-éducative." AMM Immigration 1977–1986. M Bolloré to M le Préfet, 16 July 1973. ADSSD 1801W art. 226 Letter from the Préfecture de la Seine-Saint-Denis to Bobigny, 22 August 1973. "Étude statistique des colonies étrangères du département de la Seine Saint Denis." March 1966. CANC 19770317 art. 1 Roberrini, "Rapport à M le Préfet de la région parisienne." CANC 19960311 art. 6 Conseil général Préfecture de la Seine-Saint-Denis, "Conseil général." Bobigny, January 1970.
44 CANC 19960311 art. 6 "Programme de la gouvernement de la résorption." 11 February 1970. Original French: "tous ces problèmes (de l'habitation abusive) sont liés à la définition d'une politique d'immigration."
45 CANC 19770317 art. 1 Roberrini, "Rapport à M le Préfet de la région parisienne sur la résorption des bidonvilles et les problèmes des migrants." 1 March 1971.
46 Castles and Miller, *The Age of Migration*, 204. The official concern over ethnic regrouping can be construed as a precursor to the debate over polygamy among immigrant communities in France during the 1980s and 1990s and the broader implications for integration into French society. This in turn reveals the ways in which authorities continually invest in and investigate the familial relationships and social structures of migrant groups.

47 Conklin, *A Mission to Civilize*, 129.

48 Manchuelle, *Willing Migrants: Soninké Labor Diasporas, 1848–1960* (Athens: Ohio University Press, 1997), 124.

49 For a discussion of cholera outbreaks after the revolutions of the nineteenth century, see Catherine J. Kudlick, *Cholera in Post-Revolutionary Paris: A Cultural History* (Berkeley: University of California Press, 1996). Her work demonstrates that disease and urban disorder can go hand in hand.

50 CANC 19770317 art. 1 Groupe interministérielle permanent pour la résorption de l'habitat insalubre, "Annexe II: Critères d'insalubrité." 27 August 1971.

51 Ibid.

52 AMSD 18 ACW 22/24 Ville Saint-Denis, "Extrait du registre des délibérations du conseil municipal, sixième session." 25 October 1963. "Un témoignage de M Grenier à l'Assemblée nationale: 35 dans une cave," *L'Humanité*, 24 July 1963. "Pour le relogement d'urgence des travailleurs noirs." 25 August 1964. "Situation des travailleurs d'Afrique noire à Saint-Denis." 17 August 1964. "Relogement des travailleurs noirs." 24 August 1964. "Conseil général de la Seine: réponses aux questions écrits." *Bulletin municipal officiel (Ville de Paris)*, 17 October 1964. CAN F1a 5116 "Pour une politique concertée du logement et de l'action socio-éducative appliquée à la résorption des bidonvilles." Paris 1967. CANC 19770317 art. 1 Groupe interministériel permanent pour la résorption de l'habitat insalubre, "Annexe II: Critères de l'insalubrité." 27 August 1971.

53 Manchuelle, "Background to Black African Emigration to France: The Labor Migrations of the Soninké, 1848–1987" (PhD diss., University of California-Santa Barbara, 1987)," 490.

54 Georges Mauco identifies *bidonvilles* and slums as a prominent source of insecurity for immigrant groups. The threat of eviction only added to the insecurity rather than alleviating it. See Mauco, *Les étrangers en France et le problème du racisme* (Paris: La Pénsee universelle, 1977), 80.

55 CANC 19770317 art. 1 Marc Roberrini, "Rapport à M le Préfet de la région parisienne sur la résorption des bidonvilles et les problèmes des migrants." 1 March 1971. Original French: "reloger des isolés encore en micro-bidonvilles et dans les taudis et garnis irréguliérs."

56 CIEMI *Journal officiel: Avis et rapports du conseil économique et social* session de 1964 Séance du 23 juin 1964, "Problèmes posés par l'immigration des travailleurs africains en France." CANC 19770317 art. 1 Roberrini, "Rapport à M le Préfet de la région parisienne sur la résorption des bidonvilles et les problèmes des migrants," 1 March 1971.

57 ADSSD 1801W art. 226 Letter from the Préfecture de la Seine-Saint-Denis to Bobigny, 22 August 1973.

58 APP GaA7 "Mode d'intervention et d'action des mouvements gauchistes ..." CANC 19960134 art. 17 "Le mécontentement des milieux africains de la région parisienne est exploité à des fins subversives, par les gauchistes." 25 March 1975. CANC 19770317 art. 1 Préfecture de police, "Note à M le Préfet: Agitation dans les foyers d'hébergement de ressortissants africains de la région parisienne." 8 October 1969. CANC 19960311 art. 6 "Constitué fin du novembre 1969, à l'initiative des responsables de la 'Gauche Prolétarienne.'" 20 January 1970. AN 19870623 art. 1 "Les activités subversives dans la colonie africaine francophone en France." 2 March 1974. ADVM 2018W art. 20 Letter to M le Préfet, 6 August 1970. "Intervention de la Maire d'Ivry sur Seine, sur le problème de l'immigration." 16 October 1969.

59 Catherine Wihtol de Wenden and Rémy Leveau discuss the Vitry affair of 1980, when over 300 Malians were thrown out of a *foyer* by the communist mayor of Vitry. They do not consider, however, the historical origins behind the impulse

to expel and relocate immigrant populations. See Catherine Wihtol de Wenden and Rémy Leveau, *La beurgeoisie: Les trois âges de la vie associative issue de l'immigration* (Paris: CNRS Éditions, 2001), 17.

60 CAN F1a 5116 "Pour une politique concertée du logement et de l'action socio-éducative appliqué à la résorption des bidonvilles." 1967.

61 Ibid.

62 Manchuelle argues that firms such as Renault recruited Soninké immigrants in, "a semi-clandestine fashion (for these employers never admitted to having organized these recruitments, and even denied for a long time that they employed a large number of Africans) in French harbors or in Dakar." See Manchuelle, "Background to Black African Emigration to France," 504. Archival evidence suggests, however, that by 1970 Renault executives were corresponding directly with French officials concerning the housing and employment of African workers.

63 ADVM 2018 W art. 20 Chef du service, Régie national des usines Renault to Roberrini, Boulogne Billancourt, 12 May 1970.

64 Ibid.

65 Manchuelle cites an estimate of 22,000 to 30,000 African workers in the Paris region by 1963. Because of the loosely regulated nature of African labor migration at that time, the figure of 30,000 is probably one of the most accurate counts available. Manchuelle, "Background to Black African Emigration to France," 498.

66 Michel Jacques, "Le dossier social des travailleurs immigrés manque de formation professionnelle, analphebètisme, taudis," *Le Figaro*, 29–30 August 1970.

67 Paskins, *Paris Under Construction*, 120–122.

68 Ibid., 120.

69 CANC 19770317 art. 1 Roberrini, "Rapport à M le Préfet de la région parisienne sur la résorption des bidonvilles et les problèmes des migrants." 1 March 1971. Original French: "les foyers jouent un rôle normal et nécessaire de prévention contre les bidonvilles."

70 Viet, "La politique du logement des immigrés," 98. Original French: "[l]a construction massive de foyers à partir de 1967 (près de 700 foyers en 1976) avait abouti à faire de cette forme d'hébergement le caractère le plus visible de la condition de l'immigré."

71 Ibid.

72 CAN F1a 5136 "Problème noir région parisienne." Préfecture de la Seine, 1965. Original French: "la société des travailleurs noirs est une société uniquement masculine."

73 Ibid. Original French: "le comportement sexuel des noirs Africains, très libre aux yeux des européens."

74 Mancheulle, *Willing Migrants*, 124.

75 Ibid.

76 Ibid., 123–128.

77 ADVM 2018W art. 20 "Les travailleurs africains d'Ivry ont quitté l'usine-dortoir pour vivre dans des foyers," *L'Humanité*, Paris, 10 December 1970.

78 CANC 19770317 art. 1 Marc Roberrini, "Rapport à Monsieur le Préfet de la région parisienne sur la résorption des bidonvilles et les problèmes des migrants, 1970" (Paris: Préfecture de la région parisienne, 1 March 1971). Original French: "il était trop tard pour transformer les foyers africains déjà existants et certains de ceux-ci devaient rapidement, pour satisfaire aux nécessités tribales et sous la pression d'idéologies extérieures et extrémistes, échapper peu à peu au contrôle des associations; les clandestins se multiplièrent, les locaux se dégradèrent et on passa insensiblement de la grève des loyers a l'anarchie la plus complète."

79 CANC 19770317 art. 1 Roberrini, "Rapport à M le Préfet de la région parisienne sur la résorption des bidonvilles et les problèmes des migrants." 1 March 1971.
80 CAN F1a 5136 Préfecture de police, "Nombre et implantation dans le département de la Seine des travailleurs originaires des États d'Afrique noir." 5 September 1963.
81 Ibid.
82 CANC 19770317 art. 1 Marc Roberrini, "Rapport à Monsieur le Préfet de la région parisienne sur la résorption des bidonvilles et les problèmes des migrants, 1970" (Paris: Préfecture de la région parisienne, 1 March 1971).
83 For example, a meeting reported on in the *Journal Officiel* discussed the problems posed by the migration of African workers. CIEMI "Problèmes posés par l'immigration des travailleurs africains en France." *Journal Officiel* séance, 23 June 1964.
84 CANC 19770317 art. 1 Roberrini, "Rapport à M le Préfet de la région parisienne sur la résorption des bidonvilles et les problèmes des migrants." 1 March 1971.
85 Ibid.
86 AMSD 18ACW 22/23 August Gillot to M Raymond Barbet, Saint-Denis, 23 May 1961.
87 Ibid.
88 Ibid. Original French: "d'une part le Gouvernement prétend appliquer une politique de décentralisation et, d'autre part, il continue de faire venir, ou de laisser venir de nombreux habitants de nos départements et, dans le cas que je signale, des habitants du Sénégal."
89 APP GaA7 Préfecture de police, "A.S. des expulsions de travailleurs originaires d'Afrique noire." 6 November 1963. CANC 19770317 art. 1 Roberrini, "Rapport à Monsieur le Préfet de la région parisienne."
90 AMSD 18ACW 22/23 Ville de Saint Denis, "Extrait du registre des délibérations du Conseil municipal: quatrième session administrative de l'année 1964." Saint-Denis 28 May 1964. "Questions écrites: no. 282, 312." *Bulletin Municipal (Saint–Denis)* 7 August 1963 and 27 August 1963. F. Grenier to M Pompidou, *Bulletin Municipal (Saint-Denis)* 1964.
91 CAN 19770317 art. 1 Letter to M le Préfet, Paris, 25 July 1966.
92 CANC 19770317 art. 1 Roberrini, "Rapport à M le Préfet de la région parisienne sur la résorption des bidonvilles et les problèmes des migrants." 1 March 1971. Original French: "le plus 'bidonvillisé.'"
93 CANC 19960311 art. 6 "Programme de la résorption du gouvernement." 2 November 1970. Letter to M le Ministre de l'Intérieur, Paris 12 August 1971. 19770317 art. 1 Letter to M le Premier Ministre, Créteil, 11 October 1971. Roberrini, "Rapport à M le Préfet de la région parisienne sur la résorption des bidonvilles et les problèmes des migrants, 1970." 1 March 1971. Letter to M le Préfet de Paris 13 January 1971. Letter to M le Préfet, Bobigny, 14 June 1972. AMM Foyers/Migrations 1969 à 1973 M Bolloré to M le Préfet, 16 July 1973. AMM Immigration, Ville de Montreuil. "Quelques donnés sur les travailleurs immigrés résidant à Montreuil et sur la situation des travailleurs migrants." January 1979.
94 CAN F1a 5136 "Étude problème noir région parisienne."
95 CANC 19960311 art. 6 "Déclaration des maires communistes de la région parisienne et des élus de Paris pour la liquidation des bidonvilles et pour le relogement humain des travailleurs immigrés." Paris, 29 November 1969. AMM Foyers/Migration 1969 à 1973 Assemblée nationale, Réponses des Ministres aux questions écrites no. 356, 23 April 1971. AMM Foyers/Migrations 1969 à 1973. Le Maire de Montreuil à M le Préfet de la Seine-Saint-Denis, Montreuil, 30 March 1973. CANC 19770317 art. 1 Letter from the Préfet, 9 January 1970. AMSD 18 ACW 22/23 "Conseil général de la Seine: Réponses aux questions écrites: logement no. 226."

Bulletin municipal officiel (Ville de Paris), 17 October 1964. "Le Dossier social des travailleurs immigrés," *Le Figaro*, 29–30 August 1970. ADSSD 1801W art. 227 Cabinet, Service départemental de liaison et de promotion des migrants, Préfecture de la Seine-Saint-Denis, Bobigny, 24 October 1975.

96 See Wihtol de Wenden, *Les immigrés et la politique,* 116–143, 143–189; Weil *La France et ses étrangers*, 81–101; Viet, *La France immigré: construction d'une politique, 1914–1997* (Paris: Fayard, 1998), 231–303.

97 CANC 19770317 art. 1 Letter to M le Préfet Bobigny 14 June 1972.

98 CANC 19960311 art. 6 "Violences policières au foyer africain de Pierrefitte," *L'Humanité*, 24 July 1971. Préfet de Police to M le Ministre de l'Intérieur, Paris, 12 August 1971. Letter to Ministre de l'Intérieur, Paris 12 August 1971. CANC 19770317 art. 1 Letter to M le Préfet, Bobigny, 14 June 1972. Letter to M le Préfet de la région parisienne, Paris, 2 July 1971. Roberrini to M le Préfet, Paris, 3 July 1972. Roberrini, 5 July 1972. Roberrini to M le Préfet, Paris, 13 July 1972. AMM M Bolloré, Sous-Préfet to M le Préfet, Bobigny, 16 July 1973.

99 CANC 19960311 art. 6 "Violences policières au foyer africain de Pierrefitte," *L'Humanité*, 24 July 1971. Original French: "police mettait le foyer en état de siège. Les policiers armes pénétraient dans la chambre, ordonnaient à ses occupants de l'évacuer et jetaient les valises par les fenêtres."

100 CANC 19770317 art. 1 Letter to M le Préfet de Paris, Paris, 10 March 1970.

101 Ibid. Original French: "les travailleurs africains ont volontairement choisi la dispersion plutôt que le relogement en 2 foyers qui leur avait été proposé."

102 CANC 19770317 art. 1 Letter to M le Préfet de Paris, Paris, 10 March 1970. Letter to M le Préfet, Bobigny, 19 September 1974. Roberrini to M le Préfet de la Seine-Saint-Denis, Paris, 17 April 1970.

103 Gérard Noiriel, *Immigration, antisémitisme et racisme en France (XIXe–XXe Siècle)* (Paris: Fayard, 2007), 563. Original French: "La mobilisation contre les foyers insalubres et les bidonvilles aboutit à la mise en place de 'comités de lutte' qui permettent à une partie des travailleurs concernés de s'engager eux-mêmes dans l'action."

104 CANC 19770317 art. 1 Letter to M le Préfet de Paris, 16 April 1971. Original French: "la modicité de leurs loyers et de la proximité de travail."

105 CANC 19770317 art. 1 Letter to M Fougier, Paris, 9 January 1970. Letter to M le Ministre du Travail, de l'Emploi et de la Population, Paris, 30 June 1973. Letter to M le Préfet, Paris, 25 July 1966. Letter to M le Préfet, 15 December 1970. Letter to M le Préfet, Paris, 10 March 1970. Roberrini, "Rapport à Monsieur le Préfet." CAN F1a 5136 "Étude problème noir." Préfecture de police, "Nombre et implantation."

106 CANC 19770317 art. 1 Letter to M le Ministre du Travail, de l'Emploi et de la Population, 30 June 1973.

107 CANC 19770317 art. 1 Letter to M Fougier. CANC 19960311 art 6 "Violences policières au foyer africain de Pierrefitte," *L'Humanité*, 24 July 1971. Letter to Ministre de l'Intérieur, Paris, 30 May 1973.

108 CANC 19960311 art. 6 "Faut-il résorber les bidonvilles?" *Combat*, Paris, 22 November 1971. Original French: "imposer de long trajets quotidiens à des travailleurs qui vivaient jusqu'alors à la porte de leur usine." and "disséminer les personnes appartenant à une même ethnie en les relogeant dans des ensembles d'HLM distants de quelques kilomètres."

109 APP GaA7 Préfecture de police, "A.S. des expulsions de travailleurs originaires d'Afrique noire," Paris, 6 November 1963. CANC 19770317 art. 1 Roberrini, "Rapport à M le Préfet de la région parisienne."

110 AMSD 18 ACW 22/23 Camara Galadio to les Conseilleurs municipaux, Commune de Saint-Denis, 19 August 1964. Original French: "[d]ans ce cas, je vous

prie Messieurs les conseillers de mettre à ma disposition, une maison inhabitée où nous créons un Foyer, à la fin de chaque mois, je m'en occuperais pour payer le loyer. C'est un problème majeur qui me frappe aujourd'hui, donc il est nécessaire de m'adresser à vous les élus de la commune, à la municipalité et enfin à toute la population Dionysienne entière pour trouver une solution. Je compte entièrement sur vous."

111 CIEMI *Hommes et migrations* 625, 11 August 1965. AMSD 18 ACW 22/23 Galadio to MM les Conseillers municipaux, 19 and 26 August, 1964. Galadio to M le Maire, 9 August 1964. Galadio to Gillot, 21 December and 28 December, 1964. Gillot to the Sécretariat du Comité de Ville du PCF, 4 and 14 August 1964.

112 For more on the 1974 suspension of immigration, see Viet, *La France immigrée*, 358–383.

Conclusion

In an October, 1974 report, the *Direction de la réglementation 6ème bureau* within the Ministry of the Interior reported on a trip that Sally N'Dongo planned to take to Lausanne and Zurich, Switzerland that same month. The report alleged that the *Front communiste révolutionnaire* (Revolutionary Communist Front) had contacted N'Dongo, who at that point still presided over the UGTSF, and extended the invitation. According to the *Direction de la réglementation*, N'Dongo was in contact with leftist militants since at least 1971. The *Direction* also claimed that, in addition to his work with the UGTSF, N'Dongo also oversaw the *Comité d'information et de soutien à la lutte du peuple sénégalais* (Committee of Information and Support for the Struggle of the Senegalese People), whose goal was to free political prisoners in Senegal, at his residence in Puteaux outside of Paris.[1] The seemingly political nature of N'Dongo's planned trip to Switzerland, his contacts with leftist militants, and his advocacy for the release of Senegalese political prisoners as a direct challenge to the Senegalese government troubled the authorities watching him. They noted a much more public embrace of political militancy than previously observed.

Yet the UGSTF's request for renewed authorization two years later in 1976 from the *Préfecture de police* did not indicate any sort of political activism or shift toward overtly political activities. Article Two listed the group's goals as to "strengthen the bonds of friendship between Senegalese workers in France and improve their living conditions through social and professional assistance."[2] This remained in line with the organization's emphasis on social welfare dating back to its founding in the early 1960s and also met the criteria regarding similar groups: that they were not to engage in political activities. In August of 1978, though, the Ministry of the Interior through Monsieur Cantan, the *Directeur de la réglementation et du contentieux* (Director of Regulation and Litigation), denied the UGTSF's request for renewal. This was one of several denials that Cantan issued that month to various African immigrant associations.[3] Despite the official emphasis on social welfare, from the state's perspective N'Dongo's political connections and activities posed a threat, one that could not continue to operate within France. The government's withdrawal of official authorization meant that the UGTSF could no longer operate legally in France. One of the cornerstone immigrant organizations of the postcolonial eras disappeared from the vibrant associational sphere that it helped to establish in the first years after decolonization. For his part, N'Dongo eventually returned to Senegal, where he died in 2001 at the age of 75, the same year as his sometimes ally and sometimes adversary, Senegal's first president, Léopold Senghor.

African Political Activism in Postcolonial France has covered three key themes regarding postcolonial African immigration to France: immigrant political activism, state surveillance, and social welfare. Important threads connect each one, from the influence of colonial policy to the impact of the Cold War and decolonization. We see how closely connected the state's response to African immigration was to the political activism of African immigrants themselves, demonstrating how African immigrants shaped the Fifth Republic's immigration policies and actions toward immigrant communities. N'Dongo and others became important political actors who had a deep and abiding impact on the direction of state immigration, surveillance, and social welfare policies. Political activism took a variety of forms, from more traditional union-style organizations to riots, rent strikes, and demonstrations. Approaches to political organization—including the creation of organizations such as the UGTSF—often mirrored colonial approaches to political protest and activism in both France and West Africa. The breadth and depth of politicization was evident in myriad ways which African immigrants expressed themselves and challenged the French state throughout the early postcolonial era.

African political activism in the 1960s and 1970s retained links to the colonial and metropolitan past while also shaping subsequent generations of immigrant activists. Nodding to the Pan-African nationalist movement that spanned the European, North American, and African continents across the interwar era and into the postwar period, political actors such as N'Dongo utilized the trade union model adapted in both France and AOF during the interwar period and carried it into the late 1970s and early 1980s. By that point, the emphasis on national identity within African immigrant organizations metamorphized into one that prioritized ethnicity and gender, especially as more and more African women arrived in France to join their husbands after 1974. Thus, the African immigrant activism witnessed across the 1980s and 1990s and into the 2000s was informed by and shaped by the postcolonial activism undertaken by organizations such as the UGTSF and activists such as N'Dongo. The *sans-papiers* movement of 1996 in the Église Saint-Bernard, for example, was a continuation of the types of political protests seen across the 1960s and 1970s, while the mark of the Pan-African movement of the interwar and postwar eras was indelibly there, too. The riots of 2005 in response to the deaths of two young men in a power station after an encounter with the police reflected a history of rioting and political protest in response to tragedy, as evidenced by the response to the deaths in Aubervilliers in 1970.[4] These contemporary protests have important historical roots in an immigrant community with a long history of political activism and protest spanning the twentieth century. This book elucidates African political activism in France during the era of decolonization and just after.

The French state responded in an equally multifaceted way. Each aspect of the government's policies—whether in the form of surveillance or in the social welfare initiatives undertaken throughout the 1960s and 1970s—was shaped not only by changing understandings of the African immigrant community across the early postcolonial era but also by the ways in which the colonial state addressed African colonial subjects into the postwar era. Many of the policies that emerged—from the establishment of the *Centre Bossuet* in 1963 to the anti-slum campaign—borrowed colonial-era tactics and techniques from both France and AOF.

As in the colonies and during the interwar period, surveillance often shaped the social welfare initiatives undertaken by various governmental organizations. The *Centre Bossuet*, for example, emerged out of a concern over disease and specifically the prevalence of tuberculosis among African immigrants. This organization also incorporated an important tradition of providing social welfare and medical services for colonial migrants that continued into the postcolonial realm. The programs and initiatives undertaken by the CMSB were possible in large part because the French government closely tracked and monitored the African immigrant community, gleaning where and how African immigrants lived, where they worked, and the perceived challenges that they faced. Similarly, the anti-*bidonville* campaign came about through state surveillance efforts, as officials determined where African immigrants lived and where they *wanted* them to live. In turn, events such as the Saint-Denis riot, the Ivry rent strike, and the protests that erupted in Aubervilliers attracted surveillance as officials tried to better understand this immigrant community with an eye not only on offering social welfare programs but also in seeking to control and contain this and other immigrant groups.

Several factors beyond the legacy of French colonialism in AOF and elsewhere influenced how it was that officials responded to African immigrants—the Cold War contributed significantly as well. While initially reading African immigrants as apolitical, especially in comparison to other immigrant groups such as the Algerians, officials became more and more concerned about political activism across the 1960s as anxiety over leftist influence and, specifically, the role of organizations such as the PCF and the CGT amongst African immigrants, increased. Fears over the left's perceived influence were fueled by growing concerns about the extreme Left's power in France and beyond, despite the broad spectrum of political parties and affiliations that operated in France overall. The idea that the PCF and other far-left organizations and parties were interested in harnessing the power of African immigrants' political aspirations was not entirely a fabrication of paranoid authorities. As this book has shown, although conflicted, the Left took a much greater interest in the political activism of African immigrants than previously acknowledged. This makes sense, as the PCF, for example, participated in challenging the French colonial state. That it would take the opportunity to criticize the capitalist system by helping to publicize the plight of African workers in France is not surprising. African immigrant political activism became more radical over the course of the 1960s and into the 1970s, as demonstrated by the trajectory of N'Dongo and the UGTSF as well as the protests staged in response to the deaths in Aubervilliers.

The international emphasis on human rights in the postwar era also shaped the discourse of African immigrant groups that undertook political activism after decolonization. Developments such as the Civil Rights Movement in the U.S. and the anti-apartheid movement in South Africa influenced global protest by providing various models through which to challenge official state policies that fostered racism and, in those two cases, segregation. While France never enacted legislation approaching the segregationist policies created in both the U.S. and South Africa, it nonetheless struggled to integrate a population of former colonial subjects and citizens. The separation, isolation, marginalization, and impoverishment that ensued contributed to the very political activism that authorities sought to avoid, while also shaping the social welfare programs enacted by the French state. The hope was that improved health and housing would dissuade African workers from political activism, thereby breaking the influence of the extreme Left, which the French state perceived as increasingly engaged with this community across the postcolonial era.

The period between 1960 and the late 1970s, then, proved vital in the establishment of the postcolonial African immigrant community. Building upon a long-standing tradition of migration from France's colonies in Sub-Saharan Africa, the Africans who arrived in France after 1960 found themselves facing many of the same challenges as their predecessors and some new ones as well. Housing continued to be an issue, as did disease, isolation, unemployment, and racism. As their predecessors had done in the interwar period, postcolonial African immigrants shaped public discourse on immigration and migration from the former colonies through the political activism that they undertook in response to the dire circumstances that they faced. Yet the community's composition proved ethereal—it had more in common with decades past than those in the future. By the late 1970s and with important changes in French immigration laws—namely, the suspension of labor migration in 1974—the African immigrant community's composition changed substantially. Women and children began to arrive to rejoin their husbands who decided to stay in France rather than to repatriate.

This proved to be an unanticipated consequence of the 1974 change in immigration law. Other immigrant groups—including North Africans and specifically Algerians—had come in family units prior to and just after World War Two. Until the mid-1970s, most African immigrants arrived alone. With this shift toward the arrival of women and children, organizations such as the *Centre Bossuet* scrambled to provide social welfare services to these new clients—constituents they previously rarely served because of the nearly all-male nature of African immigration to France across the twentieth century. Housing proved troublesome as well, as most African men resided in dwellings, as we have seen, that proved wholly unsuitable for families. In responding to African immigration in general after 1960 and to the arrival of women and children in particular, the French state also looked to policies and initiatives undertaken for other immigrant groups, including Algerians.

The arrival of women and children mirrored other important shifts within the African immigrant community by the late 1970s and 1980s. An increased emphasis on ethnicity emerged, as highlighted by the establishment of organizations that emphasized ethnic origin—such as the *Association pour la promotion soninké* (Association for Soninké Promotion)—rather than nationality. Cultural organizations emerged, as did those geared specifically toward women. Whereas the African associational sphere had previously been nearly all-male in composition, the diversification of the immigrant community itself led to the establishment of groups that addressed the specific needs of female immigrants. After the 1981 law that liberalized the right to association, a virtual explosion of immigrant organizations occurred, including those within the African immigrant community.[5] This carried on the important tradition of African immigrant political activism throughout the twentieth century, albeit in new forms and through new approaches.

Throughout the 1980s, 1990s, and 2000s, new generations of activists emerged: the children and grandchildren of immigrants who arrived in France during the postwar and postcolonial eras. From the North African perspective, we saw the emergence of the second-generation *beur* movement with slogans such as "*touch pas à mon pote*" ("hands off my buddy") led by activists such as Harlem Désir. The development of the *sans-papiers* movement comprising undocumented workers pioneered a new form of political visibility for immigrants without official papers. The movement hit its apex in 1996, when hundreds of *sans-papiers* occupied the Église Saint-Bernard. Moments such as these were built on an important political tradition established by immigrant communities in France throughout the twentieth century while also echoing protests undertaken during and after the colonial era. These protests challenged the French state on a number of fronts, from human rights abuses under the colonial regime to the plight of postcolonial workers inhabiting shantytowns and *bidonvilles*. African immigrant political activism also overlapped with other tensions, such as the ongoing debate over the headscarf and the multiple "*affaires du foulard*" or headscarves affairs that permeated the public sphere throughout the late 1980s, 1990s, and 2000s.

By 2005, there was once again a "riot in the night," or, at that point, multiple demonstrations and riots in protest about the aforementioned deaths of two young men at a power station in October of that year in the midst of a confrontation with police. The upheaval continued for weeks and the Fifth Republic teetered on the verge of collapse. The children and grandchildren of immigrants publicly drew attention to the challenges that they faced in navigating life in France, from racism, discrimination, and dislocation to a lack of integration. The rhetoric used throughout these protests mirrored, to some extent, that used by African workers throughout the 1960s and 1970s, which was borrowed, in turn, from their predecessors in the Pan-African nationalist movement. While the language of Marxism had largely disappeared from social and political protest following the end of the Cold War, the protestors posed important questions about how it was and whether immigrant communities could truly find a place within the Fifth Republic and French society. Across the 2000s and especially after the 2005 riots, the Ministry of the Interior imposed increasingly restrictive measures around immigration as the French public wrestled with how to address this issue, culminating in 2007 in the election as President of Nicholas Sarkozy, who as Minister of the Interior had taken a hard line on immigration. The extreme Right continued to gain traction amongst the electorate, culminating in a run-off off between the National Front's leader, Marine Le Pen, and Emmanuel Macron for the presidency in 2017. Le Pen lost the second ballot and Macron won the election. As revealed by that election, debates around immigration continue to influence contemporary politics.

Most recently, the refugee crisis spurred by the Arab Spring, the civil war in Syria, and other events in the Middle East, North Africa, and Sub-Saharan Africa continue to raise important questions about the place and role of immigration not only in France, but also throughout Europe and beyond. The international community is contending with the largest refugee crisis since World War Two, with 59.5 million people displaced by 2014 and millions more since then.[6] While France has not taken in the same number of refugees as Germany, Turkey, or countries bordering Syria, including Jordan and Lebanon, nor contributed the kind of money that the U.S. or the U.K. have toward humanitarian relief efforts, there is nonetheless an ongoing dialogue about what the refugee crisis means for France.[7] This crisis has raised many of the same questions as postcolonial migration in regards to integration, belonging, identity, and security, but with a bit of a twist. In France and elsewhere in Europe, as philosopher Thomas Nail argues, terrorism and migration have become synonymous with one another, with migrants cast as "potential terrorist(s) hiding among the crowd of migrants and the terrorist as a potential migrant ready to move into Europe at any moment."[8] Not since the Algerian War of the late 1950s and early 1960s and the bombing attacks of 1995 have immigrants in France been so closely associated with the threat of terrorism. While that association existed before the January, 2015 *Charlie Hebdo* attacks, the November terrorist attacks across Paris that same year, and the attack in Nice in July of 2016, it became amplified in France and elsewhere as a result of these and other instances of mass violence, including the attacks in Brussels, Belgium in March of 2016. Before and after these attacks, the language used by various political figures and commentators was not colonial in nature, as it was in reference to African immigrants in the early postcolonial period. But it reflects the anti-immigrant sentiment woven throughout French, European, and global political rhetoric. Terms such as "barbarians," "chaos," "hordes," and "floods" reveal the deeply negative connotations associated with the refugee crisis and those arriving from Syria and elsewhere.[9] For countries such as France and the U.K., with important histories of accepting refugees during international crises dating back to the interwar era, these developments are troubling. They signal a potential return to the politics of isolationism and nationalism in direct challenge to the postwar and post-Cold War emphasis on global integration through organizations such as the United Nations and the European Union. As the U.K. prepares to leave the European Union following the "Brexit" vote of June 23, 2016, we see once again the impact of immigration in shaping popular opinion and public policy.

As this book has shown, immigrants have a powerful ability to shape state and international policy and may do so once again if the migrants caught within this most recent refugee crisis can be thought of in human and humanitarian terms. French approaches to social welfare for immigrant communities—including those from North Africa during the interwar period and after World War Two and from Sub-Saharan Africa following decolonization—suggest that the state has an important capacity to provide programs that assist rather than target immigrant, migrant, and refugee groups. Immigrant communities—and in this case, refugees—utilize the opportunities provided through these programs in diverse and important ways.

African Political Activism in Postcolonial France has endeavored to highlight the multiple ways in which immigrants to France have shaped, and continue to shape, the landscape of contemporary French politics. In recent years, Western societies, including that of France, have struggled to address the colonial legacy as well as issues such as diversity and multiculturalism. Recently, there have been disquieting nationalist and protectionist trends in European politics and beyond that are linked, in large part, to contemporary and historical trends in immigration. Most notably was the Brexit vote, the outcome of which was linked to debates over immigration and refugees. The 2016 U.S. elections were also particularly informed by analogous questions. The rise of far-right politics in France and elsewhere in Europe serve as reminders of some of the darker chapters of twentieth-century world history. To this end, *African Political Activism in Postcolonial France* hopes to have provided much-needed historical contextualization in these conversations, contextualization that is often sorely lacking.

Notes

1 CANC 19870799 art. 25 MI 33134 Direction de la réglementation 6e bureau no. 1433 "M Sally N'DONGO, président de l'Union générale des travailleurs sénégalais en France participera aux côtés des responsables du Front Communiste Révolutionnaire a deux meetings organisés par la 'Ligue Communiste Révolutionnaire Suisse' à Lausanne et Zurich." 16 October 1974.

2 CANC 19870799 art. 25 MI 33134 UGTSF, "Buts de l'Association: UGTSF." Puteaux, 1976. Original French: "resserrer les liens d'amitié existant entre les travailleurs sénégalais en France et d'améliorer leurs conditions de vie par l'aide sociale et professionnelle."
3 CANC 19870799 art. 25 MI 33134 CANTAN, Le Directeur de la réglementation et du contentieux to M le Préfet des Hauts de Seine Direction de l'administration générale 2eme bureau, 4 August 1978.
4 For more on the 2005 riots, see the first four essays in Part 1: "Auto da fé: Understanding the 2005 Riots," in Charles Tshimanga, Didier Gondola, and Peter J. Bloom, eds., *Frenchness and the African Diaspora: Identity and Uprising in Contemporary France* (Bloomington; Indianapolis: Indiana University Press, 2009).
5 For more on the 1981 law, see Wihtol de Wenden and Leveau, *La beurgeoisie.*
6 Alise Coen, "R2P, Global Governance, and the Syrian Refugee Crisis," *International Journal of Human Rights* 19, no. 8 (2015): 1045.
7 Nicole Ostrand, "The Syrian Refugee Crisis: A Comparison of Responses by Germany, Sweden, the United Kingdom, and the United States," *Journal of Migration and Human Society* 3, no. 3 (2015): 255–279.
8 Thomas Nail, "A Tale of Two Crises: Migration and Terrorism after the Paris Attacks," *Studies in Ethnicity and Nationalism* 16, no. 1 (2016): 158.
9 Ibid., 165.

Selected bibliography

Archives

Archives départementales du Val-de-Marne

6J 105/106
2018 W art. 20
2252W art. 253

Archives départementales de la Seine-Saint-Denis

110 art. 22
1801W art. 226
1801W art. 227

Archives municipales d'Ivry-sur-Seine

134W 38

Archives municipales de la Marie de Montreuil

Foyers/Migrations 1969 à 1973
Immigration

Archives municipales de Saint-Denis

18 ACW 22/23

Archives de Paris

1206W art. 6

Archives de la préfecture de police (Paris)

GaA7

Centre des archives nationales

Objets généraux: Service de liaison promotion des migrants (1958–1969)

F1a 5051
F1a 5052
F1a 5053
F1a 5116

F1a 5135
F1a 5136
F7 16108

Centre des archives nationales contemporaines

Intérieur: Direction générale de l'administration

19770317 art. 1

Travail: Fonds d'action sociale pour les travailleurs migrants, UEO

19770391 art. 2

Santé: Direction de la population et des migrations

19810201 art. 4

Comité nationale consultatif

19810221 art. 4

Intérieur: Information sur la politique intérieur des étrangers et leur incidence en France

19850087 art. 9
19850087 art. 10 mi 26607
19850087 art. 159/159 M 26755/26756

Association pour la coopération Franco-Africaine

19850250 art. 4 liasse 417

Santé: Centre Médico-Social Bossuet

19870009 art. 1
19870009 art. 1 1965 2
19870009 art. Bossuet 1969 6

Intérieur: Direction générale de la police nationale

19870623 art. 1

Intérieur: Associations étrangères, associations françaises comprenant des membres étrangers

19870799 art. 24
19870799 art. 25

Intérieur: Pays d'Afrique Noire

19940023 art. 20

Intérieur: Pays d'Afrique Noire, 1960–1969

19940023 art. 20

Intérieur: Direction des libertés publiques et des affaires juridiques

19960134 art. 15

19960134 art. 17

Intérieur: Dossiers par pays: Afrique Noire

19960134 art. 15

Intérieur: Les dossiers, les notes de la préfecture de Paris

19960311 art. 5
19960311 art. 6
19960311 art. 7

Intérieur: Études générales sur le PCF

19960325 art. 8

Archives nationales d'Outre Mer

SLOTFOM

Centre d'information et d'études sur les migrations internationales

PCF 62/1/11

Institut national de l'audiovisuel

Newspapers and Periodicals

Agence France-Presse
L'Agence ivoirienne de presse
L'Alsace
Associated Press
L'Aurore
Bulletin municipal officiel (Ville de Paris)
Bulletin municipal officiel (Saint-Denis)
Cahiers nord-africains
Carrefour
La Cause du peuple
Combat
Le Courrier du Val-de-Marne
Le Cri des nègres
Croix du Nord
La Croix
Droit et liberté
L'Écho de la mode
L'Écho (La Liberté)
Les Échos
Esprit
Étincelle
Le Figaro
France-Soir
Franc-Tireur
Guardian
Hommes et migrations

L'Humanité
International Herald Tribune
Journal officiel de la République française
Libération
Le Monde
New York Herald Tribune
New York Times
Nord littoral Calais
L'Oise matin
Le Parisien libéré
Paris jour
Paris-Presse l'intransigeant
Le Populaire du Centre
Revue française des affaires sociales
Revue mensuelle
Revue des sciences médicales
Témoignage chrétien
The Times (London)
Le Travailleur
Union républicaine de la Marne

Dissertations and Unpublished Sources

Bernadot, Marc. "Une politique de logement: la SONACOTRA (1956–1992)." PhD diss., Université de Paris I—Panthéon—Sorbonne, 1997.

House, Jim. "Antiracism and Antiracist Discourse in France from 1900 to the Present Day." PhD diss., University of Leeds, 1997.

Keller, Kathleen. "Colonial Suspects: Suspicious Persons and Police Surveillance in French West Africa, 1914–1945." PhD diss., Rutgers University, 2006.

Manchuelle, François. "Background to Black African Emigration to France: The Labor Migrations of the Soninké ; 1848–1987." PhD diss., University of California-Santa Barbara, 1987.

Miller, Jennifer A. "Postwar Negotiations: The First Generation of Turkish 'Guest Workers' in West Germany, 1961–1973." PhD diss., Rutgers University, 2008.

Prakash, Amit. "Empire on the Seine: Surveillance, Citizenship, and North African Migrants in Paris (1925–1975)." PhD diss., Columbia University, 2010.

Sessions, Jennifer. "An Empire under Observation: French Colonial and Post-Colonial Surveillance in Metropole and Colony, 1918–1970." panel commentary at the Society for French Historical Studies annual meeting, New Brunswick, NJ, April 5, 2008.

Van Den Breemer, Rosemarie. "The French and Dutch Muslim Parcel Compared: An Institutionalist Account of Religious Governance and Secularism on the Cemetery." Politicologen Etmaal, Leuven, 27–28 May 2010.

Secondary Literature and Published Sources

Adi, Hakim. "Pan-Africanism and West African Nationalism in Britain." *African Studies Review* 43, no. 1 (April 2000): 69–82.

———. *West Africans in Britain 1900–1960: Nationalism, Pan-Africanism, and Communism*. London: Lawrence and Wishart Limited, 1998.

Agyeman, Opoku. *The Failure of Grassroots Pan-Africanism: The Case of the All-African Trade Union Federation*. Lanham: Lexington Books, 2003.

Aissaoui, Rabah. *Immigration and National Identity: North African Political Movements in Colonial and Postcolonial France*. London; New York: Tauris Academic Studies Palgrave Macmillan, 2009.

Alexander, Martin S. and J. F. V. Keiger, eds. *France and the Algerian War, 1954–62: Strategy, Operations and Diplomacy*. London; Portland, OR: Frank Cass, 2002.

Amiri, Linda. *La bataille de France: La guerre d'Algérie en mètropole*. Paris: R. Laffont, 2004.

Anderson, Benedict. *Imagined Communities: Reflections on the Origin and Spread of Nationalism*. Rev. ed. London; New York: Verso, 2006.

Arnold, David. *Imperial Medicine and Indigenous Societies*. Manchester; New York: Manchester University Press, 1988.

———. *Colonizing the Body: State Medicine and Epidemic Disease in Nineteenth-Century India*. Berkeley: University of California-Berkeley, 1993.

Attias-Donfut, Claudine, François-Charles Wolff, and Catriona Dutreuilh. "The Preferred Burial Location of Persons Born Outside France." *Population* 60, no. 5/6 (December 2005): 699–720.

Balibar, Etienne. *Race, Nation, Class: Ambiguous Identities*. London; New York: Verso, 1991.

Bancel, Nicholas, Pascal Blanchard, and Dominic Thomas, eds. *The Colonial Legacy in France: Fracture, Rupture, and Apartheid*. Bloomington: Indiana University Press, 2017.

———, Thomas David, and Dominic Thomas, eds. *The Invention of Race: Scientific and Popular Representations*. New York: Routledge, 2014.

Barou, Jacques, ed. *L'habitat des immigrés et de leurs familles*. Paris: La Documentation française, 2002.

———. *Travailleurs africains en France: Rôle des cultures d'origine*. Grenoble: Presses Universitaires de Grenoble, 1978.

Bashford, Alison. *Imperial Hygiene: A Critical History of Colonialism, Nationalism and Public Health*. Houndmills; Basingstoke; Hampshire; New York: Palgrave Macmillan, 2004.

Bates, Robert, Avner Greif, and Smita Singh. "Organizing Violence." *The Journal of Conflict Resolution* 46, no. 5 (October 2002): 599–628.

Baudry, Pierre. *Premiers résultats de l'enquête sur le logement en 1973 dans la région parisienne*. Paris: Institut national de la statistique et des études économiques, Direction régionale de Paris, 1974.

Beauvoir, Simone de. *Force of Circumstance*. New York: G. P. Putnum's Sons, 1965.

Berend, Ivan T. *An Economic History of Twentieth-Century Europe: Economic Regimes from Laissez-Faire to Globalization*. Cambridge; New York: Cambridge University Press, 2006.

Bernardot, Marc. "Chronique d'une institution: La 'Sonacotra' (1956–1976)." *Sociétés contemporaines* no. 33–34 (1999): 39–58.

Beyer, Cornelia. *Violent Globalisms: Conflict in Response to Empire*. Abingdon: Ashgate, 2008.

Bivens, Roberts. "'The English Disease' or 'Asian Rickets': Medical Responses to Post-Colonial Immigration." *Bulletin of the History of Medicine* 81 (2007): 533–568.

Blanc-Chaléard, Marie-Claude. *Les Italiens dans l'est parisien: une histoire d'intégration (1880–1960)*. Rome: École française de Rome, 2000.

———. "Old and New Migrants in France: Italians and Algerians." in Lucassen, Feldman, and Oltmer, *Paths of Integration*, 46–62.

Blanchard, Pascal, Nicolas Bancel, and Sandrine Lemaire, eds. *La fracture coloniale: la société française au prisme de l'héritage colonial*. Paris: Éditions La Découverte, 2006.

Bleich, Erik. "Anti-Racism without Races: Politics and Policy in a 'Color Blind' State." in Chapman and Frader, *Race in France*, 162–188.

———. "From International Ideas to Domestic Policies: Educational Multiculturalism in England and France." *Comparative Politics* (1998): 81–100.

———. "The Legacies of History? Colonization and Immigrant Integration in Britain and France." *Theory and Society* 34, no. 2 (April 2005): 171–195.

———. *Race Politics in Britain and France: Ideas and Policymaking since the 1960s*. Cambridge; New York: Cambridge University Press, 2003.

Blin, Thierry. *Les sans-papiers de Saint-Bernard: Mouvement social et action organisée*. Paris: L'Harmattan, 2005.

Bloom, Peter. "Beur Cinema and the Politics of Location: French Immigration Politics and the Naming of a Film Movement." in Shohat and Stam, *Multiculturalism, Postcoloniality, and Transnational Media*, 44–62.

Body-Gendrot, Sophie. "Ghetto, mythes et réalités" in Dewitte, *Immigration et intégration*, 279–290.

——— and Catherine Wihtol de Wenden. *Police et discriminations raciales: Le tabou français*. Paris: Les Éditions de l'Atelier/Les Éditions Ouvrieres, 2003.

Boittin, Jennifer Anne. *Colonial Metropolis: The Urban Grounds of Anti-Imperialism and Feminism in Interwar Paris*. Lincoln: The University of Nebraska Press, 2010.

Bosniak, Linda. *The Citizen and the Alien*. Princeton: Princeton University Press, 2008.

Bouton, Cynthia A. *Interpreting Social Violence in French Culture Buzançais, 1847–2008*. Baton Rouge: Louisiana State University Press, 2011.

Branch, Daniel. *Defeating Mau Mau, Creating Kenya: Counterinsurgency, Civil War, and Decolonization*. Cambridge: Cambridge University Press, 2008.

Braziel, Jana Evans and Anita Mannur, eds. *Theorizing Diaspora: A Reader*. Hoboken: Wiley-Blackwell, 2003.

Brinker-Gabler, Gisela. *Writing New Identities: Gender, Nation, and Immigration in Contemporary Europe*. Minneapolis: University of Minnesota Press, 1997.

Brochmann, Grete. *Mechanisms of Immigration Control: A Comparative Analysis of European Regulation Policies*. Oxford; New York: Berg, 1999.

Brower, Benjamin C. *A Desert Named Peace: The Violence of France's Empire in the Algerian Sahara, 1844–1902*. New York: Columbia University Press, 2009.

Brubaker, Rogers. *Citizenship and Nationhood in France and Germany*. Cambridge: Harvard University Press, 1992.

Brumpt, L. "Problèmes sanitaires posés par les travailleurs africains." *Revue des sciences médicales: la pathologie du noir africain en France* 162 (October 1964): 5–9.

Bryder, Linda. "The Papworth Village Settlement—a Unique Experiment in the Treatment and Care of the Tuberculous?" *Medical History* 28 (1984): 371–390.

Burton, Richard D. E. *Blood in the City: Violence and Revelation in Paris, 1789–1945*. Ithaca; London: Cornell University Press, 2001.

Buton, Philippe. "Inventing a Memory on the Extreme Left." in Jackson, et al., eds., *May 68*, 58–75.

Campani, Giovanna, Maurizio Catani and Salvatore Palidda, "Italian Immigrant Associations in France." in Rex et al., eds., *Immigrant Associations in Europe*.

Carmona, Michel. *Haussmann: His Life and Times, and the Making of Modern Paris*. trans. Patrick Camiller Chicago: I. R. Dee, 2002.

Caron, Vicki. *Uneasy Asylum: France and the Jewish Refugee Crisis, 1933–1942*. Stanford: Stanford University Press, 1999.

Castells, Manuel et al. *Crise du logement et mouvements sociaux urbains: Enquête sur la région parisienne*. Paris: Mouton, 1978.

Castles, Stephen and Alastair Davidson, *Citizenship and Migration: Globalization and the Politics of Belonging*. New York: Routledge, 2000.

———, and Mark J. Miller. *The Age of Migration: International Populations Movements in the Modern World*. 2nd ed. New York: Palgrave, 1998.

Centre d'études anti-impérialistes (Paris). *Bulletin de liaison du Cedetin*. Paris: Le Centre, 1975.

———. *Les immigrés: contribution à l'histoire politique de l'immigration en France*. Paris: Stock, 1975.

Chafer, Tony. "France and Senegal: The End of the Affair?" *SAIS Review* 23, no. 2 (2003): 155–167.

———. *The End of Empire in French West Africa: France's Successful Decolonization?* Oxford; New York: Berg, 2002.

———, and Amanda Sackur, eds. *Promoting the Colonial Idea: Propaganda and Visions of Empire in France*. Houndmills; Basingstoke; Hampshire; New York: Palgrave, 2002.

Chamberlain, M. E. *Decolonization: The Fall of the European Empires*. 2nd ed. Hoboken: Wiley-Blackwell, 1999.

Chapman, Herrick and Laura Levine Frader, eds. *Race in France: Interdisciplinary Perspectives on the Politics of Difference*. New York; Oxford: Berghahn Books, 2004.

Chiodi, Pietro. *Sartre and Marxism*. trans. Kate Soper. New Jersey, NJ: Humanities Press, 1976.

Christiansen, Samantha, and Zachary A. Scarlett, eds. *The Third World in the Global 1960s*. New York: Berghahn Books, 2012.

Christopher, Emma, Cassandra Pybus and Marcus Rediker, eds. *Many Middle Passages: Forced Migration and the Making of the Modern World*. Berkeley: University of California Press, 2007.

Clark Hine, Darlene, Trica Danielle Keaton, and Stephen Small, eds. *Black Europe and the African Diaspora*. Urbana and Chicago: University of Illinois, 2009.

Coen, Alise. "R2P, Global Governance, and the Syrian Refugee Crisis." *International Journal of Human Rights* 19, no. 8 (2015): 1044–1058.

Cohen, William. *The French Encounter with Africans: White Response to Blacks, 1530–1880*. Bloomington: Indian University Press, 2003.

Cohen, Robin and Zig Layton-Henry, eds. *The Politics of Migration*. Cheltenham, UK; Northampton, MA: E. Elgar, 1997.

Colas, Georges. "Les problèmes de l'immigration africaine noire." *Hommes et migrations* no. 625 (8 November 1965).

Cole, Joshua. *The Power of Large Numbers: Population, Politics, and Gender in Nineteenth-Century France*. Ithaca; London: Cornell University Press, 2000.

Conklin, Alice. *A Mission to Civilize: The Republican Idea of Empire in France and West Africa, 1895–1930*. Stanford: Stanford University Press, 1997.

Cooper, Barbara M. "Anatomy of a Riot: The Social Imagery, Single Women, and Religious Violence in Niger." *Canadian Journal of African Studies/Revue canadienne des études africaines* 37, no. 2/3 (2003): 467–512.

Cooper, Frederick. *Citizenship between Empire and Nation: Remaking France and French Africa, 1945–1960*. Princeton: Princeton University Press, 2014.

———. *Decolonization and African Society: The Labor Question in French and British Africa*. Cambridge: Cambridge University Press, 1996.

———. "From Imperial to Republican Exclusion? France's Ambiguous Postwar Trajectory." in Tshimanga, Gondola, and Bloom, eds. *Frenchness and the African Diaspora*, 91–119.

Copans, Jean. "Paysannerie et Politique au Sénégal." *Cahiers d'études africaines* 18, no. 69/70 (1978): 241–256.

Copin, Noël. "L'Afrique Noire au Coeur de Paris." *Études sociales nord-africaines/ESNA* 14 (22 June 1963): 526–533.

Cottle, Simon, and Libby Lester, eds. *Transnational Protests and the Media*. New York: Peter Lang, 2011.

Cunha, Maria do Céu. *Portugais de France: essai sur une dynamique de double appartenance*. Paris: L'Harmattan, 1988.

D'Arcus, Bruce. *Boundaries of Dissent: Protest and State Power in the Media Age*. New York; London: Routledge, 2006.

Dal Lago, Alessandro. *Non-Persons: The Exclusion of Migrants in a Global Society*. trans. Marie Orton. Milan: IPOC di Pietro Condemi, 2009.

Daughton, J. P. *An Empire Divided: Religion, Republicanism, and the Making of French Colonialism, 1880–1914*. New York: Oxford University Press, 2006.

Daum, Christophe. *Les associations de Maliens en France: Migrations, développement, et citoyenneté*. Paris: Éditions Karthala, 1998.

Davidson, Naomi. *Only Muslim: Embodying Islam in Twentieth-Century France*. Ithaca: Cornell University Press, 2012.

Davies, Peter. *The National Front: Ideology, Discourse, and Power*. New York: Routledge, 1999.

Davis, Belinda. "What's Left?: Popular Political Participation in Postwar Europe." *American Historical Review* 113, no. 2 (April 2008): 363–390.

Dedieu, Jean-Philippe. *La parole immigrée: Les migrants Africains dans l'espace public en France (1960–1995)*. Paris: Klincksieck, 2012.

Derrick, Jonathan. *Africa's "Agitators": Militant Anti-Colonialism in Africa and the West, 1918–1939*. New York: Columbia University Press, 2008.

Dewitte, Philippe, ed. *Immigration et intégration: l'état des savoirs*. Paris: Éditions Découverte, 1999.

———. *Les mouvements nègres en France, 1919–1939*. Paris: Éditions L'Harmattan, 1985.

Diawara, Baba. *Portraits de douze noirs de France: Portraits de douze noirs de Francei: Ni éboueurs, ni sportifs, ni vigiles, ni musiciens*.... Paris: L'Harmattan, 2009.

Doumbia, Adama, and Naomi Doumbia. *The Way of the Elders: West African Spirituality and Tradition*. Saint Paul, MN: Llewellyn Publications, 2004.

Dubois, Laurent. *A Colony of Citizens: Revolution and Slave Emancipation in the French Caribbean, 1787–1804*. Chapel Hill: The University of North Carolina Press, 2004.

Dudziak, Mary L. *Cold War Civil Rights: Race and the Image of American Democracy*. Princeton: Princeton University Press, 2000.

Echenberg, Myron. *Black Death, White Medicine: Bubonic Plague and the Politics of Public Health in Colonial Senegal, 1914–1945*. Portsmouth, NH: Heinemann, 2002.

Eichengreen, Barry J. *The European Economy since 1945: Coordinated Capitalism and Beyond*. Princeton: Princeton University Press, 2007.

Einaudi, Jean-Luc. *Octobre 1961: un massacre à Paris*. Paris: Fayard, 2001.

El Alaoui, Soraya. "L'espace funéraire de Bobigny: du cimetière aux carrés musulmans (1934–2006)." *Revue européenne des migrations internationales* 28, no. 3 (September 1, 2012): 27–49.

Epelbaum, Didier. *Les enfants de papier: Les juifs de Pologne immigrés en France jusqu'en 1940: l'accueil, l'intégration, les combats*. Paris: Grasset, 2002.

ESNA/Cahiers Nord-Africains. *Approche des problèmes de la migration noire en France*. Paris: ESNA, 1965.

Fall, Babicar. *Le travail forcé en Afrique Occidental française, 1900–1946*. Paris: Karthala, 1993.

Fall, Mar. *Des Africains noirs en France: Des tirailleurs sénégalais aux … blacks*. Paris: Broche, 2000.

Falola, Toyin. *Colonialism and Violence in Nigeria*. Bloomington; Indianapolis: Indiana University Press, 2009.

Fanon, Frantz. *Black Skin, White Masks*. Paris: Éditions du Seuil, 1952.

———. *The Wretched of the Earth*. Paris: Présence Africaine, 1963.

Farge, Michel. *Le statut familial des étrangers en France: de la loi nationale à la loi de la résidence habituelle*. Paris: L'Harmattan, 2003.

Fassin, Didier. "Compassion and Repression: The Moral Economy of Immigration Policies in France." *Cultural Anthropology* 20, no. 3 (August 2005): 362–387.

———. "Riots in France and Silent Anthropologists." *Anthropology Today* 22, no. 1 (February 2006): 1–3.

Favell, Adrian. *Philosophies of Integration: Immigration and the Idea of Citizenship in France and Britain*. 2nd ed. New York: Palgrave Macmillan, 2001.

Fink, Carole, Philipp Gassert, and Detlef Junker, eds. *1968: The World Transformed*. Cambridge: Cambridge University Press, 1998.

Flynn, Thomas R. *Sartre and Marxist Existentialism: The Test Case of Collective Responsibility*. Chicago; London: The University of Chicago Press, 1984.

Fogg, Shannon L. *The Politics of Everyday Life in Vichy France: Foreigners, Undesirables, and Strangers*. Cambridge: Cambridge University Press, 2009.

Foner, Nancy and Richard Alba. "Immigrant Religion in the U.S. and Western Europe: Bridge or Barrier to Inclusion?" *International Migration Review* 42, no. 2 (June 2008): 360–392.

Foret, François, and Xabier Itçaina, eds. *Politics of Religion in Western Europe: Modernities in Conflict?* London; New York: Routledge, 2012.

Fortuné, Félix-Hilaire. *La France et l'Outre Mer antillais: Quatre siècles d'histoire économique et sociale*. Paris: L'Harmattan, 2001.

Foster, Elizabeth. *Faith in Empire: Religion, Politics, and Colonial Rule in French Senegal, 1880–1940*. Stanford: Stanford University Press, 2013.

Foucault, Michel. *Discipline and Punish: The Birth of the Prison*. 2nd ed. New York: Vintage Books, 1995.

———. *Security, Territory, Population Lectures at the College de France 1977–1978*. eds. Arnold I. Davidson. New York: Palgrave, 2009.

Freedman, Jane, ed. *Gender and Insecurity: Migrant Women in Europe*. Aldershot: Ashgate, 2003.

——— and Carrie Tarr, eds. *Women, Immigration and Identity in France*. Oxford: Berg, 2000.

Freeman, Gary P. *Immigrant Labor and Racial Conflict in Industrial Societies: The French and British Experience, 1945–1975*. New Jersey: Princeton University Press, 1979.

———. "Migration and the Political Economy of the Welfare State." *The Annals of the American Academy of Political and Social Science* 1986, 51–63.

Frey, Yves. *Polonais d'Alsace: pratiques patronales et mineurs polonais dans le bassin potassique de Haute-Alsace, 1918–1948*. Besançon: Presses universitaires franc-comtoises, 2003.

Fyle, C. Magbaily. *Introduction to the History of African Civilization Volume 2 Colonial and Post-Colonial Africa*. Lanham; New York; Oxford: University Press of America, 2001.

Fysh, Peter, and Jim Wolfreys. *The Politics of Racism in France*. Houndmills; Basingstoke; Hampshire; New York: MacMillan/St. Martin's Press, 1998.

Gaddis, John Lewis. *We Know Now: Rethinking Cold War History*. Oxford: Oxford University Press, 1997.

Gafaiti, Hafid, Patricia M. E. Lorcin, and David G. Troyansky, eds. *Transnational Spaces and Identities in the Francophone World*. Lincoln: University of Nebraska Press, 2009.

Galtung, Johan and Tord Hoivik. "Structural and Direct Violence: A Note on Operationalization." *Journal of Peace Research* 8, no. 1 (1971): 73–76.

Garavini, Giuliano. "The Colonies Strike Back: The Impact of the Third World on Western Europe, 1968–1975." *Contemporary European History* 16, no. 3 (August 2007): 299–319.

Gardinier, David E. "Strike Movement as Part of the Anticolonial Struggle in French West Africa" in Maddox and Welliver, eds. *Colonialism and Nationalism*, vol. 3, *African Nationalism and Independence*.

Gastaut, Yvan. "Français et immigrés à l'épreuve de la crise (1973–1995)." *Vingtième siècle. Revue d'histoire* 4, no. 84 (2004): 107–118.

———. "L'irruption du thème de l'immigration dans les médias." *Confluences méditerranée* no. 24 (1997): 15–31.

Gaudilliére, Jean-Paul and Ilana Löwy, eds. *Heredity and Infection: The History of Disease Transmission*. London: Routledge, 2001.

Geddes, Andrew. *The Politics of Migration and Immigration in Europe*. London: Sage, 2003.

Geest, Sjaak van der. "Between Death and Funeral: Mortuaries and the Exploitation of Liminality in Kwahu, Ghana." *Africa: Journal of the International African Institute* 76, no. 4 (2006): 485–501.

Geissler, Rainer. *Media, Migration, Integration: European and North American Perspectives*. New Brunswick: Transaction Publishers, 2009.

——— and Horst Pottker, eds. *Media, Migration, Integration: European and North American Perspectives*. New Brunswick: Transaction Publishers, 2009.

Germain, Félix F. *Decolonizing the Republic: African and Caribbean Migrants in Postwar Paris (1946–1974)*. East Lansing: Michigan State University Press, 2016.

Geschiere, Peter. "Funerals and Belonging: Different Patterns in South Cameroon." *African Studies Association* 48, no. 2 (September 2005): 45–64.

Gifford, Prosser, and W. M. Roger Louis, eds. *Decolonization and African Independence: Transfers of Power, 1960–1980.* New Haven; London: Yale University Press, 1988.

Ginio, Ruth. *The French Army and Its African Soldiers: The Years of Decolonization.* Lincoln; London: University of Nebraska Press, 2017.

Glaes, Gillian. "'Africans against Algerians, the exploited against the exploited': Media Representations of the 1963 Saint Denis Riot." *Proceedings of the Western Society for French History* 36 (2008): 309–321.

———. "Curing Patients, Connecting Lives: The *Centre Médico-Social Bossuet*, the West African Community, and the Struggle Against Tuberculosis, 1963–1979." *Proceedings of the Western Society for French History* 32 (2005): 386–403.

———. "Policing the Post-Colonial Order: Surveillance and the African Immigrant Community in France, 1960–1979." *Historical Reflections/Réflexions Historiques* 36, no. 2 (2010): 108–126.

Glazier, Ira A. *Migration Across Time and Nations: Population Mobility in Historical Contexts.* New York: Holmes & Meier, 1986.

Gonin, Patrick and Véronique Lassailly-Jacob. "Les réfugiés de l'environnement: une nouvelle catégorie de migrants forcés?" *Revue européenne des migrations internationales* 18, no. 2 (2002): 139–160.

Gordon, Daniel A. *Immigrants and Intellectuals: May '68 and the Rise of Anti-Racism in France.* Pontypool, Wales: Merlin Press, 2012.

———. "Reaching Out to Immigrants in May 68: Specific or Universal Appeals?" in Jackson, Milne, and Williams, *May 68*, 93–106.

Goren, Arthur Aryeh. "Sacred and Secular: The Place of Public Funerals in the Immigrant Life of American Jews." *Jewish History* 8, no. 1/2 (1994): 269–305.

Gosselin, Gabriel, and Jean-Pierre Lavaud, eds. *Ethnicité et mobilisations sociale.* Paris: L'Harmattan, 2001.

Gourévitch, Jean-Paul. *Les Africains de France.* Paris: Acropole, 2009.

Granotier, Bernard. *Les travailleurs immigrés en France.* Paris: François Maspero, 1970.

Guerin-Gonzales, Camille. *The Politics of Immigrant Workers Labor Activism and Migration in the World Economy since 1830.* New York: Holmes & Meier, 1998.

Guéye, Abdoulaye. "The Colony Strikes Back: African Protest Movements in Postcolonial France." *Comparative Studies of South Asia, Africa and the Middle East* 26, no. 2 (2006): 225–242.

Guimont, Fabienne. *Les étudiants africains en France (1950–1965).* Paris: L'Harmattan, 1997.

Hage, Julien. "Les littératures francophones d'Afrique noire à la conquête de l'édition française (1914–1974)." *Gradhiva* 2 (2009): 80–105.

Hale, Dana S. *Races on Display: French Representations of Colonized Peoples, 1886–1940.* Bloomington: Indiana University Press, 2008.

Hall, Catherine and Sonya O. Rose, eds. *At Home with the Empire: Metropolitan Culture and the Imperial World.* Cambridge: Cambridge University Press, 2006.

Hargreaves, Alec G. *Immigration, "Race," and Ethnicity in Contemporary France.* New York: Routledge, 1995.

Harrison, Christopher. *France and Islam in West Africa, 1860–1960.* Cambridge: Cambridge University Press, 1988.

Harrison, Mark. *Public Health in British India.* Cambridge: Cambridge University Press, 1994.

Haus, L. "Labor Unions and Immigration Policy in France." *International Migration Review* 33, no. 3 (1999): 683–716.

Hayes Edwards, Brent. *The Practice of Diaspora: Literature, Translation, and the Rise of Black Internationalism.* Cambridge; London: Harvard University Press, 2003.

Hendrickson, Burleigh. "March 1968: Practicing Transnational Activism from Tunis to Paris." *International Journal of Middle Eastern Studies* 44 (2012): 755–774.

Hill, Ann Maxwell. "Chinese Funerals and Chinese Ethnicity in Chiang Mai, Thailand." *Ethnology* 31, no. 4 (October 1992): 315–330.

Hily, Marie-Antoinette and Michel Poinard, "Portuguese Associations in France." in Rex et al., eds., *Immigrant Associations in Europe*, 126–160.

Hollifield, James Frank. *Immigrants, Markets, and States: The Political Economy of Postwar Europe.* Cambridge: Harvard University Press, 1992.

Horn, Gerd-Rainer. *The Spirit of '68: Rebellion in Western Europe and North America, 1956–1976.* London: Oxford University Press, 2007.

Horowitz, Donald L. "Immigration and Group Relations in France and America." *Bulletin of the American Academy of Arts and Sciences* 45, no. 4 (January 1992): 9–30.

House, Jim and Neil MacMaster. *Paris 1961: Algerians, State Terror, and Memory.* Oxford and New York: Oxford University Press, 2006.

Ireland, Patrick R. *The Policy Challenge of Ethnic Diversity.* Cambridge: Harvard University Press, 1994.

Jackson, Julian, Anna-Louise Milne, and James S. Williams, eds. *May 68: Rethinking France's Last Revolution.* Houndsmills; Basingstoke; Hampshire; New York: Palgrave Macmillan, 2011.

Jaeger, Georges. "L'examen de dépistage des travailleurs africains en France." *Revue des sciences médicales: La pathologie du noir africain en France* (October 1964).

Jameson, Frederic. *Marxism and Form: Twentieth-Century Dialectical Theories of Literature.* Princeton: Princeton University Press, 1971.

Jennings, Jeremy. "Citizenship, Republicanism and Multiculturalism in Contemporary France." *British Journal of Political Science* 30, no. 4 (2000): 575–598.

Jindra, Michael, and Joel Noret, eds. *Funerals in Africa: Explorations of a Social Phenomenon.* New York; Oxford: Berghahn Books, 2011.

Johnson, Michelle C. "Death and the Left Hand: Islam, Gender, and 'Proper' Mandinga Funerary Custom in Guinea-Bissau and Portugal." *African Studies Association* 52, no. 2 (September 2009): 93–117.

Johnson, Richard. *The French Communist Party versus the Students: Revolutionary Politics in May–June 1968.* New Haven; London: Yale University Press, 1972.

Jones, Hilary. *The Métis of Senegal: Urban Life and Politics in French West Africa.* Bloomington; Indianapolis: Indiana University Press, 2013.

Judt, Tony. *Past Imperfect: French Intellectuals, 1944–1956.* Berkeley: University of California Press, 1992.

Karam, Patrick. *Français d'Outre–Mer. Dossier d'une discrimination occultée: sommes-nous à part entière ou entièrement à part?* Paris: L'Harmattan, 2004.

Kastoryano, Riva. "Negotiating beyond Borders: States and Immigrants in Postcolonial Europe." *Journal of Interdisciplinary History* 41, no. 1 (Summer 2010): 79–95.

———. *Negotiating Identities: States and Immigrants in France and Germany.* trans. Barbara Harshav. Princeton: Princeton University Press, 2002.

———. *Être Turc en France: réflexions sur les familles et communautés.* Paris: Éditions l'Harmattan, 2004.

Keaton, Tricia Danielle, T. Denean Sharpley-Whiting, and Tyler Stovall, eds. *Black France/France Noire: The History and Politics of Blackness*. Durham: Duke, 2012.

Keese, Alexander. "A Culture of Panic: 'Communist' Scapegoats and Decolonization in French West Africa and French Polynesia (1945–1957)." *French Colonial History* 9 (2008): 131–145.

Keller, Kathleen. "On the Fringes of the 'Civilizing Mission': 'Suspicious' Frenchmen and Unofficial Discourses of French Colonialism in AOF (1918–1939)." *French Colonial History* 9, no. 1 (2008): 103–129.

———. "Political Surveillance and Colonial Urban Rule: 'Suspicious' Politics and Urban Space in Dakar, Senegal, 1918–1939." *French Historical Studies* 35, no. 4 (2012): 727–749.

Keller, Richard. "Madness and Colonization: Psychiatry in the British and French Empires, 1800–1962." *Journal of Social History* 35, no. 2 (2001): 295–326.

———. *Colonial Madness: Psychiatry in French North Africa*. Chicago: University of Chicago Press, 2007.

Kennedy-Brenner, Carliene. *Foreign Workers and Immigration Policy: The Case of France*. Paris: Organization for Economic Co-operation and Development (OECD), 1979.

Kepel, Gilles. *Les banlieues d'Islam: naissance d'une religion en France*. Paris: Éditions du Seuil, 1987.

Kessel, Patrick. *Le mouvement "maoïste" en France: textes et documents 1963–1968*. Paris: Inèdit, 1972.

King, Russell, and Nancy Wood, eds. *Media and Migration: Constructions of Mobility and Difference*. London and New York: Routledge, 2001.

Kivisto, Peter. *Multiculturalism in a Global Society*. Oxford: Blackwell, 2002.

Klein, Genevieve. "The British Anti-Apartheid Movement and Political Prisoner Campaigns." *Journal of Southern African Studies* 35, no. 2 (June 2009): 455–470.

Kohn, Hans and Wallace Sokolsky. *African Nationalism in the Twentieth Century*. Princeton: D. Van Nostrand Company, Inc., 1965.

Kudlick, Catherine J. *Cholera in Post-Revolutionary Paris: A Cultural History*. Berkeley: University of California Press, 1996.

Kunovich, Robert M. "The Sources and Consequences of National Identification." *American Sociological Review* 74, no. August (2009): 573–593.

Kurlansky, Mark. *1968: The Year That Rocked the World*. New York: Ballantine Books, 2005.

Lambert, W. E., F. M. Moghaddam, J. Sorin, and S. Sorin. "Assimilation vs. Multiculturalism: Views from a Community in France." *Sociological Forum* 5 (1990): 387–411.

Lange, Matthew, and Andrew Dawson. "Dividing and Ruling the World? A Statistical Test of the Effects of Colonialism on Postcolonial Civil Violence." *Social Forces* 88, no. 2 (December 2009): 785–817.

Lapeyronnie, Didier, "Primitive Rebellion in the French Banlieues: On the Fall 2005 Riots." trans. Jane Marie Todd in Tshimanga, Gondola, and Bloom, eds. *Frenchness and the African Diaspora*, 21–46.

Lauren, Paul Gordon. *The Evolution of International Human Rights: Visions Seen* 2nd ed. Philadelphia: University of Pennsylvania Press, 2003.

Lawrance, Benjamin N., Emily Lynn Osborn, and Richard L. Roberts, eds. *Intermediaries, Interpreters, and Clerks: African Employees in the Making of Colonial Africa*. Madison: University of Wisconsin Press, 2006.

Layton-Henry, Zig, ed. *The Political Rights of Migrant Workers in Western Europe*. London: Sage Publishers, 1990.

Lebovics, Herman. *Imperialism and the Corruption of Democracies*. Durham: Duke University Press, 2006.

Levine, Philippa. *Gender and Empire*. Oxford: Oxford University Press, 2007.

Lewis, Mary Dewhurst. *The Boundaries of the Republic: Migrant Rights and the Limits of Universalism in France, 1918–1940*. Stanford: Stanford University Press, 2007.

Lionnet, Françoise. "Immigration, Poster Art, and Transgressive Citizenship: France 1968–1988." *SubStance* 24, no. 1/2, no. 76/77 (1995): 93–108.

Lucassen, Leo, David Feldman, and Jochen Oltmer. *Paths of Integration: Migrants in Western Europe (1880–2004)*. Amsterdam University Press, 2006.

Luedtke, Adam. *Migrants and Minorities: The European Response*. Newcastle upon Tyne: Cambridge Scholars, 2010.

Lyons, Amelia. "Social Welfare, French Muslims and Decolonization in France: The Case of the Fonds d'Action Sociale." *Patterns of Prejudice* 43, no. 1 (2009).

———. *The Civilizing Mission in the Metropole: Algerian Families and the French Welfare State during Decolonization*. Stanford: Stanford University Press, 2013.

———. "The Civilizing Mission in the Metropole: Algerian Immigrants in France and the Politics of Adaptation during Decolonization." *Geschichte und Gesellschaft* 32, no. 4 (December 2006): 489–516.

MacMaster, Neil. *Colonial Migrants and Racism: Algerians in France, 1900–62*. Houndmills; Basingstoke; Hampshire; New York: Palgrave Macmillan, 1997.

——— and Jim House. "La Fédération de France du FLN et l'organisation du 17 Octobre 1961." *Vingtième siècle. Revue d'histoire* no. 83 (September 2004): 145–160.

———. "The '*seuil de tolérance*': The Uses of a 'Scientific' Racist Concept." in Silverman, *Race, Discourse, and Power in France*, 14–28.

——— and Jim House. "La Fédération de France du FLN et l'organisation du 17 octobre 1961." *Vingtième siècle. Revue d'histoire* no. 83 (July–September 2004): 145–160.

Maganga-Moussavou, Pierre Claver. *L'aide publique de la France au développement du Gabon depuis l'indépendance (1960–1978)*. Paris: Publications de la Sorbonne, 1982.

Makonnen, Ras. *Pan-Africanism from Within*. ed. Kenneth King. Nairobi, London, and New York: Oxford University Press, 1973.

Mamdani, Mahmood. *Citizen and Subject: Contemporary Africa and the Legacy of Late Colonialism*. Princeton: Princeton University Press, 1996.

Manchuelle, François. *Willing Migrants: Soninké Labor Diasporas, 1848–1960*. Athens: Ohio University Press, 1997.

———. "The 'Patriarchal Ideal' of Soninké Labor Migrants: From Slave Owners to Employers of Free Labor." *Canadian Journal of African Studies/ Revue canadienne des études africaines* 23, no. 1 (1989): 106–125.

Mann, Gregory. "Immigrants and Arguments in France and West Africa." *Comparative Studies in Society and History* 45, no. 2 (April 2003): 362–385.

———. "Locating Colonial Histories: Between France and West Africa," *The American Historical Review* 110 (2005): 409–434.

———. *Native Sons: West African Veterans and France in the Twentieth Century*. Durham: Duke University Press, 2006.

Marrus, Michael and Robert O. Paxton. *Vichy France and the Jews*. forward Stanley Hoffman. Stanford: Stanford University Press, 2003.

Marsh, Kate, and Nicola Frith, eds. *France's Lost Empires: Fragmentation, Nostalgia, and la Fracture Coloniale*. Lanham: Lexington Books, 2011.

Martin, Philip L., and Mark J. Miller. "Guestworkers: Lessons from Western Europe." *Industrial and Labor Relations Review* 1980, 315–330.

Martin, Tony. *The Pan-African Connection: From Slavery to Garvey and Beyond.* Wellesley: Majority Press, 1984.

Mathias, Elizabeth. "The Italian-American Funeral: Persistence through Change." *Western Folklore* 33, no. 1 (January 1974): 35–50.

Mayer, Nona. "Is France Racist?" trans. Rosemary Morris. *Contemporary European History* 5, no. 1 (March 1996): 119–27.

Mauco, Georges. *Les étrangers en France et le problème du racisme.* Paris: La Pensée universelle, 1977.

Mazower, Mar, ed. *The Policing of Politics in the Twentieth Century: Historical Perspectives.* Providence: Berghan Books, 1997.

———. "Violence and the State in the Twentieth Century." *The American Historical Review* 107, no. 4 (October 2002): 1158–1178.

McDonald, James R. "Labor Immigration in France, 1946–1965." *Annals of the Association of American Geography* 59, no. 1 (March 1964): 116–134.

McNevin, Anne. "Political Belonging in a Neoliberal Era: The Struggle of the *Sans-Papiers*." *Citizenship Studies* 10, no. 2 (May 2006): 135–151.

Merriman, John. *Police Stories: Building the French State, 1815–1851.* Oxford: Oxford University Press, 2005.

Miller, Jennifer A. "Her Fight Is Your Fight: 'Guest Worker' Labor Activism in the Early 1970s West Germany." *International Labor and Working-Class History* 84 (Fall 2013): 226–247.

———. "On Track for West Germany: Turkish 'Guest-Worker' Rail Transportation to West Germany in the Postwar Period." *German History*, 30, no. 4 (December 1, 2012): 550–573.

Milza, Pierre, ed. *Les Italiens en France de 1914 à 1940.* Rome: École française de Rome, 1986.

——— et al, eds. *L'intégration italienne en France: Un siècle de présence italienne dans trois régions françaises: 1880–1980.* Bruxelles: Éditions Complexe, 1995.

Modood, Tariq, "The Politics of Multiculturalism in the New Europe." in Modood and Werbner, *The Politics of Multiculturalism in the New Europe*, 1–26.

——— and Pnina Werbner. *The Politics of Multiculturalism in the New Europe: Racism, Identity, and Community.* Palgrave Macmillan, 1997.

Molina, Natalie. *Fit to Be Citizens?: Public Health and Race in Los Angeles, 1879–1939.* Berkeley: University of California-Berkeley, 2006.

Morgan, Philip D. and Sean Hawkins, eds., *Black Experience and the Empire.* Oxford: Oxford University Press, 2004.

Morice, Alain, and Swanie Potat, eds., *De l'ouvrier immigré au travailleur sans papier: Les étrangers dans la modernisation du salariat.* Paris: Éditions Karthala, 2010.

Murphy, John P. "Protest or Riot?: Interpreting Collective Action in Contemporary France." *Anthropological Quarterly* 84, no. 4 (2011): 977–1009.

Myers, Daniel J. "Racial Rioting in the 1960s: An Event History of Local Conditions." *American Sociological Review* 62, no. 1 (February 1997): 94–112.

Nail, Thomas. "A Tale of Two Crises: Migration and Terrorism after the Paris Attacks." *Studies in Ethnicity and Nationalism* 16, no. 1 (2016): 158–167.

Nantambu, Kwame. "Pan-Africanism versus Pan-African Nationalism: An Afro-Centric Analysis." *Journal of Black Studies* 28, no. 5 (May 1998): 561–574.

N'Diaye, Jean-Pierre. *Négriers Modernes: Les travailleurs noirs en France*. Paris: Présence Africaine, 1970.

Ndiaye, Pap. *La condition noire: Essai sur une minorité française*. Paris: Éditions Calmann-Levy, 2008.

N'Dongo, Sally. *La "coopération" franco-africaine*. Paris: François Maspero, 1972.

———. *"Coopération" et néo-colonialisme*. Paris: François Maspero, 1976.

———. *Exil, connais pas ...*. Paris: François Maspero, 1976.

———. "L'école de la vie" *International Review of Education/Internationale Zeitschrift für Erziehungswissenschaft/Revue internationale de l'éducation* 40, no. 3/5 (1994): 319–323.

———. *Voyage forcé: Itinéraire d'un militant*. Paris: François Maspero, 1975.

Noiriel, Gérard. *Le creuset français: Histoire de l'immigration XIXe–XXe siècle*. Paris: Éditions du Seuil, 1988.

———. *État, nation et immigration: Vers une histoire du pouvoir*. Paris: Éditions Belin, 2001.

———. *Immigration, antisémitisme et racisme en France (XIXe–XXe Siècle)*. Paris: Fayard, 2007.

———. *State, Nation, and Immigration: Towards a History of Power*. Paris: Éditions Gallimard, 2005.

Nunez, Juliette. "La gestion publique des espaces confessionnels des cimetières de la Ville de Paris: l'exemple du culte musulman (1857–1957)." *Le Mouvement Social* no. 237 (December 2011): 13–32.

Olaniyan, Tejumola and Ato Quayson, eds. *African Literature: An Anthology of Criticism and Theory*. Malden: Blackwell, 2007.

Olzak, Susan. "Contemporary Ethnic Mobilization." *Annual Review of Sociology* 9 (1983): 355–374.

———. *The Global Dynamics of Racial and Ethnic Mobilization*. Stanford: Stanford University Press, 2006.

Ostrand, Nicole. "The Syrian Refugee Crisis: A Comparison of Responses by Germany, Sweden, the United Kingdom, and the United States." *Journal of Migration and Human Society* 3, no. 3 (2015): 255–279.

Ott, Katherine. *Fevered Lives: Tuberculosis in American Culture since 1870*. Harvard University Press, 1996.

Owusu, Thomas Y. "The Role of Ghanaian Immigrant Associations in Toronto, Canada." *International Migration Review* 34, no. 4 (Winter 2000): 1155–1181.

Palidda, Salvatore, ed. *Racial Criminalization of Migrants in the 21st Century*. Surrey and Burlington: Ashgate, 2011.

Pan Ké Shon, Jean-Louis, Gregory Verdugo and Amy Jacobs. "Immigrant Segregation and Incorporation in France: Extent and Intensity from 1968 to 2007." *Revue française de la sociologie* 55, no. 2 (2014): 179–214.

Paskins, Jacob. *Paris Under Construction: Building Sites and Urban Transformation in the 1960s*. New York: Routledge, 2016.

Patterson, Tiffany Ruby and Robin D. G. Kelley. "Unfinished Migrations: Reflections on the African Diaspora and the Making of the Modern World." *African Studies Review* 42, no. 1 (April 2000): 11–45.

Peabody, Sue. *"There Are No Slaves in France": The Political Culture of Race and Slavery in the Ancien Régime*. Oxford: Oxford University Press, 1996.

Peabody, Sue, and Tyler Stovall, eds. *The Color of Liberty: Histories of Race in France*. Durham: Duke University Press, 2003.

Perrot, Michelle. *Workers on Strike: France 1871–1890*. New Haven; London: Yale University Press, 1987.
Pinçon, Michel. *Cohabiter: groupes sociaux et modes de vie dans une cité H.L.M.* Paris: Ministère de l'urbanisme et du logement, Plan construction, 1982.
Pinkney, David H. *Napoleon III and the Rebuilding of Paris*. Princeton, NJ: Princeton University Press, 1958.
Pojmann, Wendy, ed. *Migration and Activism in Europe since 1945*. New York: Palgrave MacMillan, 2008.
Portelli, Alessandro. *The Death of Luigi Trastulli and Other Stories: Form and Meaning in Oral History*. Albany: State University of New York Press, 1991.
Putnam, Robert. *Bowling Alone: The Collapse and Revival of the American Community*. New York: Simon and Schuster, 2001.
Quiminal, Catherine. "The Associative Movement of African Women and New Forms of Citizenship." in Freedman and Tarr, eds., *Women, Immigration and Identity in France*, 39–56.
———. *Gens d'ici, gens d'ailleurs: Migrations Soninké et transformations villageoises*. Paris: Bourgois, 1991.
Raissiguier, Catherine. *Reinventing the Republic: Gender, Migration, and Citizenship in France*. Stanford: Stanford University Press, 2010.
Reader, Keith A. *Intellectuals and the Left in France since 1968*. New York: St. Martin's Press, 1987.
Reimers, Eva. "Death and Identity: Graves and Funerals as Cultural Communication." *Mortality* 4, no. 2 (1999): 147–166.
Rex, John et al., eds. *Immigrant Associations in Europe*. Aldershot: Gower, 1987.
Reynaud-Paligot, Carole. "Construction and Circulation of the Notion of Race in the Nineteenth Century." in Bancel, David, and Thomas, eds., *The Invention of Race*, 87–99.
Rist, R. C. "Migration and Marginality: Guestworkers in Germany and France." *Daedalus* 108, no. 2 (1979): 95–108.
Robben, Antonius C. G. M., ed. *Death, Mourning, and Burial: A Cross-Cultural Reader*. Malden: Blackwell, 2004.
Robinson, David. "French 'Islamic' Policy and Practice in Late Nineteenth-Century Senegal" *The Journal of African History* 29, no. 3 (1988): 415–435.
Roelsgaard, E., E. Iversen, and C. Blocher. "Tuberculosis in Tropical Africa: An Epidemiological Study." *Bulletin of the World Health Organization* no. 30 (1964): 459–518.
Rosello, Mireille. "French *Bidonvilles* in the 1960s: Urban & Individual Initiatives." *Renaissance and Modern Studies* 40, no. 1 (1997): 97–110.
———. *Postcolonial Hospitality: The Immigrant as Guest*. Stanford: Stanford University Press, 2001.
Rosenberg, Clifford. "The Colonial Politics of Health Care Provision in Interwar Paris." *French Historical Studies* 27, no. 3 (2004): 637–668.
———. *Policing Paris: The Origins of Modern Immigration Control between the Wars*. Ithaca; London: Cornell University Press, 2006.
Rosenberg, Jonathan. *How Far the Promised Land: World Affairs and the American Civil Rights Movement from the First World War to Vietnam*. Princeton: Princeton University Press, 2005.
Rosenhaft, Eve, and Robbie Aitkin, eds. *Africa in Europe: Studies in Transnational Practice in the Long Twentieth Century*. Liverpool: Liverpool University Press, 2013.

Ross, Kristen. *Fast Cars, Clean Bodies: Decolonization and the Reordering of French Culture*. Boston: MIT Press, 1995.

———. *May '68 and Its Afterlives*. Chicago: University of Chicago Press, 2002.

Roy MacLeod and Milton Lewis, eds. *Disease, Medicine, and Empire: Perspectives on Western Medicine and the Experience of European Expansion*. London: Routledge, 1988.

Rucht, Dieter, Ruud Koopmans, and Friedhelm Neidhardt, eds. *Acts of Dissent: New Developments in the Study of Protest*. Lanham: Rowman & Littlefield Publishers, Inc., 1999.

Rudé, George. *Paris and London in the Eighteenth Century: Studies in Popular Protest*. New York: Viking Press, 1971.

———. *The Crowd in the French Revolution*. London, Oxford, and New York: Oxford University Press, 1959.

Rudolph, Nicole C. *At Home in Postwar France: Modern Mass Housing and the Right to Comfort*. Oxford and New York: Berghahn, 2015.

Safran, W. "Pluralism and Multiculturalism in France: Post-Jacobin Transformations." *Political Science Quarterly* 118, no. 3 (2003): 437–465.

Samuel, Michel. *Le prolétariat africain noir en France: temoignages recueillis et présentés par Michel Samuel*. Paris: François Maspero, 1978.

Sargent, Carolyn, and Stéphanie Larchanché. "Disease, Risk, and Contagion: French Colonial and Postcolonial Constructions of 'African' Bodies." *Journal of Bioethical Inquiry* 11, no. 4 (October 8, 2014): 455–466.

Sartre, Jean-Paul. *Between Existentialism and Marxism*. trans. John Mathews. New York: Pantheon Books, 1974.

———. *Colonialism and Neocolonialism*. trans. Azzedine Haddour, Steve Brewer, and Terry McWilliams. London and New York: Routledge, 2001.

Schain, Martin. "Minorities and Immigrant Incorporation in France: The State and the Dynamics of Multiculturalism in Joppke and Lukes," *Multicultural Questions*, 199–223.

———. *The Politics of Immigration in France, Britain, and the United States: A Comparative Study*. New York: Palgrave Macmillan, 2008.

Schnapper, Dominique. *Qu'est-ce que l'intégration?* Paris: Éditions Gallimard, 2007.

Sebbar, Leila. *The Seine Was Red: Paris, October 1961*. trans. Mildred Mortimer. Bloomington; Indianapolis: Indiana University Press, 2008.

Seifert, W. "Admission Policy, Patterns of Migration and Integration: The German and French Case Compared." *Journal of Ethnic and Migration Studies* 23, no. 4 (1997): 441–460.

Senechal de la Roche, Roberta. "Collective Violence as Social Control." *Sociological Forum* 11, no. 1 (1996): 97–130.

Senghor, Léopold Sédar. "Négritude: A Humanism of the Twentieth Century." in Olaniyan and Quayson, eds., *African Literature: An Anthology of Criticism and Theory*, 195–202.

Severin-Barboutie, Bettina. "From the City Perimeters to the Centre of the Political Arena: Deprived Neighbourhoods and Urban Policies in Postwar France." *Urban Research & Practice* 5, no. 1 (2012): 62–75.

Shepard, Todd. *The Invention of Decolonization: The Algerian War and the Remaking of France*. Ithaca: Cornell University Press, 2006.

Shermen, A. J. "Insider Outsiders." *New England Review* 24, no. 3 (Summer 2003): 162–172.

Shohat, Ella and Robert Stam. *Multiculturalism, Postcoloniality, and Transnational Media*. New Brunswick: Rutgers University Press, 2003.

Shorter, Edward and Charles Tilly. *Strikes in France 1830–1968*. Cambridge: Cambridge University Press, 1974.

Silverman, Maxim. *Deconstructing the Nation: Immigration, Racism and Citizenship in Modern France*. London: Routledge, 2002.

———, ed. *Race, Discourse, and Power in France*. Aldershot: Avebury, 1991.

Silverstein, Paul A. *Algeria in France: Transpolitics, Race, and Nation*. Bloomington; Indianapolis: Indiana University Press, 2004.

Singer, Daniel. *Prelude to Revolution: France in May 1968*. New York: Hill and Wang, 1970.

Snow, David A., Rens Vliegenthart, and Catherine Corrigall-Brown. "Framing the French Riots: A Comparative Study of Frame Variation." *Social Forces* 86, no. 2 (2007): 385–415.

Sofi, Mirna, "La dimension spatiale de l'intégration: évolution de la ségrégation des populations immigrées en France entre 1968 et 1999." *Revue française de sociologie* 50, no. 3 (July–September, 2009): 521–552.

Spire, Alexis. *Étrangers à la carte: l'administration de l'immigration en France (1945–1975)*. Paris: Bernard Grasset, 2005.

Stoler, Ann Laura. *Carnal Knowledge and Imperial Power: Race and the Intimate in Colonial Rule*. Berkeley; Los Angeles; London: University of California Press, 2002.

———. "Sexual Affronts and Racial Frontiers: European Identities and the Cultural Politics of Exclusion in Colonial Southeast Asia." *Comparative Studies in Society and History* 34, no. 3 (July 1992): 514–551.

Stovall, Tyler. *Paris Noir: African Americans and the City of Light*. New York: Houghton Mifflin, 1996.

———. "The Color Line behind the Lines: Racial Violence in France during the Great War." *The American Historical Review* 103, no. 3 (June 1998): 737–769.

———. *The Rise of the Paris Red Belt*. Berkeley: University of California Press, 1990.

Sun Crowder, Linda. "Chinese Funerals in San Francisco Chinatown: American Chinese Expressions in Mortuary Ritual Performance." *The Journal of American Folklore* 113, no. 450 (Autumn 2000): 451–463.

Suret-Canal, J. "Strike Movements as Part of the Anticolonial Struggle in French West Africa." in Welliver, ed., *Colonialism and Nationalism in Africa*.

Taguieff, Pierre-André, ed. *L'antisémitisme de plume 1940–1944, études et documents*. Paris: Berg International Éditeurs, 1999.

———. "The New Cultural Racism in France." *Telos* 1990, no. 83 (March 20, 1990): 109–122.

Teller, Michael E. *The Tuberculosis Movement: A Public Health Campaign in the Progressive Era*. Westport: Praeger, 1988.

Thomas, Dominic. *Africa and France: Postcolonial Cultures, Migration, and Racism*. Bloomington; Indianapolis: Indiana University Press, 2013.

———. *Black France: Colonialism, Immigration, and Transnationalism*. Bloomington; Indianapolis: Indiana University Press, 2007.

———. "Fortress Europe: Identity, Race, and Surveillance." *International Journal of Francophone Studies* 17, no. 3 & 4 (2014): 445–468.

Thomas, Martin. *Empires of Intelligence: Security Services and Colonial Disorder After 1914*. Berkeley; Los Angeles: University of California Press, 2008.

———. *The French Empire Between the Wars: Imperialism, Politics and Society*. Manchester: Manchester University Press, 2005.

———, Bob Moore, and L. J. Butler. *Crises of Empire: Decolonization and Europe's Imperial States, 1918–1975*. London: Hodder Education, 2008.

Thompson, Elizabeth. *Colonial Citizens: Republican Rights, Paternal Privilege, and Gender in French Syria and Lebanon*. New York: Columbia University Press, 2000.
Thompson, Vincent Bakpetu. *Africa and Unity: The Evolution of Pan-Africanism*. London: Longmans, 1969.
Thörn, Håkan. *Anti-Apartheid and the Emergence of a Global Civil Society*. Basingstoke: Palgrave Macmillan, 2009.
———. "The Meaning(s) of Solidarity: Narratives of Anti-Apartheid Activism." *The Journal of Southern African Studies* 35, no. 2 (June 2009): 417–436.
———. "Solidarity Across Borders: The Transnational Anti-Apartheid Movement." *Voluntas: International Journal of Voluntary and Nonprofit Organizations* 17, no. 4 (December 2006): 285–301.
Tiersky, Ronald. *French Communism, 1920–1972*. New York and London: Columbia University Press, 1974.
Tilly, Charles. *The Contentious French*. Cambridge and London: The Belknap Press of Harvard University Press, 1986.
———. *The Politics of Collective Violence*. Cambridge: Cambridge University Press, 2003.
———, Louise Tilly, and Richard Tilly. *The Rebellious Century, 1830–1930*. Cambridge: Harvard University Press, 1975.
Timera, Mahamet. *Les Soninké en France: D'une histoire à l'autre*. Paris: Karthala, 1996.
Toubon, Jean-Claude. *Les conditions de logement des étrangers en région d'Île de France*. Paris: INSEE, Direction régionale de Paris, 1979.
Touraine, Alain. *The Voice and the Eye: An Analysis of Social Movements*. trans. Alan Duff. Cambridge: Cambridge University Press, 1981.
Touré, Sékou. *Experience guinéenne et unité africaine*. Paris: Présence Africaine, 1962.
Trébous, Madeleine. "Les noirs en France." *Esprit* (April 1966).
Trumbull IV, George R. *An Empire of Facts: Colonial Power, Cultural Knowledge, and Islam in Algeria, 1870–1914*. Cambridge: Cambridge University Press, 2009.
Tshimanga, Charles, Gondola, Didier, and Bloom, Peter J., eds. *Frenchness and the African Diaspora: Identity and Uprising in Contemporary France*. Bloomington; Indianapolis: Indiana University Press, 2009.
Union générale des travailleurs sénégalais en France. *Le livre des travailleurs africains en France*. Paris: François Maspero, 1970.
Vaillant, Janet. *Black, French, and African: A Life of Léopold Sédar Senghor*. Cambridge: Harvard University Press, 1991.
Van Den Avenue, Cècile. "De l'expérience plurilingue à l'expérience diglossique: migrants maliens en France." *Cahiers d'études africaines* 41, no. 163/164 (2001): 619–636.
Van Den Breemer, Rosemarie and Marcel Maussen. "On the Viability of State-Church Models: Muslim Burial and Mosque-Building in France and the Netherlands." *Journal of Immigrant and Refugee Studies* September 11, 2012: 279–298.
Van der Geest, Sjaak. "Between Death and Funeral: Mortuaries and the Exploitation of Liminality in Kwahu, Ghana." *Africa: Journal of the International African Institute* 76, no. 4 (2006): 485–501.
Van Zanten, David. *Building Paris: Architectural Institutions and the Transformation of the French Capital, 1830–1870*. Cambridge; New York: Cambridge University Press, 1994.
Vaughan, Megan. *Curing Their Ills: Colonial Power and African Illness*. Stanford: Stanford University Press, 1991.

Verdery, Catherine. *The Political Lives of Dead Bodies: Reburial and Post-Socialist Change*. New York: Columbia University Press, 1999.

Verdugo, Gregory. "Public Housing and Residential Segregation of Immigrants in France, 1968–1999." *Population* 66, no. 1 (January 2011): 169–193.

Viet, Vincent. *La France immigrée: construction d'une politique, 1914–1997.* Paris: Fayard, 1998.

———. "La politique du logement des immigrés (1945–1990)." *Vingtième siècle. Revue d'histoire* 64 no. 1 (1999): 91–103.

Villanova, Roselyne de, et al. *Immigration et espaces habités: bilan bibliographique des travaux en France, 1970–1992.* Paris: L'Harmattan and CIEMI, 1994.

Volovitch-Tavares, Marie-Christine. *Portugais à Champigny, le temps des baraques.* Paris: Autrement, 1995.

Vranken, Jan. "Industrial Rights." in Layton-Henry, ed., *The Political Rights of Migrant Workers.*

Wallerstein, Immanuel. *Africa: The Politics of Independence.* Lincoln: University of Nebraska Press, 1961.

———. *Africa: The Politics of Unity: An Analysis of a Contemporary Social Movement.* New York: Random House, 1967.

Warner, Carolyn M. and Manifred W. Wenner. "Religion and the Political Organization of Muslims in Europe." *Perspectives on Politics* 4, no. 3 (September 2006): 457–479.

Wayne, Michael. *Imagining Black America.* New Haven: Yale University Press, 2014.

Weil, Patrick. *La France et ses étrangers: L'aventure d'une politique de l'immigration 1938–1991.* Paris: Calmann-Levy, 1991.

———. "Georges Mauco, expert en immigration: ethno-racisme pratique et antisémitisme filleux." in Taguieff, ed., *L'antisémitisme de plume 1940–1944*, 267–276.

———. "L'ordonnance de 1945: l'aboutissement d'un long processus." *Plein droit* 22–23 (1993). http://www.gisti.org/spip.php?article3899

———. *Qu'est-Ce Qu'un Français? Histoire de la nationalité française dépuis la révolution.* 2nd ed. Mesnil-sur-l'Estrée: Folio, 2005.

———. "Racisme et discrimination dans la politique française de l'immigration 1938–1945/1974–1995." *Vingtième siècle. Revue d'histoire* no. 47 (July–September 1995): 77–102.

———. *La République et sa diversité: Immigration, intégration, discrimination.* Paris: Éditions du Seuil, 2005.

Welliver, Timothy K., ed. *Colonialism and Nationalism in Africa: African Nationalism and Independence.* vol. 3. Abingdon-on-Thames: Routledge, 1993.

White, Owen. *Children of the French Empire: Miscegenation and Colonial Society in French West Africa, 1895–1960.* Oxford: Oxford University Press, 1999.

Wieviorka, Michael. "Contextualizing French Multiculturalism and Racism." *Theory, Culture & Society* 17, no. 1 (2000).

Wihtol de Wenden, Catherine, "Immigrants as Political Actors in France." *West European Politics* 17, no. 2 (1994): 91–109.

———. *Les immigrés et la politique: Cent cinquante ans d'évolution.* Paris: Presses de la Fondation Nationale des Sciences Politiques, 1988.

———. and Zakya Daoud, eds. *Banlieues: intégration ou explosion?* Courbevoie: Éditions Corlet-Éditions Arléa, 1993

———. and Rémy Leveau. *La beurgeoisie: Les trois âges de la vie associative issue de l'immigration.* Paris: CNRS Éditions, 2001.

Wilder, Gary. *Freedom Time: Négritude, Decolonization, and the Future of the World.* Durham: Duke University Press, 2015.

———. *The French Imperial Nation-State: Négritude and Colonial Humanism between the Two World Wars.* Chicago; London: The University of Chicago Press, 2005.

———. "Panafricanism and the Republic Political Sphere." in Peabody and Stovall, eds., *The Color of Liberty*, 237–258.

Williams, Raymond. *Marxism and Literature.* Oxford; New York: Oxford University Press, 1977.

Wilson, Frank L. *The French Democratic Left 1963–1969: Toward a Modern Party System.* Stanford: Stanford University Press, 1971.

Winders, Jim. *Paris Africain: Rhythms of the African Diaspora.* New York: Palgrave Macmillan, 2006.

Wrench, John. *Racism and Migration in Western Europe.* Oxford; Providence: Berg, 1993.

Young, Robert J. C. "Preface." in Sartre, *Colonialism and Neocolonialism*, xiv–xv.

Index